Other Loyalties

The Life of a School and the
Education of a Teacher

Kareem Aal

DARAKEH PRESS

Copyright © Kareem Aal, 2022

First Edition, 2022

All rights reserved. No part of this publication may be reproduced or transmitted in any form or by any means, electronic or mechanical, including photocopying, recording, or any information storage or retrieval system, without prior permission in writing from the publisher.

ISBN 979-8-218-04189-2
Available as an electronic book; ISBN 979-8-218-04190-8

Cover design by Dan Tanz
Map illustration by Jesse Maloney
Book design by Kelley Creative

Published by Darakeh Press

www.kareemaal.com

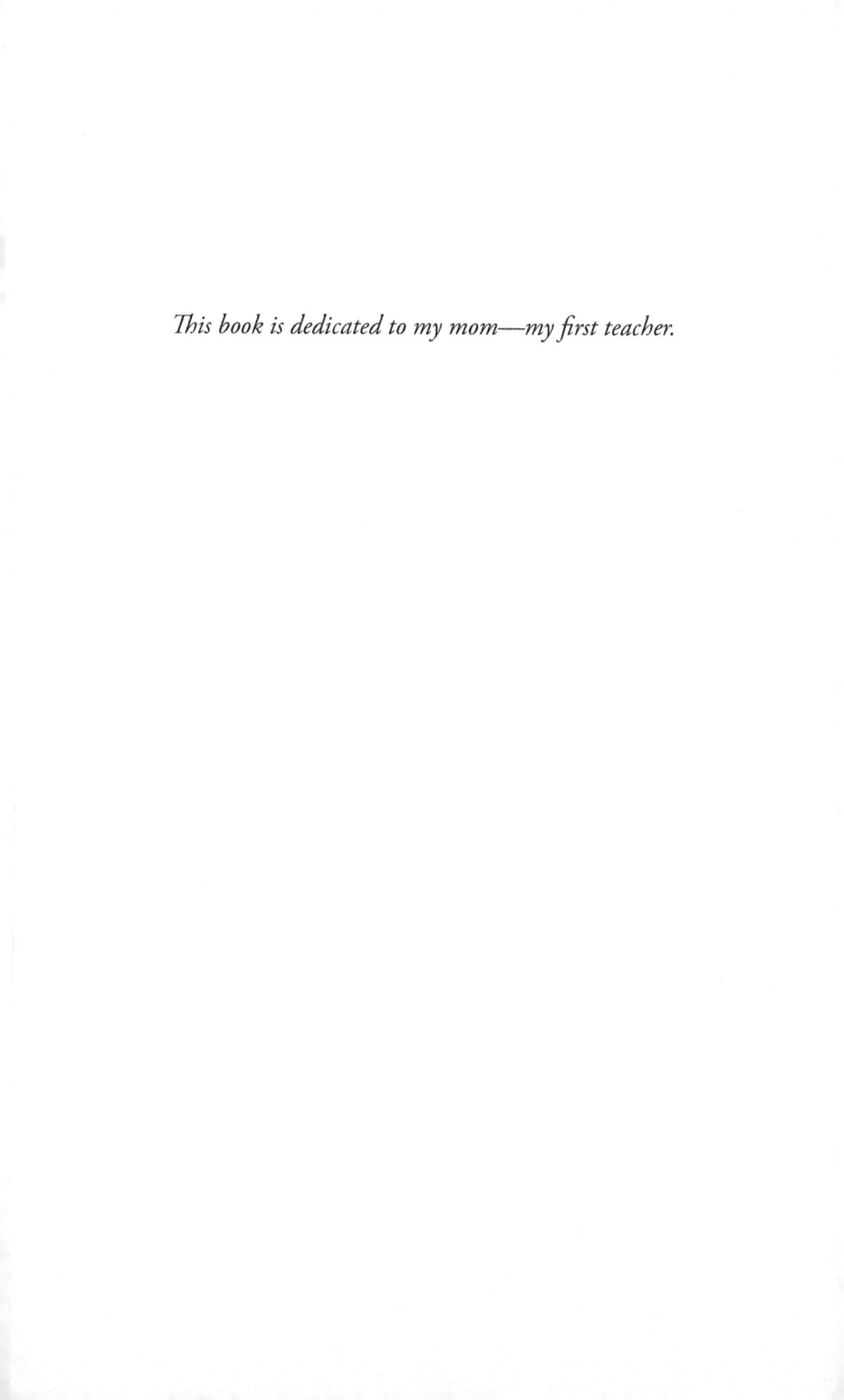

This book is dedicated to my mom—my first teacher.

Puritanism: The haunting fear that someone, somewhere, may be happy.

- H.L. Mencken

BOUNDARY WATERS
RED LAKE
TOWER SOUDAN MINE
BEARHEAD STATE PARK
MINNESOTA
IRON RANGE
FARGO
MOOREHEAD
MISSISSIPPI HEADWATERS
BLACK BEACH
DULUTH
MILLE LACS
JAY COOKE STATE PARK
NORTHWEST COMPANY FUR POST
WILD RIVER STATE PARK
FRANCONIA SCULPTURE PARK
ARCOLA TRAIL & HIGH BRIDGE
MS. D's LITTLE SCHOOL
CAMP ST CROIX
WILLOW RIVER STATE PARK
HUDSON FARM
POINT DOUGLAS CEMETERY
BARN BLUFF
JEFFERS PETROGLYPHS
WATT MUNISOTARAM

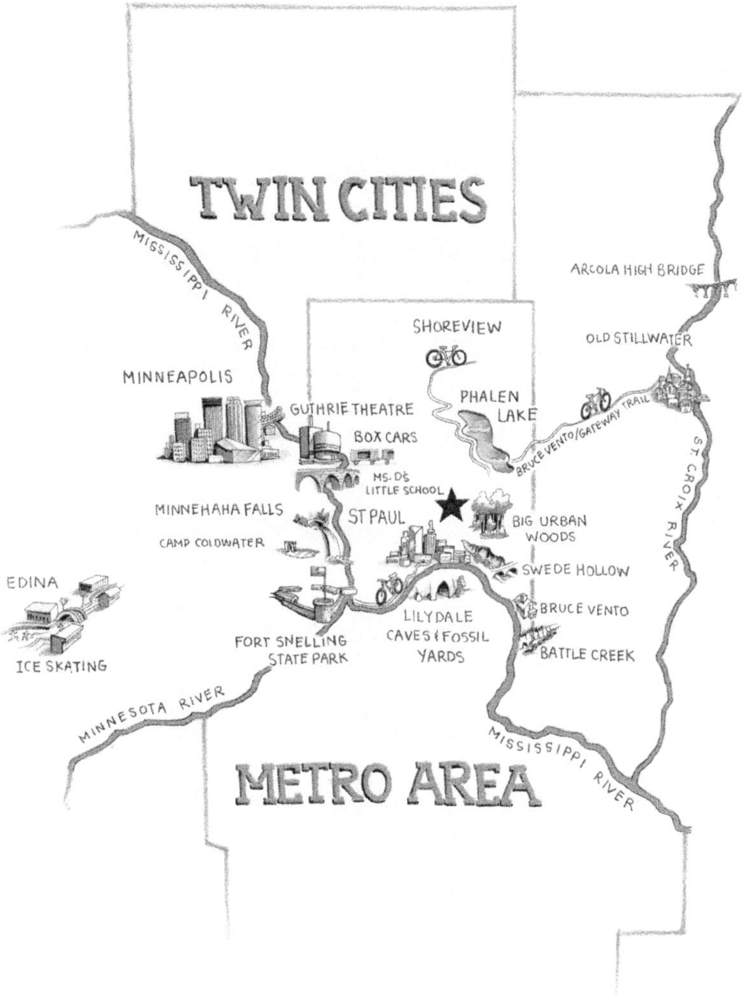
TWIN CITIES
METRO AREA
MISSISSIPPI RIVER
MINNEAPOLIS
GUTHRIE THEATRE
BOX CARS
MS. D'S LITTLE SCHOOL
SHOREVIEW
PHALEN LAKE
BRUCE VENTO/GATEWAY TRAIL
ARCOLA HIGH BRIDGE
OLD STILLWATER
ST. CROIX RIVER
MINNEHAHA FALLS
CAMP COLDWATER
ST PAUL
BIG URBAN WOODS
SWEDE HOLLOW
BRUCE VENTO
BATTLE CREEK
LILYDALE CAVES & FOSSIL YARDS
FORT SNELLING STATE PARK
EDINA
ICE SKATING
MINNESOTA RIVER
MISSISSIPPI RIVER

One

MY TEACHING CAREER had begun, and the clock was ticking—parents and students would be coming for Open House in two days. The room assigned to me was a bare rectangle without a single desk or chair. Two rows of strip lights hung from the ceiling, and when I turned them on, a dull shine reflected off the scuffed hardwood flooring.

Along one wall at waist-level, there was a cubby hole about the size of an old Zenith TV. I thought the space might have been used as an altar in days past. Afterall, the school was part of a church complex, built over one hundred years ago by Polish Catholic immigrants on the east side of St. Paul, Minnesota. Built to serve the children of the parish, the private religious school had shut down in the early nineties as enrollment declined. The old building was leased to a public charter school, and I had been hired as their new social studies teacher.

Since 1916, a group called the Missionary Oblates of Mary Immaculate had overseen the complex and the church still had a congregation and mass on Sundays. Though the public school and church were neighbors, their missions, by law, had to diverge. The relationship was uneasy from the beginning. During recess my first year, I would sometimes glimpse the priest stepping out of the rectory, a small building next to the school, and gingerly make his way out of sight. Other days I'd see the prim, white-haired laywoman, one of the "oblates," casting a side-glance at the school's new occupants as she entered the church.

Not until a decade later, when I was reading *The Golden Compass* to my eight-year-old daughter, did I bother to look up what the word 'oblate' meant. I found out from Webster's online dictionary that an oblation was an offering made to a god, and an oblate was someone who dedicated themselves to a religious life but stopped short of taking monastic vows.

Knowing now the devotion it took to pump life into a small public school it makes me wonder whether I was not becoming an oblate myself back then, by entering the teaching profession. The white-haired laywoman and I had more in common than I thought.

Looking back at myself in my new classroom, trying to get ready for Open House in the last days of August, I see the large cubby hole again. It was not clear what belonged there anymore. Back when the place was a Catholic school, white candles, rosaries, and a cross would have been purposefully set down on a green tablecloth across the altar. Crayon drawings of the Sacred Heart of Jesus might have been taped up on the wall around it—all framing the room's center of prayer.

The space was conspicuous now, just a big square hole in the wall, painted off-white like the rest of the room. What new secular relics of a public school education that might be placed there were harder to pin down. Textbooks? A copy of the UN Charter of Human Rights? A list of U.S. presidents? External hard drives? Quotes by moral leaders, stripped of religious references? A pencil sharpener?

There was another possibility. A possibility that tremored forth from the chilliest corner of schooling.

Maybe it *was* still an altar, but of another kind. Alone in my classroom, I thought of all my students that I didn't know yet. They were out there confronting the end of summer, trailing their moms at Target, buying notebooks and markers that would be lost within the month. They were junior high kids, but still young enough to beg for candy at the checkout line. Staring back at the altar, I wondered what part of their innocence and perfection would be sacrificed when they stepped through the classroom doors. And as their teacher, what role would I play in this ritual?

I stood in front of the cubby hole—altar?—and wrestled with this question. It was late afternoon, and the school was silent. Turning off the fluorescent strip lights and closing the door to my room, I walked to my car and climbed in. I left the radio off, carrying the silence of the school with me. Without knowing what I was doing, I drove past Target and into the parking lot of a hardware store. There was less a plan in my head than a feeling in my body—a reaction to my new classroom that I didn't know how to express. I walked down aisles filled with electrical and plumbing supplies, light bulbs, and door hinges, until I stood in front of a wall of aerosol cans, each with a different colored top. The first thing I did after seeing my new classroom was buy a can of black spray paint.

I DON'T HAVE any photos of my years teaching at the little public charter school anymore. There's one photo that I remember, though. It was taken on an outing with seventh and eighth graders. We were at a farm collecting wood for a sculpture that the students were going to make for the school.

Combing through the woodlands edging the fields, we found some fallen trees. Picture a chainsaw, held in the hands of a fourteen-year-old, eating into the bark. The chips shoot out as the cut grinds deeper into the heartwood of the tree. Beside the kid are two smiling adults; one is an educational assistant named Mr. Shane, the other a science teacher named Mr. Maloney.

After getting the pieces we needed, we killed time on some hay bales lined up in the field. There was a large gap between two rows, and the kids were taking turns leaping across the bales. I dropped down and watched. Bodies hurled themselves from side to side above me against a bright sky.

When I snapped the photo, I didn't know that it would capture a fresco of junior high life. In the upper half of the frame, a white pair of beat-up high tops are curled together in mid-jump. They belong to Hunter—but his body above the knee is cropped out.

To the right is his best friend Marlowe, laughing. Standing in the background is a younger student, Jeremiah. His mouth is dropped open in awe. Way in the background is a couple, Mason and Marina, cuddled together atop a hay bale.

It was all there: friendship, love, freedom, danger, and swift lessons on how to be awesome. And out of frame were the adults wise enough to let it happen.

BUT BEFORE ALL that, I was just a new teacher. Simply put, an adult with the right paperwork in order to legally watch over a room full of children. My expectations were too low, too high, and nothing in between. Standing there in my first classroom, it began to dawn on me how school could be: crowd a bunch of young people into an impoverished space and try to recreate the bounty of the outside world.

Some teachers attacked the problem with skill and confidence. They distilled just enough "real life" for students without overwhelming them. I, on the other hand, was dumbstruck about what to include and what to exclude from my classroom. By this point in history all children were welcome in a public school classroom, but there was more to inclusion than that. Choices had to be made about what stories, ideas, language, and ways of moving a body would be welcome, and which would be left out—even by just being ignored.

I woke up on my second day as a teacher and was already in a panic. How was I going to survive the first day of school which was still a week away? But I had to put my fears aside and get back to the urgent task of preparing my room.

I went about it in a haphazard way, like a college student trying to furnish an off-campus apartment. I started by checking my basement and closets for props. I just wanted items that could help decorate or at least fill the space in the classroom. Coming up empty-handed, I stopped at my parents' house in Minneapolis, still clinging to the childhood belief that they'd take care of all my problems. I went to the basement to pick up a small bookshelf, and something written on the wall caught my eye. It was the drippy red lettering of a movie title: *Bloodsport*.

When I was thirteen years old, I bought a can of red spray paint and wrote the title next to a punching bag. In the film, actor Jean-Claude Van Damme plays a young American named Frank Dux who gets whipped into shape by a Japanese karate master, Sensei Tanaka. I fantasized I was Dux and watched the movie over and over again—leaning toward the TV during the inspirational training montages.

Standing in my homemade childhood dojo, I saw some clippings of Bruce Lee from *Black Belt Magazine* still taped on the wall, curled and yellowing. I started to reminisce about one of my favorite scenes in *Bloodsport*. Frank Dux's father is sitting with Sensei Tanaka. Tanaka pours him a cup of tea and says, "Frank has told me you came to America to grow vines."

"Yes, that's right. I work at the Verne vineyard."

"I came here to grow fish in my hatchery. We both grow children. You use science to make vines grow better. Like vines, children need training. Martial science provide a way of training. It brings mind, body, spirit together."

The basement dojo was now cluttered with a table saw, old bikes, and boxed Christmas decorations. I found and dislodged the bookshelf and dragged it up the stairs. The bookshelf would help spiffy up a corner in my classroom, but I wondered if the more valuable item I carried up from the basement was the memory of *Bloodsport*. Sensei Tanaka didn't hesitate to inflict a little pain to help train Frank Dux, and as a thirteen-year-old, I wished I could have been Tanaka's student. Was it a first clue on how to teach?

I shoved the bookshelf into the trunk of my gold Mazda Protege, my dad loaded a potted palm tree in the backseat, my mom passed me a worn book from the 1970's called *Sharing Nature With Children*, and I crossed the Mississippi River to St. Paul. At first, I thought I'd taken the book from my mom just to be polite. It was another one of those things, like newspaper clippings and old mail, that my mom always handed to me at the door before giving me a hug. But as I was driving, the book made me realize that I had to start a list of things a classroom lacked. The first item on the list was a classroom's connection to the stirring sanity of the forest.

I made one more stop on the way to school. I swung by Half-Price Books and blew two hundred dollars on sixty hard-cover journals for students. Next to the cash register was a bin full of computer games. I saw a CD-ROM for a game called *Age of Empires III*, which I knew nothing about. But I had an epiphany that this could be my entire curriculum for early U.S. history. For a brief, glorious, lazy second, I thought that I could plop my students in front of an old desktop computer screen, and they'd become familiar with the places, historical figures, and thrust of the Age of Exploration and colonialism. It'd be like *The Oregon Trail* that I played in school—a game that entertained us with keyboard tasks like shooting rabbits and buffalo or dealing with dysentery and made us vaguely aware of the story of white settlers in stagecoaches moving West.

Even though I knew I would have no computers in my room, I bought the CD-ROM.

There were specific challenges teaching in the first decade of the twenty-first century that I didn't understand at the time. I started my career way after the age of the chalky blackboard and just before the digital revolution. During the blackboard era, teachers used a piece of chalk and a lectern, plus a zest for memorization and bookshelves of classics, to teach about life. The teacher stood at the front of the room and dispensed a black and white prescription for being an educated person, to students sitting in rows taking notes.

When the digital revolution arrived, classrooms filled with electronic devices through which the entire world swirled under a glass screen—displayed in over one billion colors. The iPads and laptops offered individualized learning and an end to lessons hamstrung by space and time—and teachers. Children slid their fingers across a hard surface and were fed a stream of thrills. There would come a time in my teaching career when I saw a kid watch the entire history of life on Earth on his iPad in the few minutes we had to wait before lunch. The kids to his right and left spent those minutes watching a man eat 241 chicken wings from Hooters on YouTube. While I walked around the room gathering half-completed worksheets on a single, measly, event in U.S. history—The Homestead Act—students sped ahead along the timeline. The resources of the internet allowed them to self-pace their historical inquiry, and soon they were watching simulations of the Earth burning down to its iron core as the Sun expanded into a red giant billions of years in the future.

In the internet era the teacher tries to be a sober digital curator, web designer, and tech support. But the reality is that students are both programmers and end users that have surpassed the computer knowledge of most teachers. Tapping commands, students can get immediate feedback from code that understands what they want. The interaction with zeros and ones on the computer offers students the sort of cooperation they can't always get from the people around them, or even from themselves.

I came to an important conclusion much later in my teaching career. The dashing tech innovators and their teacher cheerleaders shared a blind spot with more old-fashioned teachers—and it was in the shape of a human. The flat dimensions of a computer screen were another version of the 'black and white' world of the chalkboard. I'd watch students on iPads merge with images and music, floating away like dust motes across a beam of sunlight, *losing* themselves. Other times I'd see students sneak out their phones and scroll through TikTok as their brain stems nibbled on the crudest stimuli. After twenty minutes of their attention being harvested, they were barely able to respond when I asked, "Are you there?" Zoning out on a screen was the same as zoning out during a long lecture in an old schoolhouse. In other words, in both the chalkboard era and the digital era, there was an emptiness—an emptiness where there should have been a child.

But I had to acknowledge this about the new digital age: Students were also slipping into worlds made up of texts and livestreams from friends and family, or online clips from people who looked and felt like them. The cultural and racial communities they identified with fit in their pockets. They could also *find* themselves on their phones. But the discovery that they could exist in their comfort zone came at a price—the discovery erased the people and community that could have formed in the classroom their bodies occupied. In this scenario, the child was there, but there was an emptiness where there should have been a community.

In my first classroom at the public charter school next to the church, these issues weren't around yet. The iPad didn't exist, laptops were too expensive, and no kid had a cell phone. Expo dry-erase markers, screen projectors, and paper and pencil, still ruled. If students wanted to drift off, they had to do it the old-fashioned way and daydream. If they wanted a community, they had to open their mouths and speak to the people sitting next to them.

My students and I would be face-to-face much of the day, and subject to the friction of the physical world. When things got messy there would be no online world to hide in. We were stuck on an empty stage together, where tradition had exited but the future hadn't yet entered.

I found it hard to recover from my first impression of the classroom as an abandoned stage. I didn't know that I was like all teachers at the time—stuck in a limbo between eras. A classroom already lacked the ambient drama of the city streets, the clatter and focus of a workshop, the buzz of a shopping mall, and the latest churn and bustle of the business world. But a classroom now also lacked the stimulation of the new digital era that *had* begun at home, well before the turn of the millennium. Kids were beginning to spend more of their lives playing video games that engaged them in ways that made class time feel even more flat and dull. Life for kids outside school was becoming a personal entertainment paradise—a Hollywood blockbuster and personal arcade wrapped up in one.

Added to this list of obstacles for teachers was a re-emergence of a longstanding tradition in U.S. society: Power and authority were being challenged and renegotiated. Teachers were not being spared. Along with a growing distrust of public schools, indicated by a steady rise in homeschooling, there was also a rise in a form of indulgent parenting. This meant that a classroom also lacked a sort of order and deference to the teacher that used to be taken for granted. Holding class was now seen as a fusty play none of the actors wanted to be in, with a director—the teacher—that was quickly losing respect.

There were still hidden possibilities in the classroom, but I only saw a vacuum waiting to be filled. The little charter school had no textbooks, nor did I think I wanted them. Yet without a script and without authority, I began to have nightmares where the students and I stumbled through a grim, bare-bones improv routine under the fluorescent strip lights of my class.

The school building was mostly empty when I arrived by late morning. A few more teachers had returned early from summer break and toiled methodically in their rooms, preparing for Open House the following night. At my classroom door—with my arms full of journals, the plant, and *Age of Empires III* CD-ROM—I resembled a dad carrying a jumble of questionable supplies to the beach for his family. But setting the palm tree down on the hardwood floor in my room, I felt more like a lonely castaway. The things in my hands were random items that had washed ashore, collected by a frantic man. I wanted to piece together a small likeness of society in my empty classroom—but it felt like I was decorating a deserted island with the relics of a civilization that was fading from memory.

I eyed the can of black spray paint I'd bought a day earlier.

It was on the floor wrapped in a plastic bag from the hardware store. I fished it out, tossed the bag to the side, and broke the seal on the can. I walked over to the cubby-hole, pressed down on the nozzle, and coated the inside of the altar black.

That night, as the paint fully dried, I raided a stash of glow-in-the-dark stars I'd bought for my three-year-old son. The next morning, I affixed the stars to the black walls of the altar and hung a square of cloth across its opening.

The plan was that during class, when a kid poked their head behind the cloth and onto the altar, they would see a starry night sky. My hope was not that a part of them would be sacrificed in the name of getting educated—it would be given back. Out of desperation I'd found my first classroom ritual.

BEFORE GETTING MY own classroom as a teacher, I had formed dark impressions of school and what its physical space could do to young humans. These impressions came from my own firsthand experience as an energetic schoolboy trapped in a room, and from the couple years I spent as a special education assistant at Crawford Middle School in Minneapolis. Crawford was a program for kids labeled with emotional-behavioral disorders, housed in a windowless building in an industrial zone.

The designation of the school tells everything one needs to know: Federal Setting Level 4. Each level represents an increase in the amount of time a child will spend with special education teachers, separated from "general" teachers and students. Level 4 is the most restrictive public setting before a student is sent to a private or residential program.

At most schools, kids are denied the same things as a prisoner: their own relationship with time and movement. A path to literacy, the thing that could save children from incarceration, is also found at school. At a place like Crawford though, where many of the kids were African American, the sparse rooms, hallways, and locked doors, seemed to have more of the qualities and aims of the prison system.

To be transferred out of their regular schools and sent up the Federal Levels, some Crawford students had fought with other kids or destroyed property, but mostly it was the crime of making teachers mad. These kids refused to comply, and a simple act like not sitting down was enough to derail an entire class period. They were the students that caused some teachers to snap and say things like, "She came in hot today—I knew it was going to be one of those days" and "I couldn't even get through the lesson. She was yelling and walking around provoking other students.

She needs more *support*" and "It's not working—I'm just not meeting her *needs*."

Teachers, worried about the other students languishing there in a chaotic room, lost patience, succumbed to frustration and vengeance, and made calls to the office. An Office Referral was filled out and a ceremony began: the consecration of a disciplinary record.

After the referrals started rolling in for a student, it was only a matter time. Each "fuck you bitch," "suck a dick," threat, and fist fight, was documented and filed. Every attempt to intervene in ways that helped the student but failed, was used as evidence when the school wanted to be rid of them. The endless conflict in class drained everyone. And though the tender hearts of teachers felt remorse, they also felt relief when they saw that a student had been crossed off their roster. Everyone felt relief—teachers, principals, and especially other students—no matter what color they were. It was a cheap and temporary relief though. The catch was that a student could never be crossed off the streets, the bus, the mall, the society in which we all lived. The kid was one of *us*.

By the time students reached Crawford, they'd outdueled a long line of adults, who had become fed up and passed them along. Of course, like most of these last-resort types of schools, Crawford was filled with kind and dedicated teachers—but they were no match for the momentum that had already begun. It was hard for students and teachers alike to break free from the script. Once a boy or girl understood that they were in a school for "bad" kids, they threw themselves into the role, using their talents to make the most of it, competing among themselves for negative attention. Many were on some form of psychiatric medication that, while well-meaning, signaled to the kids that there was something even deeper wrong with them—on a molecular level.

One day at Crawford, one such student complained to me. She was seated at her desk in the dim, cheerless math room. Over the weekend her auntie had braided her hair. The extra love and care had energized her, and she was rallying to get some work done.

"Do this class make you nervous?" she asked.

"What?" I asked.

"You keep walkin' back and forth."

"I have to check if kids need help."

"You be acting like somebody's always about to do something."

"Wait, are they?" I waited for a beat but realized it wasn't a funny joke. "But seriously, I'm just restless I guess."

"You gettin' on my nerves."

"Sorry." I took a step back. "How's it going with the work anyways?"

"You know what?" she said. "Just shut the fuck up talkin' to me."

"But you…I…"

"Bye."

She raised her palm to my face and rudely waved me away. Then she lowered her head and dragged herself forward question by question across a worksheet. We both were rattling the cage in our own way. My footsteps sounded like those of a prison guard to her ears, but I was hearing claws on concrete, a lion trapped and pacing.

The reality was that most of her classmates had found ways out of the room already. Students at Crawford asked to go to the bathroom a lot or got in trouble so they could go to the hallway or time-out room. This was where students found the two African American hall monitors, Mr. Frank and Mr. Gordon, who would have conversations with them and win arguments using words that added up in the students' minds. They were father figures spread thin over a group of kids whose fathers were often out of the picture.

But back in the classroom, many of these students had no assignments turned in. As lousy, and seemingly irrelevant to their lives as some of this work was, not getting it done ended up mattering. There was enough blame to go around: a society still reeling from its history, hectic family lives breaking up under economic pressure, mass incarceration, schools that were oblivious or hostile to black culture, white teachers with low expectations, black behavior specialists and assistants who stopped short of getting the teaching licenses that would have put them in charge of classrooms so kids wouldn't be constantly leaving class to find them in the halls.

Students were also failing themselves—and in a pivotal way, acknowledging that they had a role in their situation was the only way to empower them. Calling these kids victims seemed to be adding to the way these students were getting handy with stacking failures on top of each other, until the failures reached eye-level and stared back at them from the mirror of the school bathroom. Whether to accept that reflection was a choice still within their power—but not if they were told the warped image they saw of themselves was chiseled in stone—in their DNA, and the DNA of life itself in America.

At Crawford, I could never stop feeling that many of the kids were still successful somehow. They kicked out the doors of the classroom to make their own spaces, to find their own "teachers" and way forward, in a place that seemed designed to crush them. No, they were not victims—but the *building* they were in was not their friend.

OPEN HOUSE WAS a few hours away. With the altar finished, I turned my attention to the empty walls of the room. I had remembered the cinder block walls of the math classroom at Crawford and stopped at my parents again that morning. I collected National Geographic maps from the basement, and put them in a brown grocery bag, determined to add a little happiness and color to my room.

I checked the clock again and carried the brown bag to the laminator across the hall from my classroom. The machine warmed up and the stuffy scent of melted plastic filled my nostrils. I fed the machine maps of Amazonia, battles of the Civil War, the surface of the Moon, the old city of Jerusalem, the peopling of the Americas, and thirty others. Interleafed with these was a Hollywood map of stars' homes and famous blood-spattered crime scenes, like the Manson Murders. A long skinny map of Manhattan finished its press between the rollers, and I laid it on top of the stack of maps. Central Park, the Upper East Side, and Harlem were encased between shining plastic sheets capable of withstanding two thousand years of biodegradation.

Stepping into the hallway my head swirled with polyethylene fumes. With my arms wrapped around the collective terrain of half the planet, I headed back to my room wondering where I would set the maps since I had no desks or chairs. My classroom was empty because it hadn't been used the year before. But the student population of the little public charter school was growing, and once-abandoned parts of the old school building were coming back to life but were not yet furnished.

When I opened the door to my room I saw that Mr. Brandon, the giant custodian, had been at work while I was laminating. He had wheeled in vintage steel tanker desks. The bulky desks, ubiquitous in 1950's offices, were scattered in the room like seven large metal islands in a steampunk archipelago. At least now when parents showed up for Open House, it would look like their kids had someplace to sit on the first day of school. (Even though that place now looked like an insurance office from mid-century America.)

Who were the young humans I was expecting to show up, anyways? If they were "kids," it brought to mind lightheartedness, play, babysitting, but also a dismissiveness that allowed a teacher to look upon the difficult and obnoxious, and think, "At least that's not *my* kid." Were they "students"? That conjured a serious role that a teacher was expected to help them fulfill, but also a faceless mass to be acted upon, numbers on a roster. Was I dealing with "sons and daughters"? As a father myself, this identity suggested love, care, the future of a family and the world to a teacher, but was shadowed with disappointment, anger, trauma, embarrassment—fragile and maybe doomed hopes.

If I thought of students as "animals," how would that change the way I set up my room?

Calling students animals was dicey. But it was not an accusation; it was an understanding. A description that I used for myself. What I had felt in a room at Crawford was that I was a creature stuck in a cage—under pressure but apathetic, bored but filled with energy. School offered structure that cloaked a brewing storm inside students and teachers. A fierce, inarticulate rebellion felt in the bones and building up inside our muscles like lactic acid. Was it savagery thrashing against a civilizing force, or a fight for independence, dignity, and freedom against an oppressive institution?

There is a technical word for what happens to animals in the zoo that pace or circle their cages in madness: stereotypy. It was a new word for me, but one I'd been searching for my whole life as a student and now a teacher. A shark that swims forty-five miles a day in its natural environment rubs its nose raw tracing the dimensions of a tiny zoo aquarium. A jaguar hunting in the wild covers over six miles—but the tight turns of an exhibit make it chase its own tail.

The jaguar's stalking was an endless attempt to solve a problem posed by instinct: survival. But safe in a cage, with food provided, the creature's movement served no purpose. The problem vanished but the urge to solve it remained. With natural impulses thwarted, the animal's paw prints stitched the outline of a quiet implosion on the cage floor. I was likely to *implode* like the jaguar, but other personalities, like many of the kids that ended up at Crawford, were less likely to submit to being cooped up, and *exploded* instead. When they did, they got hit with the labels of various disorders: attention deficit hyperactivity, oppositional-defiant, emotional-behavioral.

In my room I spread out the laminated maps on top of the tanker desks, working a few compelling ones to the top: the world at night, captured from satellites, with veins of light snaking away from the bright splotches of major cities; America without political borders or roads labeled—a green, beige, mountain dimpled Garden of Eden; a theme map of Indonesia.

I rifled through the maps looking for what was beautiful and mildly interesting. There was no rhyme or reason, no connection to educational standards or upcoming units of study. As the hour of Open House approached, I got out a role of packaging tape and hung the laminated maps that I'd chosen on the walls, assembling another piece of the learning *environment*. But the posters on my classroom walls only made me think of the murals painted inside zoo enclosures—the strange scenes of forests, savannahs, green foliage, and blue sky that coated the walls, sharp angles, and corners of an animal's cement cell.

The leaves of the potted palm tree seemed to wink at me from the corner, and the altar beckoned behind the curtains. The question remained though—who was this environment for? Animals? Students? Society? Spiritual beings? Sons and daughters? Kids?

MY SKEPTICAL ATTITUDE toward school caught the attention of Professor Greenwalt. He was the advisor in charge of my cohort of would-be social studies teachers at the University of Minnesota's teaching licensure program. Professor Greenwalt had a slim frame, salt and pepper hair, and a knack for introducing challenging thoughts with a light touch.

One assignment he gave involved observing how teachers managed behaviors in high school classes. I wrote about how school *itself* was a discipline policy. A policy that hammered straight lines out of the winding interests of individuals, for the benefit of society.

Professor Greenwalt wrote back: "It seems that you are on the verge of despair about this. Whatever ways that schools shape students, I'm sure that it is humane in comparison to other institutions."

It wasn't that I thought life should be a free-for-all or schools should be places without limits. Socialization had to happen somehow. As an athlete and karate practitioner, I loved disciplining my mind and body under a sensei's guidance, while honoring the other students and etiquette of the dojo. I ate up the serious tone and daily practice that honed movement—with a group who accepted the code. It was the way the body and mind were being disciplined in classrooms that troubled me. Kids did a lot of sitting. The mind was presumed to be a rational machine that just needed clear instructions, slowly repeated, to work properly. There was no sign of spirit except on "pajama day" during Spirit Week. There was even less acknowledgement—based on the hasty schedules of most junior highs that rotated students between discreet subjects every 47 minutes—that the body, mind, and spirit were related and may need some coordination. And the skill of coordinating them would require contemplation—a practice that flourishes within a more fluid relationship to time, which didn't fit the rapid bell schedule.

It took a while, but I eventually saw Professor Greenwalt's words as an admission that the institution of school was doing *something* to kids. And though we weren't entirely sure what it was, at least it was being done humanely. I just hoped it wasn't in the same way that zoos claimed to "humanely" treat the animals.

OPEN HOUSE CAME and went. After the last family left, I stood around trying to ground myself. The flurry of visits to my room had left my introverted head spinning. It was dark outside the windows of my classroom, and I saw the red taillights of a car pulling away from the front of the school.

The evening had been a blur of mute children ushered forward by their parents to meet *me*, one of their new teachers. Since I wasn't exuding confidence and competence myself, I think I bonded briefly with the kids as we stood awkwardly together under the anxious gaze of their parents. It was that moment when the kids and I both realized that whatever our true relationship would be, we wouldn't know until school started the next week and their parents weren't there. (Parents may not want to hear that their kids act differently when they are not around—but this is just how it is, and it cuts both ways. Silent kids start to talk, talkers go silent…and so on.)

Open Houses, since that time, have always felt like a lawyer's presentation of evidence to a jury of parents. The different exhibits are clean, colorful hallways, and a showcase of fancy projects or after school clubs. Then comes the walking tour where parents make contact with eager smiling staff members. This is to confirm that the staff members don't have tentacles—or Antifa and Confederate flag tattoos. I'm sure a few parents show up *hoping* teachers have one of these tattoos, but from what I've seen, most still want an ideology-free zone at public schools. They want their kids to have a chance to think and decide on their own.

Mr. Brandon, the custodian, passed by and poked his head in.

"How'd Open House go?"

"Man, it was a lot of action."

He emptied my waste basket and smiled.

Mr. Brandon had the build—and broken body—of a UFC heavyweight fighter. Over the past couple of days, I had seen him wrestling industrial cabinets and desks around the school, wearing a thick back brace. When the halls had been dark and quiet that week and I was floundering in my room, he became my first companion.

It dawned on me that as the custodian, Mr. Brandon might have something to say about spray paint being wielded in the rooms. But he had said nothing. He turned and left, and I heard the wheels of a plastic trash bin jangling away down the hall.

I've been told that graffiti artists have a code. When they come upon a wall that's already been hit by another artist, they have a choice to make. They can paint over an existing work *only* if what they are going to do will be better.

I picked up my backpack to go and saw the curtain of the altar pushed to the side. During Open House, out of the corner of my eye, I'd seen younger siblings wander over to it and peek inside. While their older brother or sister mumbled answers to my questions about how their summer had gone, the siblings had caught the first glimpse through the gateway and into the starry sky.

Before turning off the light to my room I closed the curtain on the spray-painted cubby hole—the altar.

My first act as a teacher was vandalism.

Two

I GOT MY teaching license a couple years after finishing my undergraduate degree and spent the next year applying for jobs at schools. I'd get a handful of interviews, but after encountering my inexperience and southpaw approach to questions, each was followed by radio silence.

At the time, America was in two wars against Muslim countries. It was the height of hysteria about Islamic fanaticism. I couldn't help thinking that my foreign name signaled a threat that some employers wouldn't openly admit to, as nice Minnesotans. A "nice Minnesotan" was unlikely to be bigoted to your face and may even welcome you politely as a colleague, neighbor, and even friend. Their manners were in it—and what else would serve as a foundation for understanding but manners? It was a good start and nothing to sniff at, but living in the Midwest, I needed to find a boss who would blow past my weirdness and any cultural red flags my background would raise.

In possibly the last job ever found through the newspaper want ads, I saw a post for a junior high teaching position at a public charter school on the east side of St. Paul. I applied immediately, a week before Labor Day, the traditional start of the school year in Minnesota. Ms. D was the footloose principal of the little school, attached to the old Catholic church. She was a Green Bay Packers fan with a passion for wearing red Christmas sweaters all year round. Ms. D gave me my first classroom, something I'll never forget. Especially when she needed me to speak up for her years later, when forces were lined against her, and I stayed silent until it was too late.

Ms. D claimed that her technique for finding candidates came from her old mentor, a principal in small-town Wisconsin, who would pile resumes in the back of his convertible and drive down the county highway. When he stopped, any names still left on the backseat would get a call.

I walked into Ms. D's office for the interview and heard the 80's hit "I Don't Want to Lose Your Love Tonight" playing from a boombox. We didn't sit very long before she led me down some stairs, saying, "Yep, yep," and nodding her head a lot.

I followed her through a hallway and stuttered, "I can't teach anything I don't know."

"Yep, yep. You can only teach who you are and what you know."

We popped into a room where three blonde elementary teachers, who I would come to know as the Three Sisters, and the laid-back middle school English teacher, were sitting in conversation. After introductions we cruised back out. It was a quick sizing up, and I felt the bustle of their deliberations and verdict before the classroom door shut. They must have given Ms. D the thumbs up after I left, because I was hired.

My role at the little K-8 school would be to teach social studies to fifth through eighth graders. That was the extent of Ms. D's formal directives to me pretty much the whole time that I worked there. The value of her approach towards teachers stays with me to this day: First do no harm. As an administrator she seemed to believe that before advising and instructing—it was best to consider the consequences. She gave me the gift many teachers dream of—to be left alone by the administration unless I asked for help. Letting me find out how I wanted to do the job on my own didn't translate into neglect, it gave me confidence.

Football fan that she was, Ms. D was the ultimate offensive linemen for her teachers. Protect the quarterback and let them make the play. I vowed to try to do the same for my students.

The job at Ms. D's little school had come suddenly, and I had to get my bearings physically and mentally. Physically, I had a room with some tanker desks, a bootleg altar, and random laminated maps on the walls. On the mental side I took a cue from my interview with Ms. D. I knew I could only teach who I was and what I knew. That meant I had to *understand* what kind of teacher I already was, as much as *decide* what kind I wanted to be. I tried to take stock of my approach—the lessons of *Bloodsport* mixed with the heady theories of Professor Greenwalt and other instructors in my licensure program at university, and the wisdom of Ms. Kouneski.

Noni Kouneski was my supervising teacher during my first, short student teaching gig. She had tried to put her finger on the style she thought I was using. "It's called…*discovery learning* or something like that." She waved a hand around in the air in a way that wordlessly described "a mess."

For one lesson in Ms. Kouneski's 4th period U.S. History class, I led the students through an excerpt from Nobel Laureate Doris Lessing's collection of essays, *The Prisons We Choose to Live Inside*. In "When in the Future They Look Back on Us," Lessing tells the true story of an oak tree that was associated with French General Petain, who had collaborated with the Nazis in World War II. After the war, the residents of a town in France convicted the oak tree and sentenced it to death. Besides that bizarre premise, I can't recall how I got kids to tune in to me. It felt like we were all surfing a wave that had originated at the front of the room, but was now being powered by the interest and engagement of the students.

When the bell rang and the room cleared, Mrs. Kouneski leaned in close to me and said, "How did you like that feeling? They were eating from your hand." I suppose it was the way a preacher feels when the congregation locks into the rhythm of a sermon, or that of a musician on stage coasting on the vibe of the audience. In other words, I was a performer in the zone.

"You even had Harrison Bergeron hooked," Mrs. Kouneski added.

"Who?"

"Darren. The jaded kid in the second row."

"Oh." I remembered a student looking at me funny during the lesson. His hair was unkempt and his baggy cargo pants and hoodie spilled out of his desk. "The guy who said he skipped school yesterday to walk around the city?"

"Yeah, that's what I call him. You know the short story by Kurt Vonnegut? 'Harrison Bergeron?'"

"Haven't read it."

"It's just about a dystopian future America. They pass a law where no one is allowed to be better than anyone else. The government handicaps the above-average. If you're beautiful, you have to wear an ugly mask. The athletic are saddled with weights so they aren't too graceful or fast. And if you're intelligent, they install radios in your ears to disrupt your thoughts."

"What does Harrison Bergeron do in the story?"

"He's kind of the hero that rips off all his 'handicaps' and tries to overthrow the government."

"That's Darren?"

"Well, no. Darren just reminds me of the story because he handicaps *himself*. He's so smart but just weighs himself down with stuff."

"Ohh."

Ms. Kouneski sighed and then straightened one of the desks. "Anyways, having a student teacher again is fun. It makes me want to study, or travel. Maybe go back to China."

Ms. Kouneski's colleague, a social studies teacher in the class next door, had warned me in jest, "Don't be fooled by her easygoing attitude—she's a perfectionist and works harder than all of us!" But it was too late, I had already absorbed a split image of what a teacher was: someone who appeared to be calm on the outside but was grinding like mad behind the scenes.

THE MORNING AFTER Open House I got to school early. Mr. Brandon was threading a bookshelf through the door of a kindergarten classroom, but no one else was around. I entered my room, sat on top of one of the tanker desks, and flipped through the pages of my complimentary Teacher Planner, which had been dropped off at the school by an agent of the Horace Mann Insurance Company. The calendar was filled with pages marking monthly and weekly dates. Large blank cells used for listing classroom activities, units, and assignments stretched until June.

Staring at a nine-month school year of decision-making along these lines, I became paralyzed.

As suave and fulfilling as the Doris Lessing mind-meld during Ms. Kouneski's 4th period was, I was sure it was a one-off. If I penciled in that lesson from my student teaching days in one of the cells of the teacher planner, I'd still have 165 days to fill. Besides, that lesson was courtesy of a teaching style that had become outdated. The teacher-centered world of lecturing and notetaking was not fashionable anymore. Since the mid-nineties, innovative ideas about collaboration and group work filtered down from the open-office plans of the tech and corporate world and into the agendas of school administrators. It was true that the ideas filtered more slowly to urban districts, where students of color were assumed to need more direct instruction, but interactive and cooperative learning were theoretically hip. The student was supposed to be the center of gravity in the room. But all these strategies seemed the same to me on closer inspection.

If I picked out a learning goal for the day in advance, it didn't matter if students got there in creative and cooperative ways—they all needed to end up in the same place: the destination that was meaningful to the adults who created and delivered the curriculum. I might as well just photocopy lecture notes for students and spare them the pantomime of being meaning-makers themselves. If a student had no agency in picking what mattered to them as a topic of study, it didn't matter that interactive, and engaging methods were used to learn the skills and content.

A regurgitation of facts, ideas, and mindsets, whether it was accomplished by rote or artsy activities, was still, well, vomit. You can put on an original puppet show illustrating the elegant molecular structure of a fart but it's still a fart. That was the dark power of a set curriculum that I wanted to avoid. It led students toward foregone conclusions on a calendar schedule. In my history classes, I'd end up being a tour guide at some ancient ruins—having them recite after me what others already knew. (*What "others" already knew? Wasn't that shared knowledge—common truth?*) Why was I hesitant to help my students assemble "facts"? It may have been a fear that the string of facts that needed to be imparted to them had no end. When would the individual get to step in? I worried that the kids, on our tour of ancient ruins—the narratives, documents, and conclusions of adults—would never stop to push on bricks to see if they'd open a secret chamber. Doing so might reveal a view of history I didn't know about as the teacher. Snake pits and treasures would remain walled off with me, as the competent guide, who kept them safe and knew the "important" parts to see. As a teacher following a set curriculum, my main job would be to make sure we finished on time to board the tour bus for the next stop, the next topic, the next facts.

On the other hand, if I drew only sparingly from a prepared curriculum, I would have to rely more heavily on what students brought into the room from their own lives and culture. For this to work, students would have to trust that they *had* background knowledge, and that it was worth something. Without clear learning objectives we would be setting out into the darkness, but the upside was that each of us would have to become a torch.

I knew it would be hard to stay an explorer in a room, for both me and the students. Each child has an inner expanse, light-years across, but by junior high, the school routine sets in. The inner expanse becomes shrouded. Many of the kids who would be in my classroom had already withdrawn and hardened, waiting out the day, ticking off minimum requirements. They sensed that the world of adulthood would ask that they moderate their imaginations, and interests, and accept the lie that this was what was required to pick up new responsibilities and freedoms. Like Darren from Ms. Kouneski's room, they began to dim their own torches so the world wouldn't expect much from them or even notice them.

Withdrawal from the world was a strategy that began to occur to students in kindergarten when they found out their loving teacher wanted a *certain* answer. For example, the word "cat" was to stand alone. If a 6-year-old girl wanted to add the word "queen," she'd have to wait for the spelling test to be over for the "catqueen" to reign. The hero of her imaginary world could not be enthroned using the sober words on the spelling list. A boy, asked to draw a portrait of his family, would be gently told by his teacher to erase the sword he had sketched in his hand—weapons weren't "appropriate" at school. The self-appointed protector of the family would have to disarm himself and prepare to become a peasant.

There were two things these kids could do during a school day to face the mandate that there was a right way to learn—get very, very, quiet, or very, very loud.

AT MS. D'S little school, I'd be teaching without a textbook, veteran teacher mentoring me, or head of a social studies department dictating the way it was done. This was a result of circumstance more than design. The middle school section of Ms. D's K-8 school was small and needed only one teacher for each subject. There were no textbooks, because I was a late hire and the school's first social studies teacher. A decision about buying textbooks had never needed to be made by Ms. D, and this ended up suiting me. I was more energized by projects and apt to use handmade materials and primary source documents.

Besides, social studies as a subject itself was a moving target, more so than math, English, or science. Nailing things down in a textbook was more of a temporary political act than a useful approach to history. When studying history, Professor Greenwalt had acknowledged how absurd things could get. "Every turn of the head could produce a different bias—" he'd said "—*and* lesson plan."

Indeed, the different events of World War II and the Civil War were scattered in my mind, each fueling a separate agenda. Each agenda highlighted a different identity, level of society, and narrative, and did so only by excluding the others—at least for a time. Should I focus on the decision making of a great man,

Abraham Lincoln, or the technological advantages of the North? Who would I help the kids get to know—the first black troops to fight in the war, the 54th Massachusetts Infantry Regiment, or the hundreds of women who disguised themselves as men to fight on both sides? Should I introduce them to the thirteen- and fourteen-year-old boys who ran away and joined companies of soldiers, thinking they were headed to adventure and an escape from school and boredom? Should I tell them that schoolteachers like me, were often put in charge of rounding up enough kids, like them, to fill the ranks? Would too much attention to the Confederacy's ideas secretly inspire a generation of white nationalists or open a helpful debate about states' rights? Should I just play it safe and talk about The Battle of Gettysburg—focusing on bird's-eye war strategies disembodied from politics, ideology, and the close-up horror of war?

I didn't know how I'd use the teeming historical resources that were proliferating online: archives of primary source documents, items, and photos—from the Minnesota Historical Society to the Smithsonian, to the Library of Congress. Which perspectives would get showcased just by being easier to access? Which stories would dominate my lips just because they'd been repeated more often, over a longer period of time?

In early twenty-first century America, social studies teachers found themselves as judges. Was it an honor, a duty, a blessing, or a curse?

Around the time I was finishing my teaching licensure program, I was on a run and bumped into my old kindergarten teacher Ms. Baymun. She was from India and looked about the same as when she gave me a cheetah pencil sharpener almost twenty years before. (I had kept my promise to her and said three nice things to other students that day before lunch.)

"What are you up to these days?" she had asked me.

"Getting a teaching license. Thought I'd give it a try."

"Wonderful."

"Yeah, but I'm worried it'll be overwhelming...and boring at the same time."

"How?"

"You know, didn't it get repetitive teaching kids how to read the word 'cat' year after year?"

Mrs. Baymun laughed, and we shuffled a little farther off the walking path. It was like I was seven again, standing before my teacher, and not quite clever enough yet to hide my insecurities from others.

"I worry about two things," I said. "They're kind of opposites. One is that the kids will think I know everything. If they sniff that out on me it's no good." Her head tilted and I went on. "Why would they bother learning anything themselves? You know—no one cares to go to the moon anymore, because we already know what it's like!"

This would soon be the teaching conundrum in the age of Google, which was just picking up steam when I began teaching. Any question could be asked, but since the answer was so easy to find and so thoroughly mastered by a hundred experts at your fingertips—why bother asking? I figured students would stay silent before a teacher that seemed to know it all.

"And?" Mrs. Baymun asked.

"And?"

"You said there were two things you're worried about."

"Well, the other is that I don't know anything at all."

"Join the club!" She leaned back and turned her palms skyward.

"What about the repetition?"

An airliner passed overhead. The engines roared and we stared out at the lake. I imagined a thirty-year career stretching before me, spent retelling the tale of The Battle of Gettysburg.

"I taught how to read the word 'cat' hundreds of times. How could I get tired of that? The sound of three little letters…"

"But…were…was it interesting for you?"

She touched my elbow with her fingertips.

"Each time it was like the student was naming the first cat on earth! And the best part was next—when they started to write it."

It was a hot day, and I was feeling a little guilty about hoisting my doubts on my elderly kindergarten teacher. I thanked her. She wished my family well and stepped back on the path.

As I jogged away, I noticed something in my conversation with Mrs. Baymun that had been present but was hard to quantify—warmth. What computers or a rigorous curriculum could not do was dispel anxieties with something besides information. The warmth of another being: common as a house cat or an old teacher.

FROM WHAT I remembered when I was thirteen, us junior high kids wanted nothing more than to explore the new loneliness of our changing bodies and minds…with friends. Then timidly, and sometimes brazenly, we would expose our new self-chosen identities to the rest of society at malls, movie theaters, classrooms, parties, and sports events. Society would give its own feedback about who we were: charming, smart, annoying, promiscuous, theatrical, weird, dangerous, cocky, artistic, asshole, funny, responsible. Often bad-mouthed, the judgements of others provided a mirror of we ourselves, that was ignored at great peril. Identity beta-testing: that was the true curriculum for middle school.

I wondered whether I, as a teacher, would be able to do the following for my students: thwart my agenda, political agendas, the state's agenda, the economy's agenda, and the diamond-tipped chisel of convention and leave the territory that was rightfully their own uncharted.

Many other objectives were racing for pole position in school. As the first day of school neared, the one that seemed pressing was the need to figure out how to *span time in a room with others* without infringing too much on their rights. Doubting whether I could figure out how to do that, I decided that leaving the classroom and looking back was the only way for my students and I to see school clearly and reflect on why we were there in the first place.

I would instill doubt about whether a "room" was the right place to be to learn about oneself. That would be my first approach. From the beginning, I was plotting escapes from the building and tried to sketch out a hasty manifesto to justify it. Before the kids even arrived, I was up to my neck in the fantasy world of a rookie teacher—when I thought my decisions were their destiny.

Three

AT 8:55 A.M. on the day after Open House, I heard the intercom speaker crackle to life, followed by Ms. D's voice chiding a teacher's child who had been lingering in her office. "Go on. You said you wanted to."

A squeaky voice quickly announced, "Please-come-down-to-the-meeting-thank-you."

"Tell 'em where it is."

"In-the-cafeteria!"

The intercom went dead, and I set down my Horace Mann Teacher Planner on my tanker desk. The margins of the first pages were filled with doodles and squiggly arrows branching from the words "Native Americans," "Lewis and Clark took constipation pills," "Louisiana Purchase," and "power." The boxes under the days of the week labeled "Lesson Plan" were still empty. I hopped off the desk and hustled downstairs.

Staff members trickled into the dreary basement cafeteria of the church complex. It was the Friday before the long Memorial Day weekend and a chance to bring the whole staff together one time before the students came on the following Tuesday.

First meetings of the year could be the godforsaken wastelands of adult small talk before a community was built. I had attended a couple while working at Crawford Middle School in Minneapolis. Teachers drank Minute Maid orange juice from Styrofoam cups, broke plastic knives putting cream cheese on bagels, and felt the ease of summer being hacked to death by a succession of power point slides.

The juice and dry pastries were laid out today, but there was something else in the air in that basement. I tried to place it: leadership, belief, mildew? A circle of chairs was set up and groups of two and three trading in stories and laughter filled in segments of its circumference.

I overheard the Three Sisters talking to each other. Ms. Ashley, a fourth-grade teacher, asked the other two blondes, "Did you see Rashad last night at Open House?"

"He got so tall!" Ms. Rhodes, a third-grade teacher, replied.

"I know—but he still has his chubby cheeks," Ms. Rhodes said, before taking a bite out of a bagel.

"Did you get to talk to his mom?" Ms. Gina asked.

Ms. Rhodes pulled a hand to her mouth, finished chewing and said, "Yeah—she's so great. I can't believe he's in eighth grade."

I took a seat by myself and stared into my cup. Orange liquid shone back at me like a tiny sun. I took nips at it, making sure I didn't finish so I wouldn't have to wade through the milling crowd again for a refill. My main task was figuring out how to sit on a chair and look like I belonged.

Sitting alone, with nothing to do except take sips of orange juice, there were soon just a few shards of orange pulp left clinging to the bottom of my cup. I glanced up. Three jugs of Minute Maid sat on a mobile, folding cafeteria table on the other side of the circle. My throat was dry and hands were fidgety. I thought about getting up for a refill and risking having to have a conversation.

Luckily, latecomers filled the last empty chairs of the circle and Ms. D spoke. "Let's go around and introduce ourselves—and why don't you tell us how you became a teacher and ended up at this school."

A few veteran teachers spoke about being refugees from bigger public school districts. They had gotten out before losing their passion for teaching—their initiative steam-rolled by a fussy or test obsessed administrator, or centralized curriculum planner. A few had been with the charter school since it first operated out of an old dentist's office in a strip mall.

The collection of origin stories was slowly building. It ranged from resolutions made in childhood, to being inspired by a high school chemistry teacher, to traditions of teachers in the family. By the time it reached me it had formed a base of crystal-clear purpose in teaching.

I stated my name, skipped over the biographical profile, and leaned forward.

"I guess I became a teacher soon after I was born. I pooped."

Whenever I was new to a place, I felt I still had some control about what my persona would be. One cagey statement and I could be pegged as the mysterious guy. Since I'd played the role before, and knew it well, I committed to giving it another spin.

As an introvert, that persona afforded me peace and quiet: just tack on a couple offbeat thoughts at the start of small talk and create lasting apprehension in chatty and nosy types. A tricky side effect was that it could create a niggling unfulfilled *interest* in one's personal life.

Yet I found out that I would never have to worry about prying colleagues at Ms. D's little school because the details would be filled in off-stage by speculation when I wasn't around. During my first year I heard snippets about me, Mr. A, the new social studies teacher: he doesn't sleep; he's divorced; he doesn't drink, so he's Buddhist; I don't think he has kids; he's from Puerto Rico, Morocco, Iran.

The backstory that people create for you can be so thrilling that there's nothing to do but go along with it. After a few years at Ms. D's school, I confirmed to my colleagues that I had seven wives, each in a different country. I was being sarcastic, but I was so elusive at the time, it's possible some of my colleagues believed me.

The teaching profession is dominated by women, and a man is a bit of a novelty. Because of this status I learned that men were often spared some of the nitty-gritty tasks that women had to tackle to keep a school running. From organizing events, scheduling, to making calls, to ensuring students had basic needs met like food and shelter. These duties went along with the peer pressure women placed on each other. Since there were so few male teachers, for us, there was rarely a sense of competition or the tension of keeping up with each other.

I found out that even parents had different expectations for male teachers. It was enough for parents that finally there would be someone who might empathize with their active boys, who never could sit still in class. There was also the predicament of some single mothers that factored into their relief at seeing me at the door of the classroom. More than once, I heard a mother speak into the air during Open Houses, "He's gonna have a *man* as a teacher. He ain't never had that!"

As a man in a profession run by women, I remained on the outside of many important nodes of power that relied on complex female relationships that I didn't understand. It was not enough to be polite and do your work in the pressure cooker of an urban school—there was an emotional upkeep that required transacting in pieces of yourself: vulnerabilities and joys. As a certain type of man, I didn't express those things in the same way and sometimes not at all. My reluctance to vent or cry about (and find solutions for) the problems and dramas of the day came off as aloof at worst, stoic at best.

The whirlwind of dedication, anxiety, industry and, at times, mania that descended upon the mostly white women at this urban school was disorienting. I often felt that my level of concern about a student or situation was so out of sync with theirs that I could only remain silent.

When called upon to speak about a kid that looked headed for disaster, I felt obligated to look at the bright side—which sometimes got mistaken for wisdom. Thus, I became the wise, positive guy with seven wives. It was a delicate balance.

When I talked about "poop," nervous laughter and an unanticipated wave of understanding had washed over the circle. After a period of earnest and straightforward sharing, the odd comment stuck in people's ears. It's not to say that my answer was better than theirs, more honest, or that my path to becoming a teacher was more profound—it's just the way I think.

I envied the casual willingness of the teachers to describe their lives. There was a rhythm to good old-fashioned conversation that I envied at times and could never match. But it wasn't me.

I worried that the tickled reaction to my comment about poop would lead me further into a con-game. I'd dole out provocations and insights like fortune cookies and become a caricature. I was aware as a mixed person, with one foot in Africa, and another in the USA, that I would always linger on the edge of who an American was supposed to be. If I filled the role of being an exotic foreigner at my workplace it was because I'd darkened the outline for it myself.

But I decided to press my luck and took my introduction further. I let out a small cough and continued. Afterall, the receptivity to my off-color comment was unusually strong among these teachers at Ms. D's little school.

"After I pooped, my parents had to learn how to clean it up. Then in the night, I cried, and I taught my parents patience. So, I guess, this is the first time I'm getting paid for teaching."

THE QUESTION IN my mind when I said, "I pooped," was whether you had to be aware of being a teacher to be one. There were clever definitions of what a teacher was. An old Arab joke was that a teacher was someone who kept talking when no one was listening. The definition I've held onto though was that a teacher was someone or something that has helped someone to *learn* something.

To me, there were many better and effective teachers than me around. At the staff meeting I was hesitant and embarrassed to claim I was in the ranks of these teachers. Teachers weren't always people—they were things and situations in the world. Boulders without teaching degrees that taught hardness in unforgettable ways. Waterfalls, without a single credential, taught about change and continuity.

My childhood friend Eddie, and his dad Rocky, leaving to do a paper-route in the middle of a sleep-over, taught me sacrifice, economics, and hard work. From the doorway of Eddie's house, I watched them drive off in a 1985 Chevy Impala that we called The Boat. They hadn't laid out any lesson targets, but the subjects—sacrifice, economics, hard work, were taught along the way. It was a bit of the available curriculum generated by their world. The father-son coteaching team had never been evaluated by a principal to see if they were either "developing" or "proficient" at delivering it.

Back inside at the sleepover it was a little harder to enjoy my Twizzlers and game of Super Mario after Eddie and his dad left. The tiny digital man in overalls sped across the screen picking up gold coins, ate a mushroom and doubled in size, then got stung by a *Goomba* and shrunk back down. I miss-timed a jump, died, and got sent back to the start. The stakes were never lower.

I thought of Eddie stepping into the chill before dawn, his pale legs with knobby knees sticking out of Umbro soccer shorts. Rocky would finish a hand-rolled Drum cigarette in the parking lot of the Star Tribune distribution center, his eyes blood-shot but kind. They would fill the backseat of The Boat with bagged newspapers and head for their route.

Rocky would collect paychecks from a couple other jobs only to be kicked back to start when the bills came due. In between he would write scripts for comedy sketches, read *Granta* literary magazine, and take us to downtown bars to watch the Manchester United soccer team play on satellite TV. Eddie kept pumping his scrawny limbs and leveling-up, using the value of hard work and his father's visions of art to unlock new worlds.

The ingredients for such lessons came in waves over the course of ordinary life and, to alert people, taught all one needed to know about living a dignified, meaningful life. As a teacher, I fretted that such ingredients would not be available in the classroom, underestimating the wildcard that would be right under my nose: the curriculum kids generated by being themselves.

Other Loyalties

I HAVE ONLY one memory of my first week as a paid teacher with students at Ms. D's little school. While standing among the students at their tanker desks, trying to remember my lines and unsure what to do with my hands like a mediocre actor, I feared one thing: the classroom door being opened by another adult and being exposed as a fraud.

That afternoon the door *was* thrust open. Ms. Rhodes peered around at the students. It was a gallery of postural disrepair: Xander had nearly slid off his chair, Rashad slumped over until his nose was an inch from the desktop, Angelina's head was tilted so far to the side that her hair was nearly dusting the floor. The rest were in a fog of extreme incomprehension as I went on about the nature of social studies.

Student boredom was the veto power over any schemes written out in my Horace Mann Insurance Company lesson planner.

Ms. Rhodes leaned through the doorway a little farther. She then yelled out a word at the top of her lungs that I didn't quite understand at first.

"*Diarrhea!*"

The kids, reacting with lightening reflexes, started laughing. Rashad perked up and yelled back, "Ms. Rhodes! You nasty!"

I was a bit slower. But then the word hit my center like a body blow, and before I knew it, Ms. Rhodes whooped and slammed the door. I'd been hazed and initiated.

When Ms. D's little school went down in flames less than five years later, me and Ms. Rhodes didn't see eye-to-eye about the causes. But I remembered what she gave me that day, though—the knowledge of how the fresh scent of the irreverent can transform an institution.

I HAVE A respect for the informal tribal education that rubs off from those around you. I'm a believer that learning takes place everywhere, making me more of a traditional person than modern when it comes to education. It's part of what made it hard for me to carry on the conceit that I worked for a specific, formal enterprise, that was tasked with *education* by society.

But as a parent, bedtime, has become its own sort of educational institution. It has a designated time slot each night that my wife Marie and I desperately try to stick to, and I'm always trying to use it to pass along a certain message or lesson. If I'm not careful the lessons can be contrived, and coercive—and a bit like a school lesson.

When I find myself becoming ungenerous about the project of schooling, I again remember Professor Greenwalt. During a class discussion in the licensure program one afternoon, he was speaking about differentiating the fire hose of events from daily life from the focused questions a teacher might introduce. He remarked, "With your students, it's good to remember the difference between experience and *an experience*." Meaning: the teacher's role was to bring about the conditions for certain types of experience. It was the difference between stumbling through the day reading the words on the shampoo bottle, cereal box, billboards, and street signs, and reading an intentionally chosen story in an intentional way.

It was during one of my household's bedtime story hours that the *experiences* of my first staff meeting at Ms. D's little school and Ms. Rhodes strafing of my classroom, echoed years later, in my daughter's bedroom. By having us circle up and share how we became teachers, Ms. D had gotten us to reflect on what a teacher might look like. When Ms. Rhodes screamed "Diarrhea!" into my room, it was a bright flare that signaled, "A teacher can be anything, but a *schoolteacher* must act consciously."

On that night, a stillness came over my daughter Yasmina's room when she finally climbed under the covers. She was six at the time, so this was after she had completed a pre-sleep checklist that seemed to have been co-authored by an airline pilot. It was long and very detail-oriented.

The learning space was warm and quiet. There was a one-to-one teacher-student ratio. It was what one might think were ideal classroom conditions.

Suddenly, Yasmina threw her covers off and leapt up. There was one last item on the list: French-kissing the scruff of our cat.

"If you don't hop back into bed, I'm not going to read," I called out.

She left a wet spot of slobber on the creature's fur and sprinted back to her room. She took her position at my side and saw the book I had in my hands.

"What's that?" she asked.

"One of my favorite books, *Mis Amigos*."

"No!"

"You'll like it, it has animals in it."

"Then I get to pick two more."

"Okay, but that's it."

Yasmina grabbed two more books: one about otters, and one about a magic wooden horse, both as thick as a slice of hand-tossed pizza.

My thumbs pinned open the first pages of *Mis Amigos*.

"*I learned to walk from my friend the cat…*"

The girl in the book listed the teachers all around her. The book's moral was hammered home page after page: *"I learned to watch the night sky from my friend the owl," "I learned to explore the earth from my friend the ant."*

The message became redundant to my daughter. She hooked a finger onto a toe and started rocking. Learning from animals came naturally to children. She already knew all this. Kids are like ancient Shaolin monks, mimicking the wild to bring a forgotten strength back into human movement all day long.

The two books she picked to read sat on the bed next to us. They represented another forty minutes of reading. Before closing *Mis Amigos,* I saw that the author, Taro Gomi, had a bestseller.

It's title: *Everyone Poops.*

four

I LOOKED OVER at the spray-painted altar. The curtain had been ripped off and the lamp I had put in there to charge the glow-in-dark stars had a burnt-out bulb.

A thick packet sat on my tanker desk—a printout of the Minnesota state standards for U.S. history. Westward expansion, the Antebellum South, World War II: whole eras were buttoned together in a tight sentence that was the 'Standard' of knowledge for that era. Next to this was a numbered list of important 'benchmarks' that described what students would be doing to show that they knew this standard. Lastly, there was a column of 'Examples' of topics from that era: names, laws, places, concepts, and events.

I was staring at the standard for pre-colonial America and a list of words in the 'Examples' column that read, "Trading relationships, wampum, smallpox." I tried to make a modern list that would match these words. Oil deal, World Bank, cluster bombs? Globalization, debt, suicide? Sugar industry, lobbyists, heart disease? I gave up and rubbed my hand over my face.

It was three weeks into my first year at Ms. D's little school. The month of September never felt so long, and when I looked at the next week in my Horace Mann Insurance Teacher Planner it was blank. That was when I was reminded of an incident from my licensure program. It was more words from Professor Greenwalt ringing in my ears. He had spoken them during my longer stint of student teaching under Ms. Margaret in the suburbs. I had been called to an emergency meeting with the dean of the social studies education program, along with Professor Greenwalt. We sat in the dean's office at the University of Minnesota, where I received my admonishment. Ms. Margaret had brought them concerns about my level of organization, and preparation, in other words, my professionalism.

Professor Greenwalt, looked across the large wood table at me, and said as delicately as possible, "We want you to be able to make it through September when you get your first job."

The whole time at the meeting I was kind of alarmed and excited that something involving teaching was being taken so seriously. But my pride was hurt, and I was annoyed.

I was living in downtown Minneapolis at the time and would run to the bus at five a.m. after having burned the midnight oil coming up with lessons for Ms. Margaret's eighth-grade U.S. History class. With my messy hair and wrinkled clothes, I would roll into the middle school, monopolize the copy machine like I was printing counterfeit money and head to the room with stacks of print-outs—ready to bribe the students into silence and work if need be.

A couple of weeks had passed since I took over Ms. Margaret's class, and the problem had festered. Between the late nights and my bus runs, I had repeatedly failed to provide Ms. Margaret with lesson plans at the start of the week so she could review them. We had gotten along, and she had even driven me to school a few times, but I had ignored the growing concern behind her polite requests. Foreseeing trouble, Professor Greenwalt, asked me, "You know the kindness and care you give to your students—don't you think your colleague Margaret deserves a little of it too?"

She was a respected teacher who "ran a tight ship," as they say. The students sat in rows of desks, knew their jobs, and expected to imbibe a steady flow of information. I was nothing like that, and I suspect Ms. Margaret just wanted her room back. Each day I taught her class, another bullet point on the state standards was left behind. Like a player in a video game campaign, she kept track of all the outposts in a historical timeline she would have to revisit when I left, to complete her quest to cover the curriculum.

Her approach to history was concrete sequential, the facts were settled, and ready for analysis. Mine was chaotic and speculative—history was breathing down our necks—and we were often spiraling towards the same troubles and surprises as our recent and distant ancestors.

But I think it was the lesson with the human skull that finally unsettled my supervising teacher Ms. Margaret. The night before, I had noticed the cranium resting on a Bruce Springsteen record in the corner of my apartment. Maybe this is my flaw as a teacher, but I don't assume students have any reason to listen to me. I've always been on the lookout for items that might snag their attention, for the unexpected question.

I shoved the skull in my backpack.

What was weird about the students in Ms. Margaret's class was that they had been primed by a teacher who very much expected to be listened to. Students had been well-trained by Ms. Margaret. They carefully followed my instructions as was the routine in her class. Was their discipline more than skin deep? Their voices were off, and bodies were still. They took out pieces of paper and pencils when asked. My worry was whether this outwardly regimented part of themselves could help them survive the teeming, unpredictable jungle that I knew was inside them. Their brains were organs, made of tissue, not rational machines. Brains that evolved through the illogical events and accidents of history, not the dictates of some logical programming done in isolation. I figured I ought to deal with students as holistically as possible, because human behavior and decision making was sometimes logical, but other times erratic—like a rabid beast leaping down from the canopy. I believed students needed some lessons that plunged them into this wild, shadowy part of life, where the rules were reversed. Where the teacher was as lost as them when faced with a new situation.

Rationality helped us shoo away some of the illusions that held humans back: demons, superstitions, and cumbersome religious rituals. This disenchantment of the world laid the groundwork for the industrial revolution and material comforts and got us

Other Loyalties

to look long and hard at the evidence before concluding something was real or true. But it certainly didn't help solve the big questions of life. Those seemed vexing as ever to people in the twenty-first century. In fact, rationality couldn't account for even everyday living. The way a person handled situations was tied up in emotion, intuition, instinct, biology, and a million other factors, happening all at once. We acted like we could dissemble an individual mind or society—or reality itself—and rebuild it like an engine. But we'd get turned in circles or dressed down by the unforeseen consequences of taking things apart. The assumption that we would succeed at understanding and optimizing our existence through scientific breakthroughs was part of the thrill ride of modern life. For my part, I felt life would easily hold on to its mysteries.

I wondered about Ms. Margaret's group of kids, in her organized room, following the sequential logic of her lessons. Would they crack, when the mask slipped and rationality and order was upended, and they faced the true instability of their minds—or the refusal of life to submit to a blueprint. Maybe Ms. Margaret's faith in detailed planning, and a disciplined mind, would give them the confidence that they could hack or bulldoze their way through the incomprehensible and contradictory parts of life. But I held that no matter how well-paved the path running through their suburban neighborhood and toward their future was, consciousness would remain the habitat of a playful, brilliant-but-distractable chimp who got the occasional urge to build pyramids or rip off the limbs of other chimps. When any of these kids scratched the surface they'd find an animal beneath, prowling the subconcious.

At the start of first hour that day, I stood in the front of the room, under the intense scrutiny of Ms. Margaret's attentive students—with a human skull in my hand.

"Can I get a volunteer?"

A few kids raised their hands.

"Ethan, come on down."

An eighth grader rose and took his place beside me. He smiled and waited to see what his role was. His skinny frame was buffeted by the stares of classmates, who, like evil NASCAR fans, hoped for both performance and a fiery crash. I set the skull on a stool next to the boy and asked, "So what has more power, Ethan, or the skull?"

The kids offered their comparisons.

"I think Ethan is more powerful—he can still change. The skull can't really change."

"Yeah, I agree. Ethan can like move around and stuff. The skull is kinda stuck. It needs one of us to carry it around."

A girl in the back row, whose parents had come to America as refugees from Somalia, said, "Well, the skull could be the fear of death. That's pretty powerful. It's scarier than Ethan…he's nice!"

One of Ethan's friends answered, "Yeah, but Ethan has the power to actually kill us!"

The students laughed and another of his friends yelled, "Oh God!"

"Hey, come on," Ethan protested, but remained pinned to the spot next to the skull.

It was a good moment to segue to a discussion about how the past sometimes rules over the present, and how that was the case with their families, genetics, and the US Constitution. The punchline with the skull was that "the dead govern the living."

When I got trained in Montessori later in my teaching career, I learned there was a name for my skull lesson: impressionistic. But it was just not the sort of event in a classroom that slotted into a lesson plan in a systematic way or in a way that Ms. Margaret would understand. I didn't know how to write it up in advance, and the impression it gave Ms. Margaret was that I was going off-road. I appeared to be a rogue teacher disregarding best practices and the consensus of social studies experts about what to teach kids, how to teach it, and when to teach it.

I liked Ms. Margaret, and I surely benefitted from her well-behaved classes I got to work with, but I had an uneasy feeling around her. It was the feeling I had around certain administrators. I felt like the girl who wanted to spell 'catqueen,' and was corrected by someone that knew better.

AFTER THREE MONTHS, my student teaching gig was over, Ms. Margaret got her young scholars back, and I got a teaching license. Now I was on the verge of making it through my first September at Ms. D's little school. It was an election year, and Obama and McCain were on the campaign war path. Unable to penetrate the state social studies standards contained in the packet, I seized on the election: it was an opportunistic decision, not a systematic one, because it did not fit the sequential logic of the curriculum.

Resting my elbow on the thick packet of standards that represented two hundred years of American History, I called the local offices of both main political parties. I asked if they would take any student volunteers to make calls and experience firsthand the thrill of the bloodless battle for power Americans have been blessed with for the time being.

When I had asked Ms. D if we could do this project, she did not hesitate in saying yes. I didn't know then about the red flags this would have raised in a regular public school. Was it legal for students to work on a political campaign even if it was for the purpose of learning about elections? That, along with the need for permission slips, transportation, and the logistics of being away from the school for two hours of the day, with only half of my classes, would have given most administrators pause—but not Ms. D. She understood what timely opportunities could mean to our students.

The next day I let a group of seventh and eighth graders choose who they would like to work for during the election. Luckily, they all chose the same candidate, because the campaign office of one side did not answer my call anyways.

A week later we farmed the fifth and sixth graders out to different rooms, piled the seventh and eighth graders in two vans, and headed to a shabby rented space draped with partisan banners. We were met by a young operative, an energetic Asian-American man, who would be our handler. I wondered about the calculation he was making by letting these inexperienced kids into the room—as nothing is done in politics without it.

The kids were handed a script and their own thick packets, except this one contained the names and numbers of registered voters.

We were led to an area in the back. Lining the walls were smudged banquet tables filled with rows of phones. I sat down with Billie and Kendrick. They were younger students but were favorites of Ms. D who gave them her blessing to go along. We rehearsed making a call and I stepped back. It was mid-morning, and they were met with answering machines, disconnected signals, long stretches of rings in their ears, and occasionally the elderly voice of a potential voter.

It went as expected. Confusion, misunderstandings, repetition, patience, failure: all the elements of learning that I couldn't front-load into a lesson plan. Ms. D hadn't required one. She only saw the ripe conditions—the makings of *an experience.*

After getting through to a person, and asking if they planned to vote, Kendrick turned to me, with a quizzical smile, "Man, Mr. A, why you got us calling these old people?"

Kendrick had been working his charm and was starting to enjoy himself.

Meanwhile, Billie, the dramatist, yelled, "Hell no! I'm not doing this no more. I called this one number, and they said the dude was *dead.*"

The rest of the students were hunched over their packets, checking off who was home, who was voting, and who was buried.

We returned each week until the election, when our handler passed out signs to the students and suggested we post up on the Interstate 94 overpass. Alice, a tall volleyball player, held a sign high and jumped up and down.

"Oh my God! That guy just flicked me off!" Alice yelled before shrinking back a little.

Other Loyalties

A pick-up truck disappeared under the bridge at eighty-miles-an-hour.

"Oh shit!" Billie called out before spinning around and running to the other side of the bridge to catch sight of the truck speeding off.

"He did too, I saw that," Kendrick said.

"Why would he do that?" Alice asked, still shaken.

"I don't know, G. He just probably likes the other guy," Kendrick reasoned before hoisting his sign back up.

Being middle schoolers, they now had a new game to keep score on: how many middle fingers could they get. They had each other and laughed about it.

We headed back to the campaign office. Already the air was charged with the buzz of the final round of a championship bout. Blows were being delivered quietly and privately in voting booths across the country. But that year the election was still a largely ceremonial struggle. The political elite invited the common citizen to pick between two choices that would largely preserve the status quo.

The election was peppered with rallies and debates and news coverage, and moments of inspiration, but did not quite get under the skin or consume people's thoughts. The future would not brighten and horribly darken for either Republicans or Democrats based on the outcome. This is what I hoped at least, and I repeated to the students that the fact that we got to *have* elections was what mattered.

When we arrived back at the campaign office, we didn't find the normal bustle and noise. The main volunteers were out driving people to the polls. It would be hours before election results rolled in. Our handler held out a couple of boxes of cold pizza to the kids. He had been friendly and appreciative of them, and I marveled at his conviction. He was competent and driven—someone you would want on your team.

I think that is what shadowed my view of him as I watched the students shoving pizza in their mouths. Behind the idealistic organizer something festered in a corner of his demeanor. It was subtle, maybe unavoidable, but most definitely present: raw political ambition.

When he looked at the students, I'm not sure he saw individuals, but future partisans. A ledger filling up with checkmarks on one side. For our handler, we were part of a block of voters—a segment of the population that he might put in the bank for his political party.

During our time volunteering it was important to keep in my mind the idea that this was a neutral experience—to show students how campaigns worked. When Kendrick asked, "Mr. A, who you voting for?" I gave him the answer that would become my go-to response to students during every election: "Who do *you* think I should vote for and why?"

The students sensed that there might be more on the line in elections than I believed or let on. Many of the Latino and black kids picked up messages from some parts of their communities that certain candidates didn't actually like people who looked like them. They were never satisfied when I avoided telling them who I voted for. Because without knowing my choice they couldn't be sure that I liked *them*. It was vital for me to stay in the middle, but for adolescents that didn't always appreciate grey areas, it was the same as being on the other side.

When their candidate won the election, the kids were proud. I put aside my cynicism and reserved a row at a movie theater that had been rented so election volunteers could watch the inauguration together. We were late the day of the inauguration and the owner of the theater in Minneapolis, himself a representative of Minnesota's state legislature, was upset and had been about to give our seats away.

Seeing Kendrick and Billie at my side, waiting to sit, he kindly relented. We filed in to watch the show on the big screen. It wasn't nothing for the boys to see a brown face at the top of the Capitol steps, behind the lectern. When my black students looked up at the screen, they saw eyes looking back at them that were softer than usual. It was *an experience*.

Most politicians seemed so old to my students. To their youthful eyes, politicians had faces that were already heading toward becoming skulls. But at least in that election, the flesh that covered the skull, and the 'dead' that would govern the living, looked like their ancestors.

five

IT WAS LATE February, and I was hunting for clues about what I should be doing, and how I might please the boss, again. Ms. D had loved the excited sounds students made each time they returned from working on the campaign. Many of the kids who ended up at Ms. D's little school had been unhappy or unsuccessful in regular public schools. Their parents had sought out the charter school as an act of desperation. Many were from lower-income families, where finances stretched nerves to the breaking point and housing was precarious. But parents had enough energy to take a risk on an alternative school that might work for their kids. They knew school was often going to be the most stable place in their kids' lives.

The adrenaline of seeing the boss happy with my work with such kids goaded me on.

On one bitterly cold morning I stomped snow from my shoes and entered the school. As I was bustling down the hall towards my room, I overheard Ms. D talking about her staff to Ms. Olivia, her assistant administrator, "I like the energy of first year teachers. You know, before they think they know what they're doin.' It'd be great if they could keep that *and* become professionals."

When Kendrick, Billie and other students stepped into the movie theater full of mostly white political partisans—all adults—it was a novel environment for them and me. We had to figure out what made the situation tick, sorting through the leverage gained from being connected. I thought of other environments and situations we could expose ourselves to. Going outside the room provided chances to fulfill Ms. D's wish that her teachers be both amateurs and professionals—full of new ideas, but reliable and competent.

I realized that being out in nature often required people to flip between settings: novice, apprentice, and master. The cycle was hardwired into our thought process. The extreme differences in environments early humans encountered around the world turned us into amateurs over and over again, as we adapted and evolved. Repeatedly cut down to size by novel challenges, we figured out how to survive and eventually became masters of another corner of the Earth. We were naked apes harnessing every faculty we had to make-do. (Were we using the power of rationality to succeed? Or was it something else like the capacity to pay attention, watching for what we didn't know?) At each of our thousands of stops through the primitive landscape, we forged new skills and habits, until it was time to move and start over. Necessity forced our hand, and we had to forego the comfort of being the 'pros' when we left for new habitats.

Even now, strip away the most basic safety bumpers of civilization—food and shelter—and most of us would be beginners again. But our needs would be clarified from our wants in an instant. Burning the cheat-sheet of accumulated technological progress, and going into nature occasionally, could help us remember the ability to *pay attention* that made us who we are.

One reason I loved back-country camping was that the usual signs and symbols that defined and dictated modern life were not present. It required a heightened awareness. In the city, sidewalks and streets led me from building to building, work to home, and hallways led from chair to bed. But in the forest, something could be glimpsed through the trees that had nothing to do with any of this, and I could go off to find out about it. The trail made was mine.

It wasn't enough to watch *Man vs. Wild* or *Naked and Afraid* on cable TV, where they dumped a pro survivalist or handful of bare-butted people onto a beach or swamp and rolled the cameras. In the age of Google and reality TV it seemed even more important to insist on doing things yourself. We all needed the taste in our mouths again.

I believed this would be true of my students on a smaller scale. We could all strive to be amateurs, to be more like animals trusting our instincts—the feelings in our bodies. The sight of kids stepping off a bus into an unfamiliar environment, even if it was a campaign office, was to witness their instincts, their will to survive, sparking back to life.

Of course, some of the kids who lived in unstable homes were always in fight or flight mode. They were *living* in survival mode, and expected trouble: a drunk, screaming parent, an empty refrigerator, a question mark about where to sleep that night. I wasn't sensitive to this at the time, but for my students who had experienced trauma, outings to unfamiliar settings were probably hard on them at first. Traumatized kids had to pay *too much* attention and often shut down from the overload.

But instinct was more potent and creative than we gave it credit for. Getting kids to tune in to their senses, could take them beyond their trauma eventually. Trauma led kids to believe their options were cut off, and they were cornered, and could only withdraw or fight to keep safe. I tried to keep tabs on the theory that paying attention to how our bodies felt in the classroom, versus outside of it, could lead to a wordless gospel with the potential to heal. By twisting and turning down literal paths in the woods, maybe traumatized kids could envision new ways out of their own fear cycles.

Our language skills and future-orientated thinking sped humans to the top of the food chain. It had marked us with arrogance, though. Even the students with troubled homes, were relatively more materially secure in their lives than most people in history, and certainly more than poorer people around the world. It was hard to tell if the words multiplying in the dictionaries of our species only meant more ammo to deceive ourselves. Humans in the first world especially had been sitting pretty too long. Buffered by talk of a 'knowledge economy,' stocked grocery shelves and GPS systems, it was assumed by our talkative society that we knew what we were doing, where we were, and where we were going.

Leaving the classroom would put those assumptions to the test.

There were different things that stood in the way of getting students out of a classroom. One of them was legal jeopardy. Housed in the institutional memory of schools were lawsuits filed by parents. Although crafted into a righteous narrative of keeping students safe, the verdicts from these cases became the guardrails surrounding a school, and the guardrails became ramparts over time.

At the top of the ramparts crouched the birdlike presence of lawyers. Lawyers were at the pinnacle of a culture that was at risk of strangling itself with words and technicalities that were more important than the truth. The threat of lawsuits was enough to turn away beautiful but slightly dangerous ideas teachers dreamed up. Secure within the walls of the school, students started to dry up, their life essence being drained away by risk-averse adults. And all the while vulture-like creatures circled above the icy steps of a school or the playground, waiting for bones to break.

The advantage of Ms. D's little school, which was newer and smaller, was that the institutional trauma from lawsuits did not stretch back that far. Fear of the legal system was still carried inside teachers there who had been scarred in bigger school districts: reprimanded for daring lessons, cowed by the specter of angry parents and the stifling concerns of administrators, who themselves, were badgered by risk-averse higher ups.

Even the contract hueing watchfulness of a teacher union, which Ms. D's school didn't have, could be an obstacle. Afterall, a union teacher could complain about a breach of contract if they were forced to return three hours after the last bell from a field trip. Even though the trip may have been to show kids some cool petroglyphs in the middle of nowhere, the expectation that they should get paid for the extra time could complicate the planning of such a trip.

Rebelliousness and optimism were the stilts on which Ms. D stood towering over the hand-wringing masses of educators and administrators. And a willingness to utter without shame the educational unmentionables: love, risk, and fun. The truth was that most adults in education knew what mattered most—they were just trapped like most adults anywhere. Trapped because they used their role as the responsible ones as an excuse to worry about the wrong things. While performing their duties they forgot what made life exciting and worth living. Like parents using their kids as an excuse to leave a party early or not travel, teachers were too willing to scale back the big dreams they had for their classrooms.

In schools there was a game of chicken going on that blinded the system to what mattered. A game where superintendents convinced themselves to emphasize numbers, whether it was enrollment, finances, or student performance data. Then, the administrators and principals below them felt compelled to prioritize what could be quantified. This preoccupation with the quantifiable filtered to the teachers who were given spreadsheets to fill out about students that they knew in multidimensional ways, that alas, could not be captured by even multiple data points. Teachers had to pretend to care about completing the spread sheets and the data, wasting precious time, and misdirecting energy from their most important task: inspiring and encouraging.

Ms. D, without totally disregarding the uses of test scores and data, won the game of chicken by letting her school swerve off the road and keep going to where the good stuff was—the qualitative data. For the record, Ms. D was a woman whose husband and kids cracked open glow sticks on a summer camping trip. Then, they drank the liquid to see if their urine would glow in the dark—to her applause. Neon green piss flowing under a starry sky; it was data alright. Data that showed her family was together, having a blast.

I wanted to get students out of the classroom to give myself a break, but I was also rolling loaded dice. There was a guarantee the kids would stumble upon educational content out in the world, and my job would become much simpler: just to get them to notice it. But I'd have to wait until my second year, when I joined forces with a science teacher, for my urges to get outside to fully catalyze. All it took were a few kindred points of view, to make a big dream come true.

BESIDES WORKING ON the campaign, we did take one field trip near the last week of school my first year. I don't even remember where we were going. I know that the entire middle school was loaded on two busses, and I was hanging out the window talking to Ms. D.
"Did someone pack the lunch coolers?" I asked.
"I don't know."
"And I never got Malcolm's permission slip," I continued.
"Oh?"
"Should I try to call his mom before we go?" I shout as the bus is pulling away.
I see Ms. D skipping alongside the bus in an ankle length red skirt. During each bound I can see pantyhose with one or two runs. She's waving to the kids, yelling to me and them, "It'll be an adventure!"
On the last day of school that year I had to take cover in my room. Students and staff were roaming the halls, armed with water balloons and buckets. I fancied myself as a person who understood the wide boundaries at Ms. D's school. My reluctance to join the water fight raging on all floors of the building told me I still had a lot to learn.
As students were boarding their buses, water balloons rained down on them from the window of the principal's office. Who supplied the water balloons? Ms. D. Since it was part of my duties to go out with the students for dismissal, I had to finally enter the fray. A couple students warned me that Kendrick had been searching for me. Why was he searching for *me*?
Kendrick and I had something in common; we were both happy to be alive. But we expressed our happiness in different ways. He let the world know about it, I hid my happiness behind a poker face.

That first year at Ms. D's little school, some younger students were allowed to be part of the middle school. I was first introduced to Kendrick's boyish exuberance watching him make calls at the campaign office early in the year. (When a student helps bring a lesson to life a kinship is born, one that's hard to shake, when faced with other students that might be resisting the lesson or actively destroying it.)

But there were other things I enjoyed about Kendrick. We were out for recess one day in the winter, messing around by the loading docks, when Kendrick climbed a railing. From the top he pointed at a giant mound of snow below, and before jumping yelled, "There go Jamaica!"

It was the sort of nonsense poetry flung around by children at play: his parents had roots in the island nation and their son, finding himself in a cold white world, couldn't do anything but take a leap into it.

My way of processing the carnage of the forty-five-minute snowball fight during that same recess, was calm and quiet reflection once we returned to the classroom. But Kendrick, midway through an acrobatic verbal account of how A.J. got his whole ear filled with snow, suddenly stopped and took a sidelong glance at my face, "Man, you suspicious."

"What do you mean?"

"You don't never say nothing."

"But, what if there's nothing to say right now."

He just chuckled.

"Man, *you're* suspicious," I protested.

He shook his head, "Why you *so* suspicious Mr. A?"

A master at reading people and situations, it was his way of saying that he hadn't nailed me down yet but was still trying. It became an ongoing joke until he graduated from eighth grade. I'd be standing there lost in thought and Kendrick would say, "Stop being suspicious."

Kendrick came from a family of voluminous talkers and was mystified by my silence. His ease and charm with people bedazzled me in return. His mother was a large lady I'd sometimes see around the school—her rough edges buffed by charisma. She needed them both to batter down obstacles and manage the sprawling patchwork operation required to survive poverty in America.

Ms. D, who became like a godmother to Kendrick, would say, "Well, Kendrick's mom got her ten-thousand-dollar tax return. They went to the mall and Kendrick got new shoes and five hundred dollars-worth of clothes."

It was a classic dig at poor families, but the problem was that there was some truth to it. Being poor put people behind the eight-ball so comprehensively at times that I couldn't blame a mother for giving her kids the feeling of what it's like to have enough money—getting the things they need and want and not worrying about it for once. Even if it wasn't a textbook financial decision, it was an emotional investment that had its dividends.

The real issue was that Kendrick's mom poured the rest of the tax-money into the casino. When you combined poverty with bad habits that anyone can fall into, there was little chance of getting out of the hole. These destructive patterns weren't special to black families and were found in other families at the school from the lower end of the economic spectrum. I heard stories of a Hmong girl, whose home life was a study in neglect due to her unemployed, alcoholic parents. On home visits, Ms. Gina, one of the Three Sisters, would see a lawn strewn with beer bottles and used tampons. So bad were some of the situations found there that Ms. Gina was compelled to break some rules about student-teacher boundaries, and had the girl stay over at her house until things settled down.

There was a poor white student named Ryan who had an abusive, and spiteful father. Down on his own luck, he made sure his anger at the world passed through Ryan first. Ms. D asked me once if I'd ever been on a home visit to Ryan's house. When I said no, Ms. D replied, "Oh, Mr. A, it's one of the worst, one of the worst I've seen."

Ms. D would always remind us that despite their flaws, struggling parents loved their kids and tried to take care of them. No matter what judgements I made about them as the teacher of their children, I could never come close to providing those pieces. I would not and could not, be there for them after the bell rang. And if they ended up in prison later in life—I wouldn't be the person who remembered them and showed up to visit. Even so, it was fair to say, that the sooner some of these kids broke away from their parents, the better.

One day, in late winter, we had an afterschool event for parents, in the spirit of giving them the benefit of the doubt. I'd been reading about a Brazilian educator named Paulo Freire who rallied some farmers and taught them how to read by using everyday words and ideas that related to their lives. His aim was to empower the community and humble teachers a bit. Literacy, expertise, and knowledge were not things to be owned, and should not be hoarded by teachers. They were meant to emerge from a dialogue between the two groups: teachers and community.

I thought a good place to start would be to hear from parents in a setting that was different from the PTO or conferences. Fired up, I raced to Ms. D and asked her about bringing in a couple instructors for a staff training who were using Freire's techniques at a high school in St. Paul. She cut the check and we helped two educators fund their side hustle.

Circling up in the dim cafeteria, the instructors led parents and teachers through theater exercises that brought some eyerolls from the tired staff. It didn't matter if the intentions of a professional development were dipped in gold—teachers made for awful students after four p.m. Or anytime really. But the presence of some parents that had showed up stemmed an open revolt, and lent a touch of urgency and earnestness to the gathering.

We finished two rounds of "Columbian Hypnosis," where we took turns pretending to mesmerize our partners with the palms of our hands and leading them around like puppets. Then we sat down with parents to talk about ways to make things better at the school for their babies.

Kendrick's mom hijacked the mic without a backward glance. As she began telling stories, it was like a stick of dynamite had been thrown into a fishpond. The other parents just floated there stunned, wondering how or why they would interrupt such a lady. She was empowered by the opportunity to have her voice heard, but there was an uneven quality to the situation. After not being asked what she thought for the many years her kids had been in school, the floodgates had opened.

She talked up and down the heartaches and humor of being a parent, stopping to punctuate points with deep chuckles. She finished by saying, "And I told those girls, until he graduate from high school, *I'm* Kendrick's girlfriend." Kendrick's mom brushed off the social cues that said she should probably pass the mic, and told a few more stories, keeping the narrative squared on her experience. But she had showed up for the meeting, and even after years of having Ryan as a student, I would never meet his father once. Still, after seeing how one parent could commandeer an event, I realized how fraught it could be to co-create a curriculum and direction for a school through such dialogue between parents and teachers. When you added ideological differences, it made me want to abandon Freire's ideas and keep more power in the hands of teachers—if they could be trusted.

Part of Kendrick's desire to figure me out had to do with finding a place to put me in his private map or picture of the world. Just like I was sizing up his mother and other parents, so they'd fit on my map of the world. Kendrick and I had our private maps, but we also were part of the actual world his mother had to look at unflinchingly. A white Minnesotan world full of reserved, sometimes wary Scandinavians, that made each encounter with her loud, direct presence feel like a barnstorming.

I wasn't white or black, but it was not clear what other category Kendrick could put me in.

Eventually there emerged a consensus among some students that I might be "Arabian." One class period I saw A.J., a gentle Latino kid who liked to draw animals, pretending to strap on a vest and press down on a button in his hand. The kids around him were all giggling. I got closer and heard him saying, "Allahuakbar!"

A.J. was just re-enacting stuff he saw on Comedy Central. Up late, A.J. had probably watched the recent episode of the animated series *South Park,* called 'Imaginationland.' In the episode some Islamist fanatics blow themselves up at a goofy theme park. The centuries-old stereotype of the murderous Arab had been passed along to the next generation by way of a funny cartoon series.

But I took it with a smile. The beauty of a diverse class of kids was that no one was outnumbered. Each race got stereotyped and roasted but the distribution of cultures in class stripped it of some malice. The kids asked A.J. about his taco stand, and I figured we were even. Still, Kendrick pressed on, asking me repeatedly, "Mr. A, *where you from?*"

Where did my reluctance to share about my life come from? It bothered my colleagues and students but seemed normal to me. Although I grew up in America, the Middle Eastern style of Islamic architecture suited my mindset: the architecture of the veil. Houses were designed to appear very plain on the outside. Ancient neighborhoods stretching from Morocco to Syria to Afghanistan were built from this blueprint.

From the street, in front of a windowless wall and simple door, it was hard to tell if the owner of a house was rich or poor. The idea was to demonstrate modesty, but also protect outsiders from their own jealousy and covetousness. On the inside of houses, an enclosed courtyard opened to the sky. There'd be a garden and a fountain that flowed with cool water. It was also the place where people had their private conversations. In a roundabout way, it resembled some facets of Midwestern culture—an aversion to flashiness, discretion, and an orientation towards family and religion.

Along with my distaste for gossip, this inner-courtyard approach to interactions served as a type of end-to-end encryption of my personal life. Because I didn't share with my colleagues, little was shared with me. We remained opaque to each other, opaque and free—free from having to make too many judgements about the doings of each other's lives.

The problem was that my attitude toward sharing was a liability with students. When I brought my principled disinterest in people's personal lives into the classroom, kids got the feeling that I didn't care about *their* lives. Most teachers, whether sincere or not, double-down on finding out about their students' interests and families—hoping to cash in on the relationship when the going got tough in class.

I had never developed the skills to question people in that strategic way and could only fall back on what I knew: let things play out organically and see what happens. The result was that I harmonized with some students. But for many other students, I sheepishly gambled that another teacher would connect with them.

In only my first hear I had already committed the ultimate teacher *faux pas*: I had favorites.

Kendrick never found me on the last day of school that first year. His water-balloon ammo had been spent and I escaped a soaking.

The buses pulled away. Kids were shouting out the window that revenge would be theirs next year, with the elementary teachers hooting and waving them away. Mrs. Rhodes launched one more water balloon at the last bus, and tiny fists shook at her out the window.

After a year of scrambling to keep up with the demands of working with junior high kids and trying to be a serious adult with a job, I couldn't unwind. I walked into the school with my head down, mulling over some question about this or that.

Just like the first day of school, they don't tell teachers in their licensure programs about how to act on the last day of school. What should you do with your hands? What task should be done first and last? How do you cap off the year?

"Mr. A!"

I was startled to see Ms. D sitting at the front desk with her shoes off and feet up. She was leaned way back in the chair with her hands behind her head.

"It's summer!"

Six

AFTER MY FIRST year at Ms. D's little school the value of summer break took some time to appreciate. By mid-June, parts of myself that had been seized up for nine months in lessons and the fates of young people, started to relax. But it took until the middle of July, the point farthest from the end of the school year and its beginning, for a full recovery.

I was at a fancy bakery called The French Meadow with my friend Dan, who had stayed on as a special education teacher at Crawford Middle School. We had giant breakfast burritos, coffee, and a table on the sidewalk where the sun was blessing our leisure. Parts of my identity that I recognized from before I was a schoolteacher were wheeled back out to the front of my consciousness for the first time in nearly a year.

"Having to run classes all day, for so long—it was like being possessed."

"I know. I forget to work on my music sometimes during the year," Dan replied.

"School just took over. I didn't think about traveling or writing...it was just getting through the day. Man, sometimes I felt like a trapped servant. Is this what it's like to have a real job?"

"Stepford teachers."

We both laughed remembering the Christopher Walken character in the recent remake of the sci-fi movie, *The Stepford Wives*, where husbands of the fictional town of Stepford, Connecticut, program their wives to be dutiful robots.

I raised my coffee cup, mimicking a gonzo toast Walken's character makes at the men's club that is responsible for the mind-controlling scheme. "To Stepford!"

Dan dumped some hot sauce over his burrito, "All I know is I'm never teaching fucking summer school."

In fact, at the end of the year Ms. D was asking who wanted to teach summer school. But seeing the fear in my eyes, she didn't press me. Now, feeling my limbs limber up at the alfresco cafe, taking notice of thoughts besides school, I was grateful.

By disposition, being a schoolteacher was a stretch for me. I had started that first summer off by reflecting on why teaching seemed so damn hard for me and not other young teachers. It was probably an illusion, but other teachers, even during my licensure program, seemed settled about their role as adult in charge. Their personalities aligned with the duties of the job, and they fit in. Maybe they were just first-born siblings and were used to giving orders. But the distress I felt in the role all year didn't seem to be written on other teacher's faces. I tried to figure out why.

In my early twenties, before deciding to become a teacher I traveled a lot. I was following a dream of roaming the Earth looking for knowledge, just like in the ancient stories. But I wasn't a swashbuckling traveler who sought out action. In fact, one of the first things I did after arriving in a new city was frantically look for the parks. It was a type of panic born of being surrounded by people on the sidewalks who had an aura of purposefulness—businesspeople, hipsters, even the homeless with their bundles of rags. They all kept snapping into place like Lego in a time lapse video.

Fixed eyes, set jaws, feet that moved bodies down the street in an obvious direction, made me feel that they knew how to belong. From head to toe, other people presented unified surfaces. Doubt and contradictions were inside each person, but appearances had me fooled. Their skin hid many different organs and selves but their outer expression of themselves was singular. Their faces were perfect masks. They had careers, roles in society—even if it was being a vagabond. With my car and gas money, I couldn't even pull off being a vagabond. It was clear who everybody else was, but who was I?

If it was a mystery how other people held themselves together, I was more keenly aware about what was going on inside my own skull. There was not one single mind in there but many, not one persona but many. Depending on the time of day, the situation, the weather, a team of rivals was at work in my cerebellum, each with its own emotions and reactions.

This had always made being around people difficult. Crowds were treacherous. The more people I had to try and understand, the more minds that started firing-up inside my own brain. It was like my mind was a fractal that grew a different branch whenever it encountered another mind. (This was a serious liability for me as a teacher who would have twenty to thirty-seven kids in front of me at once. Firing up a new mind to meet each kid was close to impossible.)

While traveling I wondered sometimes about the point of even going to cities where there were so many people—instead of just heading for the hinterlands. I guess that was the appeal of the American road-trip that I'd been idealizing since reading *On the Road* in high school.

As a teenager, whenever my parents went out of town, I bought a pack of sunflower seeds and jumped into my mom's Mitsubishi Gallant. It was so easy to turn onto the Interstate and drive all night. I weaved around the population centers and shot out into the countryside. The act of keeping the car on the road marshalled the various narratives in my head and at least pointed them in the same direction.

One trip I pulled onto a dirt track, drove for a mile over sun-flaked cow pies and stopped. The world went quiet. It was federal land in Oregon. I got out and walked past a rusted claw-foot tub sitting in the sagebrush. It was full of holes made by gunshot. Around it were ATV tracks, shell casings, and beer bottles, setting up a tableau I didn't fit into.

A low-key, straight-talking persona started to quiver to life inside my mind in case I ran into the triggermen. But I never would bump into the rowdy, freedom loving boys, that had claims on the open range. And in their absence the need to sustain my invented steely rural persona faded too, and I was left in solitude with the other parts of myself. One less mind, one less role to play, for the time being.

After college, when I was at parties or bars, or around any number of people, I would often get left behind. Conversation was a high-speed human event. It couldn't wait for me to sift through my lumbering reactions to what was said. Likewise, a classroom was stuffed with emotions, exchanges, and unfolding dramas that required multiple conversations on an hourly basis. A classroom, I discovered, was too noisy for my disposition. Not due to kids yelling, but because the responses to their raw humanity, the personas it took to relate to the variety of kids in an urban class, piled up inside my mind.

Towards the end of my licensure program Professor Greenwalt left a note on one of my papers that anticipated this problem. He warned of the risks I'd face as a teacher, and I knew he was right: "My only concern here is that your sharp eye for observing people does not slow you down as a teacher, where many decisions need to come quickly and intuitively."

In the hinterlands, on the other hand, I caught up to myself. There were no, apparently "solid" personhoods to compare myself to, or interpersonal events to note or mediate. Out there *I* could be the one who was observed—by the animals and myself, and some intelligence hovering within me but just beyond my purview. Was this intelligence the collective unconscious? A higher objective self? Madness?

I never thought of it before but when I was alone out in the country the sun went down silently. Yet the sky still answered it in a thousand colors. Within the quiet of the open range the many parts of myself were all still there but I could hear them clearly. My preferred role of witnessing—paying attention to—my own existence found its perfect setting.

To be a teacher I had to believe it was possible for my students to find this peace too. To feel like they could create a forcefield out of their own minds and use it to become a part of things—their bodies and every other atom around, if only for an afternoon. A word of encouragement, a small bit of space left open in the classroom for students to become themselves, might be the difference between getting in touch with all their parts or splintering.

The stakes were higher than I thought in middle school.

A kid's brain changed a lot in very early childhood, but in adolescence, another time of big developments, they had a greater ability to shape the changes happening in their brains. The forge was hot, but the young blacksmiths were impulsive and fickle. Growing up was a complex task and they needed help.

Psychologically and physically, kids were both whole and incomplete at the same time, just like adults—but with a better shot at rearranging the pieces of themselves before they catalyzed. They were more malleable and more open than adults, and I feared the results of my influence on them. I thought of the last part of Professor Greenwalt's note on my paper: "In trying to understand our students, we're taking things apart that shouldn't be taken apart—to try to understand them better. But ultimately, a teacher has to act. They have to make some choices, and students *will* be affected by those choices."

Seven

THE SOUND OF flip-flops came down the hall and stopped outside my classroom. It was morning but the middle-aged Scandinavian-American who peered into my room was already beet-red, battered by the humidity of late August in Minnesota. It was the start of my second year at Ms. D's little school.

"It smells like sawdust," she said, taking a few more steps into the room.

"That's right," I answered.

"What do you have going on in here?"

"I built those bleachers over there this summer," I said, nodding at two massive, wood boxes.

"Oh wow, impressive."

"Well, actually I was an assistant. My, well…um, older friend Dennis helped me out."

I didn't know how else to describe the father of my girlfriend, the grandfather of my son, who was a Scandinavian himself. Dennis was a Baptist preacher with rock solid values, who picked up skills during a life of poverty and service. A preacher who maintained the mental and spiritual health of vast rural stretches through weekly pilgrimages for cups of coffee with the elderly, shut-ins, backwoods weirdos, and un-befriended.

When we went up North to visit him before he became sick, we played chess and ate molasses cookies together. Cups of coffee steamed on a red-and-white checkered tablecloth—the central command of rural households—and conversation flowed. He told stories about all the near misses with death that populate life in Northern Minnesota: the chainsaw ripping off a chunk of his leg, the truck through the ice, the bear, the mining career.

I filled in the blanks of my foreign origin for him by telling stories of my father's village in North Africa and his work at a greenhouse in Faribault, a community in Southern Minnesota. My father had harmonized with the low-key rural folk there and didn't mind the hour drive each way from Minneapolis. My mother was born in the small Wisconsin town of Chippewa Falls, left after college, and never looked back, teaching in a low-income neighborhood in Chicago before settling in Minneapolis.

Small-town America was part of my origins. But growing up in the nineties in Minneapolis, I took cues from the fashionable trends of global culture filtering in from the coasts, and knew that it was cool to not be white. For years I soaked in the dismissive attitude towards the bland Midwest, that has come back to bite the country.

I was grateful, in this later stage of life, to be able to spend time with my small-town father-in-law to be, subduing my cosmopolitan and liberal conceits.

On one visit to his house up North we toured the vintage cars that were hauled to the woods beyond the field as they gave out over the better part of a century. A black Ford from the 1940's nestled against a row of tamarack pine. My father-in-law sat on the bulging wheelhouse with my son, and I snapped a picture. Later that day my wife and I had a cigarette in a gold 1964 Rambler that had a young birch tree growing up through the hood. The car was like a rare butterfly, pin-mounted to a board. The scattered cars were a living museum of the glory days of American history.

Dennis and I found common ground on the waters of Lake Namakan, near the border with Canada. Goals were simple out on the water: keep the leech water fresh, catch some walleye, and find a nice island for lunch. Out on the water it was hard to tell where the border was between two countries even. We were ordinary men again, feeling the breeze coming off a glacial lake in July.

Other Loyalties

We had boated beyond the signs and symbols of cultural warfare, the delirious right-wing talk radio, the snotty jibes of headlines in liberal papers and on cable shows. Sides and colors were being chosen like the "red" and "blue" death spiral of Crips and Bloods in Los Angeles ghettos, come home to roost in greater America. We left all that on the mainland and found our island.

It was there that we reclaimed *other loyalties*. Ones that I keep close to my chest as political hysteria threatens to make me turn into an attack dog for one side or another.

My awkwardness in naming the venerable old man to my colleague went along with my hesitancy in sharing details about my personal life. I felt that leaving a few blanks in the story gave me room to breathe, and not just politically. I always pictured social scenes like one of those cork boards on FBI shows, where notecards, photos, and maps, are webbed together. If I could prevent too many links from being made, I could avoid being trapped, domesticated, and turned into a token.

I also didn't want to be neutered as a "really nice guy" by the armies of women who populate K-12 education. By not pursuing the big money of careers that were more open to men, I felt it was assumed I must be somehow more sensitive, moral, and safe. And more boring. It was a contradiction—I wanted to be left alone but I also wanted to be interesting.

The persona I'd played with my first year had served me well, it had acquired me seven wives, after all. Eventually though I was boxed in by lies of omission. Namely, that the woman I lived with and was destined to marry, wasn't ever mentioned to the people I spent more than half my day with.

Only after three years at Ms. D's little school did my colleagues learn that I had a child. In a bid for more freedom, I had wanted to keep work and personal life separated. Yet in my classroom I hustled like an addict, trying to inject hits of life back into the dulling confines of school for my students. It was that conundrum again—what to include and what to exclude from the classroom.

The veteran teacher walked over to get a better look at the bleachers. She was one of the refugees that had fled a big school district and escaped to Ms. D's little school. She ran a hand over the green all-weather carpet that covered the bleachers and took a deep breath in through her nose.

"I love the smell of sawdust. My dad was a carpenter."

She turned, and the sound of flip-flops smacking heat swollen feet headed down the hall and into a first-grade room.

I felt affirmed that an experienced teacher had marveled at something in my room. The bleachers, like the spray-painted altar, were another stand-in for my ignorance of the curriculum. In the run-up to my second year as a teacher I wasn't prepping lesson plans and units because I was still racking my brain for a different piece of the puzzle; what should a classroom look like?

I found my answer in the memory of Ms. Jaglo's room, my raunchy sixth-grade teacher. Ms. Jaglo had short, bleach blonde hair, that marked her as unmistakably Scandinavian, but she didn't exactly fit the stereotype as reserved. Not only did she teach me my multiplication tables, but each student was allowed to put a condom on a broomstick during a sex-ed lesson. She was strict but allowed for controlled outbursts of rambunctiousness that appeased us.

Ms. Jaglo's go-to consequence for me when I made mild infractions was that I had to write a story and read it out loud to the class. The clutch detail was that she never told me that I had to use a different word than 'catqueen,' so to speak, and never told me that something I wrote was 'inappropriate,' making me erase the sword I had drawn. As a boy, she never left me defenseless in the class, taking away the tools I needed to handle life. I later learned that she kept a laminated collection of stories I wrote and illustrated, replete with color drawings of poop, for over twenty years, before giving it to my parents when she retired.

What I remember most about her classroom was that in one corner she had two large bleachers that formed a sort of mini amphitheater. In class we would gather around Ms. Jaglo on these carpeted bleachers for lessons, stories, or conversations. Often

Other Loyalties

those things were one and the same. It was a magnetic hearth that focused the dispersed warmth and attention of the kids and teacher in a big room.

The bleachers were almost too friendly and comfortable. I can now see why some administrators like desks made of metal and particleboard, topped with a cold melamine finish, spaced out in sharp rows. Because in the cozy, fort-like space between the two bleachers and the corner of the room, I got into the only real trouble I ever had at school.

Me, Cleo, Lexie, and Alisa were inside for recess because we hadn't finished an assignment. When Ms. Jaglo stepped out for a few minutes, Cleo laid out a blanket and we told the girls that we should make a baby together. This was obviously before Ms. Jaglo's sex-ed lessons, and it was the sort of joke sixth graders made when left to their own devices. We all laughed. I wouldn't have even known where to start. (Around that time my friend Tyrone told a sexual joke about a golf ball and three holes. He kept checking my face for comprehension, but I was lost.)

Cleo, Lexie, Alisa, and I were all still playing "dress-up" but on the awkward threshold of adolescence, when some of our fashion choices might start to stick if we weren't careful. The news of the would-be orgy during indoor recess reached someone's parents and I got my first and only school suspension. When we got back the class, we had a discussion with Ms. Jaglo about what had happened—on the bleachers.

What should a classroom look like?

Before thinking it through I raced to Menards. Fifteen years after sitting on Ms. Jaglo's bleachers I was going to build my own. The Baptist preacher, Dennis, rode shotgun with the Muslim father of his unwed daughter's child at the wheel. It was an American scene of Vaudevillian and ordinary divinity. It was completed when we rolled down the city streets in his light-blue Ford pick-up with a stack of two-by-two's, plywood, and all-weather carpeting, ready to get to work.

We unloaded the supplies in my garage, and I promptly stepped aside. Dennis set up two sawhorses, mapped out the project in his head, and plugged in his circular saw. I tried to make myself useful but kept thinking of this nexus of my raunchy former teacher Ms. Jaglo and my future father-in-law, a man who helped organize pressure on a town co-op to stop selling pornography on the basis that it was a community supported store.

The conservative man and the liberal woman overlapped on some choice real estate of character. Placing a premium on a type of honest companionship, their day-to-day approach to life superseded political alignment and religious dogma.

It took a few days, but we finished up the bleachers. We loaded them into his truck and drove them to Ms. D's little school. After slotting them through my classroom door like two thick slices of Texas toast, we slid them into place. Next to my brutal tanker desk and second-hand student tables, the carpeted homemade bleachers were a soft touch.

It was already the morning of Open House, and I didn't have a syllabus ready, but I felt prepared for the year. Just the novelty of a mini-stadium taking up a third of the room would rearrange student's expectations—and buy me some time. Plus, it would be a dazzling exhibit for parents to see during Open House, sure evidence of a competent teacher.

The next morning, we had our beginning of the year staff circle in the dreary basement cafeteria. Ms. D celebrated the high attendance of families at Open House the night before, which was unusual at an urban school. It was a sign that parents were buying in to the program. Teachers told their origin stories, we had lunch, and then we had an hour of 'professional development' training.

Ms. D's staff development was of a different order—not for her were the half-hearted discussions of academic articles about reading strategies, PowerPoint death marches about school policies, or videos of sell-out teachers (who we were all jealous of) hawking canned strategies from their teaching brands. Instead, Ms. D paired us all up and told us to take a walk.

Sounds simple enough unless you're Mr. Maloney, the middle school science teacher. I would soon learn that he preferred jumping, climbing, and diving. Hiking, the closest Mr. Maloney came to walking, was done at such a pace that he had to make signs out of twigs and leaves to indicate which turns he made when you fell behind on the trail.

During my first year at Ms. D's little school, I heard rumors about a science teacher who had worked there the previous year but had to take a job at another school to get health insurance for his family. Some of the teachers had a nickname for him, "Pony." From the female teachers who said it, I got the feeling it was a name born of both affection and attraction.

There was an undomesticated whiff about the stories I heard about this science teacher. I was even compared to him that first year when another teacher witnessed the ramshackle but energetic scene in my classroom. Kendrick was chasing Musah around the room with a toilet plunger, as Elliot filmed them on my camcorder. (It was their attempt at acting out an idea they had for the Halloween horror movies we were making.)

But I felt a little insecure when I heard them mention me and the science teacher's names together. I knew the other teachers missed the guy and had the sensation that although there might be similarities between us, I was coming up short next to the memory of the genuine article.

Alas, it was true. Mr. Maloney roamed on a different plane of excellence altogether, a combination of the exacting Vietnamese common sense of his mother and fierce Scottish self-sufficiency of his father. When we joined forces my second year, the best I could do was take up a position near his right hand.

Personally, Mr. Maloney palled at the crowd and clamor he found at a Hanoi market when he had visited Vietnam but retained a taste for spicy dishes and hospitality. In spirit, he preferred the vigor and solitude of the Scottish Highlands, sketching out his clan's crest badge for his students to see.

There are a few people in life that I've met who can thread the needle. Mr. Maloney was able to take impulses from the rawest parts of his psyche and shape them into wholesome experiences without smothering the danger and thrill he hungered for. With his return to Ms. D's little school my second year, outings with students would blossom under his maniacal unwillingness to leave a moment dull.

But it was Mr. Maloney's artistic side that steered his interests and ambition in a thoughtful and humane way, turning the reckless into the poetic, the brazen into the visionary. An ordinary walk with students at a regional park in St. Paul would turn into an 'urban hike' that might include entering drainage pipes or crossing creeks on homemade rope bridges.

There's a recent YouTube video of him walking along the steel arch spans on the underside of the historic Arcola High Bridge, nearly two hundred feet above the water. His footsteps drive forward without hesitation. The GoPro camera on his forehead captured a wide angle and ate up the sun-kissed ripples on the St. Croix River that flowed on at the bottom of the drop. One rogue gust away from a filmed demise, Maloney stoops to pick up a rusted bolt. He holds it up to the camera and gently chides his father, a retired welder who helped repair the bridge decades earlier, for the shoddy work of his crew.

"When did you stop being scared?" I asked him after watching the footage.

"When I was eight."

I tried to learn from Mr. Maloney's knack for taking kids into challenging environments and keeping our species on its toes. As we conspired together over the years, with Ms. D's support, to get the kids out of the building, a partnership was born. A partnership that brought terror to our fellow teachers.

It was about their desire for stability I suppose. Blame it on our move from hunting and gathering to farming ten thousand years ago. Any modern person used to watching TV with snacks crafted out of corn starch is the torchbearer of this legacy. And as such, these people, including teachers, get grouchy when you make them get up and move like some wretched nomad.

When Mr. Maloney and I asked teachers to leave their rooms to go on outings we planned, their hands tightened around their daily planners, and black disks replaced their eyeballs. What will

Other Loyalties

we *do* out there? The suggestion of the whole middle school going on a field trip also triggered the gears of a giant alarm clock. One counting down the days left to hit all the benchmarks, before the state assessment tests.

The daunting logistics of permission slips, pre-ordered bag lunches, student medications, and bus rentals, curbed most leftover motivation to leave the building. Field trips fell in the 'extra work' category of a teacher's workflow and were treated with caution.

It was often educational assistants who were more willing to support a trip outside. The truth was that us younger teachers and assistants were unaware of the amount of work that needed to be done to get students caught up, prepared for testing, and restored after this or that raw deal life had dealt them. An impossible responsibility that oppressed experienced teachers—and blinded them to the potential of leaving it all behind, at least for a day.

The other challenges were the possessions and habits of veteran teachers. They'd spent years building and collecting and making their classrooms warm and comfortable to students. Hammered-in routines that made the day tolerable for both them and students crisscrossed the room like a functioning but jam-packed roundabout. The system served the children and ironed out the chaos in their lives. But the same hard-won classroom habits could lead to inertia, stability's revenge.

At least in my case, as a beginning teacher, whether to leave on a field trip was an easy choice. I didn't know the content to my class, didn't have student behavior well-managed, and was grateful to just get the heck out of the building. I could hide my shortcomings by blending my unruly classes into a larger group. My hope was always that a firm teacher would take charge of the students I couldn't handle.

I knew my philosophizing about nature was partly a cover-up. Finding an honest way to introduce Manifest Destiny or the Indian Removal Act was exhausting. The daily planning of lessons was a never-ending task of decision-making and stagecraft. Going to bed by midnight on a school night was a blessing rarely experienced in my first years as a teacher.

I was proud of my new bleachers in my classroom, but the main show, the heart of the middle school, would begin to move outside. And Maloney and I would be the ones to blame.

BY OCTOBER, I had figured out a U.S. history lesson for the kids in the nick of time. Towards the end of September, in a moment of weakness, I'd tried to get my *Age of Empires III* CD-ROM to work on an old desktop I brought from home but couldn't figure it out. I read on the back of the package that you could play the game as either the British, Spanish, or French empires, but the Native American civilizations were not playable. However, as players were building their colonial empires in North America, they could make 'alliances' with the different tribes there by building trading posts at the camps of the different tribes. It was a dubious message coded into the actual programmatic structure of the game—Native Americans had no power or agency.

After failing to get the game to work it was put back in its case on my desk next to the packet of state social studies standards. I don't know what I was thinking. Even if I could have gotten the game to work, how many students could crowd around a single screen to play? Not only was it a bad lesson—it was impractical. It was not even really a lesson. It was me stabbing around in the dark, looking for activities to occupy the kids.

There was something else on my desk though, besides the CD-ROM and packet of standards. It was a business card that read—*Johnny Smith: Indian*. I don't remember where I picked it up—a bulletin board at a café? A resource folder from my teaching licensure program? It didn't matter. The card was from a Native American elder, from the Ojibwe tribe, and I had invited him to my room to give a presentation. This was another scheme of mine, like going on a field trip instead of giving a lecture. It served to protect kids from my lack of knowledge and exposed them to someone besides me.

Having a guest speaker wasn't the same as a trip outside, but I hoped the bleachers and Johnny Smith could change the atmosphere enough in my room, to make it feel like we had gone someplace new.

Johnny Smith showed up with his guitar on the date we had agreed on, and I welcomed him into my classroom. He was in his late sixties, had a weathered face, white hair, and lean frame.

The whole middle school poured through the doors of my room, including Maloney's. Students filled the new bleachers to capacity and crammed chairs into spaces throughout the rest of the room. A bunch of kids finally had to settle for the floor. There are few things more precarious than a critical mass of junior high kids; half are looking to distinguish themselves through acts of stupidity, and the other trying to unlock the secrets of invisibility.

Ms. D's husband, Mr. D, walked in. He was the barrel-chested, all-purpose helper of the "D" duo. He looked at me and then the old man up front and said, "Holy crap, you did it!"

"What? What?"

"Is that Johnny Smith?"

"Yeah."

"I thought so—we used to work together at the Anishinaabe Academy by Lake Street!"

"Really?"

"Yes, he's so awesome—the best guy. The kids will love him."

Teaching about Native Americans in school is a strange thing. Given the grim story of Indian boarding schools, it's like discussing the historical significance of a battle, on the battlefield, while it still rages. The tools used to nearly obliterate a people and culture are still around—textbooks that leave out voices and facts that change the storyline, teachers that are almost universally white, and a daily rhythm that is completely out of sync with nature.

Bringing Johnny Smith in was a 'hail Mary.' A fifty-yard bomb sailing over an expanse of ignorance and indifference about Native American people.

"How's everybody doing?" Johnny asked.

"Good!"

"Gucci, dawg!"

"Good!"

"Are you going to play something?"

In the back I heard a whisper, "I thought they was all dead. Wait, Mr. A, who is that?"

Johnny, dressed in jeans, white button up and cowboy hat, adjusted some strings.

"Good to hear. Yeah, why don't I just play something. I'll start out with a very important tune from my culture."

The adults in the room braced themselves to be reverent, moved, and repentant.

Johnny strummed a few cords, laid out a few lines, and then hit the chorus, "So baby, come over, and we'll *eat mac n' cheese together*. Now baby, hop in and we'll go *eat mac n' cheese together*."

The kids knew how to laugh at it, the adults wondered if it was okay to take cues from them.

"You know," Johnny said, after telling a story about a raven and a bear, "I like being retired. Just the other day I said, 'I want to see my buddy.' It was a Wednesday morning and I just drove up to the Red Lake reservation and saw my buddy."

Johnny was speaking and the students listened—neither an art, nor a science, it was an arrangement much simpler and true; just an elder fulfilling his responsibility.

"I graduated high school when I was twenty-three years old. I had quit school and tried to get a job, but I was too dumb. So, I went back and got a diploma."

I heard Javion whisper to no one in particular, "Damn, he said he was dumb."

Johnny glanced down at his cowboy boots, took a small step back and set his hat on a stool.

"My spirituality works like this: When I go back home, I take my hand drum with me and go out in the woods and sing praising songs. I sing honor songs that praise our creators for what they give us. I honor people who do extraordinary things. A traditional life to me is just doing the things I learned. Being respectful of all things. Treating people kindly. Doing the things I learned that mean something to me in my heart."

LATER IN THE year I invited Johnny back and he brought a young man who had on a grass-dance outfit. Johnny had his guitar and also brought his hand drum. The young guy looked nervous and spectacular in his breech cloth, pants, moccasins with bells and lamb fur, and beaded cuffs. Their relationship had the hallmarks of an apprenticeship, that also included pathfinding through a haunted, hostile, setting: a school run by the US government.

Johnny massaged a heartbeat out of the stretched hide of the drum. The explosive cache of adolescent hormones assembled in the room was diffused by an ancient compact in their blood. They sat entranced.

The dancer began slowly stepping to the drumbeat, re-creating how the ancestors would stomp down the tall grass, blessing and prepping it for a ceremony, a new camp, or battle. The fringes—colorful ribbons representing braided grass—started to sway, mimicking the movement of the prairie.

In the dance what was done with one side of the body had to be done by the other for the sake of symmetry. I watched the students watching Johnny and his young friend from Red Lake pound a dance circle into the hardwood floor of my classroom.

Johnny invited a couple students into the circle. I've heard that pregnant women don't enter the circle because anything carried into the circle is an offering to the creator, so I was glad it was two boys to be on the safe side. I wondered what the two volunteers carried into the circle: a stash of Jolly Ranchers, a Nintendo DS crammed in a back pocket, innocence?

There were a few giggles. But for a group of African American girls, Shanice, Jayla, and Alyssa, huddled together on the bleachers, the idea of learning a story by imbibing movement and sound accorded with something deep within them and they leaned forward.

The scene swirled with an improbable energy; a sacred moment smuggled into public education.

ONE WINTER EVENING, long after my time at Ms. D's little school, I was sitting in front of my computer. Existence had been reduced to tracking the path of a cursor, my eyes and fingertips playing a game of Russian roulette with the simulacra of the internet.

My attention settled for a second on a thumbnail image of a black woman, combined with the words "academic" and "hip-hop." I clicked. It was a TED Talk. I have nothing against the sharing of knowledge, but the filmed lectures seemed like a racket for a series of intellectual beauty pageants at best, a woozy cult of tech worship at worst.

I was wrong again. The speaker, Professor Love, described her time as a teacher in an inner-city school. She imagined what an outside person would think if they had looked in on her classroom: "'*There's no learning going on there. It is loud. It is not academic.*' And I saw it as organized noise. I saw it as kids using everything they had to learn."

Professor Love interpreted the infuriating pencil tapping of her students as drumming, saying, "They are homing in on their African and African-American spirit…There's a soundtrack playing in their bodies, and they are responding to that soundtrack."

IN SOME WAYS, inviting people like Johnny was an excuse I found for not having to plan a lesson. But it was also a way of bringing the outside in. Every morning the idea of entertaining rotations of kids for a full day, inside a box, boggled my mind and I got on the horn quick to find help.

I remembered a performer named Desdemona, who used to host an open mike called Poets' Groove at an Ethiopian restaurant called The Blue Nile in Minneapolis. During summers off from college I used to slip into a booth on Wednesday nights and watch her kickstart the event with her spoken-word poems.

I tracked Desdemona down and set up a date for her band Ill Chemistry to visit Ms. D's little school.

The whole school met in the gym, elementary school kids coming face-to-face with the late-night set of a crew of hipsters and hip-hop artists. The acoustics were terrible and the politically charged lyrics about identity flew over the elementary students' heads. The words were a flock of birds plumed with adult problems, landing on the shoulders of a handful of mature middle school students in the back. Desdemona paced the stage in front of the rows of kids in blue uniforms, calling into her mic, "You got to learn to live your life while you're *living* your life."

Full-bodied, generous, and beautiful, Desdemona worked to reach the kids, but they became transfixed on her partner, Carnage the Executioner. He was a beatboxer that provided a straight-forward translation of the bands message: there's something inside of us, and this is one way to let it out.

After the concert the middle school crowded into my room for a Q&A with the band. The kids, including Kendrick, huddled around Carnage the Executioner. Carnage was a solid guy with a crown of short dreadlocks. I watched Kendrick motormouth questions to the band, and then Carnage specifically. Carnage began to remind me of Johnny Smith, an elder from the community with a rare chance to reach the kids inside a school building.

Eight

I DON'T ASK people a lot of questions, preferring to let them sketch out the lines of their life as they see fit. I figure that just by watching someone, I'll find out who they are. But the background picture for Mr. Brandon, the giant custodian, never quite filled in. He had lived in Hawaii where he picked up jiu-jitsu and a rabid dog chased him through a sugarcane plantation. The Hawaii trail ended there. When he talked about a school age son, I couldn't make out if he lived with him, but he nevertheless acted fatherly to many students. Like Johnny Smith and Carnage, Mr. Brandon exuded enough life experience to shift the environment—without us even leaving the classroom.

I learned later that Mr. Brandon had spent time in the clink. You don't find a lot of ex-cons in schools, unless they show up for a "Scared Straight" assembly about staying off drugs and out of crime. Ms. D believed in giving people second chances, and her frequent casual visits to classrooms told me that she too found out about people just by watching what they did.

Early in my second year at Ms. D's little school, Mr. Brandon was asked to help in the classroom with two difficult students, Kai and Noah. Once they were grouped up with him, they yapped and clung to him all day—the edges of their dysfunction and immaturity sanding away on his massive frame.

I remember Mr. Brandon taking a Sharpie in his giant hand and hunching over an unspooled roll of red butcher paper. The boys sat on either side and copied him. They were adding scales

Other Loyalties

to a wall sized Chinese dragon that Mr. Brandon wanted to put up for a school festival.

A few minutes passed and Kai and Noah started wriggling like wind puppets, trying to poke and slap each other from across the expanse of Mr. Brandon's torso. He twitched his shoulder like a giant bull, and they settled. One by one they added sloppy scales alongside the precise, packed teardrops that Mr. Brandon was drawing.

I circled closer to where they were sitting huddled together.

"Mr. Brandon, man, you can draw!"

"Yeah, I always liked drawing. Used to do a lot of graffiti growing up."

"Mr. A, look at mines'," Kai said.

"Yep. Those are nice dragon scales—you must have a good teacher," I said.

Noah, missing out on the attention leaned in front of Mr. Brandon to add a scale next to Kai's. Kai drew on his hand with his black marker, and a brewing skirmish that would have taken me five minutes to settle down was ended as Mr. Brandon took a big breath. Just expanding his chest to breathe separated the two rascals.

"These two are like my little puppies," Mr. Brandon said, leaning back over to finish the dragon claw he had started.

I discovered the raw facts of Mr. Brandon's muscle and size worked wonders in a confined classroom. The desire to copy strength and the threat of being squashed pacified Kai and Noah. Like the restive subjects of a strongman dictatorship, they reeled in destructive impulses and accepted their lot.

Kai and Noah were two of the many kids I saw as a teacher that got the raw deal—family strife, poverty, fetal alcohol syndrome, genetic cognitive impairments. There were thick files on these kids. I usually didn't read them, hoping that I could avoid biasing my expectations of what they were capable of.

Chaos and distress were packed tight inside these students, ready to come out sideways any time. I could study the test results and documents to try and pinpoint the sources of their disequilibrium. But in the end, I had no choice as a teacher but to just try to put a lid on their acting out, for the sake of all the other kids.

This was when I first took part in one of the seesaws of school life. I tried to suppress mental issues for the sake of the group and counselors and social workers tried to uncork them to process. We took turns but the timing didn't always work out. Kai would be screeching and twirling his fingers in someone's face, and I'd need him to sit down and be quiet for a couple minutes. Noah, who read at a second-grade level, realized the work I'd given was too hard for him. He began chasing Kai around the room. It was an alternative assignment he gave to himself—an assignment he could do well. Kai, unable to focus himself, was happy to be chased. Unlike school, it was a game he understood.

Their scheduled meetings with one of the social workers weren't until later in the day or had already happened. They were left with their frustrations and emotions circling and swooping, lifting them off the ground and setting them down backwards. They didn't see classmates, the work, the environment, but a scene that didn't match their inner state. The only answer was to cause some silly trouble to find balance.

Instead of turning in lesson plans at Ms. D's little school we wrote out a 'Weekly Reflection.' We gave them to her on Friday and she wrote back by Monday. The sheet of paper had five sections: Highlights, Lowlights, Praise, Suggestions, and a place where she asked what she could do to help make our jobs as teachers better. I wrote to Ms. D about my behavior management struggles in the 'Lowlights' section. I was worried that with Kai and Noah I'd resort to old-fashioned strategies like fear and punishment in my quest for the fool's gold of teaching: students sitting down and being quiet.

Ms. D wrote back: "The goal is for students is to be respectful so you can teach, and others can learn. I do not care if they are ever quiet—just not so crazy—make sense?"

The causes of what made Kai and Noah act "crazy" were nuanced and deep-seated. These psychological issues could not be diffused with clever verbal redirections and offering them choices. They needed a more primitive force: gravity. Tethered to Mr. Brandon, Kai and Noah stayed closer to the ground—got a feeling for how it held them up and might be counted on.

Even though it was Mr. Brandon's physicality that calmed them the other question was whether anything mattered more than psychology. Early on as a teacher, I wondered whether the ratio should have been turned around—multiply the counselors, psychologists, and social workers and have teachers stop by and pick up kids for lessons. Teachers that looked like Arnold Schwarzenegger or Hagrid from *Harry Potter*.

ONE AFTERNOON THE fall of my second year, the doorway of my classroom darkened, and a big pair of steel-toed boots gently crossed the threshold. Mr. Brandon had on his black leather vest and stood next to the American flag, which was limp in the stuffy air. It was like having a righteous motorcycle gang leader surveying a battleground where he hadn't got the word yet on what weapons could be used.

It was after school, and I was toiling behind the last remaining tanker desk in my room. Ms. D had found me a couple tables for the kids and Mr. Brandon had wheeled out the rest of the desks during the summer. He was doing double duty now, custodial work and representing solid ground for Kai and Noah.

His soul patch jerked as he greeted me and asked politely if he could use my phone.

It was quiet, and though I tried to give him his privacy, fragments of his conversation caught in my ear. I thought he must be talking to his family at first—there were the sounds of care and trust, concern and worry.

"I love you and know that it's going to be alright."

I looked back down at the paper I was grading. It was Alice's, the volleyball player. I'd had students choose a single quote from a historical figure from the Revolutionary War period and then write a fictional story in which the context fit the quote. Alice's story quoted Benjamin Franklin, "We must all hang together, or assuredly we shall all hang separately." I left a long note at the bottom of her page that was short on direct praise. I tried to show my enthusiasm for what she had done by explaining what her story made me think about. (Later, Alice told me she didn't know what I was talking about.)

When I glanced up again, Mr. Brandon folded one arm across his chest and his vest went taut on his back. He was facing the corner with the phone still to his ear.

"I'm just out in the wilderness…"

Mr. Brandon had done some hard living and by the way he slurred and growled some words I thought he had some demons. I thought it might be an AA sponsor on the other end. But it didn't fit. It crossed my mind that Mr. Brandon might have been homeless. Small charter schools could barely pay teachers, let alone custodians, after all.

It began to sound like there may not be a person on the other end at all. The cynical side of me imagined that he was pantomiming the phone call, as some sort of missionary work. What he was really doing was performing a sermon that I was *supposed* to overhear. I'd be struck by his crosstalk with a higher power and converted to evangelical Christianity.

He was speaking calmly though, from the heart. He seemed indifferent to my presence. His voice went on, slow, and steady. Mr. Brandon was elemental—a heavy, earthy chunk of land, with a powerful, serene river running through it. Murky water, flowing past the wreckage of life's ups and downs on its winding way, but on its way.

I put another student story in front of me, and decided to ignore all the spelling mistakes and run-on sentences. Marking up all that was wrong with the writing would have made the paper look like it'd been hit with a spray of bullets from a machine gun. What was this student trying to *say*, and were they able say it, without a good grip on grammar and spelling?

I peeked up from my desk. Mr. Brandon was standing in the doorway with the phone cradled in his hand, and the cord stretched against his massive forearm.

"I'm just gonna gather my tent around my shoulders like Abraham and see where I'm called."

At that moment, Mr. Brandon resembled to me the peace of the nonjudgmental wilderness inside our school building, the peace of the open range. The sort of crusty male figure seen inside schools only when a work crew comes into plaster or paint. Visitors with toolbelts and callouses, that seem out of place—incongruent. Blue-collar workers were representatives of life choices long dismissed by the college-prep slant of American education. They should be welcomed because some, like Mr. Brandon, may be angels.

Nine

AS A TEACHER in my second year, I didn't know any better, so I didn't psyche myself out about feasibility when trying things out with students. Think of a baby's first steps into spoken language. They babble and sputter—copying every sound human vocal cords can make. By age four they've added five thousand words to their list of words.

That was how I stumbled on the tradition at Ms. D's little school of loosely structured projects and outings based on fanciful whims. I was unaware of the requirement, known by all serious teachers, that everything done during a project or on a field trip must correspond to a state learning standard. I was "babbling" and "sputtering." In my ignorance, I dragged my finger across a map of the Twin Cities metro, and then America, and just looked for interesting places to go, and things to do. At first most of these plans fell apart. But later I learned that even the plans that failed did some good. The plans set small processes in motion inside students that led to adventures for them ten or fifteen years later.

If there was something guiding me it might have been the saying, "Seek knowledge even if you have to go as far as China." Anything outside the school building was "China," as far as I was concerned. My gamble rested on faith—faith that an inner quest for meaning was inside every student. My belief was that going out would help students find counterparts for their inner quest that led down real dirt paths and adventure.

Other Loyalties

I'm grateful there was no veteran social studies teacher or department to guide me on what I was really supposed to do as a teacher. There was just Ms. D willing to authorize half-baked, wild notions. When faced with a teacher request, she was fond of saying, "If it's good for kids, do it."

One Friday afternoon in October, I wrote in the 'Suggestions' section of the Weekly Reflection that I wanted to take a road trip to California with the kids to see the ocean and the redwood trees. I envisioned a bold, life-transforming trip for my students. It would be just like the movies. Awestruck city kids, who had never even had a picnic at a Minnesota state park, would go bounding into the Pacific surf. I'd be carried over the sand on black and brown shoulders into the temple of legendary inner-city teachers. Lodging myself in their memories, they'd phone me when they were obscenely successful adults driving BMWs in Atlanta or Miami and yearning for a simpler sort of exhilaration, the kind found on a wild beach.

Ms. D wrote back, "California or bust!" I still see the green words, penned in a fast, swooping cursive. They were probably written after midnight in the passenger seat of her beige minivan as Mr. D drove back from a Wisconsin Badgers football game. It was their passion every other weekend in the fall to visit their eldest son and join the boozing crowds in the college town of Madison.

Ms. D knew that I didn't have the skills to pull off such a trip. But she said yes to everything because she was trying to cultivate something slightly more valuable than a competent teacher—an enthusiastic one.

The cornerstone of the fundraiser for the trip to California was candy, and cardboard carrying cases of it filled one of my classroom closets. At the end of one Friday in late November I reached in to get my jacket and saw the empty orange wrappers of Reese's Peanut Butter Cups. Without looking over my shoulder I opened a case, grabbed a Milky Way, and gave myself an injection of sugar with the full intention of bringing in a dollar on Monday.

It was the end of an up and down week working with the diverse junior high kids from the east side of St. Paul. First there were individual differences, then, economic ones. Add to that, cultural misunderstandings—and the incessant daredevil testing of social power that adolescents thrive on. This all played out within an age group that tries on identities like Halloween costumes. Unfortunately, two of the costumes were "asshole" and "bitch." I don't say that in a derogatory way. Students were interested in those identities because they seemed to infer a way to power in our culture.

For a teacher without a ship-shape behavior management plan, a class period was like a round of whack-a-mole: a game of Pokémon to stop here, a "roast" battle there, catching wanderers from leaving or coming through the door, hysteria over a stolen Nintendo DS, topped off with one or two daily cameos of trauma-related breakdowns.

Jayla would say, "My mom said God gave me a mouth so I could talk!" Out of respect *for herself* she would not be silenced. A precious attitude when we needed to get a class discussion going or she needed to advocate for herself, but a headache for quiet work time.

A seventh grader, Mai, refused to speak because her mom told her to not say a word in class out of respect *for the teacher*. This was wonderful for quiet worktime, excruciating during discussions and when she needed to present to the class.

Shanice, trying to button herself down to work, would explain, "See, my mom don't play. She told us if she keep her hand open when she smackin' us, Child Protection can't get her for abuse." Half the kids laughed at the obvious joke or nodded their heads while the other half went wide-eyed with disbelief.

Meanwhile, Miguel, a bulky 6th grader, leaned against the wall on his chair and daydreamed in Spanish about being back with his grandmother in San Juan del Rio, Mexico, and didn't even hear Shanice's comment.

Students were not conscious of the experiment they inherited a part in: America. They had been thrust together in a public school with people who looked different than their family and friends.

But they instinctually felt the simmering excitement, danger, and potential of it.

I wanted to shove this scene in the faces of high-flying Finns and Singaporeans whose homogenous schools and students always topped international rankings of education systems. The edgy tastes of an urban American classroom would rattle them, as it seems to rattle other parts of America itself.

The comedian Dave Chappelle has tried to explain the source of turmoil in American life—the gangly entity that is diversity: "And that's why we'll never beat China. Because everyone in America is racist, and everyone in China is *Chinese*."

Finding patterns based on differences among groups was a compulsion of the human mind. White people are like this. Black people are like that. Asians and Latinos always do such and such… It can be funny when handled by honest hands. But safely managing and combating the nastier generalizations created about these groups was the work of higher aspirations: the do-or-die project of our multi-ethnic country.

Prejudice plus power was one of the definitions of racism—but power was in flux, even if it didn't feel that way to the oppressed on the timescales that we measured our present lives. It was worth remembering that anyone was capable of racism. And the demographics were changing fast.

I didn't know if ending or eradicating prejudice was possible or even desirable. Prejudice was part of a biological tic evolution gave us that led us to mark and initially fear the new tribes wandering into the valley. Being too righteously anti-racist was a tactic that risked making saints and sinners out of a jam that all humans were in—being judges who were not blind.

When I looked out at my "unruly," loud class, filled with different shaped bodies and destinies, I knew the friction we felt in the class was *ours to own*—not to deny, blame on others or pretend we were above.

There was no immediate escape from the ancient floorplan of our biology—our eyes picked up color, our noses the smell of an odd spice in the apartment hallway, our ears the sound of a foreign tongue. The fear conditioning of our brain went to work. But other talents had evolved in humans as well. They'd been with us a long time too: cooperation and storytelling, art, and music.

There was something else: researchers had been looking into how humans see color. They suggested that our sensitivity to it had to do with reading emotion in faces and finding ripe fruit on trees, not threats. Maybe in the beginning one reason we began noticing color had to do with tracking subtle tints in the skin when someone changed from happy to sad to angry. Our eyes evolved to be able to tell if a mango was ready to eat, not whether someone could be trusted. We were judges and we would judge. Intelligence, perception itself, depended on it—but could we fine-tune *how* we judged?

I PRESSED ANOTHER fundraiser Milky Way into my mouth, like I was feeding a woodchipper. The school paid for the candy which meant it was tax-payer money that I was snacking on. I began to wonder if this was how corruption worked. Idealistic people, grinding away at the truly difficult jobs of a society bump up against the odds, and start to take a little off the top to take the edge off.

As I opened a bag of Skittles, I felt my lids close over my stinging, blood-shot eyes. Crunching into a sour handful of colored dye and corn syrup, I felt one hundred percent justified.

I was a public servant working with an age group that was misunderstood, mistrusted, and eventually ignored by society, even by their families. I discovered that junior high was the time when parents were kind of forced to let go of their children a little for the sake of sanity. It was a sort of détente. Ignoring each other was a way to take a break from arguing. Then, after leaving their kids shut away in their bedrooms, exasperated parents showed up at mid-year conferences. They wondered aloud about what happened to their child who was so studious in elementary school. Tilting their heads to the side, they looked me in the eye long enough for me to catch the accusation.

Other Loyalties

After a couple weeks, it was clear that the California fundraiser accounting book wasn't balanced. I had a well-intentioned lead sales force of sixth-graders, Adam and Javion, but they had succumbed to temptation and had joined me in devouring all the profits.

Adam was a kid with a round moon face that was covered in acne scars and belonged in a gritty British gangster movie. He had been a disaster at his other schools, and Ms. D was rehabilitating him with attention and Value Meals from McDonald's that he ate in her office, where he tried to process the feeling of someone at a school caring about him in what could be called a more visceral way.

While the California trip was unraveling, I turned my attention to more pressing local concerns, that I thought Adam and Javion should attend to. I got a volunteer from Planned Parenthood to give a sex-ed presentation to the entire middle school.

Before the volunteer started her presentation Ms. D burst into the room and did a pre-emptive strike by yelling, "Penis!"

Some of the nerves leaked out of the room in a stream of giggles.

"Penis, penis, penis! Get over it. Say it ten times with me."

She repeated this brimstone spell with the word "vagina," turned on her heels and left. The echo of the famed body parts died down. Anticipation spread across a crowd of young faces.

I was standing in the back and heard Adam whisper his version of contraception to Javion.

"Know what I do? Pull and pray. *Pull and pray*, baby."

Javion, who had probably never touched a girl, tried to muster a devious smile like he knew what Adam was talking about.

Javion was shyer and more soft-spoken, his words often coming out of his mouth muffled, like he was a five-year-old hiding behind a curtain. He had mesmerizing green eyes and a very protective mother. She must have known that many girls wanted to steal him away to the dark hallway that connected to the church to see what kissing him would be like.

Javion would volunteer at the park by his house and felt more comfortable around younger kids. In fact, I remember him repeatedly asking me, "Hey, Mr. A, do you like *SpongeBob?*" He wrote with careful, tiny words, when he did work but seemed suspended in thought much of the day like many boys his age. It was like these boys were in a waiting room, a holding pattern. There was scaffolding all around them while hormones and cells and experience were working to transform them into men. If they made a false move, the mold collapsed, and they were back talking about *Dragon Ball Z* and digging the Lego box out of their bedroom closets.

After the sex-ed presentation I asked Javion and Adam flat out, "What happened to the cases of candy?"

They looked at each other.

"And the money?" I added.

"I sold a bunch on the bus, but the money's at home. Can I bring it tomorrow?" Adam asked.

"What about you Javion, how's it going?"

"Mr. A, my little brother keep coming into my room trying to *steal* it."

"Did you sell any at the park?"

"Yeah, they all want Sour Skittles. But can I bring the money tomorrow?"

Before I could say okay, they had slinked out the door.

When it came to candy, every kid lied and stole. Between me, Javion and Adam, and other thieves, the cases dwindled, and with it the dream of heading West in a chartered bus. The dubious but perhaps accurate lesson I had taught the kids was that California was out there—just follow a trail sweetened by dreams of easy success. A trail that begins to disappear each time you stop for a snack and imagine how nice it would be there. I worried whether stating a goal and not following through really met Ms. D's standard of being "good for kids."

I had a folder going for another trip that never happened: a Civil Rights tour of the South. I even met with another charter school that pulled it off each year with the help of a long list of sponsors. They said that many of the leaders and participants were elderly and dying off. The time to go and meet people who saw those events with their own eyes was passing.

There was a porous border in students' minds between the Civil War and Civil Rights, slavery and Martin Luther King, Jr. On a timeline the events were separated, but in the tension that sometimes took over my brown and black student's bodies the events often sat on top of each other.

Each year since kindergarten, all students had been taught the story of Rosa Parks and the "I Have a Dream" speech, to use as sort of triumphant sealants on a brutal history. I wanted them to see how that history had not bled out when King was assassinated—that ordinary people lived through and carried on after those elite episodes of American history. Ordinary people were still walking around with the weight and responsibility of history in their bodies down South, and they were too.

The pressure many brown and black students felt from both inside and outside came from many places. One of them was a force that often counted on their misfortune to deal with their own status: poor white Americans. I believed that for my white students, hearing the stories of elders of the civil rights movements in Alabama and Mississippi might help them acknowledge their own yearning for lightness and respect.

This scheme to raise the consciousness of my students went on in my head and was never announced to students. The trip required organizational skills I didn't have, and I didn't know how to ask for more help. My shortcomings reminded me of an element of the Civil Rights Movement. The Movement was driven and fortified by the efforts of many unnamed black women behind the scenes. Maybe for this trip, I just hadn't asked the right people for help.

MY ROOM CONTAINED the evidence of other types of big dreams. Many of them flickered to life at Ms. D's school over the years. Most projects faded and were left in disrepair—victims of poor execution. The detritus filled corners and shelves, and was garnished with candy wrappers, dust, and orphaned hoodies.

There were two unfinished canoes jammed behind a shelf in what was supposed to be a cozy reading nook in my room. We bought the plans for building them from a website for twenty dollars and shuttled kids to Menards to load carts with glue, cheese cloth, and wood. A marriage between deadly power tools and the fickle attention spans of students somehow produced an uncanny level of focus. Something I'm sure every shop teacher has understood. I had small groups take turns building, but progress was abandoned after adding the ribs to the canoe frame. Though never seaworthy, the canoes rested like two whale carcasses washed up against the wall of the classroom, a reminder of something grand and deep.

A decade later Mr. Maloney told me he had run into Cynthia, a student who had been in my class at the time. He said she was doing well and had a job: building canoes from start to finish. A couple years later Mr. Maloney updated his report: Cynthia had married a Moroccan and was now living in the northwest corner of Africa. That was way better than California.

Ten

EVEN AT MS. D's little school, a fuss was made about numbers and test results. The reality was that if a struggling urban school could score well enough on math and reading, it was granted its freedom from educational bureaucrats from the state who could dictate ways that the school had to be run. Ms. D wanted us to be free, so she played the testing game to win it. Every month there would be a big assembly with music and lights where growth on reading and math scores would be celebrated. She believed in encouragement. Plus, she always wanted an excuse to throw a party.

Maloney and I became the go-to team for producing and hosting these assemblies. Self-appointed villains opposed to anything parochial, we pulled out all the stops. For one event, we hoisted a giant parachute to the gym ceiling and tied it off to look like a tent. As parents and students poured in, I slapped on a wig, grabbed the mic, and went into bombastic carnival barker mode for the next hour.

"Step right up! Witness before your very eyes the STUNNING achievements in reading made by seventh grader...Larry!"

A chubby kid, with a huge grin, winded his way to the stage to collect his certificate. Meanwhile the whole school was cheering for him.

How did Maloney keep his edge? How did this extra work of planning an assembly not bog him down? It was partly his personality, and the position that scientists have won in our society. They are the new wizards, and clergy, that both create and interpret reality. School tales are rife with the exploits of science teachers—the people in the building with the knowledge, materials, and license to make stuff happen.

The company they keep are shop teachers, art teachers, and gym teachers, plus a small group of teacher aides that harmonize with students via headlocks, roasts, and games of catch. Smart administrators grant each of them leeway to swear and roughhouse with students. The jostling and haranguing can tenderize reluctant learners, keeping them engaged and productive through a long school day.

These are the adults in spaces where students are allowed to move a little more like gyms, labs, hallways, and cafeterias. The dour or defiant shell teenage kids start to wear at school melts, and obscured parts of themselves resurface again. I realized that I had worn a shell too my first year at the school. I'd met great teachers like the Three Sisters but besides Ms. D, I hadn't found a co-worker who would flirt with madness and convince me to venture farther out of my room.

As a devout member of the Church of Jesus Christ of Latter-day Saints, Maloney skipped the cursing, but pretty much embraced the rest of the rough-and-tumble nature of a different type of comradery and learning, one often missing from schools. In one experiment in Maloney's room, they all leapt behind flipped over tables and donned eyewear, before literally blowing the door off his microwave.

Schools have shied away from giving standardized tests in science because it would cause teachers to focus on reading and vocabulary instead of *doing* science. Since departments of education haven't figured out how to test students in social studies, social studies teachers have, until recently, been able to sneak under the radar like science and gym teachers. Because our performance and value as teachers was not pegged to test scores, Maloney and I were able to avoid the scrutiny that math and reading teachers receive. Maybe that left us the energy to turn the gym into a three-ring circus?

What is the issue holding up testing in the social studies? One problem is that any choice about what content to add to the curriculum is part of a political agenda by definition. Even an effort to put different historical perspectives side by side is a type of agenda—a bipartisan one.

Every ten years, Minnesota and other states must parse these very agendas. Because every ten years the social studies curriculum is revised by a committee made up of parents, teachers, business leaders, and experts, and voted on by the legislature. In these sessions there is difficulty locating the bipartisan agenda, or a consensus to seek out the truth about U.S. history wherever it may lead. Instead, Democrats and Republicans angle to jam their partisan heroes into the narrative or get hold of the narrative itself. Should America air out it's dirty laundry, or not? Is America 'exceptional,' or susceptible to defects and breakdowns found in all countries? Were we founded on genocidal greed, or divine ideals, or both? Was the American Revolution fought to secure the economic interests of the elite, or did the backing of a few wealthy merchants demonstrate solidarity with the urban working class, by risking their fortunes to support their rebellion? If Ronald Reagan is mentioned three times, how come JFK, and Jimmy Carter are ignored? The testing companies and their investors are reluctantly forced to leave social studies alone because the story of America cannot be nailed down.

If U.S. history remained contested, I thought we'd be fine. The day they standardized and tested our history would be very scary indeed.

An old joke in education circles is that schools give the patriotic football coach the social studies job. Just someone solid to keep the room occupied—letting the momentum of America's self-evident greatness do the job on its own. There was no need to study history seriously, because the United States was the obvious winner. But there was another type, the crusader, that sought to liberate students from slumber through a relentless enunciation of America's wretchedness. Having students mainline the treachery, suffering, and atrocity produced by past Americans was a way of wresting history classes from a drowsy red, white, and blue, march through time. The emphasis on negative episodes however, had jolted a type of national apologist—an indignant and proud citizen—into an overreaction.

The negatively and positively biased approaches to history were turning into their own gospels. These two gospels often wrestled inside a single teacher. I was one of them. This messy struggle and inconclusiveness about U.S. history did not suit the four possible answers on the bubble sheet of an exam. We had to live with non-closure, or else fracture under the leaden certainty of one right answer. America was not a right or wrong question, it was an essay—in the French meaning of the word: an attempt, an experiment.

Meanwhile in math and reading classrooms, administrative evaluators were engaged in year-long autopsies of testing results. Students were placed along a scale: the beginning, the developing, the proficient, and the exceeding. Once a student's position was identified, efforts began to move them along that scale. Progress and data were catalogued, and the curriculum made airtight in service of improving scores. Students who lagged in math or reading were given double-doses of it during the day by replacing art or other electives with *more* math and reading—in a bid to make up for lost time in their education.

When a number was attached to a kid, it connected them to all dubious metrics; first kiss, middle child, middle-class income, life-expectancy. The metrics of all the things that went unmeasured about a child, that teachers observed with their own eyes, could not be used to erase this number that said the child was deficient somehow. And yet, it appeared that Ms. D had found a way to use numbers to get the kids to badger *themselves*—as their scores were shared with them and not hidden and discussed in teacher meetings. When they did well it was announced loudly.

At the assembly the cheering was sustained for Larry, a crowd favorite. He grabbed his certificate, high-fived a row of teachers, and jogged his way back to his spot. I adjusted my wig and brought the mic back up to my lips.

"Never before on earth, has anyone made such UNBELEIVABLE gains in reading. But believe me, my good people—Shanice has done it right here in this very building! Come on up!"

Shanice's friends screamed and pushed her towards the stage. She wrapped a curl of her thick black hair around her finger, tugged hard against her self-doubt and ascended the stage. Ms. D gave her a big hug and we were on to the next child who'd made big gains, little gains, and teeny, tiny gains.

For another assembly, Maloney toiled away on a man-sized rocket, attached it to pulleys, and a hidden container of dry ice, and somehow had it descending from the ceiling just as Daft Punk's dreamy, techno dance hit "Lose Yourself to Dance" started playing. The song was chosen by Ms. Tracy, an educational assistant, who worked in Maloney's science class. Seeing co-workers attack an "assigned" duty with such playfulness, I had no choice but to meet their energy.

In Mr. Maloney's class, Ms. Tracy was witness and aid to the construction of Styrofoam rafts that were launched with passengers on a creek, Rube Goldberg machines, science fair inventions, and a fishpond by the loading docks that contained two koi (until they were stolen one night).

Ms. Tracy, who loved to change her hair color, had enough punk rock in her to recognize the value of radical gestures. She embraced the fried insect and hot sauce eating contests, and the inspection of the frozen deer carcass Maloney pulled out of his trunk in the school parking lot.

Watching Ms. Tracy participate in the magic of learning that was Maloney's main lesson plan, was a boon for all the girls at Ms. D's little school. Maloney and Ms. Tracy ran a tight ship, but it was a pirate ship.

To do my part for the spectacle of Maloney's descending starship I packed the school van with some students and headed to Menards for supplies. At the start of the assembly, as the rocket settled on the stage in a swirl of dry ice smoke, I stepped out from behind it in the astronaut outfit the students and I had patched together: a white hazmat suit with silver duct tape wrapped around my knees, waist, and elbows; yellow, and blue glow sticks that circled my wrists, ankles, and neck; and a white motorcycle helmet.

When I picked up the mic after an entrance like that, it wasn't hard to cast a spell on the younger grades in the front rows. When their names were called after the announcement of some growth milestone, they knew it meant someone had noticed their efforts, but they really just wanted to join the party onstage.

Beyond the rows of seated parents, who were always welcome to the show, were the shadowy outlines of the cool middle school kids. The ones who had refused to sit down. The line-up of teens morphed along the back wall as their eyes darted and minds raced in a search for cues on when to take on more vogue shapes. Limbs twisted into flirtation and horseplay—Kendrick slapped the back of Billie's neck, Cynthia's ponytail was tugged, Adam smashed his knee into Miguel's butt giving him what's known as a 'corndog,' and Javion balled up sweaty fists in the pockets of his baggy sweatpants, mulling over some new private fantasy.

The middle school kids lingered in a state between elated elementary kids, and slumped, beaten-down adults.

As the line of kids ran up to collect their certificates, my eyes kept straining through the visor of the motorcycle helmet to the back wall to marvel at a Greek frieze come to life. The darkened gym became the Pergamon Altar, the ancient Greek ruin, and the stage the place for the ceremonial fire. I don't know why I kept envisioning altars at school. I must have had some hankering for rituals during the school day that went beyond sitting down when the bell rang. I was circling over some hot spot of meaning rooted deeper in our pasts.

The real Pergamon Altar was sculpted in marble over two thousand years ago in what is now modern-day Turkey. Today it sits in an island museum in Germany, having been shipped over in pieces in the late 1800's. But that afternoon, wrapped head-to-toe in laminate material and sweating, I imagined the Pergamon Altar was on the east side of St. Paul. The middle schoolers resembled the Giants, Gods, and Goddesses that were carved into the

Other Loyalties

sculptural band at the base of the altar. Depicted was the story of an epic struggle between old and new rulers in Greek mythology. As the kids struck poses, the scene mirrored that battle between the Giants and Gods for control of the cosmos.

In a fight that hinged on support from ordinary mortals, the God's Zeus and Athena used spears and thunderbolts against the Giants and the unknown and chaotic forces of nature. Yet the version of the battle I saw along the back wall of the gym was between forces inside the same individual; the half-child, half-adult, dueling with the confusion, fears and optimism colliding at this point in their lives.

The *Daft Punk* soundtrack gave way to David Bowie's *Space Oddity*, and my attention shifted.

Kindergartners started to get antsy, stretching and tangling on the floor beneath the stage, like unravelling balls of twine. I had one more round of improved Study Island test scores to announce and raised the mic to my white space helmet.

Beyond the sea of parents, I looked once again at the back wall, as I waited for a first grader to climb the stage steps. I saw Jodie M., a scrawny and horny mortal, whisper something in Cynthia's ear. She's thrilled and appalled—first slapping him, and then kicking him. Her long brown hair whipped across her face as she struck him again.

With the assembly still going, they chased each other out through the doors of the gym, and the cosmic drama on the stone frieze poured into our world. When I talked to Jodie M. and Cynthia later about their behavior during the assembly, they admitted they were proud of getting better at math and reading. But finding out what made each other tick—that was the testing they put their hearts into.

MR. K.O. WAS the star of another assembly I remember from my second year at Ms. D's school. I had met him the year before when I saw a crowd of kids gathered around a stylish older man doing magic tricks. Mr. K.O. would show up around the school, subbing for teachers and making kids laugh. He eventually came on as a full-time teacher and member of the board of directors.

As usual, without asking, I picked up fragments of Mr. K.O.'s story, the ones either overheard or shared by him. He had the good posture of a salesmen, energetic but at ease with himself, and a direct personality—reminding me of a short Paul Newman. In a previous life he had put together million-dollar deals and lived in Texas long enough to accumulate a lot of crap, marry, and divorce.

Now he was back on the east side of St. Paul to care for his ageing parents.

The fragments of his life became more colorful. With his money he had nurtured his love for travel and photography, circling the globe. He stopped in India and Southeast Asia but refused to visit China due to their misbehavior in Tibet. Mr. K.O. spoke of Vladivostok, Russia, where he met a friend to help her adopt a child.

He once showed me a picture of his cousin in a rowboat on the Ganges River. The bearded man was wearing a brilliant orange robe and the look of wise desolation that American men get who are swallowed by the "land of spirituality." The cousin looked at peace, but with a gnawing sense of displacement along the seams. Mr. K.O. wanted to make a movie about him.

A Vietnam vet, he made references to the "tall grass," and it was joked that the bi-racial Maloney was his long-lost child from his days soldiering there. Returning from the war, he taught for a few years before going into business. He had a black and white photo of his classroom from those teaching days in the early seventies. A black teenager, wearing a newsboy cap, sits serenely at a desk. Behind him tables and chairs are piled to the ceiling like a monument to the waning rebellion of the times.

One day, while picking up some of his students for some extra reading lessons, he caught me off-guard by asking, "What is Sufism?" I don't know why he brought it up, other than perhaps some curiosity born of exposure to a group of the Islamic mystics when he was in India. I had been reading a lot about Sufism, and as such was assuming I knew what the enterprise was about.

Other Loyalties

Mr. K.O.'s question hit my consciousness like a reset button. As with most things, once I was asked to articulate my thoughts about something, I realized I didn't know anything. But it was just comforting to know that someone at work was familiar with traditions I cared about and was a bit more worldly than many of my colleagues who didn't even have passports.

Mr. K.O. took on the most reluctant students. Kids that enter classrooms the way Russian trolls enter a chat room with the single aim of muddying the water. Just as the Russian state prefers to pursue its objectives under cover of chaos, some kids were not at ease unless the class was shaken so hard by their misbehavior it didn't resemble school anymore.

These kids contorted themselves and the class into unrecognizable shapes to also avoid the shame of being nearly illiterate. Some had done it for so long that whenever presented with an academic task, their face became stuck in the same scowl, smirk, grimace, or blank stare, that they had used since third grade. An expression that might take hold and last a lifetime.

When he became a full-time teacher Mr. K.O. cleared out a big closet at the end of a hall, and invited in an all-star sampling of misfits, including Jodie M. He cajoled and teased the hell out of them. And taught them how to read.

The assembly Mr. K.O. was charged with kicking off started with the sound of a loud engine mixed with The Who's song "Baba O'Reilly," known by its chorus, "Teenage wasteland." The preschoolers in the front row were startled by the rumbling and put their hands on their ears. Kindergartners and first graders popped up and crawled closer to the stage. Their teachers scooted them back on their miniature butts.

As the doors of the gym swung open, middle schoolers looked up briefly from the gossip reports being whispered in their ears. The two wheels of a machine rolled past the delicate fingers of the five-year-old kids in the front row, up a ramp, to center stage.

I heard Adam, one of the misfits, shout, "Oh, *hell no*! Look at Mr. K.O.'s old sorry ass on a Harley."

At Ms. D's little school, the communication channels were wide open. For that to happen, a place cannot be too politically correct. Therefore, the results of an informal survey about who different staff wanted to sleep with was shared with me one day. It was lighthearted of course, carried out in the same unashamed spirit as the "penis" and "vagina" incantations Ms. D had shouted at the outset of the sex-ed lessons for the students.

So and so wanted to sleep with Mr. A if "he could get permission from his other wives."

Maloney had said, "I could sleep with anybody." I didn't get the nature of his joke at first, but I eventually admired its cleverness and the innocence teased into the apparent boast. Maloney was a man with a clear conscience and a solid marriage—he could lay down and get a good night's rest next to anyone.

The problem with political correctness was not the replacing of outdated terminology, attitudes, or its original intentions of thoughtfulness around language—it's the fate it shares with most other things in this age of extremes. It's the tinge of righteousness that led its practitioners to throw the baby out with bathwater.

One day Mr. K.O. brought in a monkey doll from the thrift shop and put it in the copier room. Someone discovered that when it was wound up, it appeared to be masturbating. Mr. K.O. had set a gauntlet. A comedian, a provocateur, it was a test of his reading of the room. It seemed like everyone laughed when they encountered that cackling toy. There very well may have been a staff member who felt violated or went home feeling unsafe, but I never heard about it. Maybe they felt outnumbered. The case was open: who would get to safely be themselves, and at what price to others?

The staff culture was raunchy, unpretentious, and bold. The space may not have been optimal for everyone, but at least the pretense of a flawless professionalism was gone. It seemed that the need to project virtue and purity was what led to perversion in many institutions like the church and government. But not flaunting virtue didn't mean *abandoning* virtue and sensitivity to others. In the copier room, teachers were faced with a choice about how they felt about people showing more raw parts of their personalities, even if that included amusement at "Spanky the Monkey."

That was our gamble with authenticity at Ms. D's little school: it could reveal a horror of a human being, or an uncut gem. We cracked the lock of respectability. It was to be determined whether we opened a Pandora's box or a treasure chest.

To take this gamble required the quality I admired most as an insecure young teacher: fearlessness. I saw it in my colleagues around me. There was the fearlessness of our leader in Ms. D. The fearlessness of a comedian, in Mr. K.O., and the fearlessness of an adventurer, in Mr. Maloney. Just like the social studies standards, what *made* a teacher, was being contested not tested.

Eleven

AT MS. D'S little inner-city school, I came face-to-face with many degrees of poverty my second year. But one type of poverty transcended class; tactile poverty. It was one I traced to the transformation being spearheaded by the tech giants: the accelerating migration of life from the physical world to the screen. Handheld video game devices, gaming consoles, and the usual overdose of TV, left the kids oddly deprived of certain sensory experiences for large stretches of time. Then, in the classroom, without these screens, kids would explode with the desire to touch things.

At the end of some school days, I would look around my room and find the remains of anything that could be ripped, poked, or twisted. Shredded worksheets, broken pencils, disassembled pens, and cork boards machine-gunned to death by staples. Bric-à-brac was piled around the wastebasket—the airballs of one unending covert three-point contest.

Finally, I would see the sacred middle school mantra painstakingly carved into a table: "Bitch-ass ho."

Digging a paper clip into a surface was normal behavior for kids bored with paper and pencil work. What made it manic at times was the headlong dive into the use of computers in schools. I noticed this on the rare days that I got to borrow the new computer cart. The floors and tables would be spotless after class on those days. The cleanliness had an eerie quality; it was as if kids had never been there.

But the urge to fidget with things was pacified by the laptops only temporarily. Energy was pent up inside kids. The airy, digital fix of a day on the laptops was followed by outbursts of tactile restlessness, worksheets turned into confetti, and fresh engravings of "bitch-ass ho" on tables and walls. Whereas I could pace around the room like a lion to let out my energy, I would impulsively scold students if they roamed too much. All they could do in the room, under such circumstances, was channel nervous energy into shredding paper and marking surfaces.

I wasn't completely hostile to technology, especially the kind that encouraged movement and creativity. At the end of February of my second year, I hoped that interesting two students in video production would clean my conscience after leading a month of boring lessons in my class. I invited A.J. and Jaden to come with me after school to the local cable channel that operated out of a building in downtown St. Paul.

Jaden was well-mannered, handsome, basketball obsessed, but had always labored through his schoolwork. At the beginning of the year, it was a struggle for him to write a single sentence. But his mom worked at the school as an aide and when his dad showed up for conferences in his orange vest from a construction site, he expected to hear that Jaden had kept up, or was at least trying. And he was.

I wondered how this out of class contrivance fit with the expectations Jaden's parents had for him, but his mom was excited, and Ms. D of course was all in. When I think about why I thought to take A.J. and Jaden out to the local cable channel, I don't have an easy answer. Sometimes I think that I just wanted to observe how they acted in the world. The classroom was too busy for that. I was too involved in keeping things going, and putting out fires, to make observations. I was fascinated to see how students handled the chewy, shifting nature of real situations in the world, with people besides teachers. I felt that these trips outside the school were the only way I would get to study and *know* my students.

There was another reason I took them out. I knew enough about humans to know we are imitative. When we were out, they saw me doing much more—driving, observing, walking down the street, entering a building and making contacts—than when I was in the class. These trips allowed students to get to know *me* better too, but also provided an example of how a man might interact with the world.

At the cable channel, Jaden and A.J. got a primer on how to use the gigantic cameras and editing equipment. Meanwhile I watched the trickle of characters who filled the local cable line-up come in and expand on—and record—their artisan political views. There was a hyper guy who ran a talk-show. He cornered me with his favorite conspiracies as I waited for the boys to finish their TV production training.

"See, the Federal Reserve, that's where they really get you." The hyper man looked me dead in the eye. "I been sayin' it all along!"

Luckily it was airtime and he stepped into the studio, the cameras started rolling and he picked up right where he left off talking to me. Little did I know that within a decade, this style of long, ranting, exploratory discourse, would migrate from talk radio, and local cable, and hit primetime via the world of YouTube and podcasts.

After their training, A.J. and Jaden were authorized to use the cameras and editing booths, and we took two large camera cases back to the school with us. It was night and as we unloaded the silver Caravan it felt like we were bringing in two missiles we'd gotten in an arms deal. We were ready to start a media rebellion just like the hyper guy at the cable channel.

In March, when it got slightly warmer, we brought one of the cameras along on a field trip to Lilydale. Lilydale was a regional park in St. Paul that could meet the student need to scrape, dig, peel, and handle physical things when the urge came. Over the years at Ms. D's little school, Maloney and I contrived many excuses to go to this park on the forested floodplain edging the Mississippi. Each field trip had a discrete pretense—a search for marine fossils nestled in the limestone, a foraging hike, a poke around the historic old quarries and brick kilns. But the true aim remained the same: make sure the students got their hands dirty.

Teachers speak of "gamifying" the curriculum by using elements of video-game design in a non-gaming context to interest their students. I thought there was something back-to-front about this approach. The things that make a good game—pacing, movement, speed, storyline—were the very things being siphoned from real life onto the screen. The root cause of the tactile deprivation I witnessed in class, and was trying to heal at Lilydale, was not just the result of being stuck in a classroom. It was the result of a shift to the sedentary forms of recreation taking over their lives at home that all involved a screen.

Life itself was being gamified, stripped of all its boring and gritty interludes—the moments where idle hands did the devils work creating art, building forts, braiding hair, throwing rocks at a wall. Since the beginning, a type of restless, manual manipulation of things, has been the way humans found out which parts of the world could be remolded by their own efforts. Lilydale was a place where students could continue this legacy of trial and error.

There was a rustic rationality behind human progress that renewed itself at Lilydale. Hunter-gatherers tracking an animal would either be successful making sense of signs left by an animal, and eat, or go hungry. The city kids did their own clumsy version of humanity's first scientific reasoning by discovering that one path at Lilydale led to a swampy dead-end, one led to a small cave awash in beer bottles and old mattresses, while another up to a beautiful look-out on the river bluff.

I thought if A.J. and Jaden merged the act of collecting footage with the big video camera while participating in real life, they could have the best of both worlds. They'd be out doing stuff, but also making a video story out of it. The use of technology would be a partner in their adventure, not a substitute for it.

But I was guilty of ignoring other exciting elements of cameras, computers, and the online world—their potential to help liberate and connect people who couldn't fit into their immediate families or communities. I didn't consider this until years after I had left Ms. D's little school when I took a trip to the Apple Store with my children.

As soon as we stepped into the Apple store we were bathed in blue light. I trailblazed a path around two security guards and my son and daughter followed. All around, people leaned over devices, swiping, and tapping, performing the worldwide finger dance ritual at the oracle of the digital abyss. It was the ubiquitous, willy-nilly quest, for something substantial to hold on to, that is characteristic of our times. I bristled at the hypnotized masses; their heads bowed. Cynical and superior, I walked with my head up high. But my teenage son needed his phone fixed and so there we were, groveling at the Genius Bar.

The Genius Squad member who stepped forward to help us was dressed in the standard issue navy shirt with an embroidered white apple in the corner. Her name was Jo, and her arms were inked in a menagerie of unique symbols and images. I'm a person with no tattoos, who loves nothing more than wearing a white t-shirt day after day. But I counted on people like Jo to add vibrancy to the day and remind me of the head-on way some people live their own lives. Her hair was dyed into a rainbow, she had on a rainbow wristband, and her nails were painted pink and blue.

She sailed into the situation of our broken technology on a multi-colored ray of calm competence.

Meanwhile, there was a baby crying at the other end of the store. The father held the baby and walked back and forth past the precise machines that posed as a version of the future. He walked back and forth, but to everyone's continued dismay, not *out* of the store. The baby screamed and the sound ricocheted off the metal and glass that surrounded us. The fatigued face of the baby's father was the only surface soft enough for the scream to sink into.

Jo had heavy eyeliner on and was somewhere in the middle of the outward transition from man to woman, wherever she decided that point was. I imagined Jo trying to express herself in a small town or open up to a strict, religious family. As a teenager she might have found her only affirmation online, the only warmth and acceptance for who she was, emanating from a chat group. The only gentle landing for her emerging voice might have been a supportive stranger on the other side of a computer screen. The screens I so casually dismissed.

Jo helped my son with his phone as my daughter scrunched her eyebrows at the animated teal octopus on a display phone she'd found propped on a counter. The octopus mirrored her expressions. She was *playing* with zeros and ones, doing the sort of imitation game that I had hoped A.J. and Jaden did with me on our trip to the cable TV building.

Jo and my son leaned in together around the old phone. Two younger people at ease, oblivious to my old fart turmoil, at this crossroads in consciousness.

"It's nice to hear the baby crying," I said.

"Yeah, why?" Jo answered without looking up from her work on the supercomputer in her palm.

"It reminds us of our humanity."

"Yes—it reminds us of our roots," she agreed.

I wanted her to mean our own beginnings, as when we were babies too. But I imagined she was on to something else. Was Jo referring to a human past that was *captive* to physical and cultural limitations or *free* from them? What were our "roots"? When a man can begin to transform into woman both physically and legally—because that's what is true inside—the constraints on other categories begin to loosen. Why can't a human and artificial intelligence merge? With the ingredients available and technology capable, what variations of life could not be called life? The dissolving boundaries thrilled and liberated some people and made the heads spin on others.

Jo seemed to be coasting serenely into a transhuman reality. It was how cozy she was about technology that relaxed me. I felt myself gently lifting off the ground into a heady, deconstructed world. Anyone can be anything—didn't I want that to be true for my own kids? My students? As I looked down at this future from above a bit of panic crept in again. I worried whether it was possible to stay grounded, to maintain order in society, while snipping at evolutionary threads billions of years in the making.

Then I was startled by the scream of the wild little creature. Looking up I saw the baby wriggling in the arms of the hapless man, standing there in his puffy black jacket. Father and baby were a squishy spot pressed against the towering wall of glass at the front of the store. The two of them were a steady, organic event. But they were pinned onto a glistening, dynamic timeline, that might be leading away from them, into a different sort of future. Was this stage of development going to be left behind as part of a savage ancient history? Will infancy be remembered as a quaint beginning of poop, snot, and tears? Afterall, infancy was a vulnerability and inconvenience we'd likely engineer our way out of—an outdated byproduct of the evolutionary gamble our species made to go with the bigger brain. The big brain gave us an advantage over the other animals but required us all to be born prematurely. Starting out like that in the world left us helpless and dependent on our family for years, a family that might not understand us when we finally have the words to speak for ourselves.

The future glimpsed in the Apple store and artificial intelligence labs is one where we still have blood in our veins, but we might never see it. It will flow beneath our skin quietly like it always has—housed with all the other nasty fluids of life. But the primitive bodily potions won't determine our destiny anymore, their grip on our fate weakened by our skills with silicon and data and DNA. We might become cyborgs but will probably love it. An even bigger part of a person's education will be done before being born. Coders and genetic manipulators will be the new teachers. In fact, kids are getting a preview of this in their video games, where they can win or buy different "skins" for their character to wear, modify their personality and the shape of their face, before even starting the game.

Jo murmured something to my son and passed him his phone. He smiled and the white apple on her shirt caught my eye. There was one small bite out of it. One small bite, that's all it took for Adam and Eve to eat their way into this world in the old story. And depending on what you believed, the bite we had taken out

Other Loyalties

of our own "Apple" was leading us further into heaven, hell, or both. In other words—further into life.

But in my classroom at that time, the transhuman liberty of the future Jo represented hadn't arrived yet. My students were stuck in a dead zone—that has lasted to this day—between online personas, fantasies, and activity on one side, and physical reality, and stubborn societal norms on the other. But in one respect, there was a leak that kept draining from one to the other, from the "real" to the digital. The body was shutting down, its vigor draining away, while the mind ran free in cyberspace until wee hours of the morning. I couldn't really put all this together at the time. All I knew was that students seemed to be weirdly jumpy or despondent, and it corresponded to the explosion of personal computing and gaming at their homes. Taking kids outside to Lilydale seemed to help students find some equilibrium.

Our first trip to Lilydale would have been worth filming, but in many ways I'm glad it wasn't. It's grown in my memory like a biblical event. It turned out that the camera was way too heavy for A.J. and Jaden to carry on the hike. A few feet from the trailhead, they had handed it over to Mr. D. Mr. D then lugged that case up and down ravines for them like a porter, in the event that they wanted to get footage. A.J. and Jaden were too busy having fun to think of capturing our trip on video—an almost complete reversal of the current situation with kids and their cell phone cameras.

In fact, the camera was never taken out of its case because of a steady drizzle that started halfway through the trip. When we made it back to the parking lot, instead of giving me crap about dragging the camera around, Mr. D laughed and wiped a streak of mud off it.

Jaden and A.J. had suddenly appeared next to us, drawn towards their forgotten role as documentarians.

Glancing at the camera case Jaden said, "Man, we should have filmed that A.J."

"I know, right?"

Feeling responsible for missing some newsworthy events A.J. and Jaden got quiet for a moment. Then they both looked at each other. A.J. started giggling uncontrollably and Jaden soon joined him before they both broke into full laughter and ran off.

"What are they laughing about? Carter?" Mr. D asked.

"Yeah, I guess Carter's baptism at the waterfall won't be televised," I replied.

"It's probably better that way," Mr. D said before heaving the camera into the back of the van.

The event we were referring to happened while we were scrambling up one of the small waterfalls along a trail leading up into the bluffs. It wasn't the actual trail of course. Maloney, sniffing out the intrepid route, had veered off and we all had followed.

One by one the climb laid waste to any hopes students had of staying clean as they dug hands and feet into the rooty soil looking for holds, determined to make it to the top. Getting clothes dirty, being dirty, was a trickier proposition for the many kids in our group from the lower end of the economic ladder who had a limited clothes budget. Appearing dirty was fraught with ungenerous judgements from peers and society. It took a lot of courage and trust for students to come to terms with the fact that this was the sort of thing we were going to do during a school day.

Carter, a sweet, heavyset, sixth grader, was the last to try, and couldn't pull himself up one of the steep sections at the edge of the waterfall. The rain was falling and no matter how hard he strained, his big body couldn't solve the puzzle. His shoulders started to heave and soon tears were joining the rain drops on his face.

One by one his classmates climbed back down the treacherous slope. Some gathered below Carter and pushed up with their backs, some held onto small trees and pulled up from above. From afar it was an unnecessary, irresponsible, and meaningless risk. From the inside it was an act of impossible beauty and teamwork. It hummed along the edge of cruelty like an initiation. It echoed the lunatic Irish rubber baron who forced a Peruvian tribe to haul a dissembled river boat over a mountain in the early 20th century—a feat immortalized in Werner Herzog's film *Fitzcarraldo* and re-enacted again by some kids from east side of St. Paul on a bluff above the Mississippi. The difference between us and the insane Irishman, was that getting Carter up the waterfall was an insane act that brought out the *sanity* of those in its grip.

The field trip to Lilydale ended outside the school with an assessment of learning that was easy to grade, using data that was crystal clear. All I had to do was get off the bus and listen as students hopped off.

"Mr. A, man, I'm gonna get you. My mom's gonna beat my ass with these muddy shoes."

"Time for the old toothbrush and soap," I said.

"Put them in the washer," Mr. Maloney added.

"You crazy? That'll mess his stuff up."

"Ms. D will get you some new shoes—she hooked me up last time."

"Dude, look at my sweatpants! I got these things all the way up my butt crack."

"They're called burrs," Mr. Maloney chimed in.

"Man, I don't care! This man over here talkin' about science when I'm about to be stabbed in my junk by these things."

"They're just seeds catching a ride on you. Now that you brushed them off, we'll have some nice burrs growing right here at school!"

"Bro, stop playin'."

"Mr. Maloney, were you trying to kill us? Me and Haven almost got lost! We had to find our way back on this little path. It was *so* slippery."

"Did you see Mr. Maloney eat that brown thing—*hell* no!"

"That dude crazy."

"Ruby seen some purple undies hanging from a bush."

"Yeah, and Kiara said they looked like Ms. Conley's."

"Oh, come on guys, I have much better taste than that," Ms. Conley snapped back.

"You nasty Ms. Conley!"

Ms. Conley had taken over from the laid-back English teacher who started a new role managing the accounts of the school. She arrived at Ms. D's little school and dove in at the deep end. Though Ms. Conley left teaching for good a few years later, the year Ms. D's school imploded, she knew what kind of teacher she was from the beginning. One that belonged at Ms. D's school.

Finally, I heard a student bring up the final test question of the field trip. Kendrick, never one to tiptoe around things, blurted out with a big, dimpled smile, "Did you see Carter's fat ass trying to get up that waterfall?"

Kendrick and a few friends burst out laughing and had to grab each other's shoulders to stop from falling down. The episode with Carter was more touching than Kendrick or the other kids were willing to let on and would become a touchstone story for them.

Carter, hopping off the bus, was unfazed by Kendrick. "But I got up though, but I got up though."

"Man, we had to push your big self up. What you talkin' about?"

Then Miguel, covered head to toe in mud, jumped out of the yellow bus and yelled, "That was the best day of my life!"

THE REST OF the spring and school year sped by in fast motion. On the last day of school, the traditional water fight was raging. However badly kids wanted to hit you with a water balloon was a direct indicator of how much they liked you as a teacher. Maloney was involved in all out warfare, attacked from all sides, as were the Three Sisters. It was more touch and go with me, but sure enough, I looked up from my desk and saw Kendrick and Musah standing at my door. Each had a water balloon in their hand.

"You can't hide up in here all day, Mr. A."

"I'm unarmed."

"We're gonna get you!" Musah yelled. He raised his arm like he was going to throw as his permanent smile stretched wider on his face.

"At least give me one balloon, so you can keep your honor. If you attack an unarmed person, you will lose it."

"Man, let's go Musah, he doing Mr. A. stuff. He being suspicious."

They turned and darted back down the hall.

A bit later I headed out to send off the busses. They pulled away under a hail of water balloons, hoots, and hollers. So many arms were waving out of the bus windows it looked like giant yellow centipedes were crawling down the street.

I passed the usual cluster of kids waiting for parents who were late, slalomed through a group of sighing, drenched, and joyous teachers who had made it to the finish line, and hopped back up the steps into the school. Spinning in my head were plans for the next school year.

This planning bug is a non-stop, high-viral load infection that most teachers suffer from. The inability to stop thinking about lessons no matter where or when: on the toilet, at a museum, on family trips, reading a magazine in the dentist's office, or in the middle of the night.

The only way I found to short-circuit this bug from eating up summer was to hit the ground running in the opposite direction. I learned this technique at the end of my second year from Marie, my wife, who is a nurse and understands the consuming nature of caring for people all day. And since people are incomplete and never get enough attention, the job never feels like it is done. She had planned a camping trip and was waiting in the parking lot already, with our young son, and a packed car. It would be a clean break from the year.

I raced to my classroom to get my bag. Before turning out the lights I tipped my battered Horace Mann Teacher Planner into the trash, but I left the door open.

On my way out I saw Ms. D and the laid-back accountant walking on the sidewalk next to the school. Without stopping Ms. D called out, "Hey Mr. A! How does a $4000 raise for next year sound?"

Without stopping I managed to say, "That sounds good to me."

The laid-back accountant chuckled, and Ms. D said, "Alright, see you in August!"

I was startled because I hadn't even considered the way things work in the charter school world. There was no union and no guarantees that I'd be welcome back. I forgot that I needed to establish that I still had the job with Ms. D, then negotiate and sign a contract. In my mind, Ms. D's little school was a place I went every day with another group of adults who cared more than average about kids and tried to have some fun. But it was technically *work*, and at the end of the year, my total exhaustion finally reminded me of that fact.

IT WAS MID-MORNING on a sunny July day, just about the heart of summer for teachers. I was sitting with Dan at The French Meadow Bakery. We had polished off our breakfast burritos and were on our second cups of coffee.

Dan had left the prison-like conditions of Crawford Middle School and was now at a school in Uptown, a hip part of Minneapolis near The French Meadow Bakery. The sun shifted and Dan put his sunglasses back on. Watching an older couple stroll by with their dog he sized up the golden perk of the teaching profession.

"You can't beat these three months off."

"Did they ask you to teach summer school this year?" I asked.

"No. But they always need teachers. I just will never do it."

"Yep, I think the data shows that teachers need the break to survive."

I knew the use of data was drier and more soulless in the traditional school district Dan worked in. There were no spectacular assemblies like we had at Ms. D's little school to put the numbers and data to humane use, as a mode of motivating the kids.

"Data, fricking data. Do you know there's an IQ test called the Woodcock-Johnson?"

I almost spit out a mouthful of coffee, "*Woodcock*-Johnson? Are you serious?"

"Yes, I had to administer the Woodcock-Johnson test to the students."

"That's obscene."

"The kids walk into your classroom, and you see them, and they see you. Write that down. One of them has a runny nose and you get them a tissue. Take a note. There's some more data for you."

We had thought we'd escaped our jobs but there we were on a summer day, discussing the education system. To change the subject Dan pulled out his pen and wrote a line of poetry on a napkin. Then slid it over to me. Despite being cushioned by free time I found it hard to get into the frame of mind that poetry demanded.

I had a career and a salary, and nine more months of feeling responsible for children under my belt. I squinted hard at Dan's scraggly words on the napkin and remembered how I used to write poems so easily in my twenties, when my creativity hadn't been drained by trying to keep a classroom afloat. But Dan had a point, the summer was a time for teachers to re-direct some energy back to themselves, after a year preoccupied with others.

I unwrapped my hand from my mug of coffee and pulled out my own pen, a Uni-ball, made in Japan. I plucked a napkin from the dispenser and joined Dan writing poetry, two teachers becoming people again.

Twelve

AUGUST BECAME A strange month of the year for me when I became a teacher. The start of the month was slow, but then I realized a chain lift was gradually taking me to the top of a hill. I tried to ignore the potential energy that was building up inside. I had leisurely picnics with my family and took long runs along the river. But I knew at some point in August the roller coaster train would tilt downwards, and I'd be headed towards the school year at top speed.

I tried to squeeze in a few more midday training sessions at my karate dojo, attending the classes that I wouldn't be able to get to once school started. When Sensei Fusaro, my old karate master, found out I was a teacher, he told me I should start the new school year by breaking some boards with my hand. Sensei Fusaro never taught such stunts himself at his traditional Minneapolis dojo but thought it might leave an impression on the kids.

Teachers make a big to-do about how to start the year and establish discipline, structure, and routine in their rooms. When I was a student teacher, I overheard veterans saying things like, "It's going to take until November to *break in* my third hour," and, "Yeah, I still need to train them some more."

In my classes, students took one look at me and knew that they would be running the drills. I was a pushover, and they would have their way in my class. Like a monk setting himself on fire I would try to patiently breathe through the pain. But the noise, interruptions, and chaos of an unmanaged classroom often consumed us all.

I admired the teachers who commanded authority, but it required a certitude about the role and its importance that I did not have. Veterans suggested that you not smile "until November" and "grow eyes on the back of your head." But that meant developing an all-knowing, all-seeing vibe. Catching students in little acts of revolt and mischief required a level of multi-tasking skill that I did not have.

My first year teaching I was on the lookout for shortcuts around the time-honored need to lay down the law in class. My students and I suffered through some miserable days as I tried to pin-down activities that were interesting enough to bring the class in line on their own merit. But often we couldn't get to these activities because no students were listening to my instructions.

There were successes despite my inability to 'control' my classes. The small upside was that breakthroughs during such activities were not mediated by my omnipotence as the teacher—because I was never fully in charge. In my second year I had taken the kids to the school parking lot and had them draw different timelines in chalk to show how brief our human presence has been compared to the history of the Earth. I reminded them of Johnny Smith, the elder from the Ojibwe tribe, and his sacred drum. From him, they had gained an understanding of Native American's circular view of time, and now compared it to the long lines of chalk on the asphalt—the white European linear view of time. One was not right, and the other wrong, but there were consequences to each view of time that were not trivial—and now the students had background knowledge to think about how different approaches to time, led to different ways of living.

When activities like the chalk timelines failed to connect to students my classes came off as a formless mush. Larry, who spent downtime in class picking out his afro, was cued up by his strict grandmother to take care of business at school. He wanted a stack of worksheets that he could knock out, and was reluctant at first to embrace the messy, abstract, experiential lessons I tried to give.

But mostly it was the loud, unorganized environment that got to him. As spitballs flew and kids goofed around during unstructured project work times, I would hear him muttering, "This don't even feel like a *real* class...I don't want to be here."

Now, at the start of my third year, Larry's comment still haunted me. The last week in August arrived and all the teachers at Ms. D's little school filed down to the shadowy cafeteria. We made a circle and shared our pilgrimage to the school. The long Memorial Day weekend passed in a flash, and the school year began. By the second week in September, it was too late to develop a behavior plan for my classes. I felt I was headed into another disorganized year, where serious students like Larry would dismiss social studies as not a "real" class.

Desperate, I tried to find a gimmick. After all, the reputations and profits of entire billion-dollar corporations rested on good advertising gimmicks. I thought snapping boards with my bare hands might work.

That was how Mr. Barnett, the music teacher, walked into Ms. Allison's math room after school one day and saw my knife-hand strike splintering a piece of wood. Ms. Allison had trained in Tae Kwon Do, had a supply of cheap pine slabs, and knew how to hold them so they basically broke on their own. She was helping me rehearse. When the kids saw my raw power, they'd all think twice about ignoring my instructions.

I could have spent my time plotting the routines that would bring order to my room, typing up a classroom behavior contract, or hammering out the procedure to turn to when kids acted up. Instead, I found myself snapping boards in Ms. Allison's room.

In the end, I never demonstrated my karate chop in front of students, but I think I left an impression on Mr. Barnett. He looked at me for the rest of the year as someone who was capable of *doing* things, a great prize for American men.

Mr. Barnett was capable in ways that served his students a bit more productively. He was a gifted musician, with an iconoclastic bent. His devotion to the students endeared him to Ms. and Mr. D. In fact, he and Mr. D partnered up to moonlight as support for parole officers who had to check up on parolees at halfway houses. I would hear fragments of tales about their visits involving screams, back doors slamming shut, fences jumped, and sidewalk tackles. I think Mr. D and Mr. Barnett were armed. At least that's what I like to imagine as a nice contrast to the man who taught third grader's how to sing Beyonce songs by day. Mr. Barnett also helped Mr. D drive the morning van routes to pick up kids. Maloney told me that they would meet up early at different hotels around the city and slip in to eat the free continental breakfasts.

One day Mr. Barnett humbly murmured to me that he wrote the score for an original soundtrack to a movie. Creating a daily musical soundtrack was basically what he did for the children at Ms. D's little school over the years. He literally wrote the school song that we sang together at assemblies—the lyrics telling the tale of a freewheeling and loving family.

Mr. Barnett was a refugee from a big school district and had a dim view of some of the deadwood that filled spots on the teaching rosters there, the zombie teachers reluctantly protected by union power. Mr. Barnett would turn his face into a sour frown, and shake his jowls like Richard Nixon, before mocking these teachers by grumbling, "But I *can't* do it. I'd be missing my *prep*!"

BESIDES PRACTICING SNAPPING boards in front of Mr. Barnett, how else was I preparing for class that third year? For one, I was spending a lot of time at the Ax-Man Surplus Store on University Ave. in St. Paul.

It was a phantasmagoric place— as if a gang of anti-fascist artists looted Menards and Dr. Moreau's medical cabinet and set up camp in a plumber's basement. A local newspaper article described it as "an improbable collection of goods that are valued not for what they are but for what they might become."

Ax-Man was next to The Love Doctor Adult Store and the legendary St. Paul bar, The Turf Club. This was the club where musician Mark Mallman performed one song, "Marathon II," over the course of fifty-two hours, only stopping to go to the bathroom. I had gone to witness the masterpiece at midnight around the half-way point. Half-eaten bologna sandwiches and Red Bull littered the stage below the keyboard. Mallman's fingers were wrapped in duct-tape, and his bloodshot eyes and ragged voice transformed a stunt into a blaze of madness and glory.

Sometimes I would have a project in mind at the Ax-Man. Some creative stunt, like Mallman's, to entertain the students. But often I wandered the aisles past the dissembled bits and parts of an entire 1960s-era military field hospital, low-volt motors, severed mannequin heads, and hoped that something would speak to me.

My faith that objects could help kickstart lessons and ideas came from face offs with kids who hadn't had enough to do with their hands all day. Tactile poverty again—this was the dilemma of every age group at schools. I found this out early on when I was finishing up my teaching license and worked with kindergartners at an afterschool program in the big traditional district of St. Paul Public Schools.

In the afterschool kindergarten class, there were two assistants with me—older women, who knew the program inside and out but got paid less than me. They were kept busy hugging and mothering the kids, their bottoms squashed into miniature chairs next to miniature people. Most kids were already burned out from seven hours of school by the time I got there, but the two ladies held things together as I attempted to teach supplemental math and reading lessons to five- and six-year-olds.

One day, desperate to keep their attention, I brought in bubble-wrap for a number game. I had spent three hours the night before cutting the wrap into small squares and coloring them in for a type of bingo. I passed out bubble-wrap playing boards and recited the rules. It was the worst judgement-call in history. I was instantly ignored. The room quickly filled with snaps and pops like a giant bowl of Rice Krispies.

A couple weeks later the principal at the school came down to check on things and the only thing I remember her saying was, "Use the materials we have Mr. A. Don't…*invent* stuff."

She had probably heard about the time I brought in a box of miscellany from the kitchen section of Goodwill.

The variety and inscrutability of these utensils fascinated me, and I hauled them to the school and set them down in front of the students. They each grabbed a gizmo birthed in the most experimental reaches of the Pampered Chef's imagination. They raced away to their tables to turn the items in their hands, draw them, and make guesses about their functions.

There were diabolical-looking cookie presses, cake breakers, meat mallets, potato ricers, and herb grinders. The kids twisted knobs, cranked handles, and tested edges. The chances of a delicate finger being severed were never greater in the history of St. Paul Public schools.

"I know this!" a tiny voice called out.

I looked over at a boy holding a strange metal object in his hand.

"What do you think it's for?" I asked.

"No, I *know* this thing."

"What is it?"

"This is the thing my mom be using at night."

He held up a stainless-steel Hawthorne cocktail strainer.

The big, saintly woman at his side chuckled and caught my eye. I looked around at the bustling tables. It dawned on me that half the items were the paraphernalia of a sophisticated alcoholism: channel knives, DashDarts, beehive juicers, and Japanese-style jiggers.

My reliance as a teacher on using objects had an even earlier start than the kindergarten program. In fact, it came from Professor Rodgerson, one of my advisors in the teaching licensure program. He was like the macho shadow of the more refined Professor Greenwalt.

Rodgerson had a beard, took long Sasquatch strides across the lecture hall in Birkenstocks, and growled things about the feminization of the culture. I would float my weird theories in class, and he would respond, "You like philosophy, but I'm more of a data type of guy." His brusque manner was appealing to me as I flirted with the tail-end of growing up in my early twenties.

His backstory was that as a stockbroker he stared out the window of his office building one day and saw the different ways people were moving below. He thought to himself, "I need to figure some of this stuff out." He quit the next day and started studying kinesiology.

Professor Rodgerson was the guy who introduced me to 'affordances,' the idea that the way a thing looks gives clues about what it can do. It is the possibilities for action given to a person or animal by the environment: the surfaces, substances, objects, and other lifeforms around it. Some affordances are known, and some are yet to be discovered. But it's a relationship between things and their environment. A leaf 'affords' pulling by a worm, blowing by a person who knows how to use a leaf blower, and collecting to a child. Each time I've brought an object into my classroom I think of Rodgerson and affordances.

He taught a night class about "individual differences," and I was taking it around the time I started working at the afternoon kindergarten program. My morning job was at Crawford Middle School, the Federal Setting Level 4 school. Crawford was filled with kids who, according to the district paperwork, were severely emotionally and behaviorally disturbed.

There was a white kid there named Leo. Through troublemaking he'd worked his way through the school system and into the restrictive environment of Crawford. Leo would repeatedly dial 911 in class and tell the dispatcher, "I need TP for my bunghole!" Reciting this line from the MTV show *Beavis and Butthead* to the city's emergency hotline was a warm-up for him.

Most of the time I worked in Ms. Dawn's windowless math classroom. After having her room routinely torn up by kids, it was down to bare bones: eight desks, a metal cabinet, and the worksheets for the day. Still, a seventh grader named Daniel found a way to turn the room upside down one day during homeroom. Ms. Dawn did not want Daniel physically escorted out, so we just waited at the door as he walked in circles swiping papers to the floor and flipping desks.

Daniel was sending a legible message into the ether—this room ought to match the mess that I feel inside. He had seen his older brother shot to death a few years before, and Daniel's own innocence thrashed against the event, and what it could mean for his future. Ms. Dawn quietly put the room back together after Daniel left. Then, sometime during fourth hour, someone set Daniel off, and we watched the papers and desks get scattered back into a landscape that mirrored his suffering.

Inspired by Professor Rodgerson's lectures about affordances, I decided to do an experiment in that desolate room. I brought in seven pink, plastic snap cubes and set them on top of the metal cabinet. Without bringing any attention to them I observed their fate. Even though I was just an educational assistant, I was studying to be a teacher. Yet I didn't have any idea how to help students like Daniel and Leo and could only think of making academic observations about whether a novel object would divert them from their dysfunction.

The next day Leo was eyeing the phone and absentmindedly yelling out "Fucker!" every few minutes. When I looked in his hands, he had the cubes, and was connecting and reconnecting them.

When class ended, he left them on Ms. Dawn's desk.

Later that week a new staff member had his wallet stolen at Crawford. He was a well-meaning guy from a small liberal arts college. There was a bit of a fuss about the theft throughout the day. After lunch I saw a crowd of students gathering outside the staff bathroom.

"What is that?"

"That's nasty as hell."

"That ain't doodoo y'all."

Some kids were peering into the toilet where an unidentified shape was peeking up from the bottom of the bowl. It was like the head of an octopus, but then shifted and looked like it might have a bigger mouth.

"That bitch just moved!"

Mr. Frank, one of the main behavior interventionists, approached the scene with his keys jangling. When he got to the bathroom door, he glanced down from his 6' 4" height at the riled-up kids and snorted. He put on a carnival barker voice that I'd mimic years later at Ms. D's little school, "Look! Come see!"

The situation had to be put to rest, so I rolled up my sleeve, held my breath and reached into the cold water until I had a grip on the sewer monster. I pulled out my dripping hand with the swollen leather wallet attached to it.

There was no way any kids were going to snitch about who the thief was. But when I listened closely to them, the sounds of empathy trickled out—with a tinge of schadenfreude. It was an attitude born out of being on the short end of the stick of numerous petty crimes in their own neighborhoods.

"That motherfucker's shit got wrecked."

"Damn."

Mr. Frank shook his head and glanced down at his beeper. Before walking away, he said, "Mr. Kareem, I can't wait to be an old man."

I scrubbed my arm for five minutes and then headed back to Ms. Dawn's room. Daniel was sitting alone in a corner of the room. He liked to draw so I grabbed a blank sheet and was about to walk over. The room was eerily calm. I saw the pink cubes in his hands. He was snapping and unsnapping them together, changing their configuration—a line, a hammer shape, a horseshoe. Daniel was like a boy trapped in a dungeon, gathering up his humanity and making friends with the spider in his cell.

A month passed at Crawford—kids built and raced model cars using pressurized gas in a science class expertly led by two no-nonsense lesbians. There was a near riot when Mr. Frank was gone one day and gang affiliations flared up. The hippie teacher Mr. Bloden followed through on a threat to fart on Angelo if he kept talking and twelve-year-old Marquez put a dent in learning how to read in my friend Dan's reading class. As I went in and out of rooms, to take kids to the 'time-out' room, I got off-the-cuff

Other Loyalties

profiles of what teachers look like and do in an ordinary month, in a very unordinary building.

After my lunch break one day, I went back to Ms. Dawn's class. Leo had his feet on a desk and was reciting a line from *Predator II*, the one with Danny Glover, where the alien head-hunter prowls LA. In the movie scene, the gang leader priest of the Jamaican Voodoo Posse, King Willie, is speaking to Glover, the cop, about the killings in the city. Glover asks if he knows who the killer is and King Willie says, "I don't know *who* he is, but I know *where* he is. *He's on the other side.*"

Over and over again, Leo kept saying, "He's on...the other side. He's on...*the other side!*" laughing each time. I started saying it too, and Leo cackled hysterically, his stomach heaving inside the purple Vikings jersey that he wore every day.

In Leo's hands were the pink snap cubes, like a Rubik's puzzle that was both solved and unsolvable because the colors were the same on all sides. Like Daniel, there was no telling what sort of wreckage Leo went home to every day. This was their lot in life, and no one but them, could really puzzle it out.

After catching his breath, Leo went silent for a moment.

Holding up the pink cubes in front of his face he said to no one at all, "What the *hell* is this?"

The following summer, Dan's student Marquez, was killed in the crossfire of a drive-by shooting while visiting his cousins in Milwaukee. News of the event made me feel life was so cheap—like it was just another report of the day-to-day misery in the Gaza Strip, Kabul, or Yemen. His picture was added to a row of photos in the office—all young black boys that had attended Crawford and been lost to violence.

Marquez had lost everything, but I felt Dan had lost something too. It felt like a callous thought, but I had it. Dan had put his heart and soul into helping Marquez learn to read, and now those efforts were also wasted by some hotheads with guns. But I had to remind myself, no one can be crossed off the list in society—those 'hotheads' were *our* hotheads.

AROUND THE FIRST week in December at Ms. D's little school a student showed up at my door with a request from Mr. Barnett, the music teacher. He needed Jamiyah and a couple other students to rehearse for the Winter Concert.

I never understood the apprehension teachers had in borrowing students from my classes for special projects. I couldn't relate to teachers who jealously guarded instructional and work time in their classes, because when I scanned my room, it wasn't always clear either were happening at any given moment.

The term 'sortie,' meaning 'to exit' in French, comes from the sudden attacks a small group from a defensive position would make against their attackers during siege warfare. At Ms. D's little school there was an array of sorties being launched daily, some legitimate, and some invented by great adolescent minds. Students had found ways 'to exit' my class.

I'm more gullible than the average teacher and more than once I realized too late that my entire class was empty. Students had sped off to "do a favor" for another teacher. A string of requests had been made to me by bright-eyed kids, but I couldn't keep track: "I'm supposed to go help Ms. Rhodes, okay?" "Ms. D said I could go with her to McDonald's," "Mr. Maloney said I could go finish my science project if you're fine with it."

I had no idea where my students were.

This may horrify some, but to me it was getting close to success. It takes a village, doesn't it?

I was glad that students who felt under siege in my class by the lesson or were bored, could find excuses to leave—practicing for a solo with Mr. Barnett, decorating the gym for an assembly, helping the secretary staple newsletters.

In my mind, each sortie, every little task, reinforced within kids the jolly sensation of being useful. Hopefully, in the future, they would remember this sensation and try to be useful to their families and communities.

Two weeks into December, Mr. Barnett showed up at my classroom door, on a little mission himself. I hadn't voiced my admiration for him, and my persona among the staff as a lone wolf at the school had been established. Coupled with him witnessing me breaking wood with my hand, and the images of ex-cons from his night job in his head, he hesitated before speaking.

"Mr. A…"

"Hey, man."

"I got a request, and you can totally say no," he said sheepishly.

I'm the sort of silent person who spends vast stretches of life waiting for someone to ask me my opinion or to help them. I was rejoicing inside.

"What is it?"

"Can I borrow your bleachers for the concert?"

"Of course!"

The next morning there were two huge empty spaces in my classroom. I swept up the gossip notes, candy wrappers, and pencils that had been stuffed behind and under them. During class students were disoriented, not knowing where the center of attention should be, and where they could casually meet up with me and their friends. The big objects that served as "home" inside the class were gone.

The night of the winter concert arrived. Jamiyah stepped onto the stage for her solo. For the concert she dressed up—shedding the baggy sweats she hid under all day. Her hoodie was like a portable tent, a workshop where she was figuring out how to turn turmoil and emotion into an artistic life. But now she had on a dazzling black sequined dress. She covered "No One" by Alicia Keys and brought the house down.

The rest of the middle school kids went up for their songs. Before they started, Ms. D did a pass with her open palm stretched out. A few kids spit out their gum into it, and then they were ready to sing Jason Mraz's hit "I'm Yours."

When the middle school kids finished, a crowd of third and fourth graders walked up the steps. They filed onto the bleachers, packing it, and nearly spilling off. Mr. Barnett was at his keyboard below the stage, his eyes on the students encouraging them along, his hands hitting the first chords and adjusting the tempo to both lead and follow the kids. I thought of Jayla and Shanice listening to Johnny Smith play his sacred drum—there was something about musicians that made them natural teachers. Maybe it was just that dance and music were still taught mostly through imitation—our natural mode of learning.

The first song ended, and the little kids looked out at the clapping adults in the crowd. Many of the adults were responsible for broken homes or homes never whole in the first place. But even if they had to drag themselves there, they showed up and did the one and only thing that mattered most: look at their kids with love in their eyes.

The third and fourth graders were still young enough to be quick to cry and laugh. They sang their hearts out in the darkened gym, to their imperfect and only parents out in the audience. Mr. Barnett had chosen Timbaland's version of the song "Too Late to Apologize."

Babcock and I never completely harmonized. We got to know each other a little better over time, but there was an awkward blend of respect and apprehension. I was amazed how easily he related to his students. I could have been jealous of him. But Mr. Barnett had a sense of humor, that quality in a co-worker that's more reliable than an FBI background check in revealing who to trust.

One day he said to me out of the blue, "Mr. A, I worry about you sometimes."

"What?"

"I don't know Mr. A. You're very quiet. Are you doing okay?"

"Yeah man."

"Sometimes I think you might want to kill me."

"No man. *What?*"

"I always take your bleachers."

"But…they belong on stage."

Thirteen

THE COLOR OF early spring in rural Minnesota was moldy yellow-grey and splotchy beige. It was like the thawing skin of a plucked chicken had been stretched across the farm fields. Our school bus idled, waiting for the last students to hop on. A golden rule about field trips was developing at Ms. D's little school: never go back to the building until dismissal time once we've made it outside. The bus driver would be following directions to another stop on a day-long adventure.

We pulled out of the Watt Munisotaram, a Cambodian Buddhist temple, and headed to Point Douglas pioneer cemetery. The names of Cambodian monks living at the monastery—Dhammajoto, Kunmony, Iddhimuni—would soon be mixed in student's minds with the names of European settlers on gravestones: Amos, Permelia, Levina. The living monks meditated for years on impermanence, while the dead were gone for good, doing the trick by simply taking their last breath nearly two hundred years ago.

At school, the big stack of state social studies standards that I'd printed off sat on my tanker desk, with its list of topics and concepts that I was required to teach my students. To end up at these seemingly unrelated spots, the monastery and cemetery, the objectives for Geography and US History—subjects that were supposed to be taught in separate years—had to be mixed and matched.

Maloney had done his part for the trip by doing a Google map deep-dive after finding out I planned to take the kids to the temple. Finding an obscure nineteenth-century cemetery in the area, he added it to the itinerary, along with a nature reserve. That was the essence of our interdisciplinary collaboration—bending the scope and sequence of our curriculums to meet the moment.

The pretense of distinct subjects (science, literature, geography, art, math, history) was dissolved once we were on the road. Ms. D gave us permission to work as a true team. The sight of the math teacher sitting on the bus next to Ms. Conley, the English teacher, and talking to Mr. Maloney the science teacher, challenged the academic silos that might have been budding in the minds of students.

When we first arrived and looked up at the temple, it shattered the overcast skyline with a burst of deep red and gold shapes. Plopped down in the middle of a low-key, Lutheran, and Catholic agricultural community, the temple had an otherworldly flamboyance, like the spaceship in *Close Encounters of the Third Kind*. Cornstalk-stubbled fields laced with snow surrounded the temple like a giant homemade landing pad.

The statues of two large, five-headed *nagas* greeted students as they ascended the steps of the temple. They were half-human, half-deity, serpentine protectors against invisible forces. Gilded cornice moldings lined the roofline with more *nagas* posted at the corners—bridging the human realm with that of the gods.

We had entered past the *Sima*, a formal boundary that separates a holy temple from ordinary life. The kids were under a spell, and it was hard to tell whether it was due to the extreme novelty of the place or the force field of immortal dragons. Their heads tilted upwards to take in the magical beasts and they drifted, more than walked, over the final distance to the doorway of the temple.

What makes something sacred is belief, and the process of believing creeped into the kids as they removed their shoes by the door and stepped into a room brimming with shrines and statues of the Buddha. As I followed them, passing a pile of shoes, the smell of seventh-grader Lucas's decrepit high-tops caught in my nostrils. While the aroma lingered, I was held back in the ordinary world. Then a spicy rush of incense flushed over me, and I sailed into a higher realm.

Unlike a classroom where silence was enforced by the presence of the teacher, here they had to be quiet because it was what the environment signaled. The middle school buzz was muffled as their eyes scanned tapestries of haloed Buddhas sitting under mythic trees.

I saw the moist outlines of footprints on the cool stone floor and tracked them until they disappeared at the edge of a red rug. There was Lucas, sitting cross-legged, with sweaty unwashed socks disintegrating on his feet like medieval relics.

Historically, monasteries have served as centers for righteous seekers and devotees, but also as a refuge. Those seeking it were often tender young men taking shelter from the demands of a rough and wicked world.

I looked at Lucas, a gentle soul who didn't care much for schoolwork, liked to eat, and take it easy. Maybe he felt at home: a place where people survived off donations, tended slow rituals, and had the job of being kind.

A resident monk, draped in orange, came in to address the kids, who gathered on the rug with Lucas. The monk reminded me of a shy librarian facing up to the duty of Saturday morning storytelling hour. He began to welcome us in halting English but then stopped, smiled, and switched to *Khmer*. The rapidly spoken words popped like bubbles on a drum set, consonants vanishing into thin air. Satvar, our host, sat next to the monk and quickly translated.

"He says he is very happy you have come to the monastery… you are welcome here."

The visit to the Watt Munisotaram had not thrilled everybody. A handful of students stayed back at the school because of religious beliefs. Ms. D had to sooth some parents but didn't allow their particularities to torpedo the outing. (At another school I taught at later in my career, two teachers spent months organizing a day-long outing to Rondo, St. Paul's historically black neighborhood. It was bisected and destroyed by the construction of Interstate 94 in the sixties, but there were stirrings of a revival in the community. A week before going the principal received a couple calls from concerned parents about the safety of the area. And that was that—the field trip was off.)

For parents who kept their kids home from the monastery, the overview of Buddhism being given by the monk was probably the moment they had feared. To me, Buddhism was the castrated bull of world religions. Of the followers of all the major faiths, Buddhists seemed the most disinterested in preaching and scoring conversions. Buddhists had a take it or leave it approach that suited their worldview that wanting nothing was preferable, including wanting to convince others that they owned the truth.

But I suppose that assumption was based on a stereotype of Asians as passive and non-threatening, which misses the stern compulsion baked into the more communal societies of East and Southeast Asia. If nothing else, the recent horrors in Myanmar against Muslim minorities should put the pristine Buddhist reputation to rest. They can join the glorious but blood-soaked ranks of the other major faiths.

But at the temple, all was well that morning. We were the guests of some of Buddhism's better representatives.

The monk described his daily routine and skimmed the Four Noble Truths like a dragonfly over a lake—lightly dipping its tail to deposit eggs. I watched Kou and Henry, two Hmong students listening carefully. They were both from families that practiced Shamanism. Yet, many of the major pieces of the monk's life mirrored their own family histories: life upended by war, refugee camps, and immigration to a strange land.

To the right of the dais, where the monk was nestled in his clump of tangerine folds, were four statues. Students glanced up at the monk and then over to the Buddhas. One figure had a palm facing out meaning 'fearlessness.' Another Buddha had its thumb and index pinched together like he was inspecting an ant. The circle formed by the two fingers whittled the concept of the interconnectedness of all life down to a shape the kids were absentmindedly mimicking with their fingers.

Lucas dug his own fingers into the rug and leaned forward. Finally, he raised his hand. "So, do you…does he, the monk I mean, ever have to leave the temple?"

The monk delivered an answer in *Khmer* and turned to Satvar.

"He says that most of the monks stay at the monastery year-round. Sometimes they will go to help with a ceremony in the Cambodian community…but mostly they stay."

A hopeful vision flashed across Lucas' face before Satvar could finish translating, and he uncrossed his legs and stretched them out on the carpet.

After the session with the monk, kids broke off to explore the temple in their favorite configuration: small clutches of friends fined-tuned for giggling, complaining, and brutally inspecting differences. One group took a closer look at the four Buddha statues.

After analyzing the hairlines of beings who had reached *nirvana*, Kendrick said, "Abdi, that's you, bro." He gestured to the bulging head of one of the statues.

"Man, nah," Abdi protested. He was one of the few Somali students we had at Ms. D's little school, and like most Somali young men was attracted to the verbal speed-chess battles of urban black culture.

"That's *you*. Look at his stuff." Kendrick held Abdi's arm and pointed to his forehead.

"Nah, bitch," Abdi protested as he mounted his counterattack. "You're the one with a gap-tooth. Your teeth look like a broke down temple. Got pilgrims and shit walking in between yo' teeth."

"This man's a monk—he already a Buddha. There go your statue," Kendrick added unfazed.

Back from the bathroom, Dante joined the group a little late. Kendrick and Abdi looked at him, and his high hair line, and yelled out at the same time, "Ahhhh!"

"Oh shit. You know Dante's a Buddha!"

"What chu mean?"

"Nothing bro, let's go."

Kendrick and the group moved on, and Dante followed. There was no way he was splitting from such good times.

In another room, Brianna, Haven, and Amelie were huddled around a box containing fortunes. They were a studious trio. Brianna and Haven were petite, bespeckled Hmong girls, and Amelie was their irrepressible bi-racial leader. In another school, it's possible they would have barricaded themselves behind books and homework, anxious about grades and due dates. At Ms. D's little school, on these outings, other dimensions of their personalities flourished.

"What does yours say?" Haven asked.

Amelie read from a weathered square of red cloth, "*Your happiness in the past was hidden among the clouds...*"

"What?"

"I don't get mine," Amelie said, closing one eye to inspect her piece of cloth.

"Read yours Bri."

"*Going over the mountain with a harp means that you have hidden yourself from the world.*"

"Yeah Brianna. Stop going over mountains with a harp," Amelie teased, before rereading her own message, and scrunching her nose.

I stood near the fortune box and read a little about Theravada Buddhism, the type followed by the Cambodians at the temple. It differed from Mahayana Buddhism which was more popular in Tibet, China, and Japan.

Both types are seeking enlightenment but in Theravada the attempt is best left to the professionals—the monks. In Mahayana the common person can give it a shot, and the emphasis is on encouraging everyone to punch a ticket out of the cycle of rebirth.

I looked at it this way: a Theravadist monk will strive to break free from suffering and once they climb that wall and hop into nirvana, they are not looking back. The Mahayanists stop at the top of the wall, look back and dive back into the world to teach others how to climb. They are like rock stars who body-surf. Their fans get to touch their sweaty body and realize that a state of enlightenment is something that can be reached by someone flesh and blood like them. Mahayanists want everyone to hop on stage and jam because true ultimate happiness can never be attained until everyone's at the party.

Kendrick's group had stepped up to the fortune box.

Abdi looked up from reading a message on a yellow cloth, "Dante, I got the wrong fortune. This one's yours bro."

"What's it say?"

"You have a big head and will have to search many years to find your hairline."

"Ahhhh!"

As harsh as they could be to each other, the middle school kids were more like the Mahayana Buddhists. Always checking around for each other, to observe the suffering, but also share in it, and help ease it. I thought of big Carter stuck at the bottom of the waterfall at Lilydale.

Eventually, the strident color-schemes of the tapestries and paintings on the walls started to lose their magnetism. The candles, golden shrines, and canonical scenes from the Buddha's life started to turn into a formless slush. Like the high-end graphics of a new video game that becomes ordinary after a weekend binge, the kids' attention started to wane.

They had been respectful enough—joking, but not screaming or running around. For many, the simple request to act like they were in church did the trick. For the students who didn't go to mosque or church, or shamanic rituals, or hunting with their uncle, I wondered where they would learn to be quiet. Where could they go where the desperate sounds of the media and consumerism died down a little? Who asked them the big questions and preserved the silence, as an answer bigger than words filled the space?

I don't think religion should be taught in public school. But what schools were operating with seemed to be a strict secular humanism and materialism—a nonreligious stance that held no beliefs in beings or forces beyond the ordinary world. Ethical guidance, order, and meaning in life, were to be found through scientific inquiry and an analysis of the results of actions taken in the lives of real boys and girls.

Yet secular humanism lacked a narrative kick, a storyline that was compelling, and traditions that caught the imagination. Science had led us out of an underworld of darkness and religious superstition. To stay out of that fog, we were supposed to follow the facts. The facts did have an orientation, and it was towards more facts. The problem was that facts were ethically blind. (See, *atomic bomb*.)

Repeatedly I found myself wanting to smuggle artifacts of spirituality into Ms. D's little school—like the homemade altar I spray-painted in black, or the Native American grass-dance by Johnny Smith's apprentice. The middle-school staff at Ms. D's little school had a sense that kids needed something larger than life. When we could, we took kids to places like the temple under the humanist guise of 'cultural anthropology,' or into nature, where the trees offered a nameless take on divinity.

A temple and nature were places where a setting imposed itself on students—hitting them with ancient symbols or life-affirming greenery. The experience of the sacred didn't depend on accepting the doctrines held by a particular religion, it banked on an unseen power. Young people needed something *larger* than life to help them appreciate just how large life was. Kids had a yearning in school for experiences that if not religious or spiritual, were at least connected by some thread to the transcendent spooky joy of our tribal past. I saw this in my own my kids. Around Halloween I got a note from my daughters' schoolteacher when she was in third grade:

> So many kids have expressed interest in showing off costumes. Tomorrow during morning meeting if they would like to wear a costume, we would love to see it. This is an optional activity, so please don't feel pressured in any way to come up with a costume if you don't have one avail-

able. I also told the children that they are welcome to wear a silly hat or do their hair in a silly way if they don't have a costume."

This was during the pandemic, and all kids were at home, so maybe there was more leeway to give in to the kids demands. I can see how my daughter's teacher was balancing religious and socio-economic sensitivities, walking the inclusion tightrope that is the strength and challenge of a public-school education.

My daughter's teacher wanted to give in to the primal urge we all have to wear a mask and slip past the gates of ordinary life. To put on horns and become a beast or a demon and remember those things are in us. To carry a plastic sword and cut into other dimensions.

THE YELLOW BUS was idling at the gates of the temple. I was standing near a brown statue of the *Metteyya* Buddha: a Buddha from the future who has not yet come to Earth. Supposedly he's coming when the oceans have shrunk, people live eighty-thousand years, and everyone has forgotten the truth. How close were we to this future? The oceans were rising and life-expectancy in America was going down, and the truth was up for grabs. Lucas was dragging his feet past the statue, and I urged him on.

Every kid had boarded the bus except Billie. He had one of the cats from the temple in his arms. As living things, they came and went as they pleased, getting the royal treatment from the monks.

"Billie, there's no way in hell you're taking that cat home on the bus with you." Mr. Shane, a man with a soft spot himself, was amused by the ridiculous request, but had put his foot down.

"But it likes me."

"No, Billie."

"*Come on.*"

"Billie, put the cat down."

"Mr. A, can Billie take this cat home?"

I shrugged. I never knew how to deal with these situations—in my head I was thinking, why not?

"Just call my mom. Ask her if it's alright!"
Mr. Shane dialed his mom.
"Hi Ms. Smith. Yeah, everything's fine. It's just that…Billie wants to bring a cat home from the temple." Mr. Shane held out the phone.
"Mom, I'll take care of it!"
"Your mom says 'no' Billie. Now put the cat on the ground and let's go."
"The monk said I could have it. He the monk!"
Mr. Shane shook his head and waited.

Billie stroked the cat's fur one more time, gave it a kiss and set it down. Stepping on the bus, he looked back at me and Mr. Shane, unknit his angry eyebrows and cracked a smile, before calling out, "I thought this was a free country!"

Our school bus made its way down the county road. Passing truck drivers glanced over and saw faces of color filling the windows. I imagined we were in one of those beautiful 'jingle trucks' in Pakistan. The ones covered in calligraphy, floral patterns, camel bone ornamentation and mirror work. Out in rural Minnesota, our diverse group was an unusual sight: the Watt Munisotaram on wheels—a traveling monastery containing hopeful novices, like Billie, of the American creed.

The bus crossed a bridge and pulled into a triangle of land at the confluence of the Mississippi and St. Croix rivers called Point Douglas. Change had arrived to the area in the 1840's. The fur trade had collapsed, and a treaty signed in 1837 with the Dakota tribe signaled a pivot by the U.S. government to another resource available, which was timber. The white settlers ventured into the newly 'opened' land, worked the sawmill at the river and headed to the interior to farm. They opened a post office and mercantile, and then checked off the hallmarks of their civilization: church, schoolhouse, hotel, train station.

Once the big trees were logged off upriver, the town lost its mojo as a supply hub and its transition into a ghost town began. It was not even the end of the 19th century. All that was left of Point Douglas was a cemetery. Under the ground in the middle of a field were remains; they were the bone ruins of a world that lasted just forty years.

The bus took the exit to The Carpenter Nature Center and half of us jumped out and jogged across the highway. We crunched through the frosty meadow that surrounded the Point Douglas cemetery, spreading out like a search team combing the ground for a body.

Jeremiah, a sixth grader, was trying out an identity as the goofy, gung-ho guy, leaping over grass clumps like a white tail deer. In thirty-degree weather he only had on the blue short-sleeve polo and black slacks that were the school uniform. As he bounded ahead the earflaps on his Kermit the Frog beanie swung wildly under his chin.

At a full sprint Jeremiah was the first to reach the cemetery. He slowed to a jog and was very quickly standing still. The story of death was being told by pioneer tombstones—a tale so self-assured and enthralling that it didn't need to be spoken aloud. Jeremiah went over to a white semi-circular headstone leaning against a burr oak. Moss and lichen were beginning to color in the open pages of The Book of Life that was carved into the limestone marker.

Jeremiah bent down close to the writing, wanting to be the first to share a piece of interesting information with the group—the Indiana Jones sweepstakes.

The rest of the kids scattered around the small plot peering at names and dates. Haven and Brianna were staring down at a flat, lawn-level stone.

"Charles E. Hone."

"Born 1858. Died 1865. Wait what?"

"Oh my god, that's…he was like seven years old!"

Adolescent kids grasp mortality in their characteristic way. For some it was a horror movie thrill, detached from real life. For others, it was a force that greased the wheels of life—hurtling them swiftly and unstoppably towards the end, making them want to live wild and free. If this taste of mortality came while they were trapped in a dark emotion—when sadness filled all of creation—death felt like something bearable. The teen suicides that seemed so sudden and rash betrayed a range of pain and feeling we didn't give them credit for. The same existential crisis we respected at middle age was dismissed as teen angst.

In the cemetery, for a few quiet minutes, pain and meaning, joy and meaninglessness, vividly coexisted for the kids. After a while, I hoped the kids would play their wildcard. The one that beats back the dark thoughts of the fatal hand dealt to every person. Flirting.

Irreverence did kick in. I saw hats snatched off heads, hands cocked back for slaps, and unzipped hoodies flying behind kids as they fled and re-entered the hormonal dogfight. A couple kids fretted about trampled graves and spirits as we pointed the group back across the frozen field towards the nature center.

"Did you see that?" Billie stopped and was pointing at the ground.

"Look! Look!"

"That's a rat!"

Jeremiah tried to pounce on some critter in the tufts of grass. Brianna, Haven, and Amelie, each in a colorful jacket, formed the first ring around this face-off. The hunt was dramatized by whoops and shrieks as more kids gathered around.

Maloney stepped forward and removed his newsboy cap. With a few deft maneuvers he corralled the field mouse and scooped it up.

The kids huddled around the furry beacon, which was breathing rapidly, crouched in a fold of Maloney's cap. Little colorblind eyes stared out at the massive, grey-toned shapes peering down on it.

"Does it bite?"

"Can I touch him?"

"It's so *cute*."

"Wait, do it blink? Cause that thing staring at me."

It was true. The mouse's gaze was steady. As Maloney cradled it in his newsboy cap, I wondered if its physiology gave it an advantage over us; unblinking eyes that couldn't turn away from the suffering that was a part of life. Were these vermin on the path to enlightenment?

We crossed the highway and joined up with the other half of the middle school. They'd been at the nature center, ogling turtles and raptors. There was still time, and no reason to go back to the school. We headed along a path covered in leaves that had been under snow for the past five months. Stopping at the banks of the St. Croix River, Maloney spotted a buoy still locked in the ice. He picked up a stone, aimed at the buoy and missed. A challenge was on. In quick order, kids found their own stones and a barrage was launched at the buoy. They all missed.

Mason, a self-possessed kid who spent the first couple years I knew him in the same hoodie and a backpack he never took off, made his third attempt. The stone bounced, slid, and struck the buoy with a faint thud. Incredibly, he had beaten Maloney at a throwing contest. The kids cheered and hooted.

Proudly and silently, Mason entered the ranks of apprentices that were pushed by Maloney's impromptu physical challenges, an Army Ranger mishmash that over the years would involve making homemade bridges out of driftwood, collecting fiddleheads from young ferns to fry and eat, and filling a Mountain Dew bottle with ticks on a bushwhacking hike. After high school, Mason even spent a miserable night testing whether a deep-sea wet suit Maloney gave him would keep him warm without a tent in the middle of winter.

Adolescence was the sparring phase of life—a chance to step into the ring with various experiences without the risk of a knock-out. Maloney put the kids in situations that they would rarely find themselves in again—like jumping off a cliff into the freezing waters of Lake Superior. The feeling of competence in dealing with these situations was likely to sustain students more than any safe pursuit back at the school.

Sparring wasn't all about face-offs with danger and physical feats, it was also learning how to sidestep the frantic pace of modern life and engage in a poetic cranking of the brakes. It could be called parrying. I saw Maloney teach this mental self-defense technique to Mason on a special weekend trip we took with some of the kids to Northern Minnesota to visit an underground mine. We had a destination and raced towards it until Maloney took a sharp turn down a gravel side road for a bathroom break. Our campsite was still an hour away and it was late afternoon—I wanted to hop back on the highway and hit seventy-miles-per-hour again until we reached what I thought was our goal. After waiting at the van for fifteen minutes with the other kids, I went to check on Maloney and Mason. I found them crouched at the roadside, their hands scouring the pebbles in search of agates.

Not that Maloney didn't teach inside the classroom. He covered his bases, and I'd see his classes bent over difficult tests and quizzes, to see if the marsh-mellow guns they had constructed out of PVC pipe, had driven home any physics concepts. They had to spar with reality after all—being able to pass physics in high school to get a diploma, design, and test prototypes in college, and then for a few, build machines that didn't blow up or bridges that didn't fall down, for the rest of us.

The group worked its way along the shore of the St. Croix led by Ms. Conley and Ms. Tracy. On the Wisconsin side of the river a channel had opened, and water was visible. A long ridge had popped up where huge sheets of ice had collided, creating a miniature mountain range in the middle of the frozen river. Jake was still back trying to hit the buoy, getting tips on throwing farther from Maloney. He let a stone fly and it joined the armada of stones scattered around the buoy.

"Okay. I suck," Jake said.

"It's alright," Maloney said. "What matters is that you're aiming for something."

Jake paused for a second, before running off to join Adam, Javion, and Miguel struggling with a huge log.

"Come on dawg! Help us out!" Javion called out.

Maloney and I took one end of the log and on the count of three we swung it onto the ice. It was worth helping small dreams come true, even if they were a death wish on closer inspection.

Adam took one step on the log, it shifted under him, and he jumped back to shore.

"Hell no!"

Self-preservation spared Maloney and me the lame job of warning the other boys not to give it a try. Ahead, the rest of the group scampered back up the riverbank into the woods to find the trail.

"Let's go dude," Jake yelled. "It's probably time to go!"

The log rested on the ice. Jutting into the river only seven feet, it was a bridge to nowhere—but still pointed to the other side.

ON THE BUS ride back to the school someone shouted, "You *asshole!*"

I heard the squeaky sound of a winter puffer jacket being pounded by open palms. I turned around to take stock and saw rows of tired, thoughtful faces. Near the back Cynthia was completing a brief beat-down on Kendrick. They settled into their seats, both smiling.

The smell of cold fresh air still emanated from clothes and hair.

Billie was sitting across from me sulking.

"Billie, what's going on man?"

"I could have fed my cat with that mouse."

Fourteen

LATE SPRING ARRIVED, the air warmed, and we were all involved in a conspiracy: to stay out longer at recess. Kids, staff, and especially Ms. D, did their part to help the conspiracy succeed. The fact that we had recess was already a coup—usually students had it inexplicably yanked from their schedule when they reached middle school.

An epic game of two-hand touch football neared the length of an official NFL game, as teachers sensibly postponed the futile attempt to hold classes after lunch.

Maloney had brought out a hacky-sack, and the regulars formed a circle. The hippie pastime using the little beanbag was new to the kids, but a few had caught on. We tried to keep the bag up in the air without using our hands for more than two or three times. When keepie-uppie started to drag, we switched to a game called 'pelt.' The basic goal was to throw the bag as hard as you could at your brethren. After a couple rounds of pelt, I saw Lucas lift his shirt to show AJ a red welt on his back like it was a mark of pride.

Mr. Shane was a fixture in the circle. He was an enthusiast before it was something people put on their social media profiles. Only Maloney could match the schemes rampaging around his restless soul. I would hear reports about him and Mr. Shane climbing fences after midnight to explore abandoned sites around the city *during* the school week.

The two of them would meet up with Lizzie. Lizzie was a parent with kids at the school, and part of a cabal of urban explorers who had a special key that unlocked the tunnels crisscrossing beneath St. Paul. Even though it was my third year at Ms. D's little school, when it came to making connections with my co-workers outside of school, I opted to keep up the reserved persona, often saying no to social meet ups. I think it came across as stand-offish at first. I was fascinated but asking for details about cave exploration was a roundabout way of seeking out an invitation. The truth is that I'm a bit claustrophobic. I kept quiet. Instead, I settled for highlights, caught in the crosstalk between Maloney and Mr. Shane.

After one expedition I heard Maloney say, "Getting to that one cave was tough. Lizzie had a nightmare that she flipped and was stuck upside down in the passage. She flailed her legs, suffocating, until she woke up."

"It *was* narrow. I had to caterpillar my body to get through." Mr. Shane rippled his torso to illustrate how he had made it through the tight squeeze.

"Ha! But I'm kinda glad we skipped going to the bigger chamber. Didn't they find a sacrificed dog in there one year? No thanks."

"I think a Satanic cult took over that one."

"Can you imagine being stuck down there, and then seeing a silver blade reflect in your headlamp?"

The joke was that because of my silence, and the fever-pitch of Mr. Shane's imagination, he assumed that I was up to much more daring exploits on my own.

"Mr. A probably has the entire Labyrinth memorized," Mr. Shane said to Maloney, looking at me and not expecting a reply. The Labyrinth was the supposed holy grail of exploring in the Twin Cities, a system of tunnels twisted up beneath St. Paul like a clump of worms.

"Yeah, you know how those cab drivers in London have to memorize the streets and then take a test called, The Knowledge; that's Mr. A."

One day my path was suddenly blocked in the hallway by the robust shape of Mr. Shane.

"Dos Equis!" he shouted.
"Dos Equis?"
"Dos Equis!"
"Wait, what?"
"*I don't always drink beer, but when I do, I prefer Dos Equis.*"
"Is that a commercial or something?"
"Are you kidding? You haven't seen the ads about '*the most interesting man in the world?*'"
"Uhh."

Mr. Shane shook his head and bounded away, declaring, "That makes it even better, you don't even know. The most interesting man in the world probably watches ads about Mr. A! Unbelievable."

I didn't have a television at the time, and it wasn't until I was in the hotel room of a cut-rate waterpark that I saw the beer advertisement Mr. Shane was referring to. I was with my family, eating pizza and dressed in threadbare boxers. It was the opposite lifestyle of the silver-haired gentlemen who starred in the beer ads. 'The most interesting man' is a James Bond type of figure, shown with a cigar in a nightclub, and surrounded by beautiful women. A voiceover recounts the outlandish feats performed in his life, as they are replayed in black and white clips: he finds the fountain of youth but doesn't drink from it because he isn't thirsty; he runs a marathon because it is on his way; and while sailing around the world, he discovers a short cut. My favorite is when he has an awkward moment just to see what one feels like. In my own life I suffered awkward moments daily, so it was also the most bittersweet of the ads.

The full scope of my conventionality would have to be kept hidden if possible. I was motivated to be more interesting by Mr. Shane's outbursts of flattery but felt weirdly pressured at the same time. Despite my desire to make my classes novel and engaging, I had a taste for ordinary routines in my own life: movie night, dessert, and three-mile runs on the same route along the river.

As recess stretched past its official ending, the staff looked around at the self-governing miniature world the kids had made

Other Loyalties

for themselves; penalty rulings were being accepted in the football game; two jump ropes churned in a game of Double Dutch, and a four-square game raged that was so consequential kids were diving on asphalt to try to dethrone Mr. David, the lanky educational assistant who was the 'king.'

The hacky-sack game ended, and Maloney, Ms. Tracy, and I watched nerdy Harry Potter fantasy realms and anime battles twirl into finer resolution near the playground. Suddenly, Mr. Shane was sprinting towards Cameron with his head lowered and arms thrust behind his back.

It was the ninja style of running popularized by the Japanese manga hero *Naruto*. Cameron, the older of two autistic brothers, immediately recognized the attack and responded with a 'Twin Dragon Shot' from the manga world of *Dragon Ball Z*. It was a crossover battle between forces from two different manga universes, and it ended in a draw.

Mr. Shane retreated.

"What was that?" I asked Mr. Shane.

"Don't you know Naruto?"

"Who?"

"*The teenage ninja.*"

I hadn't taken much notice yet, but the anime version of the character had taken the Cartoon Network by storm and now the kids were obsessed with the Japanese import. Naruto's story revolved around his self-absorbed quest to find his place in his village. Obnoxious but desperate for approval, he was a great adolescent character.

I began to find thick *Naruto* manga books left behind after class. I'd thumb through the noisy, hyperactive drawings and set them aside. Hours later, right before the school day ended, some kid would often run through the door like he was packing for a wartime evacuation, gasping, "Have you seen my Naruto book?"

Recess stretched into its second hour. Ms. Conley, who was over by the game of Double Dutch, raised her whistle to her lips but then put it back in her pocket. In the distance I saw the white-haired missionary oblate exit the rectory and walk purposefully towards the backdoor of the church. She disappeared through the door, and into some configuration of her unending service to the church.

In a corner of the parking lot a game of soccer had sparked to life. There was a sure way to earn the respect of middle school kids: be very, very, good at something besides teaching. For me, it was soccer. One dazzling performance in a recess pick-up game at Ms. D's little school would make me worth something in the eyes of all the Latino and Hmong kids. It would also earn a begrudging honorable mention in the eyes of black kids who took stock of individuals who could run the table at any endeavor. I believe this came from the astute reading many black kids made of a society that seemed to reward non-whites backstage passes to power only through audacious displays of excellence. I hopped in the soccer game, and schooled all the kids with skills honed over a lifetime. I was bolstered each time I heard more sideline commentary—"Oh shit! He broke your ankles Leng!" "Oooh, Mr. A got skills!"

Spring was a time when I thought a lot about my old soccer coaches, some of my most important teachers. A cast of regular guys devoted to youth and the world's game. Dave Lawson, a small, wiry Nigerian, was one coach that left an impression. When I was fourteen, he told me that when I dribbled the ball in games I "painted myself into a corner." It was true on many levels. When I thought, I thought too much; when I wrote, I used too many words and lost my way. Only someone studying your actual movement through the world can give you information like that. It hadn't happened in most classrooms I'd been in as a student.

As a teacher I was supposed to see and educate the "whole" child—but it was not possible for a kid to fully embody themselves sitting quietly in a room. The view of who they were in that state was very truncated. I tried to listen closely to get glimpses of what was really on their minds, when I saw them looking so bored in class.

Boys would talk and write about sports. It was not that boys didn't have anything better to say. I had a lot on my mind in junior high, but when I read essays that I wrote at the time, that my mother saved in her basement, many of them drone on about how I wanted to be a pro soccer player. Reading the old essays, I figured that I, and now my students, dwelled on athletics because it kept us in touch with a part of our life where we felt competent and alive. In my classes, relying on sports to harness attention became so predictable, that I developed an involuntary tic when I talked to some boys about essay topics. "So, what do you want to write about?" Before students could answer I'd blurt out, "You know in World War I, there was something called the Christmas Truce, where the English and Germans soldiers stopped killing each other for a day—and even played a game of soccer. That'd be a cool topic! Sports!"

Tom was another coach I imprinted on. He was a conservative guy with a nerdy haircut, no girlfriend, and had attended an evangelical college in Illinois, founded by abolitionists in 1860. I never wanted to disappoint Coach Tom, my upright soccer coach. I had a regard for him built through conversations on long bus rides, where he told me I'd reached the next level. "You have to be good every game now, but also great once in a while."

Tom berated us at practice for being "prima donnas" when we were cocky and lazy, and lifted us during half-time speeches when victory was all but out of reach. Tom played cards, drank Mountain Dew after July fitness sessions, and laughed at himself as we harassed him about the amount of syrup he put on his pancakes at Perkins. But his seriousness about the game, signaled to us that we should be serious about life.

Tom was the coach of my team when we travelled to France for a tournament in a small town, three hours south of Paris, called Garchizy. Our accommodations were at a place called Espace Bernadette Soubirous. It was an old convent, turned sanctuary, in the bigger nearby town of Nevers. Only years later did I read that Bernadette Soubirous was a Catholic saint.

The story goes that in 1858 Soubirous, then fourteen, was out on a walk with her cousins. She heard a rush of wind, but nothing moved around her except for a wild rose. Then from inside a grotto near a stream in the woods a dazzling white apparition of a lady showed itself to her. Soubirous felt compelled to return to the spot day after day to pray. It became known in Catholic lore as *la Quinzaine sacrée*, "the holy fortnight."

At the time, Soubirous' mother was embarrassed, and the townspeople had spasms of conjecture: she had a mental illness and belonged in an asylum because she had seen the Virgin Mary. What I liked about the story was that when some townspeople insisted that she was seeing the Virgin Mary, Soubirous kept repeating that all she saw was *aquero*, meaning "that" in Gascon Occitan, her language.

When Soubirous had asked the apparition her name, the lady only smiled back. Her experience reminded me of eighth-grade girls on the fringe of womanhood whose honesty and passion seemed to have a hallucinatory effect on them at times.

We faired okay in the tournament, hung out in Garchizy's cafés, and got a big laugh when the French stadium announcer butchered our names and said them back-to-front. Our bad-boy forward from Texas, Nick Choppy, became, "*Euh*…Choppy Nick!"

On our last night in the convent, we had a team meeting to discuss the tournament and plan for the next day. We were ready to disperse and fill the convent halls with farts, games of one-on-one, and crumbs from chocolate croissants.

"Guys, one more thing," Coach Tom said as players started to leave. He had a couple pamphlets in his hands. "I'm just going to put these here in case anyone's interested."

The majority of players, most of whom were nominally Christian, filed past what Tom had set down on a low table. The Muslim in the room (me) and my friend Johnson, who was, as far as I could tell, a brand of no-nonsense agnostic, lingered to take a look.

Everyone left including Tom, Johnson and I each picked up a pamphlet and thumbed through them quickly before putting them back down and walking out. The pamphlets were bright primers on Evangelical Christianity.

To Johnson and me it didn't matter what symbol was guiding Tom's way: cross, crescent, star, hammer and sickle. He *had* a way. We admired him, and we were happy to travel on our own paths in the wake of his.

Bernadette Soubirous herself was eventually swallowed by the church—the details of her visions micro-managed by the Vatican. Her story was investigated by Catholic authorities, deemed "worthy of belief," and co-opted to reenforce the new mid-nineteenth century church dogma stating Virgin Mary was born free of original sin.

Soubirous did not care for the attention she was getting and went to work as an assistant in the infirmary of the hospice school where she had learned to read and write. Eventually she joined the Sisters of Charity. When asked about her visions she said simply, "The Virgin used me as a broom to remove the dust. When the work is done, the broom is put behind the door again." After hearing Soubirous' story, I always linked it to my humble coach Tom, who was burning with faith and the compulsion to preach it to the world, but instead funneled it into being a model for us.

The never-ending recess at Ms. D's little school flowed on. I popped the soccer ball over Mark's head, rolled it between AJ's legs and scored a goal. AJ yelled, "Damn it! How did you do that?"

It was turning out to be a gorgeous day. Ms. Danika had walked a group of eighth grade girls to a bodega owned by a Hmong family, and they returned smacking on chips and drinking orange pop. On the slow stroll, Ms. Danika was filled in on what new RnB songs the girls were wrapping around themselves like soft comforters, made of the silky voices of Usher and Mary J. Blige. Ms. Danika also found out which disagreements were headed to the red zone. Jamiyah told her of an ongoing issue with another girl, "And she better not put my name in her mouth again or she's gonna get smacked." Just having a wise woman hear it put many conflicts to rest. A long recess and a couple questions from Ms. Danika could help a girl clarify her feelings and give her the time to tell her story. Wisdom took different forms as Ms. Danika listened—a loud laugh to humble, a groan to make the girl think twice, to a personal responsibility reality check in the form of a brisk "Well, you know better, that's on you."

Ms. Danika had a daughter that went to the school and Ms. D's style was to ask great parents to come on as employees. Now Ms. Danika was secretary, choir and dance teacher, educational assistant, and unlicensed therapist to half the middle school girls.

After another twenty minutes, Ms. Conley finally cracked, blew the whistle, and called all students who had language arts to follow her inside for fourth hour. We knew she was right and accepted returning to the building. I flicked the soccer ball into my hands and Mr. David confiscated the four-square ball. We were on a slow march to the school doors mourning the end of recess.

I looked up as the last stragglers followed Ms. Conley inside the building. "There goes the tail end of Conley's comet," I said.

"Did you hear that, Maloney?" Mr. Shane said. "It takes late-night-show writers like two weeks to come up with something like that and Mr. A just spit it out."

It was another flattering Mr. Shane exaggeration. Mortified that I'd now be expected to produce some wit, I shuffled off and busied myself with rounding up students. Not only did I feel like an imposter among the staff, but I still felt that in front of students I was a fraud. Besides the full-bodied demonstration I'd just put on during the soccer game, I had little confidence in what I was offering students in class.

Nothing as a teacher seemed as clean and straightforward as what I got from my old soccer coaches. I didn't know how to be a "broom" like Soubirous or Tom, brushing the dust aside to reveal an assured model of how to be in the world.

Even though it was April of my third year, I would go home each day, perform my duties as a family man, and then burn the midnight oil trying to figure out what would be worth doing the next day in class. There was no one hundred percent truth to draw from. Straight facts may exist more comfortably in a math class—one skill builds on another, and the verity of the equation doesn't change based on the social status of who is using it.

Other Loyalties

And in science labs, would-be scientists can tiptoe along a path of disinterest, ignoring what their experimentation and innovation might really mean for society. Scientists can stay hitched to where the results lead, and aloof from their effects on the broader world. Even the interpretations of poems and stories in language arts class could seem innocuous, a plaything without political consequence.

Facts didn't settle so easily in a US history curriculum. Historical truths were partial, and if one was given too much attention—in repeated lessons and assignments for instance—it became as good as a lie over time. This was at the heart of the public's fierce opinions when it came to social studies in schools and the distorting effects of bias; spend too much time studying the work ethic and resourcefulness of white Protestant settlers and ignore the plight of Native Americans and enslaved people, and even the legitimate qualities and admirable values of those settlers becomes suspect. Likewise, exclusively focusing on slavery and genocide, and dismissing the innovation, progress, and promise of America, begins to eat away at the accuracy of even those foundational facts of theft and horror. Afterall, a work ethic and resourcefulness were qualities that enslaved people and Native Americans had also, it's just that the payoff for them was survival, instead of wealth. Focusing on the damage done misses out on that incredible accomplishment—survival—and the values that must have been embodied by enslaved people and Native Americans: dignity, bravery, ingenuity, forbearance.

In my class, no matter what I did, a deformed, biased, fragment of our history would emerge. As bored as kids could get in social studies, the telling of history was painting a picture of where they came from and therefore who they were. Starting the story of black people with slavery then, was fraught beyond belief. No matter how I held the topic, it cut.

I harped on students about how events in history are told from a limited point of view, but once an event like slavery or Columbus landing in America was described *a certain way,* it sunk deep into the students' minds, because it was what *really* happened, wasn't it? I could follow it up with gory descriptions of slavery or what Columbus did to the Arawak Indians, or even back up in time to explore what life was like for Africans before being enslaved or Native Americans before Europeans arrived. While the U.S. became a country and gathered economic and military strength, I could use slave narratives or oral tribal histories as counterpoints. But Native Americans' existence still seemed to have meaning only against the backdrop of Columbus. His crimes, and the era they began, seemed to define their whole reality, and in turn, our current reality—how could that be the truth? If it was, how would we face it?

I found myself often avoiding our national history and had students investigate their personal history instead. When I asked them to go home and record a story from someone in their family as an assignment, I thought my hands would be clean. How could I be indoctrinating them into a Euro-centric view if it was the people that loved them telling them their own history, and introducing topics that mattered to them? Wasn't it beneficial for Alice, a white girl, to hear the recording of Jayla's black grandmother telling the story of moving from Mississippi to Chicago? Didn't Jayla benefit from hearing Alice's grandfather talking about his time as a soldier in Vietnam?

At the time I didn't realize how offloading the complicated task of describing our national history, and opting to cater to personal histories, was a bit of a cop out. The customer of a public school is not parents, or individual kids even, but the entire community. The purpose of social studies at a public school is to encourage democratic habits and values, illuminate and strengthen shared institutions, and highlight parts of our culture that benefit everyone, and examine the parts that are causing harm.

At a price, hand-selected private schools were available for parents who wanted specific, religious, or exclusive stories told to their kids. A public school had a responsibility to the entire citizenry. But nagging in my mind was the question: If a public school was for everyone, did it end up being for no one? Why were teachers attracted to Ms. D's little charter school, a school in between public and private? And why had I felt it necessary to build an altar?

Besides personal histories, I began to lean towards philosophy to avoid the challenge of an American history that took *everyone* into account. Inclusion was necessary and noble, but on the way to enhancing America, it was making it hard to find a shared purpose. In class, the best I could do was sketch out a question, a direction, leave huge pieces of white butcher paper and markers on the tables, and see where kids went with it. I'd ask, "What knowledge do you need to be a citizen? What knowledge do you need to be a woman? Man? Adult?" or "How do you know you're human?" One day I told them to think of someone they would *not* want to be in America and explain why. Then they had to write a story as if they were that person.

Sometimes the "big-picture" questions would go nowhere because students didn't have enough background knowledge to mold opinions and thoughts. Other times questions would veer off into absurdity. After showing students a video about the differences between natural and human-made features of the Earth, I had them get in groups and write on the butcher-paper their thoughts on the question, "Are humans natural or human-made?"

Adam got a confused look on his face, and said, "What chu' mean? That's *easy* Mr. A."

He then grinned at Javion and made the infamous PIV hand gesture for sex, poking his finger in and out of a circle he made on his other hand with his index and thumb. I thought I had wasted the day and wrote about it in the Weekly Reflection to Ms. D.

On Monday, I got her response, "Miguel was moved by the video and questions—you may want to hear his perspective—I found it very reflective!" Miguel was Mexican American, and his family was Catholic, and the question set off thoughts for him about creationism and evolution, but also how much we are or are not in control of our destiny.

In the same Weekly Reflection, I asked Ms. D if we could do an urban hike in a couple weeks. She wrote back in swoopy green ink, "Plan it!" with a big smiley face next to it. Getting outside again was the best way to deal with my conflicted view of what should be done about American history and all its jagged and grand fragments. Taking the diverse kids down a wooded path turned them into a single tribe in real time, and all we had to do was try to stay together. Like the premise of a Hollywood disaster movie, we'd be an odd squad, tossed together by circumstance, and forced to survive our plane wreck without eating each other. In the classroom I had been "painting myself into a corner" as coach Dave Lawson said, and it was time to escape.

As always, the middle school staff was onboard for the field trip. Some pressure was off Ms. Conley and Ms. Allison because at the end of March students had finished taking the MCA's (Minnesota Comprehensive Assessment tests in math and reading.) The year before, the school had improved its test scores enough to be released from a sort of probation, which involved scrutiny of the school's operation by officials from the State Department of Education.

We wanted to keep our newly granted autonomy at the school and made sure the kids knew that they were helping themselves, but also the school they loved, by doing their best on the high-stakes MCA tests. This might seem like added pressure on the kids, but what it did was give them a purpose for doing well on tests, that could be otherwise blown off or soul-draining.

A COUPLE WEEKS later, the sun was shining, and we were heading to St. Anthony Falls in downtown Minneapolis for our urban hike.

The silver Dodge Caravans drove out in front of the yellow school bus on Interstate 94 like dolphins at the bow of a ship. Mr. Shane was behind one wheel and Mr. J, the other. Mr. J was Mr. Shane's counterpart, driving van routes in the a.m. and p.m. and taking care of kids and errands in between. Each van was filled with fast-thinking students, mostly eighth-grade boys or girls, who were also willing to use force to get a seat in the vans instead of the bus.

Other Loyalties

We arrived at St. Anthony Falls and screwed around near the one-hundred-thirty-year-old Stone Arch Bridge. Descending a long set of steps from street level, we entered the overgrown mill ruins left from when Minneapolis was the flour capital of the world. A couple students followed me as I walked along the edge of one of the waterpower canals leading from the Mississippi River to a mill. A snapping turtle the size of a large Weber grill stirred in the muck of the canal.

"Look, it's Morla!" I shouted.

"Who?" A.J. asked.

"There—right between the tire and the bike."

"Oh shit! What is that thing?" A.J. stepped closer to the crumbling retaining wall of the canal.

"That's a big-ass turtle!" Abdi said pointing.

"It's Morla!" I insisted.

A.J. scrunched up his nose, "Who the hell is Morla?"

"Don't you know? The ancient one who lives in the Swamps of Sadness?"

"Bro, what are you talking about?" Abdi turned, balanced on the ledge of the wall, and followed it down to the river.

I'd have to pencil in a Friday viewing of the film, *The Neverending Story*. It's a tale about a boy warrior who must go on a quest to save the world of Fantasia. Along the way he must solicit advice from Morla, the 'wisest being,' who ends up being a sort of grouchy, nihilistic Buddha, in the form of a hill-sized turtle.

"How old is that thing?" A.J. asked.

"Probably thirty years."

"Whoa! Are you serious?"

The turtle nudged past a metal shopping cart from Target and sank beneath the brown water.

A.J. and I caught up to Abdi, who had found the rest of our group beneath the bridge. Maloney pointed to the segments of the stone piers at the waterline and casually assessed what students had absorbed from a geology unit. A few yelled, "Granite!" A couple others, "Igneous!"

A part of the spring line, where the arch of the bridge began to curve away from its support, made for an inviting target. Soon we were all trying to land rocks on the half-foot wide ledge that wrapped around the pier. The task was unnecessary, and that's why it absorbed us so effortlessly. We were using our bodies, eyesight, and judgement about trajectory to launch projectiles to the place where we wanted them to go. I guess it was pointless in the same way getting a spaceship to the Moon or Mars is pointless.

In between throws, Jake peppered Maloney with questions.

"Hey Mr. Maloney, what's the difference between a stone and a rock anyways?"

Maloney often avoided the robotic, encyclopedic responses expected of scientists. Instead, he opted for a Socratic approach. "Well, in the Old Testament, you don't see people getting 'rocked to death.'"

Jake, tuned in to the Bible reference, said, "Yeah, I know, you get stoned to death, but is there a technical difference?"

"When you're buried up to your knees and receiving blunt force trauma, does word choice matter?"

"Ha. Ha. Dude, come on."

"Have you heard of the Rock of Gibraltar?"

"Yeah, I saw it on a travel channel show. Doesn't it have monkeys?"

"Could you throw that thing?"

"What?"

"The Rock of Gibraltar."

"No. What? What's your point?"

"Bro, you slow as hell," Kevin had jumped in the conversation.

"You explain it to me then, wise guy," Jake replied, staring at Kevin.

"He saying that a rock can be *big*, like a mountain," Kevin said. "Stones can be small, like your stuff." Kevin pointed to Jake's crotch. Jake smiled. Any sexual reference was welcome, even at his expense.

Maloney took up the thread, "Yeah, I'm guessing the difference has to do with size, and maybe how a human hand changes…"

"Whoa Mr. Maloney! A human hand changes the size of *what*?" Jake's eyes were gleaming.

"You nasty, you would be thinking that," Kevin said, as he prepared to make his throw.

"Oh, and your comment about my stones wasn't 'nasty'?" Jake shot back.

Maloney ignored them both. "Well, it might have to do with how the work of a human hand changes a rock into a stone. But I don't know," Maloney made a toss that smacked the pier and dropped into the river. "Dang it! Why don't you ask Ms. Conley, she's the English teacher?"

Ms. Conley, who had been looking at a green stone Jayla had found, said, "Whatever, Maloney."

Just then, a stone left Mason's hand, arced high in the air, bounced against the pier and settled on the ledge.

"You bastard," Jake muttered towards Mason.

"Man, but I got close on my last one. You saw that Maloney?" Kevin playfully pushed Mason. "Go on somewhere. You a cave man."

Mason just lifted his hand slowly towards Maloney, who shook his head, accepting defeat.

Maloney probably had favorites when it came to students, but what was undoubtably true was that *he* was a favorite. But it was an earned status, and there was no resentment among the other teachers. Girls, hungry for an exemplar of how to put a curious mind to work in the world, found one in Maloney. Boys trying to figure out how to be men, and desperate for models, found Maloney as well.

Jake, Mason, and others competed to be most worthy apprentice of Maloney, but Kevin had the current edge. Tall and wiry with an afro tied back in a ponytail, Kevin had his fingers in all sorts of things. In eighth grade, after I spent a month establishing that Native Americans had complex societies before Europeans arrived, he took me to task. "Mr. A, we been learning the same damn thing for three years." Kevin needed new questions.

The novelty and challenge of Maloney's ever-fresh science class satisfied Kevin's mind in a way my class never could. I was happy. Reaching and harmonizing with every student was a pretense I had to leave behind.

Fifteen

AT ST. ANTHONY Falls, there were still a couple hours left in the day and we were hueing to the golden rule at Ms. D's little school: never go back to the building once out. We crossed the Stone Arch Bridge and went to Gold Medal Park, a grassy space with a spiral walkway leading up a huge mound, inspired by the Native American mounds found throughout the Midwest. Once we crossed back over the bridge, many kids were spent and ready to just chill on some picnic benches.

I checked in with Maloney who nodded towards the railroad tracks.

"Let's go look for a dead body," I suggested to Brianna and Haven.

Brianna pushed up her glasses and said, "Okay."

I'd begun to understand, that beneath the quiet exterior of the Hmong girls in my class was a pugnacious willingness to take on the world, and in this case the underworld.

"Hey Jada and Quiana, do you want to come?"

"Oh no, not one of you and Maloney's things."

"Come on, we're gonna see if we can find a body."

Quiana tugged Jada off the picnic table, and they joined up with the small group of us that still had energy. We started down the railroad tracks next to the Pillsbury Flour Mill. I have a private belief that every adolescent kid should get to take a trip like the boys in the film *Stand By Me,* based on the Stephen King novella, "The Body": a trip along the rails to face death and the unpredictable next steps into adulthood—all in the company of bawdy friends who love you.

A short way down the tracks we found an open box car and climbed over every inch of it. Mr. J had brought his huge camera along for the trip, and he did the sneaky thing photographers do and became invisible. From the edges he captured Hunter and Marlowe sitting on top of the car like teenage hobos in the Great Depression, Mason staring into the middle-distance, and Jada and Quiana, huddled against each other inside the boxcar whispering an endless string of secrets.

Suddenly I saw Mr. J lower his camera and thrust his staff ID that was around his neck high in the air. He shook it twice and the keys attached to it jingled. Then he raised his camera again and turned it slightly to the right and left. Before being asked, Mr. J was identifying himself to someone.

I turned around, and rolling along the service road was a squad car from the Minneapolis Police Department. Even though we were trespassing, the officers sized up the innocent situation and wisely passed on, but not before time stood still for a moment for all of us. It's just a reflex I think a lot of people have around figures of authority—a skip in the record when the boss or principal walks in. Did time stand still longer for Mr. J?

This relatively pedestrian episode along the train tracks would have passed from my memory, if not for a tragic incident that occurred a couple years after I'd left Ms. D's little school. I was teaching at a different school in St. Paul, but it was summer break. After another year of teaching middle school, I was enjoying my three months off, with a conscience so clear that I could have been sponsored by Windex.

My son had just had his eleventh birthday party and one of his friends, Bryce, an experienced sleep-over specialist, was still going strong after staying up all night. The other kids had gone home, fuzzy, and bedraggled, stained from head to toe in the red-hot chili dust of Taki Fuego Tortilla Chips.

I turned on the radio and surveyed the carnage in the kitchen. I tipped a plate of half-eaten pancakes into the garbage and stopped to listen to a report on Minnesota Public Radio:

> A St. Anthony police officer shot and killed an African American man during a traffic stop
>
> Wednesday night in Falcon Heights with much of the bloody aftermath apparently captured on Facebook Live.
>
> The man killed was identified by family members as Philando Castile, 32, a cafeteria supervisor at J.J. Hill Montessori School in St. Paul.

The phone rang. It was Bryce's mother.
"How did it go last night? Did they have a good time?"
"Yeah, they had fun."
"Did you get any sleep?" she asked.
"I just gave up patrolling them around two and slept."
There was a pause. I peered out the window at my son and Bryce who were sprinting through the neighbor's yard and then into the street. Each of them was armed with a bright yellow and orange Nerf gun.
"Did you hear?" Bryce's mother was still on the other end of the phone.
"Yeah, I just heard."
"I don't know how to tell him," she said, her voice wavering.
"I could talk to them…I mean if you want me too, I can tell them what happened."
"Yes, thank you." She paused. "I'm just too shocked right now."
"I know."
"I have to swing by the store and then I'll be by to pick up Bryce."
"Sounds good."
I dried my hands and stepped out the front door. In the middle of the street the boys were emptying nerf darts into each other from five feet away. Our neighborhood is blissfully, irritatingly

quiet, and as usual there was no one else out from one end of the block to the other. Still, I glanced around nervously.

Bryce pumped his neon shotgun one more time, and his chubby face smiled under a canopy of dreadlocks, as two blue darts struck my son in the butt.

"Hey, can I talk to you guys for a second?"

After eighteen straight hours of fun, they braced for the worst: the news that it was time for Bryce to go home.

How do you tell the story of a murder? I could check the Cliff's Notes version of *Crime and Punishment*, listen for clues in Bob Dylan's *Murder Most Foul* about Kennedy's assassination, search YouTube for interviews of a victim's friends and family clawing in the dark for meaning. There was no way to be sure, so I just spit it out.

"A guy who worked at your school was killed by the police last night. Philando."

"What?" My son hadn't quite registered the words.

"He was pulled over and something happened, and he was shot."

"Who?" Bryce asked, squinting in the sun.

"Philando Castile."

They looked confused. Then glanced at each other.

"You mean Phil?" Bryce asked.

"Mr. Phil?" my son added. "From the lunchroom?"

"Man, that's *sad*," Bryce said.

"Yes. Your mom called. She heard about it and wanted me to tell you. I just heard a report on the radio." We stood staring at each other in the street. "She's gonna come by in a half-hour or so to pick you up."

The boys turned on their heels. A cloud darkened the future for a fraction of a second, they hesitated, and then ran off to collect the darts scattered about.

It's about what you'd expect from fourth graders. The implications aren't elaborated on. They would notice a cafeteria, where Philando memorized 500 student names, that was a lot colder and quieter and wonder why—but kind of know the answer at

Other Loyalties

the same time. Some ceremonies would take place at the school and death would take shape as some weird, unfair visitor from another world.

"Guys!" I yelled. They froze in the street and lowered their guns for a second. "Just one more thing. Can you just stay in the backyard for your battle?"

IT WAS FRIDAY afternoon, the day after our urban hike at St. Anthony Falls. Mr. J was standing beside the silver Caravan in the school parking lot. As the busses folded their doors open for students I overheard him speaking into his cell phone.

"I said, 'Officer, I entered the intersection and left the intersection when the light was yellow.'"

A tired working dad walked past, and he and Mr. J shook hands. Still on the phone, Mr. J signaled to him that smoking a joint would be nice right about now. The man laughed, nodded his head, and continued up to the front doors to pick up his kids.

Mr. J finished his phone conversation, caught my eye, and held up a finger like he had something to show me.

Outside the busses, students were getting in their last jokes with friends. A few were hanging out of the windows, begging for handfuls of Cheetos for the road home. It was fun being a teacher, but all the kids had to be gone before I could let my guard down—go to the bathroom, eat, notice my own thoughts, breathe.

"Mr. A, check these out." Mr. J had reached into the driver side window and pulled out his camera.

He flipped through the digital images of our trip to St. Anthony Falls. He lingered on a shot of three fierce but physically delicate sixth grade girls inspecting the brutal, rusted components of a freight train. Amelie was reaching for an enormous coil spring, Brianna had her palm on the cold tracks, and Haven was running a tiny hand along the manganese steel of a wheel nearly taller than her. Like a railyard crew of fairies their focus nearly coaxes movement out of an ancient metal beast banished to a forgotten spur track.

"That's a nice one."

"Yeah, I like that one too,' Mr. J answered.

A red-faced kindergartener with freckles ran down the wheelchair ramp from the front door of the school. He headed for the van door, but Mr. J stopped him.

"Hold up man! How you gonna run past without showing me no love?"

The boy turned, and his huge backpack spun with him. A smile crept onto his face, and he shuffled over to Mr. J who put an arm around his shoulders. He broke free and scrambled into the van.

As the door slid shut and the boy disappeared behind tinted glass Mr. J said, "You know Stanley? That's my boy right there."

WE ALL HAVE our favorite conspiracies. We get a morsel of information that tips us off to plans made behind our backs, and search for the fall-out all around us.

Quiana's dad, who drove one of the school busses, would pop into my classroom in his white t-shirt, and promote the underground hit *Zeitgeist: The Movie*. It was released for free online and aimed to expose the Pagan roots of Judeo-Christian beliefs, questions the orthodox view of 9/11, and analyzes how six corporations are determining the fate of the planet. The mixture of truth and conjecture had a mesmerizing effect.

There's another type of conspiracy—the one where common people join up to help each other make it through daily life. At the start of school days, I'd often see some of my black students link up in animated clusters. All groups of junior high friends do this. They drape themselves over each other and clog the halls.

There was nothing special about these meetups. So why did I view the laughter of the black kids as so unaccountable? Why did their sharing together seem so intense and mysteriously consequential?

Trying to pry a group of black students apart so they'd head to class I said, "Man, do you guys really have that much to say to each other? Is there that much news since yesterday? What's so important? What am I missing!?"

Other Loyalties

Of course, I was summarily ignored or teased, "Mr. A, stop dippin'. Go on somewhere and play soccer."

Having been on the wrong end of actual government and corporate conspiracies over the years, many black people were game for certain enterprising theories about the secret way the world worked. From plots involving the Illuminati popping up in hip-hop lyrics, to claims that AIDS was designed to target black people, the grapevine hummed.

Then there was the nebulous force called 'The System.' The 'System' was incarnated in a figure called 'The Man,' who stood firm in the control room of American power but still couldn't be pinned down. Both were cloaked in the bland names and faces of rich men or plastered within the sheetrock and boring regulations of corporations, political institutions, banks, and courts.

The ways people defied these negative forces were often home brewed, and only required each other. For some white people, hearing a sudden outburst of laughter from a group of black people betrayed sources of strength, grace, and joy that were enviable. Black culture pressed out gems of music, art, and expression that could only be created if your spirit was in a vice. Black people were not special, any more than white people were. But the dire economic situation of many black people forged specific qualities, and empathy came quick with a lot to suffer in the community.

Mr. J discretely signaling to the tired working dad was part of this legacy, this conspiracy. And so was the love and attention he showed the little white boy Stanley, who Mr. J knew for a fact had an unhappy home life.

Ms. D's little school was its own conspiracy. We had a team willing to empathize with people hurting from the injustices of our society but agreed to drop the guilt and resentment and accusation. Ms. D never dwelled on equity. Was the term not cresting yet in education circles? Was it a conscious omission? We never had heavy conversations about race and privilege. Was it because we were in denial or stuck in a naïve colorblind fantasy? Instead, I think we were too busy outfitting individual students and setting off *in* the promised land not *to* the promise land. The promised land was not a utopia or place out in the future that could only come into existence after crossing a mountain of conflict and blood. It was a forcefield we carried with us. It was *very* local—it was Mr. J and Stanley, and what they knew about each other. Our flaws were real, but I swear we found a promised land under our feet for a few short years.

Stanley got buckled in and the other kids were starting to pound on the windows to get Mr. J's attention. But before hopping in the silver Caravan and driving his route, Mr. J showed me one more picture. In it, Teddy, one of the autistic brothers, is some ways down the train tracks from the group that was hanging around the old railcar.

I could tell when the photo was snapped that Teddy was doing the dance he did to self-stimulate. After fluttering his arms like a baby bird practicing flying, he would do a short hop. It was what he did when his mind was deep in the cascade of a happy idea.

In the foreground of the photo is a sign, "NO TRESPASSING."

As the buses pulled away, I saw clusters of white women lingering and talking together on the sidewalk. What was there left to say after a long day? What were these white women up to? What was the topic? Mr. J's van hung a right onto the street and disappeared.

I stood alone—maybe it was just me.

Sixteen

MY BAD HABIT is that I like to keep my shoes on all the time. Showing up as a guest at someone's door and seeing a pile of shoes fills me with dread. Usually I hesitate, hoping that the host will offer me a reprieve—and tell me I don't have to take my shoes off. I just have this feeling that I need to be ready to go.

Before setting off for a journey, our distant ancestors didn't have these issues. They didn't have to take off or put on shoes, clothes, or even turn a door handle. They just stood up, dusted off their butts, picked up a spear and started walking.

In this spirit, I usually hung a backpack by the door of my house, pre-packed with beef jerky, apples, and two water bottles. This was my plan for an easy escape. My son used to get nervous when he saw me reach for the backpack. He knew that I was plotting an outing. It meant that we may be out for the rest of the day. I'd start stalking around the house like I stalked around the classroom—sniffing a way out—and agitating students who just wanted to work or sit peacefully in a daze.

One Sunday morning I made my final threats to my son to get his shoes on, and we were off. Pulling away in my Mazda Protege, the computer screen could be seen through the front window of the sunroom. The colorful homepage of PBS Kids was filled with the wholesome animated characters from the nature show *Wild Kratts*, and they were blinking on loop to the empty chair where my son had been sitting.

We drove to the Arcola Trail, forty-five minutes away, near the town of Stillwater. It was nothing fancy, just trees and an unpaved trail leading to the St. Croix River. My son quickly recovered from the sedentary funk of the house. Letting loose a barrage of battle orders he leapt into the underbrush. The forest floor sparkled with organic weaponry he could forage and was soon strewn with the corpses of stormtroopers.

As my son got older, the enticements and threats lost their effect. To get him out of the house, I couldn't pull on the thread of his enthusiasm to find a good stick for a gun, because he'd found other interests. Mostly it was hanging out with boys his age. But even though he kept mum about it, I knew that these other interests included new types of thoughts about girls. It was simple biology—hormones mobilizing for the next stage of life.

In general, there is a pattern set for mammals. Besides grey wolves and beavers—most mammals don't mate for life. And biologists have found that males travel more than females in those species that don't couple up for life. What did this mean for humans? According to a study by an anthropologist at the University of California, men in a traditional South American tribe traveled more than women, but only during adolescence, when they were most actively seeking romantic partners. Wanderlust was the voice of instinct, and plain old lust for a mate was at its root. It was the genetic rationale for the incest taboo that was found in all cultures. Before trying to reproduce, a person must travel beyond their immediate family, to avoid weakening the gene pool. Since a human's sense of direction steadily declined after the teenage years, there was an urgency to this quest.

The modern world has freed us to reshape our expectations about gender, and recent studies by the travel industry show that young women are traveling *more* than men. Even if there were tendencies anchored deep in the biological roots of a person's sex that affected how and why they traveled, both men and women had an urge to set out for unfamiliar territory to find the most basic keys to life: food, shelter, and mates.

My teenage son's reluctance to leave the house was strange from an evolutionary biological perspective because for all but the tiniest sliver of human history, the only place to meet girls would be outside of the family dwelling. Not that I was going to take my son out cruising, but I had an itch to push him a bit further into the world.

The sexual desires of teens are unmentionable in a teaching handbook. Our modern culture prefers to extend childhood way past sexual maturity through labor laws and mandatory schooling. These customs slow the onset of motherhood and fatherhood and allow kids to develop and educate themselves to be ready to fulfill the roles of a complex society. But this doesn't change the dictates of evolution that tell kids that once they have the bodies, they should use them. As usual, the corporate world was ahead of the game—happy to acknowledge and exploit teen interest in sexuality if it helped sell products.

Changes in hormones turned middle school into a weird cauldron of childhood and adult fantasies, a toy gun that fired real bullets. From this perspective a classroom was a torture chamber for adolescents—the lack of movement unbearable because of the new horny energy pulsing through them, especially for boys. The trend of success in school for girls was something to cheer, but the toll of the model on boys was unappreciated. They were unengaged and failing more than girls according to any number of statistics.

Schools have recently found a stopgap that might prove lasting: the headlong and haphazard adoption of technology in the classroom. It came with a benefit that no progressive or conservative teacher would admit to—the pacification of troublemaking boys. A strict demand for obedience, enforced by wrapping knuckles with a cane, was not an option for discipline that the culture endorsed anymore. ADHD drugs and an iPad were a more subtle oppression. There were now classrooms across the country full of boys plugged into some online game or another. It was the fulfillment of every exasperated teacher's tinpot dream of having a class that was sitting down and being quiet. The screen became a glowing morphine drip, easing the pain of fitting into a learning environment that did not know what to do with the tendencies of many boys.

I tried to remind myself that the characters in video games that kept boys transfixed were digital composites of bodies in the physical world. When boys moved the characters onscreen, they got a sense of motion that fulfilled a need for exploration on foot that went back to the beginning rhythms of their role in life. The quests and challenges in video games echoed the age-old 'call to adventure' that has inspired the hero's journey for ages. But what invigorated the boys online, neutered them in the real world. From the most innocent world-building of Minecraft to the most brutal war games; from the zombie slaughterhouses to the vigorous acrobatics of the porn clips they secretly binged; the sensitivity and tension in the limbs of boys drained through the game controllers and their eyeballs, into the ether.

I'd see the boys Monday mornings after forty-eight hours of gaming and watching pornography over the weekend. Their exhausted faces greeted daylight with the look of young men coming back from a hunt. They were empty-handed though, of mates thankfully, but, more troubling, also of experience.

One day in April, I showed my class Richard Attenborough's nature documentary, *Planet Earth*, where a male Superb Bird-of-Paradise, deep under the canopy of a New Guinean rain forest, calls out to invite a female to watch his display. After setting the scene the drowsy British regality of Attenborough's voice goes silent. The camera angle focuses on one end of a branch, as a small grey-and-brown female bird, lands on the other. We're in the front row of a Darwinian version of *The Bachelorette*. The male suddenly turns his wings inside out so that a neon blue pattern spreads across its black feathers. It exactly resembles a smiley face. Hopping back and forth on the branch, squawking, it performs one of the wackiest courtship dances in nature.

Malaciah, a young Jehovah's Witness, made me rewind the scene three times. Each replay he got closer to the TV, hysterically laughing, until kids yelled at him that they couldn't see. I wondered how a jumpy, horny bird like that would fit into the Watch Tower Society brochures he pressed into the hands of strangers during his missionary work. The cover of the brochure featured a dreamy green pasture, where animals and humans sat in harmony, in a paradise where there'd be no need for such frantic attempts to get attention.

Like the bird, I'd seen boys and girls try out courtship dances. Adam would stand on a chair, sing, recite the wit and social commentary woven into hip-hop lyrics, and make noises. He would cinch his hoodie tight around his face and spin around in the middle of class to maximize focus on himself. Some girls laughed but others were not impressed by this type of display. They were tuning into other courtship dances like conversation, which a few boys were finally able to offer girls by eighth grade. I heard Amelie and Mark discuss the finer points of *Harry Potter*. Mark was reading at the college level and displayed a broad vocabulary. Their dialogue had the dressing of intellectualism, but it was its own brand of feather fluffing. One day in seventh grade Mark gave an unsolicited twenty-minute presentation defending Viking culture in class, and the kids begged for more, because it was an impressive performance—a show of skill that aroused both boys and girls.

There were girls who resisted the courtship dances of the middle school boys altogether. Some were just interested in girls. They thrilled at the sensuality of Amelie's description of the young wizard Hermione, or Jamiyah's voice as she sang quietly to herself in the corner—and gushed their compliments when the boys were gone. Other girls diverted talent and energy into schoolwork and other interests. They formed solid bases of self-esteem for themselves, and in the end often coped with middle school better than their classmates who were more actively unpacking their sexuality. But they wanted to seek and be found too. Everyone wanted attention—even the shy girls and boys who dreaded it. Who doesn't want a tap on the shoulder, one saying "I choose you"?

To pathologize sexual courtship, mark it as shallow and exploit it, or worse, ignore it, was no match for a biological tradition reaching back millions of years. The goal of life was life—and a majority of the young adults were compelled to fall into place. Handholding, kisses in a stairwell, racy note-sharing, feverish daydreams, pointed to a purpose that we tried to edit out of life—like the lions mating in the outtakes of a National Geographic show.

As a young teacher, what I was always trying to figure out was why girls seemed to be able to make their peace with sitting still in the classroom better than boys. It's a truism that, when asked, kids say that recess is their favorite time of the school day—and this answer is kind of scoffed at by the adult questioner. The adult assumes this shows that the kid is missing the point of school. But remembering my own foot starting to tap in sixth grade as recess neared, I knew that recess would be the moment that many kids could show what they were truly made of, from head to toe. It was the place, that as a boy, I could work on my relationships which involved doing things with friends more than saying things.

I sought refuge in evolutionary biology to explain why one gender was able to tolerate the sequester of a classroom better than the other. It boiled down to prehistoric roles still percolating in the DNA—men left to hunt or find mates, and women stayed closer to the cave to take care of the young and gather berries and roots. Girls were maybe able to find ways to relate, connect and grow in closer quarters. (Characteristics beings exploited and twisted in the new social media landscape.) But the reality was that the whole tribe would be on the move much of the time, the soothing rhythm of heartbeats and footsteps over a dusty path were drummed into male and female infants alike.

At Ms. D's little school, I would see girls tap into the joy of our field trips with their own deep memory of long strolls across the savannah. Sometimes I think that what we were all doing running around places like Lilydale, St. Anthony Falls, and Carpenter Nature Center, was remembering.

When we were on the move, girls, boys, two-spirits, and every identity in between, were nomads again; free. I thought of Jo, the gender fluid rep at the Apple Store and how she found freedom in augmentation, transformation, and technology. Her allies sought to amend the written law to make room for her in society, but she herself was charting a new biology—a pliable future that was as vast and unknown as the land beyond East Africa was to our ancestors.

I was more specifically terrified that technology would make physical movement itself obsolete. I had a bleak view of a humanity immersed in a digital world, a physical reality interfaced with technology at all levels of life, severed from its links with natural rhythms and places. But Jo from the Apple Store showed me that what I called 'natural' would also evolve.

For the time being, though, in my classroom, I was mostly confronted with the ancient patterns of life; males and females negotiating a divide between them, so they could meet up and life on the planet would persist as it had for millennia.

The odd thing about the urban, modern world was that potential mates were plentiful, and right inside a co-ed classroom, but an adolescents instincts told them they needed to leave to find one. The impulses to leave the room or stay and court someone who was already there, pinged around the room. Some boys and girls became manic, bothering everybody with their noise and movement. Others were silent and immobilized, because after a certain point during puberty, seeing the one you were attracted to would turn you to stone. Until kids could get up the courage to talk to this person, a terrifying supernatural power surrounded the object of their fascination. The face of a girl could stun a boy, but until a boy looked her in the eye, he wouldn't figure out that Medusa was not deadly but beautiful and laughing—a partner.

Heroic journeys to find mates, confrontations with the godly power of beauty—to deny that these ancient dramas laid siege to the internal life of adolescents was to have not seen Edgar on his last day of eighth grade. The silver Caravans had dropped the last of us off outside the school. After the graduation ceremony the night before, we had driven to a campground for an overnight to celebrate. Backpacks, pillows, and sloppily tied sleeping bags sat in clumps, or spilled out of garbage bags onto the sidewalk and front steps of the school.

One by one kids disappeared into waiting cars, all their belongings piled on their laps. They had been awake all night running around the woods, and most were too exhausted to be emotional. Except for Edgar.

Near the parking lot, I saw Tabari and Jeremiah with their arms around someone who was sobbing. Edgar's curly dark hair gave him away. He was the sort of kid who got left behind in conversations because he was thoughtful. As the banter and flirting took place around him through the years, he would be cycling up into his own mind trying to think of what to say. He was a sweet, artistic kid that became one of my favorites.

As I got closer, Edgar's red eyes told a story that I knew. Unexpressed passion; the doom tale of every shy, polite, and unswaggering boy in middle school.

"She's gone!"

"Edgar, *Edgar*, bro. Who?" Tabari asked.

"She left…I'm not gonna see her again." Another wave of remorse swept over him, and his face squeezed into a grimace. More tears. He spun away and his buddies stayed with him.

"Edgar, dude," Jeremiah pleaded, leaning in closer.

"Who's gone?" Tabari asked again.

"I didn't tell her. I never told her."

I checked behind me for who was still around and who had left. I had been Edgar's teacher since he was a little round ball in fifth grade. Now I wondered myself which girl had been marching along the fault line of his heart in a pair of checkered Vans for four years.

"I can't ever tell her now."

"Bro! It's gonna be alright."

Edgar shook his head, started walking but then violently turned around. The gyroscope that had guided his orbit through many fantasies, was now spinning wildly out of control.

"Who?"

"Just tell us, dude."

Edgar stared out long and hard at a landscape being cratered by lovely thoughts crashing to the Earth at great speeds.

Then he just shook his head.

Seventeen

BESIDES THE RAMPAGING dramas that accompanied a sexual awakening, there was more than one reason the elementary teachers at Ms. D's little school were wary of the middle school kids and teachers. There was an unspoken détente in a school that contained both preschoolers and eighth graders. The presence of small people who were more vulnerable tamped down the rowdy aggression that can overcome a middle school. In return the small people got to be around models of what it took to grow up.

It was more of the *avant garde* bent of our middle school staff that fascinated and disturbed the elementary teachers. We'd return from our outings and elementary teachers would be excited but almost afraid to ask where we'd been. Elementary school education in America is the dominion of competence. The classrooms are staffed overwhelmingly by women who are backed by the confidence of communities that have entrusted them with the job. By sheer cultural expectation, it becomes a conventional role, a stabilizing force in the society—but also a keeper of the status quo.

Many women, with the talent and drive to be trailblazing CEO's, architects, and senators, guide themselves into first grade rooms to secure the literacy and civility of a nation. The hard work, organization, and certitude of purpose—the devotion and sense of responsibility, made me really uncomfortable. In fact, it shamed me.

When I walked into an elementary room at Ms. D's little school, the charts, alphabets, labeled bins, and number lines betrayed a pinpoint clarity of goals. It was all part of a colorful management system that was dialed in before the first day of school. When I saw the single file lines of kindergartners stepping quietly through the halls, I had the urge to kidnap a few and take them with the middle schoolers into the woods. I reasoned that if the mind was a jungle, those straight lines of elementary kids in the hall only represented a cosmetic sense of order. Beneath was the real kid, ready for adventure and what one might call freedom. If the six-year-olds in line got the chance to act on their own, they would be zigzagging everywhere, causing havoc, getting hurt, and seeking out informal teachers left and right for learning that suited them. But the rooms, hallways and rules of a school were the format the kindergarten teachers had to work with. Taking turns getting drinks at the water fountain, that were timed by the other kids, was the first expectation that a bit of common courtesy should be observed in public—it was learning that benefited everyone. I had to concede that not only was there was more talent and skill present in the women of the elementary school, but more responsibility. They were doing the heavy lifting of society—balancing the scales of civility and freedom at a foundational level.

Meanwhile in my room, the state social studies standards were buried inside my tanker desk, and my lessons veered between topics like a drunk at The Field Museum of Natural History in Chicago. As the middle school teacher, I was supposedly in charge of a curriculum that more explicitly aimed to shape civic habits. But I had the guilty feeling that I was wasting the precious time students had to prepare for high school *and* citizenship. Cardboard boxes and milk crates spilled over with the scraps from old projects. Completed dioramas rested on the radiators or were tucked into corners. Stacks of completed weekly five-paragraph essays sat on my desk about a hodge-podge of themes: the Arab Spring, arguments for and against Black History Month, the value of the 'big picture' perspective, the election, recent middle school outings. What was missing was the sense that we were building sensibly towards something. What they call in educational parlance: scope and sequence.

As a teacher, the witching hour for me was not midnight, it was Sunday afternoon. On one of those Sundays, after a Nerf sword battle with my son, I came into my house for a sip of water and saw my school bag. I realized I was staring down the barrel of an unplanned week of school. With spring fever setting in, I had to move fast or pay for it by spending a week simmering in junior high chaos. It was time to come up with a random project. My son knew there would be no second round of sword battles and nestled in among his Lego; his dad, a teacher, had work to do.

Building on my efforts with the spray paint, I brought up five leftover paint cans from my basement and picked up a few more colors at Menard's. I'd blown through the two-hundred-dollar tax break I could claim as a teacher early in the year and took the hit to the wallet. It was a personal investment in a project that might occupy my students and save my sanity.

On Monday, my first class pushed the tables and bleachers to the side and taped down two layers of butcher paper on the floor next to the walls. Student groups of four and five claimed six-by-four-foot sections of the walls above the chalkboards. Each group had picked a question from a list that I came up with in the middle of the night, on the toilet, and while driving to school that morning: *What makes humans different from animals? What can a human do that a machine can't? How do we know we're human? What will happen to humans in the future?*

Students still thought states were countries and the Declaration of Independence was signed ten thousand years ago. They held a network of eye-widening misunderstandings, but I made it my mission to ask them other types of questions. Basic knowledge would have to resemble something else in my room—it was less about the branches of government and more the Tree of Life.

For the next three weeks students took turns climbing five ladders propped around the room and adding to their murals. The aprons they wore were borrowed from Maloney's science class, and got speckled with paint each day. Eventually the aprons became abstract reflections of each mural.

One day while we were working, Maurice, an 8th grader who had transferred mid-year to Ms. D's little school, kicked over an entire can of white paint by accident. Within minutes, Mr. D appeared and was helping Maurice wipe it up. On the last day of school Maurice pulled me to the side. "Mr. A, thanks for not yelling at me about that paint I spilled." How could I have? I'd gone from vandalizing a cubbyhole to covering every wall in my room with paint, and Ms. D hadn't scolded me.

In the end, the murals turned out hideously. We hadn't planned well, and gobs of paint ran onto the wooden frames of the whiteboards. But in each one, lost in the deformed shapes of animals and spaceships, there was the same fizzing spirit of thought and creation found in all those scrappy cave paintings across the world.

The students who didn't think of themselves as artists worried that their messy additions to the murals would earn them a bad grade. I never talked about grades with students and wondered why they persisted on badgering me about them. In truth, I couldn't figure out a grading system that made any sense for a group of students that ranged so broadly in skills, interests, and types of intelligence.

I would tell students that there was no way they could 'fail' *social* studies. That would be the same as failing as a member of our society. It's not possible. No matter what a person does in our country, they can't get an 'F.' Suppose a man or woman was given an 'F' as a citizen. We still live with them. They can be labeled "failures" on all the paperwork but will still pass us on the streets. They're part of our community, whether they're greedy bankers, homeless addicts, reckless drunk drivers, gamers stuck in a basement, or murderers rotting in a cell. They are people who contribute to our reality just by existing, in spite of themselves or how we label them. A student who walked into the classroom, slept, or rabble roused, and did none of the assignments, helped define the room, even if I wrote them off.

I told students that social studies was just the study of humans and what they do together—i.e. if they were human they would be good at the class and have plenty to add to our success.

All they needed to do for the mural assignment was climb a ladder and make their brush strokes. And when they stepped back, they saw the details they added were part of a colorful and messy heritage. The murals stretched along the top wall, circling our entire classroom—a mysterious halo of drying household paint depicting the stabs their generation was making at big questions.

As usual, this sort of gambit explaining my grading philosophy went over the heads of most students. And the mural assignment itself didn't quite feel like work. Some students weren't convinced that they would pass the class. Around conference time, Maurice had come to me and said, "Mr. A, I need to get my grades up."

These last-second hustles to tidy up report cards turned me off. It reeked of the game-playing needed to survive the traditional school system, not a lively quest to seek knowledge. But I knew Maurice was dutifully repeating a line from home. Maurice had been sent on an errand to take care of business at school by his family. They were doing their best to offer what they assumed the teacher wanted: a student worried about good grades.

"Suppose I tell you that you will pass this class *no matter what*. What are you going to do now?"

"What chu' mean?" Maurice asked. Kendrick, who was at his side, was starting to laugh.

"What do you think I want out of you in class?" I asked.

"Man, I don't know."

Kendrick, who had been dealing with me for a couple years, rescued him. "Bro, he just want you to use that big head you got."

Maurice lined up a comeback, but then hesitated. Kendrick tapped him on the arm and started walking out of the room.

"We gotta go—Mr. A gonna get *real* suspicious soon."

WHEN I SWITCHED rooms a year later, I didn't blame the art teacher who moved in, for painting over the murals. She had

Other Loyalties

taste. All the murals vanished behind thick coats of beige paint: the drippy scenes of humans showing off their writing and architecture to a crowd of animals, the blank-faced robots unable to love, and a cascade of high-tech weapons and carnage piling up along a red timeline stretching into the future.

At the time, I was proud of the mural project and my head swirled with transcendent accomplishment. But it could have been just the paint fumes that I'd been smelling all day. I remembered the anecdote described by the early twentieth century American psychologist William James. A man on laughing gas came to know the secret of the universe but forgot it once the gas wore off. One day, while still under the influence, he was finally able to scribble down the secret before it dissolved. When he went to read it after regaining full consciousness, the words he had written were this: "The smell of petroleum prevails throughout."

Still, I charged ahead with these projects, but Maurice's question nagged at me. Why was I not preparing him to win the game of school? Would he lack the skills to trudge through bullshit and graduate high school? Was I just high on artsy fluff and calling it meaningful work?

I wrote about the murals to Ms. D in the Weekly Reflection. I admitted that it was nice to watch students "work on a bigger scale," but had my doubts about whether it was making the most out of the little time we had with them. Ms. D wrote back, "Interesting Q's—Makes them Think! Thank YOU." The "thank you" was underlined four times. I'd gone with my gut again and Ms. D's affirmation told me it was what a good teacher did.

LATE IN MY third year at Ms. D's little school, I approached first grade teacher Ms. Catherine about doing reading buddies with my classes. She looked like a suburban mom but had the vibe of a worldly folksinger—like Joni Mitchel in pumps. I was still a bit insecure, imagining that the high-functioning elementary teachers shook their heads when passing my room. It had been three years since Ms. Rhodes screamed "Diarrhea!" into my room, but I still thought a classroom was supposed to look a certain way. Any adult peeking in would have seen my class, more often than not, in the shambolic throes of some messy project like the murals. The students weren't bored—but any minute it looked like the wheels might come off.

My request was handled with generosity by Ms. Catherine. The warmth and receptivity inside the elementary classrooms felt real to me—all those years of practice welcoming and comforting frightened kids. I rejoiced because if a competent veteran elementary teacher agreed to partner with me, it meant the idea had merit—she wouldn't risk wasting time on a flighty project that wasn't likely to help her kids get better at something. Ms. Catherine got three other elementary teachers on board so each of my classes would have reading buddies.

For the program to work the way I wanted it to I needed good stories. I had contacted Hoopoe Books, an educational charity that got its start shipping illustrated adaptations of thousand-year-old teaching tales to poor Afghan schools, and now to underfunded urban schools in the US. The stories had been retold by Idries Shah, one of my favorite authors. They included titles like, *The Boy Without a Name*, *Fatima the Spinner*, and *Neem the Half-Boy*. The charity sent me a classroom set of each title.

Every Wednesday each of my social studies classes would spread out to different elementary rooms with a copy of one of these tales. I had primed my students by saying that they were now a link in a chain of transmission reaching back a thousand years. They were storytellers and had a sacred duty to be a good host to their audience. In this case it was one or two tiny children sitting cross-legged next to them.

On the first day, when Ms. Catherine was pairing kids up with an older buddy, I saw many of the kids gazing up at Maurice and Kendrick who were standing at the front of the room. They resembled the rappers and sports stars their dads, brothers and, uncles worshipped. Many of the Hmong boys dreamed of playing in the NFL. Two kids, one Hmong and one black, smiled and jumped up to follow Kendrick when Ms. Catherine pointed to them. I thought about how to assess this experience in the gradebook. How do you grade the fundamental process of one generation performing its responsibility to the next?

I believed in the pedigree of the old stories I gave my students to read, not as an act of faith but by reflecting on the ancient need for economy. The stories had been passed on through the oral tradition, and I saw no reason that they would be kept alive over the centuries by countless retellings unless they had some value that was hard to corrupt.

The branded gimmickry of many of the book series I saw for young kids disgusted me. They weren't stories but concepts, cooked up by enterprising businesspeople, and constructed by teams of marketing experts at big publishing houses. It depressed me to see kids imbibing a hollow sales pitch in the form of a storybook. Magic kittens and Lego Ninjago books: they were helping kids practice reading, the same way eating a Twinkie teaches a kid to practice eating. Even the giggly nonsense and bouncy optimism of Dr. Seuss books wore thin after a while.

The time-tested tales from Central Asia exposed kids to unexpected combinations of events that went beyond a magic camp for fairy kittens, or a cat in a hat for that matter. For example, the hero in *Neem the Half-Boy* confronts a dragon but instead of slaying him negotiates a trade with him. The words of the story combined in subtle ways that created context, lighting up the right side of the brain and preparing kids for the unfamiliar events that would meet them in their own lives.

I was making a judgement, like a teacher who would correct the young girl who wanted to spell, "catqueen." But I was ready to make a stand against the vacant picture books that I saw flooding the Scholastic book fair and library shelves.

I read the stories to my own son and would wonder which dimensions of the human mind the old storytellers were weaving into the action. I was willing to make a leap of faith since the stories didn't always follow the usual plots of children's stories, and this intrigued me. In *The Farmer's Wife*, for instance, the woman begs different animals and objects in the farmyard to help her get an apple that fell in a hole—only to have a gust of wind blow it out in the end. At times, my son, and the students, expressed a hunger for the straightforward moral satisfactions of Disney, and endings that didn't feel so unresolved. At the end of some of these story's my son would say, "Wait, is that it? What *happens?*"

During one visit I circulated around Ms. Catherine's room but there was nothing to do—the big kids were taking care of the little kids and the situation was in the slipstream of some natural order. (A much different order than the straight lines of kindergartners I saw in the halls.) I came to a stop next to Ms. Catherine and put my hands on my hips.

"They seem to be doing alright," I said.

"My kids love it. All week they ask me, 'When are the big kids coming?'" Ms. Catherine replied.

"Oh good."

"Where did you get those books anyways?'

It occurred to me that I was engaged in evangelism again. Just like the visit to the Watt Munisotaram, I was inculcating values by stealth. The visit to the cultural site had alerted them to the benefits of a life of meditation and reflection. Now it was a reading buddy program that brought more Eastern philosophy into the public-school classes being held in the old rooms of a former Catholic school.

I took my hands off my hips and dug them into the pockets of my vest, finding a balled-up tissue in the corner. "The stories—" I said, glancing quickly at Ms. Catherine "—they're just old tales that have been popular in Central Asia for centuries."

"They're really cool," Ms. Catherine said before tending to a tiny girl at her side asking to go to the bathroom.

Across the room I saw Maurice holding up the book, *Fatima the Spinner,* so his little buddies could see the pictures. It's about a girl who struggles through shipwrecks, kidnapping, servitude, and despair, only to find that each of these trials gave her knowledge that were the makings of her ultimate happiness. Almost a fairy tale straightforward enough for Disney.

I insisted on having my students reread the same story to their little buddies, envisioning new parcels of precious insight into human behavior, drifting into their ears after each reading. After a couple weeks reading *The Boy Without a Name,* my students prepared and brought the materials for a project. In the story the boy and his friend are shown two boxes by a wise man in their village; one collects dreams that they don't want anymore, the other contains all kinds of new dreams. My students helped their little buddies make and decorate two boxes of their own. Then, like the boys, they dropped in a dream they were ready to get rid of in one box and pulled out one they wanted from the other.

There were deeper meanings hidden in the action of the stories, like money sewed in the lining of a jacket. Once the stories were safe inside the subconscious, a knife would slide along the stitching, and the payload would take root. Because we think and dream in stories the image of this unconscious transaction was not outlandish in my view. Expecting a story to work on our minds when we weren't looking, did not require a leap of faith I realized—it was normal and involuntary as breathing.

I was half-consciously addressing the cultural shortcomings that I felt were damaging the mental and spiritual well-being of American kids. I was on the loose, and Ms. Catherine and my colleagues, most of them Christians, wouldn't stop me. Why? They must have sensed the intentions of my agenda. Teachers are very protective of their students, especially elementary teachers. Any whiff of a religious or ideological crusade to convert or coerce the young in a public school, would have been forcefully ended.

I knew teachers had religious and personal beliefs and those bled into their teaching, but at a *public* school, teachers had to trim the fat off their private beliefs before they were expressed to students. The choices teachers make are shaped by faith or philosophy—personal conclusions about the purpose of life. The influence of a creed shows up in lessons, but the brand and dogma are left out. The professional constraints are taken very seriously by most teachers—they know it is their duty to teach skills and how to think not what to think. A public school setting served as a purifying sieve for teachers; their actions and character got through to the observant kids, but the vows, certainty, formal traditions—and outward dressings of religion—were caught and left to the private world of the teachers.

At their best, public schools, by forcing discipline on religion, helped clarify questions of morality and invigorate the question of how best to live. Every time a teacher arrived at school, it was like a tiny reformation. They had to decide what was essential about their belief system, and then nail it to their classroom doors. When Professor Greenwalt still taught high school he told us his rules for class one year were, 1. Try and 2. Be Nice. In the hurly-burly of a classroom, religion was conduct.

The beauty of storytelling was that it was an art that had perfected passing along ideas and values in a quiet way, that didn't raise red flags by being blatantly ideological. Our own story project ended with a final visit where the first graders had cookies and milk ready for their big buddies. I saw Maurice read the purple thank you card one of his buddies had made for him. The little boy's hand was on Maurice's shoulder, and he leaned in to watch Maurice read his message. They both laughed and I peeked over their shoulders. The boy had tried to spell the eighth graders name the best he could: "More-Rice."

The last days of May went by in a swarm of spring hormones, joyous walks and picnics at parks, water fights, and weepy good-byes after graduation. The spray-painted altar in my classroom had long ago fallen to ruin, and the cubby hole was filled with debris from the year. But still visible behind the junk, was the black sky, and a few glow-in-the-dark stars. My goal that an education would give students back more of themselves than it would take away, was still holding. It was hard to admit to myself, but by the end of my third year, it was possible my lessons were working. But I was far from sure.

If I was a data type of teacher, it might have been easier to see the results of my efforts. A reading score improved, an equation got solved, a line on a graph wiggled upward towards progress, or plummeted. Maybe it was me, or just the nature of social studies, but capturing what my students got out of my class was tricky. Too much about what we did was fluid, open-ended, discussion- and experience-oriented. Adolescents were not always the most forthcoming about their learning—even though I had them write reflections each week—so I was left guessing. The doubts lingered, and the year ended with me still thinking I didn't know what the hell I was doing.

Summer arrived like a giant spaceship, lifting me off the beautiful, exhausting planet of work called the school year. It swept me into its sunny cargo hold and sped into the sky. This year, instead of heading to a campground with my family, I hopped into my friend Dan's Honda Civic, and we flew fast down Interstate 35 Southbound.

Dan and I weren't more than one hour into rural Minnesota, near the border with Iowa, when we saw a long line of wind turbines crossing the farmland. As if to confirm in our minds that we now had free time, we pulled over to the side of the road. Dan popped his trunk and he pulled out a fancy new digital camera. This summer, Dan would transform from special ed teacher to filmmaker. He lined up a shot of the turbines, locked his tripod, and got two minutes of footage of the huge blades sweeping through the air.

We sped on towards Texas, stopping in a small town, where Dan's grandparents had opened a department store in the 1940's. We stood on the black-and-white checker tiles outside the double-doors and peered into the abandoned building on main street—toying with the alternate reality that would have Dan as rich businessman instead of teacher.

After spending a few hours trying to sleep in the car at a steamy truck stop, we barreled on to New Orleans, taking turns reading out loud from Sam Shepard's book of short stories set in the southwest, *Cruising Through Paradise*. It was a book full of dusty loners staring out into the desert, a great anecdote for two men recovering from being pierced by a thousand student requests and general social overload of the school environment.

When we arrived in New Orleans the watermarks on buildings from Hurricane Katrina were still visible five years later. Dan parked and we roamed the city before stopping to catch a free jazz show at a bar. Outside the bar there was a woman who had a typewriter set up on a small table on the sidewalk. She was offering to write original poems for a small fee. Dan and I struck a deal with her and handed over our own original poem we'd written on the back of a napkin in the bar. After typing furiously for ten minutes she handed back a light blue sheet of paper with her poem for us.

The night wheeled on. We found ourselves at the 24-hour, open-air, Café du Monde. Dan started a conversation with another street artist, this time a musician. We bought her a glass of orange juice as a compliment to her sweet songs. She downed it and headed to her friend's house to crash. It was midnight.

After the singer left, I romanticized about her sleeping on her friend's couch, satisfied with a few crumpled dollars collected from a night of busking. I recalled the sidewalk poet, and the guy playing trumpet at the bar.

"Man, wouldn't it be nice to live the artistic life?" I said.

"Yeah, but…making a living playing music—it's a hard, hard, grind."

We mulled over different careers, comparing my sister's globe-trotting poverty teaching English and working in cafes, to the long hours of the high-paying tech support work his brother did, living out of hotel rooms in Ohio half the week.

Dan took a bite out of his beignet, loaded with powdered sugar, and washed it down with a sip of coffee. Finally, he said, "Summer, damn it! You cannot beat paid summers off."

"So, you're saying teaching is still the best choice?"

Dan raised his Styrofoam cup of coffee towards the lively street scenes of New Orleans. I felt in my pocket for the folded blue sheet of paper with the poem. Maybe teaching was the best of both worlds. It required art, paid the bills, and rewarded both with months of luxury living on a ship called summer.

Eighteen

MY FOURTH YEAR at the school had begun like the others, all of us gathered in a circle a week before Labor Day in the gloomy cafeteria. Ms. D liked to build on the core staff she had, giving introductions of us that spelled out the roles and qualities that made the school what it was. She lavished praise on the Three Sisters, her blonde acolytes who anchored the third and fourth grade; singled out Ms. Soraira, a teacher-aide from Venezuela, battling cancer but beating the Grim Reaper to the punch by blessing us with an angelic presence before she ever passed; Ms. Paige, who ruled her Kindergarten kingdom, with a twinkling eagle-eye; Maloney, for invigorating kids in a madcap scramble for experience and scientific knowledge.

She pointed to me and said, "This is Mr. A. I don't know what he does."

It was one of the best compliments I have ever gotten. It made its way into my ears; the whisper of full confidence sneaking in with it.

It reminded me of the central figure in the documentary *Dakota 38*. The film follows the story of Jim Miller, a Dakota elder who had a dream that he was riding across the great plains of South Dakota. Just before he woke up, he saw thirty-eight of his Dakota ancestors reaching out for each other before being hanged. Although he didn't know the story of the largest mass execution in US history, he knew it was a vision that came from the Creator—and though he tried, he couldn't ignore it.

It inspired him to lead a group of Dakota men on a yearly 330-mile horseback ride in winter from Lower Brule, South Dakota back to Mankato, Minnesota—their homeland and the site of the actual execution of the "38" during the Dakota Uprising against the US government in 1862. The entire ride and making of the film followed Native healing practices and the film would not be used to gain a profit.

The filmmaker, a young white New Englander who was asked personally by Miller to film the ride, was working on a shoestring budget, carrying his stuff in a backpack, and sleeping on couches. He was often insecure about how to proceed during the filming and spoke to Jim Miller about his apprehension.

Jim Miller looked at him and said, "You know what to do."

I flipped Ms. D's comment over in my mind. She didn't need to know what I did because *I knew* what to do. Was it possible? Was I going to be trusted with the education of the nation's children for another year? The first week with the students that year, I put this trust through the wringer. After reading a book called *The Junkyard Wonders* to my son, I decided to start the year with a bright idea. The book tells the true story of a classroom full of oddball students, gifted but ill-suited for the "regular" classrooms of the time due to physical and psychological differences. One day the teacher passes out small glass vials to each student which contain different aromas: lavender, lemon, mint, rose, and so on. Their task is to find the other students in class with the same aroma as them and form a team.

I spent Sunday night dousing cotton balls with my wife's supply of aromatherapy scents and putting them in small Ziplock baggies. The next day students in each of my classes stumbled around the room holding cotton balls up to each other's noses trying to find their matches. Adam, sensitive to smell or just looking to ham it up, took one whiff of his sage-scented cotton ball, gagged, and seized the moment to run out of the room to the bathroom. The rest accepted, by some primitive sensory calculus, that these would be their groups for different projects.

I had needed to buy an economy size bag of cotton balls and the next day decided to use them to up the ante on the premise that I knew what to do. I decided I wanted students to envision what kind of atmosphere they desired the class to have. What did it *really* feel like in my classroom in the first place? Mustering all my authority as their teacher, I ordered them to stuff cotton balls up their noses, block their ears with their hands, and squeeze their eyes shut.

"I ain't puttin' no cotton ball up my nose. Mr. A, you got me messed up!" Kiara yelled. But she was already giggling and twisting the cotton balls in her hands, so they'd fit her nostrils.

In the makeshift sensory deprivation tank, without their eager eyes and ears at work, I hoped they'd tap into how they actually felt in the room. Did they trust each other? Did they trust me to keep them safe but still give them the tough training them needed, like Sensei Tanaka in *Bloodsport*? Brianna peeked up with two cotton balls bulging out of her tiny nose, caught my eye, and smiled. It was too silly of an activity to risk transforming into a cult initiation. I smiled back. But if an average person off the street walked into my classroom the first week of school that year, I'm sure they would have reported me. This was not what a classroom looked like, and this was not what a teacher did.

With grace, it was not the average person who ended up walking in, it was Mr. K.O.

He took one look, said, "What the...?" chuckled, and walked out.

THE NEW ADDITION of note to Ms. D's unaverage staff my fourth year was Mr. Duvall from Teach for America, a program that accepts fewer applicants than Harvard Law School. They place young strivers in the shabby corners of rural or inner-city schools. There had been another candidate, a woman from New York City, who had been taking the subway since she was eight. My own bias, based on the ship-shape classrooms of the female teachers, made me wish at first that we had gotten her as our new middle school math teacher.

Mr. Duvall was tall, muscular, polished, with the full expectation of being successful, and whenever I passed in the hall, I had to do a double take. It was more than a bonanza for our largely female staff. I had not been in the world of education that long, but I knew this sort of executive talent rarely chose a school to express it—unless they had their eyes on becoming superintendent.

Trying to understand the blue-chip charm emanating from Mr. Duvall, I asked Dan how ambition and excellence could converge so thoroughly in a man. Dan said it mostly came down to the parents; they set out a shape, like a bottle, and a kid grows into it. Mr. Duvall's father was a lawyer, and I overheard Mr. Duvall one day saying that his father had made a pact about weekly runs with him that Mr. Duvall had kept for the better part of his teen years and into his twenties. I took it as a snippet of some enlightened plan to get the best out of his son.

Mr. Duvall was at Ms. D's little school for just two years, the tour of duty for his program. During his time, students made gains in math that were suspiciously grand. It was all legitimate—the result of Mr. Duvall's intelligence and a missionary zeal that couldn't be sustained. More than once, when I came in early to school, I'd see Mr. Duvall stride out of his math room with a toothbrush—he'd spent the night there sleeping on a cot. Unless all the Mr. Duvalls of the country were persuaded to take stock options in the future of America's youth, and stayed teachers for the long haul, I feared the progress would be temporary.

Early in October the newly enriched staff met up at a Mexican restaurant for a baby shower. We crowded into a side room around a table packed with jubilant decorations modeled after a couple snazzy parenting boards from Pinterest accounts. One of the party games required the handful of men there to drink milk or juice from a baby bottle—through the nipple, no unscrewing the cap. Whoever could drink the most bottles in two minutes was the champ.

Maloney and Mr. Duvall faced off. They raised the bottles high above their heads, squeezing and shaking the last drops of milk

Other Loyalties

out of the bottles before slamming them on the table. We all cheered, thrilling at this domestic version of a roadhouse whiskey drinking showdown.

As the clock wound down, I could see Mr. Duvall's biceps flaring as he gripped a bottle with two hands. One of the Three Sisters pinched the arm of another, unable to contain the joy of watching the sexy spectacle.

"Whoo! Go Mr. Duvall!"

At that moment I had an evil vision that had nothing to do with Mr. Duvall's kindness and devotion to the kids when he was at Ms. D's little school. A powerful man, using all the strength and advantages that life has provided, swallowing down nourishment meant for the children.

At the school Mr. Duvall quickly formed a team with Ms. Conley. When there was an update to the staff fantasy league of who wanted to sleep with who, Ms. Conley, the English teacher, and Mr. Duvall, the math teacher from Teach-for-America, were assumed to want to shack up.

Ms. Conley had endeared herself to the kids through fun lessons, a willingness to answer texts at midnight, and an array of killer outfits, that included leopard-print high heels. She dove headfirst into the dramas that consumed many of the girls' lives, and with Ms. D and Ms. Danika was part of the triage force that attended to the daily crises of some of the girls.

This 'crisis team', which included Mr. Duvall, was indispensable when Maloney and I recklessly blazed ahead on field trips. I, myself, had decided early on to keep up with Maloney on these trips. Maloney would not stop and count heads, pat kids on the shoulders, and remind them to sip their water. What he had was an abiding faith in a human's desire to stay alive. Lost out on the trail, few people will just sit and wait to die. Most will try to survive—even if they are walking in circles until they do succumb to the shame of being mortal. I was interested in this approach that cut against the usual fussing about safety when it came to kids.

There are few culturally defined rites of passage for adolescents these days. I figured Maloney wanted to see what kids were made of by taking treacherous trails, at a break-neck speed. He pushed hard—believing instincts kicked in even on these short school expeditions. Of course, he would often be the one who brought extra gloves and hats, the first to notice someone missing and the first to apply first aid. And in a real-life case from a trip that I won't elaborate on—the first to pull a kid out of a hole in the ice below a frozen waterfall.

Yet Maloney and I still counted on Ms. Conley, Mr. Duvall, and Ms. Danika, responsibly pulling up the rear, making the calls for the injured kid to be picked up and encouraging the laggers. When we got off the bus at the outset of a long hike, the kids needed some adjustment time, and this team of teachers brought laughter to it. Students would be led away from the malaise of their stationary home lives and up to the starting gate of a strenuous exodus into the woods, with teachers they could count on.

The Darwinian workout class being led by Maloney had a twist to it. The rest of the staff knew that though there might be winners and losers at an educational institution and in society, there couldn't be in a healthy family; everyone pitched in to get the tribe home safe. I've never been sure what the phrase "it takes a village" really means, but watching our staff gave me insight into how fragments become a whole. When Maloney yanked the kids into situations out of their comfort zones, Ms. Conley and Mr. Duvall made sure they didn't fall apart there.

Mid-October arrived and instead of getting colder the temperature rose into the seventies. We were blessed with a second summer. Maloney acted fast and plotted a bike trip from our school on the east side of St. Paul to Fort Snelling, near the border of Minneapolis. He expertly dispatched all the background work that it takes to make a field trip work, including hustling a car trailer off one of his in-laws. The trailer was insurance for a predicted number of bike malfunctions and biomechanical revolts in the limbs of unfit students. The week before our trip, the school cafeteria steadily filled with the ramshackle dirt bikes and ten-speeds kids brought in early, so they wouldn't forget on the day of the ride.

The morning of the trip Maloney raced around the cafeteria doing final tune-ups on the bikes. Most bikes were fit for a five-block ride to the corner store, but we'd be attempting a twenty-mile trip. A few daredevils were already biking around the cafeteria, swerving around trash cans, stone pillars, and each other. I tried to make myself useful.

"You got a helmet Adam?" I asked.

"Nope."

"Ain't no helmet gonna fit his big head," Kevin said.

"That dude need two helmets on top of his head," Kendrick added.

"Bro, that don't make no sense," Kevin said, disappointed in Kendrick's sloppy roast of Adam.

Standing up after tightening the brakes of a bike that looked like it had been dredged from a river, Maloney pointed to a few extra helmets.

"Got those at Value Thrift."

"Oh, hell no," Adam protested, after one glance at the geeky road bike helmets with ugly air vents.

"Two dollars a-piece."

"That's bogus Mr. Maloney. You gonna make me pay?"

"Well, you know, you could have bought one. I was just there yesterday and there were about five more left."

Maloney waited a beat after saying this, and then made a weighing gesture with his hands.

"You could buy a cheeseburger at McDonald's or protect yer noggin. I don't know. Your choice."

It was the sort of brusque but elegant laying out of the facts Maloney had mastered. Adam shuffled over, selected a helmet, and tried to jam it on his head. Without paying, Adam walked away with it perched on his head like a turban, as Kevin and Kendrick relentlessly dressed him down.

"We about ready?" I nervously asked.

"Seems to me," Maloney said, shoving an Allen wrench in his pocket.

That's when I saw Ruby standing next to a purple banana seat bike with high ape-hanger handlebars. Ruby was skinny as a chopstick but had a loud voice that was amplified by some store of confidence in her bitty chest cavity. She was one of the students I habitually let down in my room. Never able to grasp the abstract analogies I made, and not a confident reader, she often milled around the room waiting for something to make sense so she could work. One of her hands held the bike frame and the other was raised to her mouth, where her thumb was being gnawed on, and then suckled. On her feet were pink jelly shoes.

The hope for a single peloton dissolved as we left the school parking lot. Emilio did a wheelie, jumped the curb and vanished down the street. Jada and Quiana said they forgot something and disappeared into the building. Elijah had slammed his brakes and was staring at the dropped chain on Ben's bike. There was only one thing to do: keep moving in a direction and not look back.

I was so inexperienced at long-distance biking I guessed that we might try to stay on the sidewalk until we hit dedicated bike trails. The bikes bumped over yards, and in between parked cars, and onto the street, in a breathtaking melee of freedom, like an anarchist parade on May Day. In the crowd I saw Ruby cruising, with a lollipop in her mouth now and one hand high on her handlebars like Henry Fonda in *Easy Rider*.

The group quickly elongated along the middle of the street and into self-selected packs. Over several blocks, we stayed together much like a long necklace: chunky, unique, steel-framed beads strewn along a cord of asphalt. I only vaguely knew where we were going. As we turned past Swede Hollow Park, the truth of our route to the Big Rivers Regional Trail along the Mississippi dawned on me. It would take us right through a corner of downtown St. Paul during morning rush hour.

Near the Union Depot under a bridge, somebody wiped out on some sand. Ms. Conley called Mr. Kou, a jack-of-all trades educational assistant from the Hmong community of St. Paul, who was driving the trailer. He swooped in, loaded the bike and shook-up kid, and sped off.

Maloney and I had carried on with our lead group, not because we didn't care, but because we were so far ahead. We didn't learn about the crash until reaching Fort Snelling. Mr. Kou and Mr. J met us there with the lunches and gave the full casualty report. Leng got a flat tire, Lucas's handlebars fell off, Jada and Quiana were found hiding in the bathroom and were now helping Ms. Rhodes do a project with her class, and so-and-so who'd wiped out was in Ms. D's office laughing, stuffing envelopes with the school newsletter and drinking a milk shake.

The ass-covering the staff did for each other was heartfelt and done with incredible grace. It was almost taken for granted, just like in a family.

The make-do attitude required for these outings can be illustrated by an example from a different bike trip we took the kids on the next year. It was a route that passed through a regional park north of St. Paul that included a narrow strip of land splitting a suburban lake, like the path of Moses through the Red Sea.

Maloney and I had to stop at the turnaround point to fix the busted pedal of Tabari's bike. Maloney shaped and whittled a stick so that it fit the hole in the crank arm. I gave Tabari my bike and hopped on to test the modified pedal with a few pumps. It was janky but worked.

I could tell Maloney wanted to take a turn on the broken bike and we traded it back and forth every mile or so until the stick broke. Then the question was who would get to take on the challenge of riding the one-peddle bike for the better part of the ten miles we had left back to the school. It was the closest I got to the macho stare downs of brotherly love and competition that I had seen in action movies growing up. The students who watched this unfold got a glimpse of the outlook Maloney and I had as men and teachers: don't stop thinking, stay close to those willing to push you, and go the distance on one leg if you must.

We didn't spend much time at Fort Snelling, but it was enough for one ugly incident to occur. The students behaved most places we went, and I would often receive calls the day after field trips getting compliments about our students from park rangers, history center representatives, and other contacts at the places we went. At Fort Snelling though, it was an adult security guard that misbehaved.

Helen was sitting on a stone wall just outside the Fort Snelling visitor center, finishing her lunch. Helen had a shaky self-esteem, but faced most days with bright, hopeful eyes. Afterall, she'd made it to Fort Snelling on a bike, after deciding not to join Jada and Quiana's plot to stay back. Nibbling on the last bit of her sandwich, she seemed lost in thought as she looked out at the green river bottom and Mississippi River below. Suddenly, the harsh voice of the visitor center security guard yelled out, "What are you doing? Get down from there! Off the wall NOW!"

Startled by the guard's escalating behavior, Helen hopped off and ran to her friends, leaving the wrapper of her sandwich on the wall. As if to confirm her judgement of Helen the guard walked over shaking her head, grabbed the wrapper and threw it in the trash. When people blow off talk about how small acts of violence add up, I always remember the look of shock and hurt in Helen's eyes. Most troubling to me was how fast the beautiful landscape that had opened to Helen, was ripped from beneath her nose. She would recover—the scolding wouldn't scar her for life—but a life is made up of moments, and the security guard had ruined this one for her.

On the way back from the Fort Snelling bike trip, we took the less scenic route along Shepard Road. Emilio was pedaling slowly with a serene quiet about him. By this time any deviant impulses he had were squared away by the effort needed to make it home.

I squinted at a large shape moving slowly in the sunny distance. It was Mr. Brandon. His huge body balanced on a steel frame. Biking next to him were Kai and Noah, like two elephant calves under the protection of their mother on the rocky savanna of Namibia.

A couple more bikes went kaput, and Mr. Kou was called in. The students were disappointed they couldn't finish the twenty miles with their friends. But once they accepted their free ride back to school, the door of the truck slammed shut greedily. The upbeat and reliable Mr. Kou tapped the horn and sped off. The rest of us continued cycling along the wooded riverside bluffs.

It'd be another close call—the time was nearing when the afternoon busses would be arriving at Ms. D's little school. The line of bikes stretched along the riverbed trail that passed below the Science Museum of Minnesota. At this point we were guided by an unspoken calculation; students who knew the way back would take it, and those who didn't, would stay close to those who did.

We were two blocks away from the school when dismissal time came. Pedaling past a line of yellow busses, we rolled into the parking lot. It looked like we'd pulled off the trip—all the little bike groups were there.

Then I realized someone was missing.

"Has anyone seen Ruby?"

A couple kids sitting on a patch of grass, exhausted, shook their heads. I took out my pink Nokia cell phone. The kids would make fun of it even as I insisted it was 'salmon' colored. Just when I was about to dial Mr. Kou for a report, one of the kids pointed down the street.

Looking up I saw string bean legs, the color of caramel, pumping the pedals of a tiny purple bike. It was Ruby. Somehow, she had another lollipop in her hand. Behind her was a strapping white man, on a high-end road bike—Mr. Duvall. The scene dared one to make judgements. All the wrong and right ones we make when black and white are side by side.

She hopped off, passed the bike to Mr. Duvall, and gave him a high-five. She turned back and said, "Thanks G!"

Running, she then yelled at her bus, "Hold up! Hold up!"

Before catching up to her bus she stopped at another. Through a window at the back, Kiara, one of her friends, poured her a handful of Hot Fries for the ride home.

The last thing I saw were two pink jelly shoes lifting off the ground, one and then another, into the waiting bus.

It was a Friday and warm—the mood was light. The last middle schooler, Jodie M., was chased onto his bus and the doors closed. The teachers waved goodbye and then stood around chatting. Who were these adults gathered on the sidewalk and steps now that their students were gone? The elementary teachers had held down the fort at the school while we were gone, responsibly laying the foundations of reading, writing and arithmetic. What would Ms. Paige do now? Put her classroom in order? Prepare an immaculate schedule for next week? Go home and sleep? Have a beer with friends and gripe about the little turd in her class? Was her personal life run with the same cut-throat efficiency, purpose, and competence?

Ms. Conley, Mr. Duvall, and Ms. Danika were laughing about something. They were all sharp, driven people, but were willing to slow the pace of their own lives down. They backed up and let their thoughts, decision making, and actions sync up with young minds. On the bike trip, Mr. Duvall stayed in a low gear that kept him side by side with a spindly girl on a banana seat bike over the course of twenty miles. Was it patience that made these people teachers? Ms. Danika and Ms. Conley were loved by the kids because they embedded themselves in the thick of it, administering encouragement, and reassurance, along with sharing gossip, Doritos, and jokes. And what about Mr. Kou, Mr. Shane, and Mr. J? They would pop up in the right place, at the right time—teaching the importance of timing and service to others.

Who were Maloney and me? What were we up to as teachers, racing ahead, stressing kids out? Making them think if they didn't pick up the pace they could be left behind. As these types of outings accumulated, I started to let go some of the pressure I'd put on myself at the start of my first year of teaching at Ms. D's little school. I remembered fighting myself to a standstill, worrying about my responsibility to not indoctrinate the students with a warped version of history. I spent hours trying to fill the empty slots in my Horace Mann Teacher Planner, with experiences that were engaging and meaningful. Was shifting stress, the good kind, from myself onto students, a turning point in my teaching career?

Going on trips together as a middle school had become a dynamic generator of "stressful" situations for kids. All along the kids observed how it worked: the planning, the problem-solving, the support, the discomfort acting upon personalities in different ways. After the bike trip, I started a project in my class to honor and assess these outings—a new timeline. We already had one for US history on the wall. For that one kids were invited to research an event, write it up on a notecard, and convince the class that it should be added to the timeline of US history that ran along the corkboard just below the murals.

The new timeline didn't include Ancient Egypt or Greece, the Kingdoms of the Middle Ages, Columbus, or miraculous scientific discoveries. It was a timeline of Ms. D's little school, and the history we were making there on our adventures. When told kids they could all add to the timeline Mark promptly took a notecard out and summarized an event from his sixth-grade year: the time Carter got up the waterfall with everyone's help.

Since Mark was white, was history at risk of being recorded from one point of view—just starting all over again? This uptight reading of the situation didn't cross my mind at the time. When it comes to race—if you look for trouble you will find it. Besides, certain details of the Carter epic had been kept alive by the storytelling virtuosity of Kendrick and other black students. It was an ensemble memory that created the first entry on the US history timeline.

Within a month the new timeline for Ms. D's little school was shaping up. Ruby had written a few scraggly sentences and drawn a picture of herself on a bike next to Mr. Duvall, and it was stapled to the wall.

Nineteen

AFTER THE BIKE trip, we didn't have to wait long to get out again because Ms. D had penciled in a three-day trip to Camp St. Croix near the end of October. It was our second year going but it already felt like one of the cornerstones of our program. Camp St. Croix was just over the border in Wisconsin, barely a half an hour away from the school, but for many of the kids it was like being air-dropped into the Amazon.

Nerves and haphazard preparations preceded the trip. Jaden had his mom race out and buy him a new pillow, two large bags of Doritos, Nike slippers, a pack of socks, and bright white t-shirts. Bumming around the internet one afternoon I found an academic study that might have helped me understand the anxiety some of our black students had about the yearly trip. A nineteen-year-old named Pharaoh responded to a question about outdoor recreation: "So, nature is not something for black people, um, they killed us a lot in nature. They would do a lot of wild things, like on plantations... Yeah, they would hang us in trees, so maybe that's why black people don't go to the forest, don't want to *see* a tree."

A Kenyan I know, who grew up in Nairobi, told me that she never went camping as a child. "Camping means getting eaten by a lion." For some black people in America, the threat outside the city was perceived to be other humans who were unwelcoming and potentially hostile. The forest setting was often haunted with the terror of a lonely death, not a peaceful refuge. But hunting and fishing in the woods had also been one of the ways for enslaved black people to lay claim to their own time after a day of labor and also helped feed their families. Some were even able to secure a small income, and taste of independence in what has been called 'the slaves' economy.' It was a strong tradition that continued after emancipation and only began to fade after the Great Migration. That was when millions of rural blacks in the South made the move to Northern cities, to flee racial violence and take advantage of factory jobs being offered in Chicago, Pittsburg, Detroit and New York. In the North, black people didn't have the same access to the outdoors. The new arrivals had to leave their country way of life behind, and unlike urban whites, didn't have cabins or family still living in rural areas nearby. For black people, there was no easy way back to their old recreations.

Hmong students often had family members who were avid fishermen and hunters, and their families were familiar with camping. They were more at ease in the woods than many of the black students, but it wasn't a cakewalk. Many of the Hmong kids had heard chilling stories from their elders about the forest that reached deep into the realm of spirit beliefs. This all played out on a backdrop of tension between white and Hmong hunters in Minnesota and Wisconsin. There was a mistaken assumption among many white property owners that the Hmong didn't respect land rights. The reality was that Hmong hunters would just occasionally get lost and wander off public lands onto private property.

For white hunters, private land took on a sacred aura during the hunting season, and they could get very touchy about it. If certain blocks in the city were "owned" by black and Asian gangs, the midwestern woods was the turf of white hunters. In 2004, this battle over turf had exploded when a Hmong man, confronted by eight white hunters in Wisconsin, opened fire, killing six. He had climbed a deer stand on one of the white men's property and had violated a boundary.

I understand feelings about the need to protect hunting grounds. The hypervigilance around land didn't begin in America with white settlers' ideas about property. It was already present in native tribes that needed to protect their hunting grounds to survive, and fought for them. The self-sufficient attitude that is part of the culture of white settlers—who these white landowners were descendants of—also had its roots in a desire to get meat for the family. The borders of their pioneer settlements often had to be marked in blood for any hope of making it in a land they knew they were strangers in. And like it or not, white settlers had their own code of honor—albeit one backed up by the US cavalry.

In Minnesota, there are remnants and concessions to the old ways of life for Native Americans. Treaty rights allow members of the Ojibwe tribe to harvest wild rice, spear walleye, and shoot larger numbers of deer during the hunting season. My wife, who grew up next to a reservation, told me about a Native classmate who bragged about shooting seven deer. That was more than he needed. Honor was not genetic, even though trauma might be, and young tribal members were capable of losing their way.

The great-great-grandchildren of white settlers were plagued with a loss of honor too. Their sense of ownership of the land remained, but many of them were being muscled off of it by developers, banks and large agricultural corporations. They were not at home in the city or suburbs, and not able to be productive enough on small farms to compete in the market. These descendants lived in limbo on the rural outskirts with a fantasy of living off the land. The less hearty ones risked growing bitter at life, and stagnating as shut-ins, having forgotten the hard work and willingness to move and reinvent themselves that their ancestors had.

The through-line made me both smile and wince; Native Americans, white hunters, Hmong elders, black city dwellers, all had a sense of the violence and precious bounty of the wild. Whether they stayed far from it, wandered along its perimeter, or even through its holy shadows, they all hoped for a reward they could claim through their own effort.

Some roamed the wild with weapons drawn. The threat felt by the Hmong hunter, surrounded by angry men on ATV's calling him slurs, had a lethal racial backbone running through it that

Other Loyalties

the all-white jury at the trial couldn't grasp and found irrelevant. Since he'd shot four of the hunters in the back, any claim of self-defense was undermined, and he was sentenced to life without parole. A headline in the Minneapolis *Star Tribune* at the time of the event read, "Two cultures, two traditions, at peace in the outdoors. Until they met…"

The strange thing was that three full years before the hunting tragedy, a Hmong filmmaker, Va-Megn Thoj, had written a screenplay for a movie titled, *Die By Night*. Many of the encounters in the film were based on personal experience or stories Thoj heard from other Hmong people, about uncomfortable face-offs in the forest with white people. Many of these encounters went unreported because the Hmong people involved preferred to let it slide, handle it themselves, or were unsure what could be done about it if they went to the authorities.

The screenplay begins with four young Hmong people from St. Paul heading to the north woods for a camping trip. At a gas station along the way they are harassed by some hunters, speeding off as a shot is fired.

After setting up camp they sit around a fire. A young woman and man on the trip start flirting, but since they are clan cousins, they risk breaking a Hmong incest taboo. One of the older guys starts to worry about a demon that preys on lost souls in the forest by tearing their guts out.

During the night they are picked off one by one. They believe that the "creature" rustling in the bushes is indeed a demon that followed them to the US from Laos in Southeast Asia. By dawn, only the woman is alive. In the light she sees that their tormentors were the four hunters from the gas station in ski masks.

Thankfully, Camp St. Croix was a controlled environment. The black and Hmong students we brought there had white escorts so to speak, both students and camp staff. We hoped that we were enough of a family, a strong enough mixed tribe, to get through the three days in the woods together safely. It was a twisted calculation, but I always felt that the white kids that went to our school—the Cynthias, Masons and Jakes—had unwitting roles as buffers when we left the city limits. Without them knowing it, their white faces made sure we would have a shared fate.

When it came to "camping," Camp St. Croix was equipped for relative luxury. It had heated cabins, a mess hall, and a supply closet full of extra jackets. The challenges were spectral: demons from Laos, tree limbs hung with ghostly nooses reaching out from a brutal past, the insecure ranting of AM talk radio crisscrossing the rural airwaves above the camp, and the ominous silence the students found in rooms that were without computers and TVs.

But the truth was that we were safe; the rural people that surrounded the camp had other things to do than bother a bunch of city kids. Namely, living their own lives in the style they preferred—a slower pace, in a setting that was more spacious and quieter than the city. Most of my fears about taking the kids out of the city really were spectral. I had to admit that some of the supposed bad vibes rural white people were giving our students, at parks, gas station bathroom breaks, and on trails, were in my head. They were a part of my own prejudice. And when the prejudice was real, we'd all know, and close ranks—including the rural folks who had a sense of decency.

Days at Camp St. Croix were spent following the lead of counselors who took students in small groups to explore nature and do team-building activities on ropes courses and climbing walls. The kids put up with this mostly, but the temperature had suddenly dropped again and the cold gnawed at them over the long hours outside. I trailed a group of ten students from station to station, piping up from my own creeping boredom during naturalist lectures, to mutter words of encouragement to the freezing kids.

Jada and Helen stood to the side as a white twenty-something environmental education intern showed us how to analyze water samples from a pond. They had one fleece blanket wrapped around both their shoulders and were so cold that they had stopped whispering secrets and were solely focused on shivering.

I let them run off to warm up by Ms. Danika and Ms. Maura who were posted up next to a giant outdoor fireplace. Ms. Danika, who loved the woods, was a key bridge for many of the black girls on our expeditions. She heard them, loved them, and kicked their butts back to face the cold.

We were lucky during the afternoon session and got a veteran counselor who knew that the only way to a middle schoolers heart was through humor. Brian was a large man whose thick bare feet were pressed into camouflage crocs in near freezing weather. Gathering the kids close for a meeting he said, "I have a very important message for you guys."

He let out a sharp dry fart.

Kids scattered, yelled, and forgot they were cold. It was a type of chaos that brought kids back for more. A guided pattern of mayhem known as student-engagement. Brian directed all this from under a hat that had a skull-and-crossbones on it.

He took the time to uncouple the symbol from its outlaw and biker gang reputation when asked by Leng if it was from *Pirates of the Caribbean*.

"So, you think I'm a pirate?" Brian asked.

"It's the 'jolly roger' flag," Hunter replied. He was a seventh grader with an advanced, feisty, and overly righteous understanding of society, that could only lead to one thing once he was in high school: punk rock. He and his buddy were tuning into the authentic character of Brian.

"It's an ancient symbol that predates piracy," Brian said, as he led us to the archery range.

"So what does it mean?" Marlowe asked.

"*Memento Mori*."

"What?"

"Remember that you have to die."

"Cool."

The other kids, a bit younger, had lost interest after Brian uttered the Latin phrase. They were kicking the dirt and spinning around with their hands in their pockets, hoodies pulled tight over their heads. They were ready for the archery session to begin. There was no telling which way their frozen fingers would send the arrows, but at least they'd be aiming at something.

After the archery session ended, we met back up with all the other groups. With a couple hours of daylight left, kids spread out on an open field. I saw a football tossed through the air and land in Kendrick's hands. Lowering his head, he cleared a path through scrawny defenders until he was finally dragged down by Mason and Javion. The outsider boys and girls played soccer. A circle led by Hmong girls kept a volleyball up. Nerdy Pokémon battles raged among the trees.

Tight packs of girls were broken up by Jodie M.'s cowabunga raids, his messy hair flying as they tracked him down. He laughed in ecstasy as the girls caught and beat him down. I saw other boys watching, trying to figure out how being obnoxious could lead to such great rewards.

The sun hadn't set, but plots to storm each other's cabins at night festered inside impatient adolescent minds. The dam broke and soon kids were running and yelling, "They're trying to get in our cabin!" A group of girls ran to barricade their cabin door with mattresses, but it was a false alarm.

This hour or so before dinner was a jubilant free-for-all. A dreamy time with their friends and almost no rules. I kept busy playing soccer knowing that any issues that came up I wouldn't be able to deal with anyways. Problem solving was outsourced to staff like Ms. Maura, Ms. Conley, and Mr. Duvall, who seemed to enjoy, and be capable of giving, confident speeches about right and wrong. But issues were few and far between when everyone was doing what they wanted.

A call went out and everyone filed into the mess hall to eat lasagna. Afterwards we sat through a sleepy raptor presentation by a naturalist, who went through the motions like someone who'd been dragged away from their favorite TV show. A hawk swooped low over the kids heads and a bit of life entered the room. The kids who regularly stayed up past midnight on school nights shrieked and ducked. The kids who had standard bedtimes at home, managed by parents, were looking a bit disoriented sitting in a large room with birds of prey flying about at seven o'clock at night. I wondered how this latter group would make it—we still had a night hike and campfire planned.

When the presentation finished a few kids scrambled back to the dormitory to get warmer clothes, and then we divided up into our groups again. Kids were directed to put away all flashlights and we followed a winding trail into the woods.

After about ten minutes the camp counselor stopped and handed each kid a mint Lifesaver.

"Don't eat these yet."

A string of random comments flew from the dark.

"What's this for?"

"Give me my Lifesaver 'B'!"

"Can I get one more, dog?"

"Okay, get a partner and watch inside their mouth as they bite down on the Lifesaver."

"What if your partner's breath stank?"

"Well," the counselor said matter-of-factly, "it won't for long."

All around me I saw little flashes of light begin popping from the tiny caves of open jaws.

"Mr. A have you done it yet?" Amelie asked. She was the sort of mature student more at ease talking to adults.

"Nope. Here check it out." I crunched down and shattered the chalky candy in my mouth.

"Ah, that's cool!"

"Okay, let's see you do it."

Amelie put the Wint-O-Green Lifesaver in her mouth and bit.

"Did you see it?"

"Yep."

"What did it look like?"

"A tiny green galaxy."

We hiked a little deeper into the woods. Helen and Jada clutched each other, hooting and giggling as they stumbled over roots. Whatever evil force came spiraling out of the shadows they would not face it alone. At least that's what they thought.

The counselor slowed down near a stretch of the path lined on each side with thick undergrowth. Our night vision had kicked in and twenty yards ahead we could see that the trail disappeared around a bend into a stand of pines.

"So, what you're going to do is challenge yourselves to walk a short distance alone."

"Hell no!"

"Wait, what? We have to hike alone?"

"Yep. I'll have your teacher post up about fifty yards down the path."

"I'm gone. I ain't about to get murdered in no woods."

"What if we get lost?"

"Your eyes are adjusted now, and you'll be able to see the path. Now, when you're walking, I want you to listen to the forest around you. If you're very quiet, you might get to hear some nocturnal animals."

"Some what? What'd he say?"

"The Candyman comin' to snatch you and cut you up."

"Shut up! Don't say that."

"You'll be fine. You can do it." The counselor stepped back and asked for the first volunteer as I ran down the path, and around the bend. I debated how far I should go. I loved this idea of a test and took to it with an expectation of rigor and high standards that was never present in my classroom. In fact, it was the end of October, and I still hadn't given any quizzes or tests back at school.

I reached a spot in a clearing, stepped around in the dry dead grass, and decided that it would mark the end of their challenge. When I tilted my head up, I saw the moon like a patient cat sitting on a ledge, waiting for me to notice. Once I did, it fixed me in a bright, unblinking stare.

Thinking of myself standing alone in the dark, waiting for my students to find me, I am reminded of a backpacking trip I took with my daughter on the Superior Hiking Trail in northern Minnesota. I sometimes wonder how being a parent influences my teaching, but this time it was the other way around.

At the campsite my daughter and I were pulling off some birch bark to help start a fire when an enormous earthworm poked out from a rotted crevice. It moved with startling strength and purpose. When it started to move with speed, we realized our mistake; it was a baby snake. It wriggled free and disappeared in the tessellated shadows of the undergrowth. It spooked me, because I was reminded the forest held surprises, especially at night.

We heated up some naan bread I'd brought along on the hot stones of the fire ring and devoured a package of Tasty Bite Madras Lentils for dinner. We were watching the yellow packet melt in the fire, when my daughter turned her shoulders to the darkened woods.

"Let's go on a night hike!"

"Sounds good," I answered but she had already jumped up.

Yasmina was eight at the time and it was hard to keep pace with her striding ahead on the trail. She was flush with the superhuman powers of a child up past their bedtime.

Within minutes of setting off on our hike, Yasmina's long legs had quickly plunged her into her own hidden realm. She began to open some real distance from the campsite, and from me. I was feeling self-satisfied. I had raised someone who wouldn't become, as she said, "a girly girl, who's always worried about make-up."

She had been wearing the same pink stretch pants and purple shirt for three days, but the color was bleached out by darkness. All I could see was her fuzzy shape darting around rocks and over the tentacled root splay of trees crossing the path. She led us to the top of a ridge, where we entered a grove of cedars. The sharp lines of their trunks were just visible by starlight and airglow, but their woodsy, aromatic scent enveloped us. Oddly, cedar was the scent of pencils, too. But we were as far as could be from school, dead center in the heart of a summer forest.

Having stopped for a minute, the mystery and menace of night, reasserted itself, closing in on us—as if movement itself had been a torch.

"Wow Baba, it's so dark."

"Yeah."

"It's kinda scary."

"A little."

She put her hands on her hips and swiveled around, taking in the humbling silence anchored by the cedars, so comfortable in their own skin. Yasmina was still wearing her pink snap-back hat. As she turned to me, the sequined grizzly bear embroidered across the front panels gave off the faintest glint.

"Well, for the trees it's not scary."

I smiled and asked, "Why not?"

"To them it's normal. This is their house! They're just in their house and we are too."

She started hopping along the path again—in the opposite direction of camp.

"I think you're right," I cheerfully answered, mentally preparing myself for a charging mother bear and claw across the face.

Yasmina was nearly out of sight again. Then without turning around she yelled, "Yeah! If the trees aren't scared, we shouldn't be either!"

As a father, without knowing it, I had presented challenges to my daughter that I'd given to my students, as a teacher.

A lot of time went by as I stood on the path at Camp St. Croix. I imagined a kid at the other end of the dark serpent of dirt being encouraged by the camp counselor. They were probably edging up to the line, taking a breath, and telling someone to shut up. The unknown was especially horrifying and tempting for middle school kids. They were on the verge of adulthood; the vices, threats, and adult joys of the world, were becoming more visible to them, like secrets that had been hidden in plain sight.

Someone had taken the first plunge into the solo hike because a small, quick-moving form was approaching. They had wrapped their head around the low probability of getting axed to death by a maniac, or mauled by a phantom, and had put their trust in the guidance of elders. Pushing off from a solid sense of her own identity, Brianna had made it through first. Breathing heavily, she walked into the clearing. Under the moonlight, her face became visible; surprise and satisfaction flickered across her features.

"You made it."

"Yes."

We high-fived in the dark. An old Hmong folktale tells of a time when Hmong women had wings, and then they were cut so they couldn't fly away. I wondered if America, for all its flaws, held the conditions for this second-generation Hmong girl to regrow them.

One by one, kids skittered out of the dark woods to the clearing, took a breath and turned back to peer into the void they'd just passed through. From the far side we heard a scream—like someone was jumping off a cliff.

Helen came running out of the darkness.

"Lord Jesus! Lord Jesus!"

"Girl what you still screaming for? You ain't dead," Jada told her before they wrapped each other in their fleece blanket and laughed. Helen's theatrics made it exciting and fun for everyone—revealing to the reserved students what their own feelings and thoughts looked like when exposed to air.

We finished our night hike and met up with the other groups at a large firepit. Mr. Maloney had sparked some tinder and now a bonfire was reaching high, lighting up the pines and benches that ringed the firepit. Sharp skewers were being waved around my face as kids waited for marshmallows. I expected to see one of my eyeballs roasting over the fire any second.

A few traditionalists held out sticks that they'd grabbed from the surrounding brush. Ms. Conley and Mr. Duvall took over the s'mores operation from me and brought it some much-needed efficiency. I took out my knife to sharpen a few more sticks.

Within seconds, fireballs of sugary gelatin were being yanked out of the flames, shook in the air, and blown on. Kids headed back to Ms. Conley to ask for replacements.

A marshmallow dropped from a stick and sizzled on a log, bubbling out of itself, and tripling in size. For a moment we were all mesmerized.

"That one look like Kendrick," Kevin said, pointing to the now-blackened marshmallow on the log. He slid three marshmallows onto the tines of a pitchfork Maloney had carved for him.

"Nah. That's Dante's burnt self," Kendrick answered, skirting a head-on clash with Kevin, and opting to attack the easier target.

"Man, you guys are bogus." Dante had just taken the hit. He knew his pecking order in the skin-tone hierarchy, amongst his friends. Skipping the marshmallows, Dante bit into a Hershey's bar. "Y'all don't know about this chocolate though."

"Chocolate? You ain't chocolate. You charcoal!"

DANTE WAS MR. K.O.'s favorite student. He loved the kid, and they spent the day harassing each other while Mr. K.O. snuck in reading lessons. Dante was on the move most of the day, up and down and around. His string-bean arms flailing towards trouble, a high-pitched voice announcing he'd found it. Part of it was his personality, the rest was avoiding work that he thought he would never be able to do.

Zion was a gentler friend to Dante than Kevin or Kendrick. He was a tall kid that seemed sleepy and slow-moving. But he just had the elegance of a natural athlete compared to the fidgety and clumsy kids around him. Self-contained and purposeful, he'd get fed up with Dante when they did projects together. I overheard them one day in class.

"You were supposed to do that part last night."

"Come on man, I forgot," Dante pleaded.

"Mr. A, can I do this project by myself? Dante don't be doing his work."

"Well…" I stuttered.

"No dog, come on. Don't leave me like that."

"*Damn man*, I'm tired of your disorganized self."

It was true that Zion had his act together more than Dante did, but I'd also find Zion leaning way back in his chair letting the class period expire. He was deciding for himself how long he could go without doing the work before his mom made him catch up, or Ms. D gave him a pep talk in her office over a cheeseburger.

There's no exact science that told me what Dante and Zion did for each other as friends. They had been linked together probably sometime in elementary school. One morning before a field trip they got under each other's skin and had a half-fight, half-scuffle. I didn't want to repeat this scene at the place we were going so I told them they'd have to stay back.

"Look what you did dude, now we can't go," Zion said to Dante.

"Hold on. *Me?*"

They walked calmly down the hall next to each other, to see Ms. D. Before they were out of earshot, I heard Dante trying to get Zion to share the blame.

The rest of the middle school soon filed down the hall and headed out the doors to load the busses. In the foyer Dante and Zion were slumped in two chairs staring out the windows.

"So, Dante and Zion, I have a question for you," I asked.

They looked up from their stew of remorse.

"If I let you go, what are going to learn? That I'm a chump or that it's better to forgive?"

"It's better to forgive!" They yelled together already out of their seats and halfway out the doors.

I saw a tiny glance between them that said, "*He's a chump.*"

Ms. D was standing near the secretary's desk talking to Ms. Maura, one of her assistants.

I got nervous and wondered if I'd usurped their administrative power by wiping out the consequence. Was I also setting them up for failure by not making them pay the price? The only thing I could think to do was run out the doors behind Dante and Zion.

"That's why I love you Mr. A!" I heard Ms. D call out, as Ms. Maura chuckled.

Choosing which consequences fit a situation was a mystery to me, but other teachers seemed to have some approaches to the question at least. Mr. K.O. was one of them. There's an infamous photo of Dante duct-taped to a chair in Mr. K.O.'s class. There's a crumply piece of notebook paper in front of him. Scrawled on it are the words: "Duct-tape discipline." There's a big smile on Dante's face.

Dante got another dose of Mr. K.O.'s maverick behavior management system when he and Kevin started to scuffle in my room. Fed up, I sent them both to Mr. K.O. for a three-round boxing match. He'd picked up two pairs of oversized gloves at the thrift shop, and they'd become the most efficient mode of conflict resolution for boys at the school.

Kevin laced up the blue gloves, and Dante took the red. They stepped into the makeshift ring on the school stage. Mr. K.O. rang the bell and the fight was on. After taking a few big looping swings at each other they were exhausted. By round three they were laughing, gasping for air, and laying the groundwork for a friendship that has lasted into their twenties.

Back then, Dante had the air of a kid on the brink—one misstep away from heading towards becoming one of the charismatic, unemployed local characters of the Frogtown neighborhood of St. Paul. His mom was so tired, like a character in a post-apocalyptic road movie trying to guide a child through a wasteland to a precarious brighter future. Frogtown was a community blessed with loyal friends and resilience but cursed with poverty and crime. "Losers" who had given up on themselves lingered on every corner. Dante was about to become a young man out in this world, where he'd have to hop-scotch around the destroyed and fallen of his community to make it out.

Dante's mom kept picking up the phone, showing up for conferences and meetings, and agreeing to try and oversee this or that at-home reading scheme. Everything most mothers would do, but under a type of strain only poor families endure.

One Friday night after a school concert that fall, Dante needed a ride home. It had been a long week. The extra hours were piling up and red spider webs had been spreading across my eyes since Monday.

"Man, Dante, you didn't set up your ride?"

"Mercy, Mr. A."

It was after nine but instead of directing me to his apartment we drove to a church where his mom had signed him up for a late-night activity. She came to the car and thanked me. Reaching for his shoulders she had him in her arms for now.

AROUND THE CAMPFIRE at Camp St. Croix were rows of amphitheater style wooden benches rising six or seven rows. They were filled with giddy cabin groups waiting for their turn to perform skits. Maloney and Mr. Barnett warmed things up with a masterful enactment of a Mulla Nasruddin tale, a trickster figure from the Middle East.

"I can't find them?" Maloney mumbled as he searched on his hands and knees in the dirt next to the fire for something.

"What are you looking for?" Mr. Barnett called out.

"My keys."

"Where did you lose them?"

"Over there."

"Then why are you looking here?"

Maloney sweeps his hands back and forth over the dust. "Well, there's more light here."

I was tickled that someone else had heard the tales that I'd grown up with, and it made me feel closer to Maloney and Mr. Barnett, like they also knew the wise fool who was my private tutor.

Ms. Danika's cabin of girls stepped up and somehow found a way to nail an RnB hit a-cappella style after just a measly half-hour of practice time in the cabins. Like a master cook, Ms. Danika whipped up confidence out of the uneven ingredients of adolescent girl magic, self-consciousness, and nerves.

Alicia Keyes song "No One" never sounded better than when Jamiyah sung it in her sweatpants under the starlight—a backup crew swaying and stepping behind her at the edge of the firelight.

My cabin was up next. I had perhaps influenced the boys during rehearsal time when I supplied them with a bag of balls for a prop. Sitting down on one of the bunks, I muttered one double-entendre that I hoped they'd miss. Jake, a kid who reached peak horniness at a young age, caught my joke and cackled maniacally.

It was downhill from there. Along with the feverish mind of Curtis, who claimed Smokey Robinson was a great-uncle of his, a line-up of testicle gags involving the mesh bag of dodgeballs was locked down for the fireside talent show.

After the first inappropriate joke there was an initial gasp of disbelief from the audience, a skip of silence, then Ms. D's loud laughter. Following was a cascade of hysterics that rocked the amphitheater. Even some sixth graders, still submerged in the simple world of fart jokes and Ninjago, became enthralled by the way innocuous words could be deviously arranged inside sentences.

"Hey Billie, how many balls do you need to play?"

"It works with one, but it's good to have a back-up."

Curtis stretched out on the ground next to the campfire and rested his head on a of couple orange dodgeballs.

"Jake, I can't sleep, my balls are squished!"

"Dude, get some new ones from Billie, he has an extra one in his bag."

Not only did it cross the line of inappropriateness, but it also circumnavigated the globe. Floating on a sack of foam balls, a Magellan-like voyage captained by Jake, Curtis and Billie, sailed across a sea of innuendo. The only lifeboat they had was plausible deniability.

I fretted about whether I was training future sexual harassers or people who knew how to safely have fun with words.

The skits were over, the marshmallow sugar rush was spent, and the fire burned low. Maloney took a reading of the situation and decided to not add another log. Like most things at Ms. D's little school, we followed the youth. Kids were cold and itching to tear into their stashes of chips and candy back at the cabins.

The walk back began, and as the clumps of kids moved into the darkness the memory of what happened the year before amped up the energy. During our camping trip the previous fall, Ms. Allison, the former math teacher, had peeled away from the amphitheater early and no one had noticed. She suited up in a costume she had stashed in the bushes earlier. As a group of kids passed under the black silhouettes of some giant oaks, a hairy beast leapt out at them.

Without a second thought Dante's reflexes, keyed to the tough neighborhood of Frogtown, got him swinging. Soon Zion joined in, and a few others rained down punches until the screaming face of a blonde woman appeared from under a gorilla mask. By then the boys had sprinted off to safety.

The risk of getting jumped was part of the bargain when zipping up inside a gorilla suit and going on the prowl. For Maloney and me, it clearly was a case where the boys were due clemency for acts done at times of war. But the shock of getting punched by her own students triggered a reaction and there was going to be hell to pay.

Ms. Allison couldn't find many enthusiastic supporters in favor of the drastic punishment of sending Dante and Zion home early from camp. And it would fall to her on a lonely afternoon after we returned to school to give the speech that she felt the boys needed to hear.

This was one of many weird moments as a teacher where the pressure to take sides in a situation that was too complicated, left me silent. When Ms. Allison approached me to spitball consequences, I hoped my thick, scrunched eyebrows revealed my inability to choose. I didn't like being an unsupportive colleague, but I hated being a judge against others more.

After that episode the year before, kids and staff were prepared for mayhem, and we went all out. After the campfire, Maloney and I broke away from the tail-end of the group and outflanked the kids through the woods. My specialty was laying in the leaves off the path and making a demented rattling sound with my tongue. Adam, Cynthia, Maria, Javion, Kevin, and a couple other good targets came walking by.

"Did you hear that?"

Their flashlights scanned the woods, and from my hidden spot I hissed again.

"Oh snap!" Adam screamed.

There was a flurry of grabbing and pushing as they fled—everyone for themselves.

Maloney had hopped into navy coveralls and a Michael Myers hockey mask. He had a knack for stalking by stealth—appearing silently from behind a tree, watching kids run for their lives, and then when they thought they were safe, stepping out from around the corner of their cabin before they could reach the door.

Just like in a classroom we differentiated the lesson in terror. Teddy, Jack, Cameron, and some other kids who were on the Autism spectrum, had been safely ushered into their cabins before we began the slaughter, by Mr. Shane. Rubber bands were rolled off Pokemon cards and a battle was on. Haven, Brianna and Amelie displayed bravery during the night hike but were now in their jammies playing a PG rated game of Truth or Dare in Ms. Conley's cabin.

Back in the danger zone, I saw Edgar from the trees—peacefully walking to his cabin with his poetic thoughts—and spared him.

Just like in the movies, we hunted the "cool" guys and girls who were trying to raid each other's cabins. Jodie M. carried on his lifelong flirting campaign at the window of Ms. Danika's cabin filled with girls. He was sent screaming when Maloney showed up a foot behind him wearing the pale face of the psychopath.

There was also a meta-challenge going on; Maloney and I tried to creep on each other. As I was waiting in ambush for some kids he materialized at my periphery and I got spooked, asking nervously, "Wait, *who is that?*"

After an hour I thought surely the night must be over. Everyone had been scared into their cabins. In my own cabin I gave some solemn lectures about needing to be rested for tomorrow's sessions, and watched a few heads vanish under sleeping bags.

I peeked outside and saw Jodie M.'s bushy hair bouncing through the shadows. Walking to Maloney's cabin to check in, I saw mattresses laid across the floor like a WWE wrestling ring. On either side were sweaty boys in stretched and ripped

Other Loyalties

t-shirts. Maloney was waiting in the middle for the next wave of challengers.

In Mr. K.O.'s cabin the kids had laid out a buffet of chips and two liters of grape and orange Fanta. Larry, an eighth grader, had a handful of barbeque chips and was talking smack with Mr. K.O.

"All I know is I'm getting my own bed," Larry said while shoving some chips in his mouth.

"I'd rather sleep on the floor than share with you and have to wrestle your big butt for the blanket all night," K.O. answered.

"You'd be wrestling with something bigger than that all night," Larry quipped.

"Ahh, nasty. Larry you are so wrong." Mr. K.O. shook his head and grimaced.

Larry was a student everyone was rooting for. He was indomitable, cocky, but would fix you in a stare and ask how you were doing. Most students don't ask teachers that question—imagining that you walk into a closet in the corner of the classroom at the end of the day and turn yourself off like a robot.

When Larry was wavering academically as a seventh grader, the whole middle school staff piled into Ms. D's office and told him that we cared about him and loved him. From that point on, whenever a kid was coming up short, we would convene among the framed sentimental sayings and photos, with the hits of the 70's and 80's softly playing from a boombox.

It was like that thing they do in Baptist churches to break you and convert you. We called it, "Doing a Larry."

On my night walk around Camp St. Croix, I wasn't too worried about my unchaperoned cabin. With the lights out Jake was most likely talking about breasts. The more reserved kids, half-asleep, listening with dreamy fascination.

I continued my walk and I saw Mr. and Ms. D and Ms. Maura, holding a vigil by the giant cobblestone fireplace across the field. In the quiet I heard my shoes brushing the grass. The administrative staff had already dealt with an issue that I didn't even learn about until the next day. A student had done the classic move of bringing some cigarettes, was caught, and sent home in the silver

Caravan with Mr. J, who soothed and chided them the whole way back to St. Paul.

When I started teaching, I assumed there was a rulebook for everything. A trusty map of right and wrong. A time to get out work, put work away, admit to a lie, agree to say sorry—brush teeth and go to bed, so to speak. The rulebook would include a collection of lines to say when any problem arose: scheduled and packaged moral responses that veteran teachers knew, and more capable rookies picked up quickly. Maybe it was like that at suburban schools, or traditional schools in big districts, but I didn't know any better and hadn't seen any lists of black-and-white rules at Ms. D's little school.

At Ms. D's little school everyone was surfing. It was a school were adults and kids were stoked, feeling their way with heart, and daring. And rules were applied case by case, based on an unspoken code to aim for the good. Conversation and relationships guided how we saw the world and laid out justice. The spirit of the law reigned.

In the middle of the grassy field, I looked up at the constellations. Maybe they were conceived the same way. Ancient tribes marked out pictures in the stars that fit their world and told stories in a specific way that gave guidance and meaning to their lives. Over time the animals and heroes in the sky changed as the heroes of the tribes did, but the truth of the storytelling act remained the same—carry forth the best of a people. The completed figures in the sky were not lasting, nor as important as the minds that could connect the dots in new ways for the new circumstances a tribe found itself in.

"Mr. A. My favorite person," Ms. D called out when I arrived at the hearth.

"He would be the one roaming in the night," Mr. D added.

"Mr. A is the hidden watcher, guarding us all," Ms. Maura said before taking a sip of tea.

"That's right," I gave the answer I had found for these situations where I was embarrassed by a compliment or qualities projected on to me. I've never been one to know how to sit and shoot the breeze, so I smiled, waited, and then turned back to cross the field.

There's so much noise in a teacher's life. Even when the fabled moment arrives on occasion and the class is humming with work, quiet and content, there is still an awareness in the room that teachers must tend to. Even in a wild free-for-all at camp, vigilance and responsibility weighed on a teacher.

I savored the wide silence I found myself in, as an entire middle school drifted off to sleep in cabins on the other side of a misty field. The stars, steady and present—took over the role of watcher and filled the sky with new heroes waiting to be found when someone connected the dots.

I glanced back at Ms. D wrapped in a gaudy Packer's blanket. Ms. Conley and Mr. Duvall had joined them, each with a steaming mug in their hands.

A darkened cabin marked out my home for the night and I walked towards it. A Rumi poem came to mind, "Out beyond ideas of wrongdoing and rightdoing, there is a field, I'll meet you there. When the soul lies down in that grass, the world is too full to talk about." We were making it happen at Ms. D's little school. A group of teachers were meeting up in a field, and—without coercion or righteousness—were letting the greatest good unfold how it would. The world was full, but how long could that last?

Twenty

A FEW DAYS before Halloween, I brought my Sony Camcorder to school to use for student films. We had just returned from Camp St. Croix and the afterglow of enduring an ordeal together permeated the middle school. The tradition of filmmaking started my second year when I'd run out of lesson ideas in October. Now in my fourth year, I was ready to help them make horror film masterpieces.

The first class of the day began, and I walked around my room dropping screenwriting packets onto tables.

"What's this?" Kevin asked.

"For your script."

"Man, do we have to do this? We already know what we're about to do," A.J. added.

"Yeah, just sketch out the plot and characters. Get some lines down and list the props you might need."

"Mr. A, I got it all in my head though!" Kevin pleaded.

When I first heard this line as a teacher, I chalked it up to a student not wanting to do the actual work and grind out the writing. It went into the category of 'student attempts to avoid work' that included the line, "But I already *know* this, why do I have to do it?" This could mean that a student remembered watching one documentary on the History Channel and therefore "knew" about the entire Civil War. Or maybe they did a coloring sheet in kindergarten on the Civil Rights Movement, so they "already knew it" and didn't need to read or write about the Voting Rights Act.

Over time, I started to suspect that some students did have a lot sorted out in their heads, because they processed things differently than me. And for students like Kevin, who were smarter than me, it was possible that he really did understand a topic on the level of the assignment I'd given. I started to worry that my demand that he write things down in such cases was an academic pretense at best, busywork, or at worst cultural insensitivity. But at the very least I thought schools should let kids know that despite their background or cultural knowledge, private conclusions, and learning styles, things were more *complicated* than they thought.

I insisted on a screenplay. Because I'd also learned that one hundred percent of the student movies made ended with a character getting jumped and beat down. I wanted to make sure there was enough dialogue and plot points in their movies before it happened.

When it came time to film there was nothing to do but swing my classroom doors wide open. Students spread out all over the school and outside to rehearse. I crossed my fingers; classroom management would be outsourced to themselves, and their focus and good behavior dependent on a desire not to make a lame movie.

I'd circle the school with my camcorder to check on the groups and record the shots they needed. Rounding corners, I still half-expected to see them messing around and wasting time, but instead found kids intensely debating how to make a scene better or taking the risk of sharing a bright idea in front of their peers. At the far arc of my loop around the school, I came across Jada, Quiana, Ruby, Dante, and Zion in a darkened back stairwell. They were yelling and screaming, but it was all part of a plan.

"Mr. A, we ready!" Jada yelled out.

On Halloween day the school was one big party zone. There was none of the apprehension found in big traditional school districts about offending cultures that don't celebrate Halloween. Prohibitions about dressing up were the result of adult over meddling. What kid from any corner of the world wouldn't love Halloween? I swung by my parents' house looking for a costume. It'd been a while since I'd rummaged in the basement for supplies there. I found a tight, sequined vest and a wig that I'd worn three years in a row for Halloween, when I was a kid. Not knowing what to pair them with, I spooned some powdered sugar into a baggie and drove to school. In the parking lot I brushed the tip of my nose with powdered sugar.

Ms. Danika was at the front desk, dressed as a witch, talking to Ms. Hannah, our new secretary. When Ms. Danika saw the sequined vest and the powder on my nose she said, "Oh no Mr. A, *you didn't?*"

Ms. Danika knew the pop diva that I was going for, shook her head, and smiled as I passed.

I saw Ms. Hannah glance at Ms. Danika, sizing up the 'norms' at her new school, and say, "Is he really dressed like…"

"Mm-hmm," Ms. Danika said before she could finish. "That's the middle school—you just wait to find out about them!"

Downstairs, Maloney's science room was transformed into a haunted house that the elementary classes toured. Two girls dressed as demented dolls, painted their faces, and sent some third graders home with nightmares. My classes would be watching the movies they had made. I had stayed up late editing the clips together, polishing the good ones, and trying to save the terrible ones with some choice sound effects.

Kevin, Mark, and A.J. had made a 'revenge of the nerds' type fantasy. Some real production value was added when Kevin brought in his skateboard and kicked it out from under A.J. for a scene. A.J hit the asphalt hard as Kevin ran away screaming, "GD on 9!" I still don't know what that meant—maybe it was a line about the Gangster Disciple gang he'd overheard in his east side neighborhood.

In another film, Mason plays a custodian in a school. He's in a dark hallway in the basement sweeping when he says in a sing-song voice, "*Just doing my job.*" Marlowe or Hunter, somebody in

Other Loyalties

a mask, lunges out of the shadows and quickly dispatches him, leaving a body lying next to a broom. The cheery line said just before his murder became a mantra for Mason the rest of the year. I'd hear him cap off a joke that fell flat or punctuate a lull in a conversation with the line, "Just doing my job."

It was as exhilarating for the students to see themselves on screen those days as it is today, but there was a unique communal payoff to our Halloween movie party back then, as we huddled by the small TV in my classroom. The single screen and limited video content, ushered in a closeness both physically and emotionally for the students. It's something that has been lost these days as each kid sits alone specifying what they want to see on their personal device. With the current flood of expert individual content creators, a humble, shabby group effort at making a horror film seems quaint and too "cringy" to be attempted at this point. But at the time, students would beg me to burn them DVD copies of the Halloween movies. They were still self-conscious about being in front of the camera, but it was so much fun they let it go and took solace in the fact that it was just for us—not the entire world.

AFTER CAMP ST. Croix and the Halloween movies there was a fallow period. November, until the two weeks off for Winter Break in December, was a precarious time of year at a school. It was a mini version of the accelerating chaos in the spring when kids and teachers started stampeding for the door of summer vacation. Whenever I felt this coming on it was time to turn to the "expert" content creators that I just badmouthed. In this case it was expert feature filmmakers. I selected films to show, and with beady eyes, crossed off multiple days in my Horace Mann Teacher Planner. I tried to relate the films to what we were supposed to be studying, but the guiding principle was to just show good films—and kill time.

When not playing video games most kids were on a steady diet of *Shrek* and *Fast and Furious* movies. Their real addiction though was *SpongeBob Squarepants*. They spent hours watching the bouncing, jittery onslaught of surreal humor—popping the episodes like a king-size bag of Sweet and Sour Skittles. Spongebob was innocent, optimistic, valued friendship and imagination, and even sang a song called "The Best Day Ever." It stimulated a part of themselves that they feared they might lose growing up.

I had a nagging feeling though, coming from the worst didactic parts of me, that the quiet themes that might underwrite a more meaningful existence for my students, couldn't survive the brainwash of endless hours spent in Bikini Bottom, the town under the sea where SpongeBob and his friends lived.

The fact that I am a cinema snob can be blamed on my sister. I spent many delirious nights at different film series she put on both in college and after. Entranced, I watched filmmakers with visual panache pushing narratives to the breaking point. Sitting there in dark theaters I would be administered Godard's classic *A bout de Souffle*, Fellini's *8 ½* or Bruce LaBruce's satire about a struggling pornographic filmmaker, *Super 8 ½*. Other nights, Antonioni's *Blow- Up* or Melvin Van Peeble's *Sweet Sweetback's Baaadasssss Song* rearranged my expectations of films.

In fact, the first film my son saw in theater was a film by the Soviet director Parajanov called *The Color of Pomegranates*. My sister had reserved the elegant Varsity Theater in Dinkytown, Minneapolis—a hundred-year-old venue in the Art Moderne style. The place was drenched in red velvet, and an Egyptian musician named Abu Solh warmed the room with the calligraphic swoops of Arabian scales on the violin.

The film was about an eighteenth-century Armenian troubadour named Sayat-Nova. Images filled the screen in such an honest weirdness that the Soviet authorities, fixated on realism, had banned the film at the time it was made. Angels appear with flattened halos and wooden wings, a foot squishes grapes on an ancient tablet, pigeons flutter down onto a sea of candles on a marble floor. It was like Sayat-Nova's soul was being x-rayed by Parajanov and the poetry inside of it was being brought to life in discrete tableaus put together with relics, fruit, and kabuki actors.

Other Loyalties

The American filmmaker Martin Scorsese said viewing it was "like opening a door and walking into another dimension."

When I walked out of *The Color of Pomegranates* I had a minty sensation in my mind—unexpected waves of images having battered it clean. My son was five months old at the time but wouldn't have understood the film any better if he was twenty-one or eighty-one. The film itself recreated the cartwheeling sensations of one's first and last days on earth. As a new father I was thinking a lot about what it meant to grow up: to get older and somehow understand the world. But did adults understand the world better or worse than children? The things children do instinctively—learn, love, care, be present—adults need entire philosophies and prophets and wellness retreats to reinforce. (I hesitate to say it, but those strange films might have been no different than the cherished non-sense of *SpongeBob*.)

As my son got older and was joined by my daughter, my thoughts about what it meant to be an adult and responsible didn't necessarily become clearer. Even a few years after I left Ms. D's school for another middle school, on my way to becoming both a veteran teacher and parent, the conclusion that approaching the world as an adult was preferable to the way children did it, was still debatable.

You see, at my house, I'm supposed to be in charge of breakfast, which usually means a bowl of Honey Nut Cheerios for my kids. I thought it was a responsible choice of cereal, one a thoughtful parent would make. The reality was that a bowl of Honey Nut Cheerios had more sugar than three Chips Ahoy! cookies. It's hot on the heels of Fruity Pebbles in sugar content. It was too late to rehabilitate the approach to breakfast at our house. One Saturday morning my daughter slept in and if I didn't serve Cheerios fast for breakfast, they'd end up being lunch. Yasmina sat on a stool munching them and looking at baby cheetahs in a National Geographic Kids magazine.

To make myself feel better I slid a plate of sliced avocado across the counter to her like a bartender from Sesame Street.

Yasmina was seven and had been fixated on figuring out how the age gap between her and her brother would play out over time.

"So when I'm 15, he'll be 21. Right?"

"You do the math."

"No Baba! Tell me!"

"You were right."

"And when I'm 80 he'll be 86."

"Yep."

"It's so weird! Khalil will be an adult!"

"I don't know. What makes someone an adult?"

"When they buy a house and have kids."

"So you're saying your auntie isn't an adult? She rents an apartment and doesn't have kids. I'm telling."

"*Fine*, tell her."

A few Cheerios floated in an inch-and-a-half of sweetened milk. She fished around for them with her spoon.

"Baba, when did you become an adult?"

I closed the dishwasher and paused in a very pretentious way. When I lined up what I thought was a profound answer she was already more interested in our cat. Gliding in on soft paws and sitting serenely beneath Yasmina's stool, it was a humbling counterpoint to my intellectual machinations—and my need for attention.

"I became an adult when I found out there *are* no adults." But at that point I was speaking to myself.

IT WAS THREE weeks before winter break and I had to get four classes of kids safely to the finish line. I found that I now had my sister's missionary zeal when it came to films. It was part of an unspoken, devil's pact with adulthood; I was trying to *complicate* kids view of the world to prepare them for life. *SpongeBob* and *Shrek*, I decided, were the creations of some big studio version of childhood—the sugar content was too high. In other words, I felt I was doing my job as a teacher—offering what they didn't seem to be getting from their home environment—films with character, ambiguity, and bite.

Here is a list of some of the films I showed at Ms. D's little school over the years, and what I thought they offered the kids:

Ghost Dog: Way of the Samurai. Forest Whitaker plays an urban loner, who keeps pigeons on his apartment rooftop and lives by the words of an eighteenth-century Japanese guide for warriors called the Hagakure. His character provided a model and code of honor for the geeky outsiders in the room.

What's Eating Gilbert Grape? Leonardo DiCaprio's portrayal of a mentally impaired kid living on an Iowa farm universally transfixed the kids. His dysfunctional and loving family hitting home.

Ghengis Blues. The documentary of a blind blues singer from San Francisco who goes to Mongolia to take part in a traditional throat-singing competition. Mr. K.O. celebrated when he walked in to find the kids glued to the TV following one of his favorite eccentric tales.

The Trippletts of Bellville. The animation about a boy dreaming of entering the Tour de France introduced them to the leering, droopy characters of French animators, and the value of animation with sparse dialogue. This contrasted with the babbling frenzy of the cartoons they watched on the Cartoon Network. There's a scene in the beginning that includes a glimpse of topless cabaret dancers parading onstage. It was a tricky moment, but my rule of thumb for films was if I showed it to my children, I would use the same judgement at school.

Duma. A more standard children's movie, but still a long way from the loud shenanigans of the *Madagascar* and *Ice Age* franchises. Until he graduated Kendrick asked every few months if we could watch *Duma* again. Ripkuna, the black South African drifter who helps a white Afrikaner boy on his journey to bring his pet cheetah to a game reserve, touched a nerve with Kendrick. Ripkuna's gruff, fatherly wisdom appealed to him.

La Haine. A film that follows three friends in a poor suburb of Paris for twenty-four hours following a riot after a young man is hospitalized by the police. My ruse to get them to read more by showing films with subtitles was given an added boost by the vulgar street dialogue of the characters. They strained to keep up. Moonfaced, foulmouthed Adam reflected on this film more than any assignment I ever gave.

Children of Heaven. Another subtitled film, this one from Iran. The story revolves around a boy who loses his sister's shoes. To avoid punishment from their parents and to keep attending school, the two of them must share a single pair until the boy can figure out a way to replace them. More than one student could relate to heartache surrounding a pair of sneakers.

From bike trips, to camping, to wishy-washy stretches of time before breaks. The school year went like that for my classes: feast or famine. If we weren't on an adventure or doing a project, we became bored and restive. That's when it was time for a film festival. It was the closest to an embodied experience kids were going to get if we weren't outside.

When I showed them *Into the Wild,* based on the true story of a recent college graduate who donates all his money to charity and sets off for the Alaskan wilderness, I found out there were astonishing personal connections kids would make to films. The story doesn't end well for the young man who runs low on food and mistakenly eats a poisonous root. He becomes stranded at his camp—a bus that he had found on the trail that had been converted into a hunting shack.

Teddy, one of the brothers on the autism spectrum, placed his chair right beneath the TV. As the young man, Christopher McCandless, starts to starve, his body thinning, Teddy began to forcefully shush any side conversations. His conviction was taken seriously, and kids joined him in watching death stalk the character they'd seen hitch-hiking with a smile across America.

When McCandless curled into his sleeping bag for the final time, tears were streaming down Teddy's face. I learned later that during the Vietnam War, his mother had to run from soldiers when she was a child and hide in the jungle. Her family was about to starve. To feed themselves they burned a field down to flush out mice to eat.

Meanwhile, Abdi, the Somali student with refugee parents of his own that had escaped war, had a different reaction. He couldn't get over his belief that McCandless was incredibly stupid. With the start in life he got, he should have just gotten a good job and counted his blessings. He was, as Abdi put it, "childish."

Twenty-One

WHILE I WAS getting through December by showing films, Mr. Barnett was preparing for the winter concert. I knew he would be coming for my bleachers any day. This time I had a trade offer to make him. Mr. Barnett had microphones, speakers, and a database of hip-hop beats that I wanted to use for a songwriting assignment in my classes.

Mr. Barnett accepted the trade and brought the equipment to my classroom. In my Horace Mann Teacher Planner, a presentation day was circled in red, and I rejoiced—there were no empty lesson plan slots left in December. The last two weeks of December had already been slashed with a Sharpie, since they fell on winter break. Now I had an entire month covered—a teacher's version of 'Bingo!'

Next, I instructed students to sum up the past twelve months in rhyme. I set up the microphone stand at the front of my class a week before the due date. It looked like a skinny crucifix—a symbol of inspiration for the performers in the room, and a sign of coercion and terror to come for the shy kids. Either way, the sight of the microphone made all the students bend over their notebooks to finish their lyrics about the year's most important events.

Square-jawed Mr. Hank sat next to Curtis and helped him corral some of his irreverence into a coherent hip-hop song. I had borrowed a couple laptops from the cart and the two of them scoured websites listing the Top 10 News Stories of the Year.

Other Loyalties

Along with Mr. Duvall, Mr. Hank, an educational assistant, was a new addition to the middle school. Looking at the two muscular All-Americans, I wondered if it was some brilliant scheme by Ms. D to keep the women of her elementary staff happy. Not anything untoward, just the daily boost of passing very handsome men in the hall.

The thing about adults who work with kids is that sexual drama and office intrigue are suppressed by a mountain of colorful construction paper, Elmer's glue, and actual freaking work. This was aside from the general fear of saying or doing something racy with young eyes and ears all around. There were no long lunches out on expense accounts, hotels, or schmoozing at the next cubicle. Late nights at the office meant fondling stacks of ungraded work in your own classroom or undressing a complicated concept for the next day's lessons. I remember hearing that the librarian and fourth grade teacher at my old elementary school fell in love and got married after about two decades of smoldering attraction tempered by the asexual façade of teacher professionalism.

Maybe I just watched too much *L.A. Law* as a kid, but I imagined that jobs where you were surrounded by adults had stretches where there wasn't really any work to do. I envisioned whole floors of companies bloated with pretend jobs. There was kind of a masquerade in the business world of dressing up and heading to the office. There would be intense moments of deal-making, a few phone calls, setting up fantasy sports leagues, and then gobs of time that tempted co-workers into acts of infidelity.

I was also hopelessly out of the gossip loop at Ms. D's little school. For all I know the shred of a rumor I overheard one day was true: the saucy tale of two staff members stealing away in the night to a nearby motel while the middle school was at Camp St. Croix. But working at a school meant that one couldn't lie and deceive, or pretend to work, very easily—you had to show up or there'd be a room full of young witnesses to your absence, and the acute sense of a broken promise.

Presentation day arrived. Curtis, with his bright eyes, baggy jeans, and big underbite stepped up to the mic. Mr. Hank, in a tight white t-shirt, joined him. Tabari, who was acting as DJ, put on some headphones and hit a button on Mr. Barnett's sampler. A beat crackled to life from the speakers, and a chord progression got Mr. Hank and Curtis bouncing and swaying.

Mr. K.O., who took turns with Curtis calling each other "sorry ass," walked in and smiled at his student. I remember Curtis hounding me about something one day in the hall. Mr. K.O. passed by, pulled out a tiny sponge ball, and began bouncing it off Curtis's forehead. Mr. K.O., still bouncing the ball said, "That's how you deal with this character."

"Quit Mr. K.O.!" Curtis had said, but in his eyes were the words, "Man, finally a teacher without a stick up their butt."

In my room for the performance Mr. K.O. folded his arms. His suit jacket tightened on his back, and he bobbed his head to the beat. He was a teacher getting down with the stuff I was doing in my class. There were the kids to consider when assessing whether a lesson was working, but the affirmation of a fellow teacher—a peer—nothing surpassed that.

Curtis and Mr. Hank passed the mic back and forth, trading lines.

"Steve Jobs got cancer in the eye..." Curtis began.

"...from using *too much wi-fi*," Mr. Hank finished.

The beat drop in Mr. Barnett's sample kicked-in and the kids in the audience yelled, "*Ohhh!*"

The other performers took turns describing the tsunami and Fukushima nuclear meltdown in Japan, U.S. commandos killing Osama bin Laden in Pakistan, and the Occupy Wall Street protests in New York and Oakland. A year on Earth was sized up by nervous kids behind a mic.

Mr. K.O. yelled, "Alright!" and clapped. Seeing a well-dressed older man in a room full of rapping kids made him look like a record executive scouting talent. There was a reason Mr. K.O. wore suit jackets to school; he'd spent a good part of his life as a salesman. Teaching was another sales job in many ways, and he was a master. His former life had required a lot of traveling and this came in handy when I tried to set up internships for a few of the eighth graders after winter break.

I needed Mr. K.O.'s help because when students came back after winter break, the post-holiday blues hit hard. The temperature sat below zero for days at a time, and even Mr. Maloney and I struggled to rally the troops outside. The best I could do was plan to save a few students by using a connection Mr. K.O. had with a travel agent on the west side of St. Paul. The woman agreed to host Kevin and Jaden as interns once a week for a month or two. I got Mark and Javion spots working at the Central Library downtown.

Before driving them in the silver Caravan for their first day of work I stopped by Ms. D's office. "Hey, since the kids will be working for two hours what should I do? Come back to the school?"

"No, go to a café or something. We got your classes covered."

"Really?"

"Yep. Ms. Sasha's got it."

Ms. Sasha had been with me since the beginning of the year and single-handedly dealt with all the problems out of my league. Barely twenty-one, she was clear-eyed about what kids were up to and quickly became deputized into the drama triage force headed by Ms. Danika.

Getting two hours alone during the school day is unheard of for a teacher. But now, with Ms. D's permission, I was free. I would have to eat my words about how the workday of the business world was a joke, and just a fancy setting for run-of-the-mill courtship rituals. In the middle of the day, I would have a chunk of time for myself like the businessmen and women that I had pegged as fiends loaded with disposable time.

I seized my chance to go mix with the corporate set of downtown St. Paul, Minnesota on their lunch hour. After dropping off my students I found a parking meter and walked to a nearby Starbucks. I was already a happy family man, so it was strictly for the benefit of my imagination: What was it like to be downtown, with nothing to do but make sure the ratio of milk and honey in my coffee was precise, and that the business class hotties noticed me?

The only problem was that I was dressed like a junior high teacher that did painting and papier mâché in class. I had on the same dirty cargo pants and fishing vest I wore every day. To the handful of decked-out women who came for their specialty drinks, I was indistinguishable from the downtown vagrant, nursing a cup of dark roast in the tattered easy chair of the café.

I was invisible to them as a person—just like my profession was. A form of existence that was out of sight, out of mind, like a soldier sitting in a Humvee in Al-Anbar province in Iraq. Or other people in jobs that serve, like nurses—people just not on their radar until they had kids in school, or their fathers had heart attacks.

I consoled myself by watching a group of hipster kids. They were from the downtown arts high school across the street. They were toying with a version of identity dress-up like my own junior high students, but with more refinement. They donned overalls, fedoras, dreads, and blue hair. A tackle box's worth of accessories dangled from their backpacks, and patches and buttons announced their multiplying alliances with slogans and symbols.

Tipping my cup in the trash, I walked to the library where Javion was charming the children's section staff with an earnest work ethic. Mark was at home in the teen section organizing and reminiscing upon the fat fantasy novels he'd devoured for the past year.

We got in the van and swung by the travel agency to pick up Jaden and Kevin. I hopped up the steps and found an office packed with Guatemalan, Chinese, and West African souvenirs. Kevin and Jaden were at a small circular table canvassed with brochures from all corners of the globe.

I wondered how much time the world-traveling older woman who ran the place had spent with people like Kevin and Jaden, young black men from the other side of her own city.

"How did it go?" I asked.

"Good."

"Great."

"They helped me out a lot trying to get these brochures into albums." She turned to them. "I have more work for you guys. Are you coming back next week?"

"I think so. Are we, Mr. A?" Jaden set down a pamphlet and glanced up at me. I leaned over to look at the pamphlet and saw a picture of three dark men, dressed in blue robes, standing on a sand dune.

It reminded me of an assignment we had done in class, my second year, when Jaden was a sixth grader. Searching around for compelling stories that would engage students like Jaden, I settled on great explorers and expeditions. It would help students trace out some of the geography of the world and demonstrate how incomplete maps of the world were back then. To get them started I told the story of Mansa Musa, ruler of the Kingdom of Mali in the fourteenth century and known as the richest man to ever live. He inherited the throne from his brother who had sailed off to explore the Atlantic with two thousand ships and never returned.

Scholars believe Mansa Musa owned half of the gold in the Old World. On his religious pilgrimage to Mecca, his generosity during a stop in Cairo ruined the economy of the Middle East for ten years as the value of gold plummeted. He literally thrust the Kingdom of Mali into the global consciousness. News of his caravan to Mecca spread to Europe and suddenly an African king on a golden throne appeared on a Catalan atlas map in 1375.

The griots, the storytellers of the West African kingdom, did not always like to tell the tale of Mansa Musa, because he left too much wealth outside of the empire. It's like erasing Jeff Bezos from the corporate history of Amazon for spending too many billions on philanthropy or his space travel side-project, Blue Origin.

One thing that historians know about is Mansa Musa's love of knowledge. He brought back scholars from the Middle East and established Timbuktu as a center for learning. Even still today, some of the greatest manuscripts in the Islamic world can be found in the dusty desert city.

The story of Mansa Musa was the sort of historical stuff I could almost impress junior high kids with. Jaden was one of them. As a skinny sixth grader, he had thumbed through an illustrated book showing Mansa Musa's caravan setting off into the Sahara with one hundred camels loaded with gold. I see Jaden's dark hand pointing to a picture of a dark king.

"Damn. That dude got all kinds of bling."

Almost three years later Jaden was in the office of the travel agency. He and Kevin, starting to fill out a little, had polished off a bowl of candy set aside for customers. I see the same dark hand attached to Jaden except it's a little bigger. The hand of a young man. That's how it was as a middle school teacher; one day I'd try to be getting through to the child inside a student, other times I'd need to get to the man.

Jaden had just set down the pamphlet with the picture of the men in turbans standing in the sand. The pamphlet was entitled, "Festival au Désert"—a celebration of music and culture in the ancient land of Mali. The festival, which began in 2001 and lasted a little over ten years until security concerns shut it down, featured Tuareg music groups. The Tuareg are the tribe famous for their blue robes, who have led a nomadic lifestyle in the Sahara and Sahel region of northwest Africa for centuries.

The Tuareg were, and still are, a deeply caste-based society. They continue to have a servile and enslaved caste of black Africans that are beholden to masters in many areas of Mali. But the Tuareg are also often as dark as the people in this lower caste due to intermarriage and mixing over centuries of the sub-Saharan slave-trade. The Tuareg's origins began in the north of Africa, but they had been blending, culturally and genetically, with people of the sub-Sahara for ages.

Why did this matter? And how did it get into my head watching one of my eighth-grade students handle a tourist brochure in the twenty-first century? Mansa Musa, a black king, bedecked in jewelry, and held high by both legend and history, had been a valuable image to put before Jaden's eyes. But the story of the Tuareg reminded me of the inconvenient nature of history, and the sinews that link far-flung geographical locations: Africans played a part in the path that led to the Southern plantations of the American south. In fact, some leaders, and kings of West African nations have issued formal apologies to African American communities for their ancestors' role in selling war captives to white slave merchants.

When I think of the road to racial reconciliation in America, I couldn't help feeling that this was part of the puzzle. When you think of historical injustice, some were more guilty than others, but if you searched around just a bit, you found that many, many, pairs of hands were dirty. When could Jaden hear the part of history that told the story about how people that looked like him had sold out his ancestors, ancestors that once ruled empires? And if Jaden could hear that, why then, couldn't my white students face up to what their own ancestors did to others? There was enough brutality in the past to dishonor us all. Everyone was owed an apology, and needed to make some themselves—was that not reconciliation?

Twenty-Two

JANUARY WAS SNOWY that year and the winding side streets of St. Paul made it impossible for the plow crews to keep up. The rule at Ms. D's little school was that when she made the decision to declare a "snow day," each teacher oversaw calling their homeroom students. If a kid showed up at the school then you would have to drive in and take them home.

I missed the message myself one day and pulled into the empty school parking lot. When I opened the front door to the school, I saw Ms. D having a coffee at the front desk with the phone in her hand.

"Good morning Mr. A! Didn't you hear the news?"

"Ah man."

"Look, there's Mario."

I turned and a kid hunched with his bare hands in his pockets peered into the building.

"He's all yours!"

"What should we do?"

"I don't know. Go out to McDonald's together and have some breakfast."

Mario jumped in my car, with his sneakers already wet and filled with snow. He was a smooth-faced Latino kid who had moved up from Texas and started his seventh-grade year with us a bit late. I didn't know him that well, but he had watchful brown eyes and was still doing his best to make a good first impression in class.

Other Loyalties

There was something else about him that I never liked to admit I saw in children—a coldness. I was kind of scared when I felt this in students. Something mean had already found a pathway through their bodies. It had come from the outside, a jerk father or crazy mother, but now it was the child's burden. He had a choice to host the meanness or try to fight it.

The lousy truth was that little assholes grew up to be big assholes, and the momentum of that fate was not easily derailed. It was hard to tell exactly what set it in motion—the origin story. Teachers get an uncomfortably close look at what it might be: the snapshots of a shambolic family life gleaned from conversations, student essays, home visits, conferences. That thirty-year-old man honking and flipping people off—teachers had him as a child in class day after day, met his creepy stepfather and overburdened grandma, and saw what he did to other kids when we weren't looking. Road rage was another symptom of a coldness that began in childhood and turned into an icy resentment of the world over time.

As we sat having breakfast at McDonald's, I hated myself for having the thought that Mario was the type of person I would avoid as an adult.

"How are things going so far?" I took a sip of super-sweet orange juice and tried to ignore the flash of images from Hollywood movies about teachers who save kids. How much encouragement would it take to overcome the trauma of his life? I looked around the restaurant at the lonesome men chewing on egg McMuffins in plastic booths.

"Alright," Mario said. "I just don't have that many friends yet."
"Yeah, that's rough."
"Yeah, but it's okay."
"Did you like your school in Texas?"
"I did but I kinda would get in fights sometimes."
"Really? You seem like a pretty low-key guy."
"Yeah."
"What were the fights about mostly?"
"It's just when people make me mad."

"People. Yep, people are good at that."

"Well, also, I have an anger problem. I think that… Well, I heard that my mom's boyfriend like hit her in the stomach when she was pregnant with me. I don't know, but it's maybe why I have a temper."

There are school social workers and counselors that have training about what to say next. I didn't know and tried to quickly wrap up our breakfast. The cynical side of me imagined that Mario had already laid out for himself excuses for future bad behavior. But if I could have been more generous that morning, I'd have seen that it was mature and insightful for him to be trying to trace the roots of his turmoil. But instead, I made a mental note to have Ms. Maura check in with him.

I always hoped that counselors worked the same slow-motion magic that teachers did. When the results of classroom efforts surfaced years and years later. When the rageful man flipping people off on the road decides to drive away and take "THREE DEEP BREATHS," instead of pulling his gun. I doubted whether the patience shown by teachers, or quaint calming techniques given to angry students by social workers and counselors, could divert a long-building fury at the world. But it's possible the slow magic of anonymous school staff members across America is one of the few things protecting us from more frequent spasms of violent mayhem and societal decay.

I dropped Mario off at his house, and waited until he got in. He was just a young man trying to understand himself, and I could only offer him my own selfish desire to escape his heaviness and go home to my cozy house. I was a bit cold myself.

There were a few more snow days in January, followed by the deepening frost of February that always numbed my spirit like Novocain. It was time to resist. There was nothing to do in a Minnesota classroom in winter, with everyone falling into a depression, except start a project.

On a Saturday morning I had experienced a home invasion that every teacher understands. It happened like this: while peacefully going about my personal business, an idea for a lesson popped into my mind—we'd start building models of ancient civilizations in class on Monday. Next thing I knew I had thrown my son into a pile of Lego and headed to the garage to jigsaw some plywood. After that I headed to the Ax-Man and Menards.

The year before I had students make models of a scene from Minnesota's early history, and it had gone well. The students had formed landscapes out of chicken wire, papier mâché and cheap tempura paint. Like a big sloppy feast, they piled it all on the squares of plywood I had cut.

Billie had built a farmhouse on the prairie out of popsicle sticks and hot glue. Then he brought in some large rubber action figures, stars from the World Wrestling Federation, to act out the role of white settlers and Dakota warriors. He was intent on recreating the incident that sparked the US-Dakota War of 1862.

After methodically displacing the Dakota people and restricting their hunting rights, the US government was starving them on their reservation. Four young Dakota warriors, out looking for food, saw some eggs at a farmstead and dared each other to take them to prove they were not afraid of the white man. A gun fight ensued, and five settlers were killed. The men fled to a nearby Dakota village and asked for protection.

The Dakota elders had a grim choice to make—knowing there would be retribution they had to decide whether to try one last time to win back some of their land. Knowing that they were outnumbered, many Dakota bands did not take part in the battles that ensued. Nevertheless, the US army used this as a pretext to put all Dakota in a concentration camp at Fort Snelling and eventually expel the entire tribe from Minnesota.

The wrestlers John Cena, Rey Mysterio, and The Undertaker were arranged on some brown felt Billie had glued to his board to represent the plowed fields of the farm. He made some eggs out of clay, and a flashpoint in history was brought to life in a mash-up only a middle schooler could conjure.

On the other side of the room, Haven and Brianna made a beautiful diorama of a Native American village. Using toothpicks and bits of cloth, they had strips of buffalo meat drying, teepees, and a hide stenciled with the minute symbols of a 'winter count,' a Dakota way of record keeping. Their precise and careful work was a counterpoint to Billie's sloppy make-do, but not necessarily superior storytelling.

All of this was the result of a glorious and messy month where I didn't have to plan a single lesson—just spend an hour cleaning up after school and another driving around town to replenish the art supplies. A trade-off I'd make again and again.

While I was just trying to make winter less painful, I must have been stepping along stones a teacher had laid down for me in the past. The only one I could think of was Ms. Jaglo, my sixth-grade teacher again. We'd made puppets in her class, mosaics, ceramic bowls, and countless illustrated books featuring our own stories. Other school years slip out of my mind so easily but when it came to Ms. Jaglo's, there were handholds to latch on to. I used them to climb back into that magical year and mined it for my own classes. It's not that I wanted to seal my place in my students' memories, I just didn't want their time spent in my room to be a gaping void in their life.

The model I remember the most from the previous year, besides Willie's, was Edgar's. Edgar, also had to make a scene from Minnesota's early history but he went a different direction. He had divided his board in sections. In each section was a story—one geological, the other mythological. For one geological story, Edgar made a glacier out of clay that was melting and turning into a painted blue river that spread around three big rocks also made from clay. These represented the granite boulders that had been dragged onto the southern prairie of Minnesota by the retreating glacier. Geologists had a name for these rocks that were out of place in that landscape: *erratics*.

Opposite this was the mythological story. Edgar had brought in three real rocks and had placed on top of each a clay model of a girl. According to Dakota tradition, there were three sisters who hid during a fierce battle. The last two chiefs killed each other and that would have meant extinction if not for the maidens hiding behind the rocks. The three rocks that feature in both stories sit

Other Loyalties

beside the sacred Pipestone quarry in Southern Minnesota. It's a place still used by tribes in the area for ceremonies and for gathering material to carve pipes.

The Pipestone quarry itself was part of another section of Edgar's model. On one side of his board, he made a mound of red clay—the Sioux quartzite rock of the real place, and on the other side was a slain Dakota warrior. He lay in a wavy pool of blood Edgar had cut out from red cellophane. A Dakota legend holds that the Great Spirit sent a flood to cleanse the world and the red pipestone that remained was the blood stains of their ancestors from that great battle.

Across Edgar's plywood board, stories walking the edge of fact and fiction played out. In them the early Native Americans of Minnesota survive the raging waters of a melting world at the end of the last ice age by finding high ground. Resources become scarce and fighting ensues. A small band hides, survives the slaughter and ensures the continuation of the people.

I figured I was doing the same with my recollections of Ms. Jaglo's room, stitching together fact and fiction, to create a narrative that told a story of a transformative school year—where I was given the chance to become *more* than what I thought was myself.

I LOADED UP at Ax-Man, Menards, and ArtScraps, a volunteer run store in St. Paul. With fresh rolls of cellophane, brown and green felt, cardboard tubing, used spools of thread, and a huge bag of hot glue sticks, I was ready for a month of blissful hands-on work. Most of the students had been to my classes the year before and remembered making their Minnesota history models, so they didn't feel overwhelmed by my instructions to research an ancient civilization from somewhere in the world and build a model of it. There was despair from kids about their lack of artistic skills, but eventually the projects were close to completion. Temples, symbols, and monuments from far-flung civilizations filled the plywood squares I had brought in.

I had zeroed in on the 'culture' component of the state geography standards, to justify spending so much time on one assignment. Also, the looting of treasures from Iraqi museums during and after the US invasion was still on my mind. Priceless artifacts and proof of some of the world's first and greatest civilizations—Sumerian, Babylonian, Assyrian—were destroyed or sold on the black market.

Destroying a country's link to their ancient heritage seemed a surprisingly high-minded act for men with guns, but it was happening. Allowing the erasure of cultural artifacts was part of some political calculus that must have been dreamt up by the fabled army of social scientists that work for the CIA and the Kremlin, as well as strategists from upstarts like ISIS and the Taliban. The Taliban's demolition crew had dynamited the Bamiyan Buddhas in Afghanistan, leaving the world's largest Buddhas in rubble. ISIS fighters had bulldozed numerous ancient Assyrian statues in Iraq and Syria. Destroying monuments cast doubt on the historical claims that a people could make about the land. The destructive act also served as a blow to the cultural pride of a people. In the power vacuum, and more importantly, historical narrative vacuum, mightier countries and brutal forces had their way.

Was the destruction of monuments always bad? Not according to many groups in America today fed up with living in the shadow of Confederate generals from the Civil War. Some cultural monuments needed to fall or be renewed. But it was something to be done with caution, and foresight—just in case even worse figures aren't raised in the void left by the statue.

"Oh, here we go again." Mr. D had stopped in my room and saw the models of ancient civilizations covering every surface.

"What?" I answered a little roughly—still insecure about what I was doing in the classroom each day.

"You're the guy that's filling garages."

"Wait, *what?*"

"You know—parents get their garages filled up with big art projects from school."

"Is that good?"

Other Loyalties

"Well, yeah! It's great. They *can't* throw them away!" Mr. D did a quick tour and then darted off on some mission for his wife.

I invited the elementary rooms to tour the models and ask questions. They had enjoyed it the year before and the teachers liked checking up on their former students. In the eyes of the elementary teachers, my students were frozen in their first or fourth grade forms: precious, innocent, bubble-cheeked and fully engaged with school. And because they were looked at in this way, the grizzled old junior high kids always softened up when their old teachers came in.

The Three Sisters were especially interested in the fates of their recent students. It was uncanny how well they knew them. When a vulgar note or some graffiti was found in a bathroom, we called them in, and they'd identify the handwriting of students they had two or three years ago.

When I saw the blonde hair of the Three Sisters, their benevolent power over the kids, and sense of ownership in the school, I always thought of the "Norns" of Norse mythology. They are three sisters who live in Asgard, the home of gods and goddesses. Their duty is to take water from the Well of Fate and pour it over the tree of life each day, making sure it stays healthy.

If this were not enough, the Norns have another task that is hinted at by the meaning of their names, Urd, Verdandi and Skuld: "what once was," "what is coming into being," and "what shall be." They ascertain the destiny of each new baby by showing up at their birth and observing them. They take notes from a shadowy part of the room on the child's lifespan and fate, good or bad, and weave it into a thread of life.

They *observe*. That caught my imagination—Norns were like a Montessori teacher watching out for a child's interests, inclinations, and potential to emerge. These qualities got nurtured by merely being noticed, and then were woven into the tapestry of an irreversible storyline. A teacher's expectations of a student was the paranormal force in education.

I liked that image of elementary teachers as visiting angels and grim reapers wrapped up in one. Every parent that connives to get their kid into the "good" teacher's room, by endearing themselves to the school through volunteer work or strong-arming the principal, confirms there is a truth to the mark teachers leave on a child's fate.

Ms. Ashley, one of the Three Sisters, showed up at the classroom door with a trail of fourth graders dressed in blue and black uniforms behind her. Spreading out to marvel at the skilled craftsmanship of older kids, I noticed a weird phenomenon; the younger students didn't gravitate towards the best constructed models but the best storytellers.

Kendrick, whose thick fingers couldn't pull off the intricate claywork, sat next to a deformed landscape of beige felt, splotched with glue. A cracking, pile of red clay, representing a ziggurat of ancient Mesopotamia, rose in the middle of the board. All around him were kids listening to the story behind these ancient step-pyramid-like structures.

"So this here was like a staircase up to the top. It's like a big ol' temple."

"How old is it?"

Kendrick looked sideways at the tiny questioner and flexed his dimples.

"Man, why you over here asking me all these questions? Go on somewhere else."

"Yeah, how old is it?" Another chimed in.

"Older than the pyramids. Them Egyptians probably stole their idea off these people."

"Whoa!"

That was too much. For an elementary school kid nothing beat the pyramids. They were the ultimate big old thing—pounded into their heads each year as their teachers grasped around for the easiest, ready-made social studies lessons. It was Pyramids, Declaration of Independence, and Martin Luther King Jr—the entire elementary school social studies curriculum in a nutshell.

The kids were ushered away from Kendrick's model by their teacher. They did find many more things to be amazed by but there was only one that beat the Mesopotamian temple.

Other Loyalties

Kids were leaning very close to Luna's reconstruction of an Aztec temple.

I heard Ms. Ashley talking to Luna, her former student—a sweet work machine with a sassy streak.

"Luna! What did you make?"

"Hi Ms. Ashley!"

"Oh my goodness—that is *a lot* of detail. Luna!"

"Oooh. That's nasty! Look at that!" A kid yelled.

"That's *tight*!"

"Mr. A, I need to talk to you," Ms. Ashley said in mock horror.

She was joking but I still winced. She was the type of woman that I withered around due to her unwillingness to waste time. I was a slow talker and by the time I collected my thoughts for a response she moved on, guiding a couple stunned kids to a model of Mohenjo-Daro, the four-thousand-year-old city in the Indus Valley in India.

Luna sat behind her step pyramid made from strips of cardboard. A black plastic headband with a pink flower held back long dark hair, and her round face was smiling.

I looked at Luna's project again, this time through the eyes of the uninitiated. On top of the pyramid was an Aztec priest in robes with his hands held high above his head. Below the priest was a clay man splayed on a ritual stone slab. The man's chest is ripped open, and his heart is already gone—it's in the hand of the priest, offered while still beating to the gods. Red drops of tempura paint spill off his body onto the slab, and down the steps of the pyramid.

Chills went through the fourth graders still staring. Such a weird and scary place was the world the middle school kids lived in. So exciting. Just like the Aztec sacrifices that numbered twenty-thousand-a-year, the danger nourished the middle school kids like the gods and kept the sun rising.

If the sun kept rising, it meant the world was turning, and they were growing up too. Despite their parents' (and teachers') desire to keep them sheltered—the fourth graders had to get ready for their lives.

Twenty-Three

IT WAS THE evening shift at St. Joseph's Home for Children, my first real job after college, and first time working with kids. My co-worker Brian and I were sitting around the staff table. We were youth counselors on the residential treatment unit. Most of the residents—pre-teens and teenagers court-ordered for half-year or year-long stays—were in bed.

I was hoping for a calm shift. The night before a kid had broken into the nurse's office and swallowed a bunch of pills. I had to sit with him in the emergency room until two in the morning, as he drank down a black goo to flush his stomach. I wasn't sure back then what kids really needed to help them grow up or "get ready for their lives." It was more a matter of holding on and surviving, until the craziness in their heads and lives settled down. (For some, I had the feeling that it never would.) As adult staff we had to be a container—holding the line, so kids didn't destroy themselves or others.

The quiet night with Brian was interrupted when a voice called out, "Brandon's over here being inappropriate!"

"Go to bed Devon," Brian said.

"I can't. He's farting and saying nasty stuff."

"Go to bed Brandon." A chubby face poked out of a doorway one last time and disappeared.

Brian could handle things casually like that. If it was just me on the unit this little incident could have spiraled out of control.

Afterall, Devon broke a pool stick over a kid's head a couple months before after becoming frustrated over some taunts.

Like many black men who end up working with kids, Brian was a former athlete whom the kids naturally admired. That wasn't enough though, and he added love and a gentle way of listening to seal the deal. You knew a shift with Brian would be mostly peaceful.

He leaned back in his chair. "*Kareem*. I don't know what to do about this mortgage!"

"Well…"

"We have to decide by tomorrow."

Brian and his wife were looking at a house in Lakeville, a suburb of Minneapolis. I didn't care for the suburbs, but after spending his own childhood dodging bullets on the way home from school on the Southside of Chicago, Brian wanted a boring place to raise his kids.

I didn't know anything about mortgages at that point in my life and eventually we were talking about my plans to join the Peace Corps.

"So, you want a go somewhere and help people?" Brian said, cradling the football he was using as a worry stone.

"Senegal. I've always wanted to check out West Africa."

"I know a place on 46th and Chicago where you can help people."

It didn't register with me until I was riding my bike home at midnight after our shift. Brian had told me the address of the building where we had been sitting.

One afternoon at St. Joseph's, a place where plenty of people needed help, I walked the kids out to the field to fly kites. Brandon and Devon ran around together trying to get some lift. Charlie sat untangling his string. Gordon poked Andrew's big belly. A hideous, metal filled smile, spread on Gordon's face when Andrew made a different noise each time he was poked.

In the distance I saw Will, another tall black man on the St. Joe's staff and the lead counselor on another unit. He was strolling towards us.

"So, I saw the social worker Dawn looking out the window at y'all," Will said before reaching me.

"What's going on?"

Will turned his head towards the sky where there were more clouds than I had seen on our way out. There were still large patches of clear sky. I didn't know what Will was getting at.

"You ever heard about a 'bolt from the blue'?"

"A what?"

"Yeah, the storm looks far away, but then lightning travels across the clouds and comes down somewhere different. It kind of surprises people."

I looked at the kids, running with their kites flopping along the ground. Finally, one started soaring in the air. The string was attached to Devon's hands who was laughing, as Brandon celebrated with a jiggly dance.

"Oh shit."

"When I see a brother with his dong hanging out I just gotta' tell him."

After working at St. Joseph's Home for Children, working in schools was the next chance to observe differences in how people worked with kids and approached institutions, depending on their backgrounds. It was easier to understand why some black kids didn't like school: the principal and most teachers didn't look like them, the language being used was kind of dry, and the topics often didn't relate to the task at hand: economic and bodily survival.

When I saw Mr. J working at Ms. D's little school, he seemed to be putting his stock in people first—the institution and larger academic project of schooling was peripheral. When I try to remember Mr. J talking with kids, I see him getting straight to the point: "Girl, what's with you this morning?" or "Are you good—what's goin' on?" Verbalization of feelings and issues was done in real-time, not noticed and brought up as a point of "concern" three days later when a student's name surfaced at a staff meeting. Mr. J, as a result, developed relationships with kids in weeks that took me months to build.

Mr. J's relational approach led to tangible advantages in the world of adolescent education. Being able to empathize with and cajole a variety of personalities, were indispensable qualities working with teenagers. They already have a mistrust of adults and according to some studies have a biological tick that makes them misread facial emotions, making constant communication key.

I've worked with both black and white staff members who were duds. Ms. D wouldn't let them stick around long but I caught a glimpse of the type: half-asleep in the corner of a classroom, only rousing to check their phones. Lethargic men and women who seemed wholly uninterested in the subject matter, who felt their job was being a body in the room that spat out threats on occasion.

But even those staff members taught me something about teaching. I hadn't made it clear that what was going on in the class was worth their attention. It was painful to admit but when I did a lesson and saw that a black educational assistant was bored and disengaged, I knew that is how many of my black students felt. I could blame it on a lack of intellectual curiosity, which was always the case with a percentage of people no matter what their color, but maybe the subject matter and the manner in which I was teaching it, was failing the most basic test: relevancy to their lives.

I noticed a not entirely unrelated phenomenon on field trips. Often the group that was furthest behind on a hike had a higher percentage of black students. The general reason would be that all teenagers liked being the farthest they could be from adults and lagged back on purpose. But often black staff members would be there in the back too.

Ms. Danika herself, was up for hikes. There was no doubt about that. Her reason for being in the back during outings wasn't a dubious feeling towards what we were doing—it was bad hips. Ms. Danika was an engine of laughter and joy along the trail, making the reluctant students forget their worries. And she was the first to encourage full participation in whatever we were doing when everyone finally caught up.

Ms. Danika was ready to support beauty, adventure, and art, whether it was a nervous sixth grader going to camp for the first time or a superstar diva stepping onto the world stage. In fact, I remember walking in the doors of the school the Monday after the Super Bowl and finding her at the front desk.

"Did you see the half-time show?" she asked.

"I missed it."

"Ooh. Beyonce killed it!"

It was hard to describe the presence of Ms. Danika. She seemed to emerge like a goddess out of the best energy and impulses of the school. Her positivity was always present, but she wasn't a predictable cheery person. Sitting by the ocean one knows the waves are going to roll in and make a sound when they crash—this is knowledge that can be counted on. Its consistency doesn't make it dull, and the hue and size of the waves change with the weather and sunlight and the phases of the moon.

Basically, Ms. Danika was a hippie, like me and Maloney, catching a ride on this great surfboard we found—Ms. D's little school. I had learned that Ms. Danika knew how to hang loose early on, when she laughed off a jam I had gotten into with parents my second year at the school.

I had walked my classes to the local library and got cards for all the kids who didn't have their own. Then I did what you're supposed to do at a library—let students roam around and pick up books that caught their interest.

A group of girls checked out some fiction books. When we walked through the doors of the school, I was riding high, as Ms. D saw the thick, serious, novels in the student's hands. The next week I was even more pleased with myself when the girls begged to go to the library again.

We walked over and they came back with a new load of higher-level reading material. This went on for a few weeks until Ms. Danika pulled me aside, chuckling.

"What you got these girl's reading, Mr. A?"

"I don't know. They seem to be really into some series."

She pulled out one of the books, and for the first time I read the title: *Torn Between Two Lovers*.

"Oh, sh…"

Ms. Danika let out a booming laugh.

"Yeah, so I got a call from Quiana's mom, and she's like, '*Where is Q getting these books?*'"

"Man."

"And she goes on telling me about how Quiana was reading so much and always in her room reading and everything."

"Then…"

"Then her mom took a closer look."

"Uhh…"

"That's some *steamy* urban romance!"

"Oh man. What did Ms. D say?"

"Well, you know Ms. D. She was happy the kids were reading!"

Ms. Danika liked the way Maloney and I rolled but could upbraid us when we got reckless with the communal well-being. Our boyish excitement caused us to outrun the capabilities of the group to keep up on some trips.

This became clear on a trip to the Arcola Trail. The trail was one of the many heirlooms from Maloney's family treasury of adventure spots that he shared with us. It led through a grove of cedars, ruins of a hunter's shack, to a view of a historic railroad bridge.

The trailhead itself was unassuming, and our big yellow bus barely fit the dirt pull-off on the county road. The two silver Caravans, driven by Mr. Shane and Mr. J, bookended the bus like they were secret service vehicles protecting the presidential limo.

After a few hundred yards the usual grouping was taking place. Mr. K.O. kept an eye on Jodie M. who was standing on a log so the girls could see him better. Ms. Danika was with a group of girls and boys, half of whom were making the usual threats about what would happen to me if their shoes got messed up. Ms. Conley had downgraded to stylish sneakers, having left the heels behind, and was sharing the news with Mr. Duvall, Ruby, and Kiara.

Maloney and I were in the lead with Amelie and her crew. Duane and Leng, in his leather bomber jacket, and some other Hmong kids who were at home in the woods, were at our side. Jeremiah was there. Seventh grader Valentina joined us with her amber tinted glasses. She had the cool demeanor of a self-possessed thirty-five-year-old. Her friend Lucia, who would rather have been chilling in the back, hustled forward to be with her.

Ms. Tracy brought up the rear of this faction. She drank the Maloney Kool-Aid long ago. She had her own burning curiosity about the world but had a better sense of external order and was the perfect partner for him in class, and on the trail.

As our group started down the trail without hesitation, a few other kids joined us, including Kevin, Mason, Tabari, A.J., and Jake. They were banking on the Spartan challenges guaranteed to be offered by Maloney to the kids who kept up.

There was one problem: a T intersection in the trail. Our lead group didn't think twice as we took a left towards the spring and bridge. After just a few hundred yards we were so far ahead that no one from the other groups saw us. They turned right. Most likely it just happened naturally. Jodie M. was probably being chased, and to escape getting slapped he scrambled in the wrong direction, and everyone just followed.

Tabari and Kevin were black, and with us up front, but it was undeniable—a large part of the group that had started down the trail at a different pace and therefore went the other direction, were black. Was this an equity issue? I figured we were in the clear on that one. I mean in the sense that there can be equality of opportunity but not of outcome. Kids could have kept up and gone with us. And what if each way on the trail led to the same place, the riverside? Could I say this honestly, knowing that Maloney probably knew cooler things to point out in the direction we had went? Did the other group really care? And why *were* we so stretched out on the trail anyways?

My mind spiraled back in time looking for an explanation to this. What I came up with wasn't flattering, because it threw into doubt the whole edifice of public schooling—that presented itself as a place equally good for all. Could it be that in America any endeavor not organically proposed by the black community was tinged with the coercive specter of a plantation? Could the exciting hike, or day out removing buckthorn from the neighborhood greenspace be echoing with the sounds of forced labor or the makings of a chain-gang? To my mind, that seemed like going too far, but what was the slow walking and apparent reluctance to get to where we were going all about? Trust?

Maloney and I oversaw these outside excursions and would sometimes try to analyze the fates and motivations of different batches of kids strung along the trails. I don't know what Maloney concluded but I wondered if the slow walking brothers and sisters were passively resisting *my* agenda. Like their enslaved ancestors who purposely slowed down the tempo of work in a sugarcane field—were my students carrying on acts of resistance by marching to the beat of a different drum? Was I plain wrong to overlay the harsh experiences and survival mechanisms of enslaved people of the past onto the fresh faces of my students today? It was as if a black thirteen-year-old in my class must be compelled to exist only as part of a four-hundred-year-old storyline of black suffering, with everything that happens or doesn't happen to them in their lives funneled back to that narrative. Maybe the kid walking way in the back was not "behind" but just where he wanted to be on the trail, with the people he wanted to be with, telling the most entertaining stories.

Even now, writing this, I feel like I'm tiptoeing around something but not saying it out loud. Yet this is where social studies teachers spend a good deal of their time. We are supposed to be guides on the alternating pathways of the American story, one moment the narrative is sharp edged, inflicting pain all the way back to the beginnings of the country, the other moment a well-trodden trail of successes, leading us to an exalted present. Social studies teachers are supposed to offer up the facts along both these paths and allow children to judge which combination leads to a better future. But the facts are anything but neutral.

I thought of other cultural differences that would explain why our middle school was so stretched out on the trail. I noticed some differences myself as somebody with a cultural background other than the linear, goal-driven world of Western culture and education. As someone with roots in North Africa it wasn't the activity or destination that troubled me when doing things with my white colleagues, it was the *pace*. But that fast pace was what allowed Europe to advance economically, wasn't it? Or did rapid unreflective progress lead them to rip each other apart more efficiently in two World Wars? Which was it?

There's a story recounted in travel writer Bruce Chatwin's book *Songlines*, about a colonial British explorer charging through the jungle trailed by a group of African porters. At one point the Africans stop, sit down, and refuse to carry on. The Brit asks them what the issue is about. One of the Africans replies, "We can't go on until our spirits catch up with our bodies."

Though students were sometimes uninterested in where I wanted them to literally go on field trips, there were also doubts about the final destination of some of the content and ideas in my lessons. While bringing up time periods in history like slavery, some kids refused to come into the room, a defiant act supported by their parents. Those were times when they felt it wasn't clear the trajectory of the conversation was beneficial for their children. The degradation of slavery was easy to spell out with facts and artifacts—whips and chains, and auctions that separated families. But what would be used in class to illuminate the actual minds and desires of the dark bodies jammed under the deck of a slave ship and set to labor in a strange land? Slave narratives? Trickster tales starring Brer Rabbit? Negro spirituals? The imagination of Toni Morrison?

I thought that I should keep rolling the curriculum back in time before the Atlantic slave trade, all the way to the great kingdoms of Africa. I don't know whether adding royalty to the family tree was convincing to the parents of a black child. But I felt that without pushing past the negative orbit of slavery, the story might be a psychic trap for their children. They would get stuck in the sorrowful belt of debris that has America locked in its gravity—has us all in frantic motion but just goes round and round.

A child's sense of pride in their heritage, a blood claim to the achievements of the ancestors, gave black students an origin story of heroes they could model themselves after. The same way an Iraqi kid, walking around the rubble of a suicide bombing, needs to be able to step inside the National Museum of Iraq. He needs to be able to look up at the four-thousand-year-old headless statue of an ancient Sumerian king and imagine his own sitting on its black granite shoulders.

And here was the tricky part: a white student also needed to feel proud of their heritage and see heroes that looked like them.

When me and Maloney's group reached the grove of cedar trees at the top of a ravine, we decided to slide down on our butts. As I bounced through a carpet of green ferns, I noticed rusted barbwire poking up between the shoots. I expected a yelp of pain to come from one of the kids slashing downhill. But everyone made it to the bottom safely and we climbed along moss-covered logs above a small creek toward the St. Croix River.

At the spring the kids had an odd reaction. When told they could take a drink of water trickling up from the ground they balked. It was not a faucet, nor labeled "Dasani" or "Evian." Maloney crouched, removed his newsboy cap, and took a gulp. After splashing his face clean like a cowboy for good measure, he looked around.

"Who's next?"

"You gonna get the runs boy, you know it," Kevin said smiling as Tabari reached his hand to feel the water.

Tabari, who had been in the Boy Scouts, was one of the few black kids who had been out camping and hiking a lot. He didn't flinch. Scooping a handful, he took a big drink and passed his wet hand over his head.

"Ooh, it's cold. It's extra fresh!"

The kids slowly lined up on the muddy slope for their own baptism.

They had been in Maloney's science class long enough to take his word when he said something was safe. But he had to do something in front of them for it to sink in. Foraging was common practice, and they'd collected and eaten seeds I swore were poisonous, tapped and boiled sap from maple trees, made tea from sumac berries, and ate whatever Maloney gathered from clearance bins at the Double Dragon Asian food store and put in his deep fryer on "Fry-days."

Maloney's authority came from some other sources too. He never swore—even using the laborious "H-E-double hockey sticks" for "hell." If kids said "shut up" in his class, they knew that there was no way of getting around writing ten alternatives. Ms. Tracy would hand them a dictionary and sheet of paper, and that was that.

Kids pick up on self-mastery but as far as I know they didn't poke around for the source of Maloney's discipline. His upbringing: the tough Scottish father and exacting Vietnamese mother had something to do with it. By the time he met his wife the raw materials were there, maybe even the outline of a complete man. The practice of Mormonism that she brought to his life seemed to help polish something already present and kept him anchored to a rich family life—as he was liable to wander off into the backcountry of the Wind River Range or Black Hills with a Bowie knife.

As with my old soccer coach Tom, kids were not concerned with *what* he was using to guide his life but that his *life was guided*. As the old adage goes, kids don't listen to adults, they imitate them. Some students assumed he was just born like that and tried to copy what they could. They never suspected that he may have gotten guidance, a sense of purpose, and even secrets, from a religious tradition that he kept to himself as a public-school teacher.

Maloney was like the namesake of the place my soccer team stayed at in France, Bernadette Soubirous, and understood discretion. When Soubirous was hounded about the details of her visionary experience with the "lady in white" later in her short life, Soubirous said, "During the fifteen days she told me three secrets, but I was not to speak about them to anyone, and so far, I have not." However, this humility did not stop Soubirous from having an enormous influence. She is Saint Bernadette after all, and the grotto where she had her vision now consists of an area dubbed The Sanctuary of Our Lady of Lourdes. The shrine built at Lourdes is now visited by millions of pilgrims each year, many of them sick and dying. They arrive with the belief that the water from the spring Soubirous dug near the grotto is holy and has the miraculous power to heal. Hope was a distraction—a precious one that allowed people to carry on living.

After drinking from our own spring at the end of the Arcola Trail, we rock-hopped across the creek and followed it to the river. I don't know what the textbook definition of health is but if it means that you look alive, then students were healthy. They spent a half-hour skipping stones and poking around the foot of the bluff. We were having so much fun I didn't think at all about our comrades—the other groups that turned right at the T-intersection. It was negligence for my part, but Maloney noticed and had determined the terrain was safe enough that the other adults could manage the hike.

Maloney did not have a habit of underestimating people. From the old ladies selling Scandinavian pastries in small-town Minnesota, to young Congolese immigrants in the slums of Paris that he met on his missionary trip, to all his students—he gave each individual their due. His brutal quest to find the limits of his own potential instilled a belief in the ability of others to manage in the world—even grow new skills if survival depended on it. And for our co-workers, that meant leading middle school kids on a trail they didn't know. But Maloney was also an empathetic warrior and conceded that there were different tolerances for suffering. So, he jogged back down the trail and returned with the rest of the groups an hour later. Everybody had their chance to drink from the spring.

At one point I saw Ms. Danika down by the river's edge. Her warm-up top was tied around her waist and her hands were pressed against her lower back. Najah, a beautiful, soft-spoken girl standing at her side, pointed to a bulge of land in the river.

"Ms. Danika, is that an island?"

"It looks surrounded by water. So yeah. What? You want to go out there?"

"That'd be tight!"

"Alrighty then, you better start building yourself a boat. That can be Najah's island."

Valentina and Lucia were sitting on a log nearby and overheard them.

"Hey, we want to go out there to!" Valentina said.

"You better make yourselves a bigger boat then," Ms. Danika answered.

"Yes, come be guests on my island," Najah said, sweeping her hand across the water.

The four of them got quiet. They were flushed in golden royal light as a cloud moved past the sun. My mind reeled and for a second, we were standing along the Volta River in the Ashanti Empire of West Africa.

I understood something then. I thought that my struggle was to link students up with historical heroes who had skin like theirs. This was admirable, necessary, but at times insufficient. Even dare I say, shallow. There was a different type of ancestor they could learn from right before their eyes. Death and passing years were not enough to define an ancestor. They could be living people who had searched and found some of the best characteristics of humanity itself. Ancestors could be the teachers students were around every day, like Maloney and Ms. Danika.

AN HOUR LATER we all were milling by the bus because one group had eluded Maloney's initial regrouping effort at the spring. They had Mr. K.O. with them, the intrepid world traveler, so we were not worried.

Mr. Shane and Mr. J were both on their phones getting dispatches from home base. Personalized instructions from Ms. D about whether Stanley would be dropped off at his mom's or

Other Loyalties

grandmas on the p.m. route, and if one of them could stay for the basketball game.

Exhausted, most of the kids climbed into the bus. Settling into the dark green vinyl seats, they felt how people feel when the body is burning clean.

Jayla opened a back window on the bus and asked casually, "What we waiting on?"

"Mr. K.O. and Jodie M.'s group. They're M.I.A," I replied.

"M.I.A.? Who dat?"

"M.I.A. Missing-in-action."

"Missin'? Mr. K.O.'s old self be missin' teeth. He better come on. My feet hurt."

"But you're on the bus—you can just sit."

"My feet still hurt," Kiara poked Jayla's butt and she ducked back into the bus.

Maloney and I were about to jog back down the trail when we saw big hair attached to a scrawny body bound towards us. Jodie M.

Mr. K.O. was the closest to irritated that I ever saw him. He wiped his forehead once with the back of his hand.

"Where'd you guys go?"

"K.O.!"

"Man, I had Jodie running around in the tall grass. I was having Vietnam flashbacks."

"Ha!" Maloney coughed out.

"You can't leave us like that. Jodie just about ran off the edge of the bluff!"

Now that Mr. K.O. was on the board of the school—the unthinkable had infiltrated his mind against his will: the specter of a lawsuit. I pictured Jodie M. floating off the edge of the cliff, his curly *Jungle Book* hair not quite enough to serve as a parachute. Maloney and I exchanged glances. Our belief in self-preservation was confirmed—Jodie had stopped himself after all. But it was hard not to think that there was another companion with us: luck.

Mr. K.O. was already chuckling again. He took off his hat and swatted Jodie M. who dodged it. Jodie M. jumped on the bus, found the seat with the two cutest 8th grade girls and shoe-horned his bony butt between them to sit.

Ms. Danika looked beat and was leaning against Mr. J's Caravan.

"*Mmm.* You gotta watch out for these two." She fixed Maloney and I in her benevolent crosshairs.

"Mr. A and Mr. Maloney will leave you…In. The. Dust."

As much as she liked these outings Ms. Danika was happiest working with her singers and dancers back on the school stage. She would slip below a talented but insecure girl's radar, meet her where she was at, and gently but surely nudge her into the spotlight.

That was one-on-one work, but then there'd be the choir to sort out. I passed through the gym during rehearsals before a concert one time, and it was chaos. Kids were in hyper conversations with each other and turned every which way. Najah was standing in the middle row with her hand over her mouth.

Mr. Barnett, waiting at his keyboard, deferred to Ms. Danika.

Ms. Danika's voice boomed, "Okay, y'all!"

A few days before the concert, like any middle school performance, it looked headed for disaster. But then, like a sonic Rubik's cube, the different sounds twisted into shape. I saw Najah drop her hand from her mouth.

Ms. Danika was someone they didn't want to disappoint, and they found their voices in time. She was their queen, and she was in the flesh.

Twenty-four

"LIFE IS *NOT* that good!" Yasmina yelled at the TV.

"Why not? What do you mean?" I said. I was still hoping that my eight-year-old daughter believed life would be an endless stream of unicorns, fuzzy cats, and laughing, uncomplicated relationships with her pre-adolescent friends.

"It's just not like that. Like they showed in the commercial," she insisted.

My family had rolled the dice and fled Minnesota for a week in October. We strapped our face masks on, boarded the plane and flew straight to San Diego. It was a generic destination but getting out to the ocean during a global pandemic seemed sexy enough. My son could hit the dope skateparks of Southern California and my daughter could test her mettle against the shore break.

At night, sitting in a shabby surfer's pad by South Mission Beach, recovering from the good times, we were watching TV together, something that we only get to do on vacation.

Commercials fascinated Yasmina, and the one she was talking about had been on a steady loop. In it, a handsome man in a chunky sweater puts a kettle on to boil, picks up his keys and heads to the door. A hot, earthy woman smiles at him, and a Basset Hound sits up on a comfy mat as he passes. We see the man hop in a Land Rover and drive off. He stops at the harbor for fresh fish, a farm stand for eggs, and the bakery.

The Land Rover pulls back in the driveway, and he walks in the door just as the whistle starts blowing on the kettle. Over a simple breakfast of toast and eggs he checks his phone, while slowly stirring his tea.

The camera pans out to reveal a tiny Norwegian island the size of one city block.

Sure enough, after ten minutes of a show, the Land Rover commercial came on again. My daughter held a miniature Famous Amos cookie near her mouth, waiting for the idyllic scene to perfectly resolve itself again.

My daughter scrunched her face, lowered the cookie for a moment and said, "*See*. Life is *not* that good!"

This was years after I had left Ms. D's little school, and I was wondering whether when I looked back on it, I was idealizing everything because it was like a tiny fantasy island. I was discontented at my new public school, the one I ended up at, and often compared it to Ms. D's charter school. There was an extraordinary cast of teachers at my new school, but somehow, we were being stifled and flummoxed by conditions out of our control—by decisions made in a district office by people who neither understood nor in some cases supported the experiment of offering a public Montessori middle school education to city kids. The building was way overcrowded, and we were unable to get the daily schedule that suited the aims of our program. As creative, dedicated teachers burned out and left the school one by one, I had the ominous sense of a missed opportunity.

If my daughter, on an oceanside vacation sitting under a pile of chocolate chip cookies, could recognize that sometimes "Life is not that good," I thought I should think again about my time at Ms. D's little school. Afterall, I was a social studies teacher, and needed to know what could be learned by keeping tabs on the troubles that are part of any story.

One memory of turbulence that came to me happened when the middle school staff was gathered in Ms. Conley's room after school. It was an informal meeting; people had their jackets on and were standing or sitting on tables. I didn't know why it was called, and I waited for someone to start talking.

"Okay guys, let's figure this out," Ms. Conley broke through, assertive and bright.

"Yeah, so we had a plan to take the kids to do this thing and the vans were gone," Ms. Tracy said.

"Where were they?" Ms. Conley probed.

"Mr. Shane took some kids to look at skateboards."

"I think he promised he'd take them yesterday," Mr. Duvall said.

"But we just need to work on communicating that to each other. You know, so we don't mess each other's plans up," Ms. Tracy reasoned.

There was an undramatic sense of agreement in the room.

Mr. Shane walked in bursting with energy. I could tell he had a wild story on the tip of his tongue and wanted to tell Maloney. He took a seat. A few heads turned, with the slightest hint of reproach.

He tuned in to the vibe and asked, "What's going on?"

"We're just trying to figure out how to not step on each other's toes doing stuff with kids," Ms. Conley said.

One too many heads turned towards Mr. Shane.

He looked around and said, "Wait a minute, what the hell is this, an *intervention*?"

Everyone laughed, even Ms. Tracy, who had friends battling addiction. She could have gotten haughty and pressed the issue but bringing it up was enough. Life went on.

That is to say Ms. D's little school was not without its issues. Since I was not plugged into the grapevine, I usually didn't know the half of it. There was such a critical mass of good things happening that the problems were easy to ignore. But like any place where the main currency was relationships—damage was done.

One afternoon a new third grade teacher who was in the room next to mine stopped in, looking pale. She'd only been at the school six months.

"I'm being fired."

"Man, I'm sorry."

"I don't know what I did wrong."

She searched my face one more time to see if I had some insight. I just stayed with her eyes until she turned and slumped out. After she vanished down the hall, I kicked aside a milk carton that had been on the floor since first period. She was a more experienced teacher than me, and I still couldn't piece together how I was managing to survive. Was I catching breaks because I was a man? It was my fourth year, and I had no routines down in my room. Simple agenda items like having students clean up at the end of each class, descended into a frantic round of badgering until students just bolted and left me with a mess.

Ms. D's instinctual style meant that if she went into a room and sensed that what was happening in there was not good for kids, she didn't hesitate in making staffing changes. She was willing to overlook the lack of procedures in my room because something else was compensating. I knew the fired third grade teacher had those routines down, so what was it that she was missing?

When Ms. D had to dismiss a staff member it wasn't easy for her. There were jokes about the emotional state of Ms. D each time she had to do it. The weeping and catharsis were legendary, sincere, and ratcheted up depending on how long a teacher had been there.

One longer-serving kindergarten teacher was sideswiped by the news of her own dismissal. I was friends with her. My first year at Ms. D's little school, she told me that even though she'd been teaching for fifteen years she was always nervous at the start of the year. I was so thankful to hear that from a veteran.

The meeting in Ms. D's office where she was dismissed was painful. The hits of the 70's and 80's played from the boombox in the background, and Bucky Badger stuffed animals sat snug on a rocking chair. But none of that softened the blow. The office became a stage for an Italian opera: anger, gratitude, red and teary faces, and a long, long, hug as the finale. Afterwards, there was nothing for this teacher to do except get out the banker boxes and start packing up all the happy, colorful paraphernalia that makes a kindergarten room.

Ms. Soraira, the Venezuelan angel, worked as an assistant in this teacher's room. She and I met up in the hallway together after the kindergarten teacher's departure.

"*Meester A*. I talked to her. She so sad."

But we kept our faith in Ms. D as a leader.

When spells of pandemonium struck the middle school several times each year—with multiple kids suffering from disequilibrium at once, I worried for my own head.

There would be a crack of thunder and I'd hear Ms. D shouting down the hall. Kids would be scrambling for cover. If they were caught, they'd try all their little charms and excuses: "My head hurts," "I lost something," "I have a stomach-ache," "I need to call my mom," and "They keep messing with me in there." When Ms. D was not in the mood, these endearments got slapped away like blaster bursts by a light-saber wielding Darth Vader.

"I don't want to hear it. Get your butt in class!"

Rashad was being a pill in class, cursing at other students and antagonizing Quiana because he had a crush on her. Before we went into the gym for an assembly, I stopped at the front desk to have him call his mom. When he handed the phone to me, I beat around the bush, and his mom wasn't getting the message. I found myself in an argument. It was the sort of combative, defensive dance parents who are tired of phone calls from schools become experts at.

Ms. D passed by, grabbed the phone, and shouted, "Your son said 'fuck' in a classroom. He cannot say 'fuck' in a classroom." And hung up.

Anyone who works with adolescents understands these spells of madness. A full moon that only appears above middle schools. It's a sort of mass psychosis, where teachers stare at each other in emergency staff meetings with bloodshot eyes. Interventions and solutions are brainstormed and logged in the annals of lost causes.

Imposter syndrome hit me hard during one of these spells. In my class, we were in a lull between projects, and I'd handed the kids an article I'd come across that morning that was too difficult for them to read. It was literally titled, "The Worst Mistake in the History of the Human Race."

The author of the article, Jared Diamond, makes a case that the discovery of agriculture, pegged as the first step towards a better life for our species, was really a catastrophe. The ability to produce surplus food meant we could settle down and have time to think about our future. Farming was the lodestone of civilization, leading to religion, technological progress, the arts, architecture, nations and…schools.

Nearly ten-thousand years ago we faced a choice: limit population or increase food production. Humans chose the latter. It was a *no-brainer*. And that's the crux of it. Our stomachs made that decision. We banked on the ease of stored bushels of wheat, and the easy pickings of domesticated goats and sheep, to fill us up the year round.

The trade-off was that it gave growth to things that weren't present in hunter-gatherer tribes. Unintended consequences like famine, warfare, tyranny, the zero-sum competition for resources, and a boring classroom packed with young energetic people on a gorgeous spring afternoon. Those were the wormy fruits of civilization.

The students who couldn't read the article were either staring into space or shooting spitballs onto the ceiling. I ran around trying to provoke them with the premise that cavemen were better than us.

I went up to Kevin, who I knew could read well, and said, "Just read a little and you'll see that fur loin cloths were *Gucci*."

"This article's boring as hell," Kevin protested.

"You gotta get into it. We make fun of primitive people, but they were able to spend more of their day chilling than we do. We work ourselves to death…"

"Okay, okay, just go bug them over there," Keven gestured towards another table. "They ain't doing nothing. They over there throwing pencils out the window, and walkin' out the class, and you over here messin' with me."

An excruciating hour passed that way. I hopelessly bounced between outbreaks of mischief at each table. Even the few who attempted to read it in each class, like Mark and Amelie, became disinterested in the long article. My Plan A was so slipshod, that a move to Plan B would have been called for within the first ten minutes of class. But I had no Plan B.

Earlier that week I'd heard Ms. D yelling in the hall, "Just do your damn *job*." As I surveyed my class and found only one-fifth of them reading, the line rang in my mind. I decided Ms. D's shouts in the hall were a form of crosstalk meant to warn and encourage us—a type of incidental staff development. It was the most sober advice she could give at times of crisis. The best option was to hold on, keep showing up, and at a minimum just do my "damn job."

Another warning came more gently from Ms. D as a note on my Weekly Reflection. Floating in the margins in green ink, next to my confessions on how bad things were going, were the words, "Don't wing it!"

I *was* winging it but not in the usual fashion. I had tried and failed again to decipher and use the Minnesota state social studies standards. The way it works is that every ten years volunteers, including teachers, apply to be on a committee at the Minnesota Department of Education that revises what should be taught in social studies classrooms. The bullet points lay out time periods but also essential knowledge—and this is where they start to take on the tint of the political climate. The meetings and period of public comment before being approved are ideologically raw because the terms by which the story of America will be told are being negotiated.

I didn't envy those committees. Fans of Ronald Reagan clashed with acolytes of Jimmy Carter; inheritors of German settlers brushed off objections by the outnumbered descendants of exiled Dakota; the champions of a triumphalist America listened impatiently to those submitting the truths of a checkered past—genocide, displacement, slavery, internment, exploitation, and military aggression.

The catch-22 of this committee work was that by making these hard judgements about what to include and exclude for the students, it was depriving students of this intellectual exercise themselves. It was an engaging battle for meaning that energized participants and the public alike. But it was adults benefiting from the process.

At any rate, a new revision of the standards had just been approved by the Minnesota legislature and I printed it out—determined to do my "job." Yet each time I sat down at my tanker desk to find guidance in the standards, I felt I was looking at discrete items in a kitchen cabinet: a bottle of vanilla, bleached flour, salt, a bit of brown sugar getting rock hard in a bag, and a small dispenser of food coloring.

I knew these items, or standards, might make something when combined but would it be something the kids would eat? The admirable thing about the standards was that its creators conceded that teachers would have a lot of say on how they exposed students to the concepts and historic episodes in their own classrooms.

The problem was that in my head a whole different set of ingredients were begging to be used. I'm guessing this was how devout Christian teachers felt in a classroom. They had their school lessons, and then they had other lessons that they felt would *really* serve their students. The same went for partisan Democrats, Republicans, and libertarians; atheists, and Wiccans; nihilists and saints.

A single veil, the tenuous public school teacher's code of honor—to stay neutral—protected students from wholesale indoctrination by these other lessons once the classroom door was closed. Yet holes were poked through all the time and were maybe the only way to let a different sort of light in the classroom. But also, a very familiar sort of darkness—the teacher's private prejudices and with them, the nation's most vile traditions. In the end, there was nothing stopping me, as a teacher, from quietly infusing my lessons with my worst interpretations of the world.

The holes I was poking in the veil were sanctioned at Ms. D's little school because Ms. D must have trusted me to not cross the line completely. When I took the kids to listen to a monk at the Watt Munisotaram, she didn't flinch. I had invited Johnny Smith, who sang sacred Ojibwe songs in my taxpayer funded classroom, but the intentions were not to win any converts in either case.

I tried to remind myself during the low points, and crazy full moons, that Ms. D appreciated my lessons, even the not-so-sacred ones. In the 'Weekly Reflection,' I told Ms. D about my class spending two weeks sewing moccasins to play an Ojibwe gambling game. There were real stakes on the line: Jolly Ranchers. My general point to the students was that fun and relaxation were a part of Native American life too.

Ms. D responded by telling the story of her own sixth-grade class in Wisconsin. They had read *Touching Spirit Bear*. The story follows a teenager who gets steered towards the Native American path of restorative justice after beating up another boy. To avoid prison time, he's banished to an island in Alaska where he's left alone with his anger. One of the tasks prescribed to him by the elders was carrying a huge rock up a hill, representing the struggles of his ancestors. When he reached the top, he was to push it back down—as a symbol of releasing his anger.

Sure enough, Ms. D walked her students to a hill in rural Wisconsin and had them all haul a rock to its top. Risking complaints about cultural appropriation, and on the other side, grumblings about doing Pagan rituals at school, she gave students a day at school that they wouldn't forget the moment the bell rang.

After reading Ms. D's note I had renewed faith. I rehabilitated my lesson about "The Worse Mistake in Human History." Recalling a *Star Trek* episode where Captain Jean-Luc Picard is put on trial for the crimes of humanity, I rearranged my class into a courtroom.

Farmers were going to be prosecuted for the birth of civilization that was the cause of the sorry state the world was in. The students were all given roles and two days to prepare for the trial.

When the court date came, my student teacher, dressed as the bailiff, announced, "All rise for the honorable Judge Isaak!" A red-cheeked 7th grader in Ms. Conley's college graduation robe strolled in.

The lead prosecutor, Rebecca, dressed in an electric blue blazer, prepared to call up her witnesses: a victim of famine, a crushed subject of tyrannical rule, and a happy member of the last hunter-gatherer tribe. He was the star witness—flush with leisure time he was assumed to not have in the false narrative of the brutish Stone Age struggle to survive. Lastly, she grilled the farmer, played by Jeremiah, who was dressed in overalls.

The defense team, dressed in their Sunday church clothes, called forth their own witnesses: a formidable cast ready to tout the glory of settling down and filling the granaries—an artist, architect, doctor, scientist and comfortable, educated, citizen of modern society.

Judge Isaak, holding a Stanley hammer that I'd brought from home, slammed it down hard on the table after closing arguments. The jury, titillated by the drama, had listened carefully to each side. As a testament to the strong arguments made by Rebecca, the jury ruled in favor of her side, even though she was new to the school and was up against three popular kids.

Excited students ran to Ms. D to talk about the trial, and I knew I was home-free. Because of Ms. D's power to hire and fire at will, the school was kept lean. I'd shaved off the fat of my lazy lesson by recycling the article on the "Worst Mistake" and opting for role-playing.

Ms. D just wanted teachers with the energy to pivot when necessary. Therefore, the spiritual dead weight of burnt-out staff that traditional public schools had to drag around as their penance for strong unions, was severed quickly. The downside was that beloved employees, like an administrative assistant who was Ms. D's right hand for a couple years, or my friend, the kindergarten teacher, were let go for reasons that were sometimes hard to grasp. For them, there was no recourse, no union to appeal to, no security.

Other Loyalties

This dynamic worked because Ms. D was a visionary and wielded her power for the benefit of kids. In other hands, charter schools can be dysfunctional autocracies. Worse, they can be hollow business ventures—nothing more than branded gimmicks. Formulated by businesspeople posing as educators, these charter school "leaders" were only interested in franchising and profit. And indeed, the lower pay compared to union schools, high staff turn-over, and dubious missions meant that many charters teetered like new businesses—scrambling to find lower rent and reliable employees to stay aloft. In many cases, when these type of charter schools closed, their students were left out to dry.

All charter schools are beholden to sponsors, who can be universities, non-profits, independent boards, or local school districts. They authorize and monitor a charter school's finances and student performance and sign three-year contracts with the group running the school.

Some baked-in pitfalls of traditional big district schools were headed off by simple decisions that Ms. D had more freedom to make as a charter school leader. The advantage of an empowered leader allowed them to follow through on bold missions to shape something new in education. The box-checking, red tape, and one-size-fits-all directives of large public-school districts, serve as quality control, but can stifle great ideas in return.

I remember walking around my first year at Ms. D's little school looking for the teacher's lounge that I'd seen on TV shows. I wanted to glimpse the crusty veteran with coffee breath, that would size up the teaching profession for me with a shrug of resignation. There was no teacher's lounge nor crusty veteran around—Ms. D had remodeled both the human and physical infrastructure. She was bringing her vision to life.

I feel blessed I never met the archetypal veteran and his or her brand of cynicism, lack of awe, and lethargic mix of boredom and competence. They were not welcome at the school and would not be, until a sad day when Ms. D was forced out of the school.

It was a time closer than we all could have imagined.

A mounting power struggle that I was only vaguely aware of was raging between Ms. D and the school sponsors. The sponsors had a rigid streak and Ms. D was having trouble managing their desire for control, and their disapproval of the freewheeling activities and style of the school. It was a bit of a *Footloose* situation, the 1980's movie about the tensions of a town that outlaws dancing.

For the time being, our school remained a working experiment in family style, joyful learning. One of Ms. D's favorite lines was "Babies rule the house." And we did our best to put kids first. A symbol of this for me was that the teacher's lounge, a potential vortex of bitching and intrigue—remained a classroom for kids the whole time I was at Ms. D's little school. There was no comfy place with vending machines to talk behind kid's backs. If kids needed to be roasted, it was best to do it to their faces.

Another decision that revealed to me early on that even the building was set up with kids in mind, was that there was no "Time-Out Room" for misbehaving students. Ms. D had turned it into another space for learning. As a result, there never developed a group of jaded students who plotted only to get out of class to reach this safe zone of pared-down expectations. Teachers and students had to try and work it out in class together. There was no easy way of ejecting a kid from the room.

If kids acted up too much, they would spend time with Ms. D. The consequences were unpredictable, and case by case. If these students needed help finding their calm center or renewing their self-esteem, she put them in the elementary rooms. They would tutor kids and help tiny hands cut out clean shapes with their amazing thirteen-year-old dexterity, under the supervision of their old teachers who knew them from when they were a little and cute.

Ms. D would often "love and logic" the crap out of students, so that they returned to class humbled and battered by affection. Sometimes the "logic" part of this formula meant that they returned to class with a genuine consequence hanging over their head. (Just like teachers, students could be easily booted from

Other Loyalties

charter schools. But since most kids loved going to school here, they would do a lot to shape up.)

Ms. D's staff loved teaching at her school, too. One reason is that she had a genuine respect for our time. We didn't have regular staff meetings or team meetings. We met as needed. There was rarely the sensation that we were together against our will, fulfilling contract hours, being exposed to some required information that was meaningless to us, just to fulfill an administrative itch. (We did have those emergency meetings during junior high full moons—which of course, were useless.)

There was an inherent danger to teacher meetings in most schools, I think. Handwringing at meetings had its place when a child's precarious existence became the subject. But adults liked to make performances out of their concern for children. It was all very unnecessary. The mere fact of working in a public school was certification that one gave a hoot.

My sense of alienation in the few meetings Ms. D had, as well as at the other schools I've worked at, came back down to being one of only a few guys present. The way women solved problems, in a sort of triangulated communal way, through conversations taking place on multiple tracks, bewildered me. I never knew how to contribute. It was something Maloney was able to do with ease that always mystified me—stepping into a conversation as a man without stepping on toes. The tough-as-nails survivalist was more in touch with his feminine qualities of empathy, collaboration, and intuition, than I was.

The dirty truth was that there were times that I just assumed a group of women, plus Maloney, could tackle problems more efficiently. I sat back on purpose—sparing myself the extra opportunities for burnout that pepper every teaching career. During some meetings, personal issues fed into an urge to try and fix *everything*. There was a stubborn refusal by some women to acknowledge that we were only a tiny slice of the influences in our students lives. It was a case of empathy run amok.

Women have run every school I have ever worked at—organizing incredible classrooms and experiences, but when it came time for someone to emcee an assembly, many of them became terrified. The extreme confidence and competence went away in a poof. It made no sense to me. Except remembering my sister complaining about not liking the sound of her own voice.

Introverted and terrified myself, I thrust my chest forward and grabbed the mic during these assemblies. I could finally be of use, and the show went on. The man who remained silent during the daily give-and-take required to govern a school, was willing to have his voice amplified to the crowd. Knowing what I know now of the brewing trouble between Ms. D and the school sponsors, perhaps it would have been better for me to participate in more gritty day-to-day conversations about the politics and emotions deciding the fate of the school. Could I have tapped into aggressive masculine qualities to help defend Ms. D from her detractors?

Instead, I satisfied myself with the fleeting attention I got as the star of assemblies. My words boomed out of the loudspeaker and filled the gym. It was April, and our last assembly of the year to recognize math and reading progress. We recycled the carnival theme because it had been such a hit my second year at the school. To raise the big top, Maloney and Mr. Shane hoisted the multicolored parachute to the gym ceiling once again.

I brought the mic to my lips and got into character: "Ladies and gentlemen! Boys and girls! You are about to witness the most shocking, incredible, inexplicable vanishing act you have EVER SEEN! There are kids here who used to *tremble* at the sight of a math problem, or a book, but now, through some sort of mysterious force called 'effort,' that fear is gone! GONE! And no one has seen it since!"

The kids and teachers cheered. Another contraption Maloney had attached to the ceiling was triggered, and balloons floated down on everybody. None of us knew that less than a year later, there would be a "vanishing act" involving Ms. D, that was itself shocking, and to many of us, inexplicable.

Twenty-five

TOWARD THE END of my fourth year, Ms. D's little school was starting to get some attention in the charter school community and the press. Test scores were way up, and kids enjoyed coming to school. Innovation and iconoclasm were bearing fruit, and Ms. D was rightly recognized and consulted about her formula at conferences and workshops. There was one conference the whole staff attended called, 'Gap Closed,' showcasing schools that had bridged the so-called achievement gap between white and black students.

Ms. D was not afraid of the mic. She gave speeches around the state and loved the opportunity to share how proud she was of our school. But she knew that the formula that worked at her school couldn't be extracted from the flesh and blood of her staff.

The problem with a good school, as with anything organically grown, was that it was not scalable. Without Maloney, Ms. Soraira, Mr. Barnett, Ms. Conley, Ms. Tracy, Ms. Danika, Mr. Duvall, the Three Sisters, and so on, there was no way to franchise our success. As a staff family, we were firing on all cylinders. There was a sense of things speeding up and all things pointed to glory. Even if it was glory reserved for a single building on the east side of St. Paul.

That spring, I rose each day before dawn, headed to the basement, and did a two-hour workout for ninety days straight. It was called P90X. I had to do something to at least be able to stand in the same hall as Mr. Duvall, Captain America himself.

I ran into Mr. K.O., who was in his sixties, one morning and asked him where he got his energy.

"Push-ups, sit-ups—the whole Rocky routine," he answered.

"Really, that's great."

"Oh yeah baby! If I don't do that every morning, I'm dead in the water."

Jacked with muscles and high on the collective energy of the school I became more alert to the number of experiences we had that belonged on a highlight reel. I began stacking video clips on my new camera phone of each school adventure: Maloney and Jake facing off to see who could climb the underside of a bridge, Hunter jumping that huge gap between the bales of hay, Brianna and Haven being surrounded by goats on a pioneer farm.

We hiked to the top of Barn Bluff in Red Wing, a town an hour or so from the school, taking the trail that was closed due to erosion. It was the more dangerous path up, but it had alchemical qualities for the kids. Their demeanor changed. The way the mass of Mr. Brandon calmed Kai and Noah—exposure to steep cliff drops pacified the rest of the students.

At one chokepoint the heights were freaking some kids out. Luna was in tears. She was genuinely scared but reveling at the attention. The Carter dynamic went into effect, and everyone rallied to get Luna across the muddy strip of trail. When the path widened again, Luna started laughing and they all turned back into goofballs and flirts. The unstable route was a suitable seesaw for the silliness and seriousness that adolescents zip between.

Here's an analogy for what it's like being on such a trail with teenagers: the concept of a 'temporal pincer.' It comes from a film about warping time called *Tenet*, that infuriated most filmgoers with its too-clever plot. I don't have the mental chops to understand most of the film, but I did get one idea.

A 'pincer movement' in battle is when two groups of troops attack a target simultaneously from opposite sides. In the film, people in the future have figured out how to invert time and can move both backwards and forwards through it. Therefore, they can attack the past with knowledge of the future. A '*temporal* pincer' is when one troop attacks moving forward through time and another moving backwards through time. It was ridiculous plot device but illustrated something particular about middle school kids. When I think about crossroads in life, the one where childhood and adulthood met was the most intense. Colliding within my students were the raiding forces of their past and future selves. As a newer teacher I had some of these contradictory vibes myself. I was scared, overwhelmed, and frozen at times, like Luna. My past, in which I was a mediocre student skeptical of school, put pressure on the future image I had of myself as a demanding teacher. But all the while, I was kind of loving it.

We made it to the top of Barn Bluff, with zero percent of our students plummeting to their deaths, but retained our one hundred percent record when it came to kids getting scrapes and bruises. Once again, I referred to my childhood oracle, the film *Bloodsport*, to guide my teaching philosophy. In it, a gruff character named Ray Jackson responds to someone at his gym asking whether he is going to Hong Kong to fight in a tournament: "I love anything with full contact. Need a few more scars on my face." Teenagers from the city, hoofing it on a trail, qualified as "full contact." And the scratched shins and forearms, and mud stains on new Nikes were definitely viewed as "scars" by the kids.

Barn Bluff itself was considered a sacred place by the Dakota, because of the burial mounds present there. At the top, I couldn't read the terrain well enough to know where the mounds were, and my eye caught on a tall flagpole that was cemented firmly in the middle of an open grassy area. From it, an American flag snapped in the crisp air. Below us was the town of Red Wing.

The kids spread out, rolling on the grass and chasing each other. Luna stomped her feet on solid ground. With tiny fingers Gao-Jer and Dena stood shoulder to shoulder and traced the path of the Mississippi below, until it twisted out of sight.

Landon was a white kid with long hair who had been recruited to the school by his buddies Mason and Marlowe. He seemed relieved, like many of us, that he had found a place to belong at the school. I saw him standing with his gaze cast out, mapping the islands that dotted the river, reflecting on the landscape like the nineteenth century writer Henry David Thoreau, who was one of Minnesota's first tourists.

Thoreau, who suffered from Tuberculosis, was prescribed a change of climate by his Victorian era doctors—the same remedy as the British patients sent to heal in the dry desert air of Egypt when it was under their colonial rule. Thoreau had visited Barn Bluff, which the Dakota call *He Mni Can,* in 1861, the last years before the entire tribe was exiled from Minnesota.

The exploited and stolen lands that had morally compromised white men, and economically devasted Native people, held the key to the physical and spiritual rebalancing of both cultures. It's the *Dances With Wolves* narrative that I've always felt was compelling. In it the suicidal Civil War veteran, broken by the savagery of the war, seeks solitude at a remote outpost on the frontier. He earns the respect of the Lakota tribe in the area, who seem to be living in a culture that is confident and whole. Eventually, he embraces the wisdom of the Lakota way of life, even though it's far from perfect.

It was easy to see how the 360-degree view from the top of the bluff served as a sacred compass for the Dakota people. The seven directions honored during their prayers were clear; above, below, North, South, East, West and a seventh direction deemed to be difficult for non-Indians to understand.

I didn't pull many punches when it came to the brutal dimensions of the white European settlement of the continent. My approach as a teacher had started out mildly enough. Ms. Allison, the math teacher before Mr. Duvall took over, had taught summer school, and picked up a book and CD called *Flocabulary*. It was created by a Brooklyn outfit that turned American history into a set list of hip-hop songs. Ms. Allison passed it to me at the end of August, a week before the first day of school, my second year teaching at Ms. D's little school.

Flocabulary's first song, "Who Discovered it?" began with Columbus calling out, *"Wow, I just discovered America."* A chorus of Native Americans responds, *"You didn't discover it we were already here."* The song tells the story of how ancient hunter-gatherers crossed over a land bridge from Asia to North America during the last Ice Age, 20,000 years ago. For an assignment, I challenged the kids to memorize the song. Late one night I got a call from Helen, who was in sixth grade at the time.

"Mr. A! I did it!"

"What? Who is this?"

"I did it! I memorized the song from class!"

"Is this Helen?"

"I memorized it, and I taught it to my friend. She go to another school—but she know it by heart now too!"

"Man, that's great!"

"Okay—Bye!"

When Johnny Smith, the guitar playing Ojibwe elder, came to visit, Helen excitedly asked him about that ancient migration from Asia. He paused, rubbed his chin, and said, "Yes, but we don't believe that. We have always been here. It's where the Great Spirit created us." It was a good reminder that the liberal, well-intentioned Brooklyn rappers, didn't necessarily know the score, and were telling a story that an Ojibwe elder didn't recognize. Johnny's answer didn't disappoint Helen. Because of her knowledge of the song, she was able to take part in a conversation. That the conversation made the story of Native Americans more complicated was a win—simplification had made violence against them much easier to do throughout U.S. history.

I became so obsessed with establishing the Native American presence in North America that Kevin called me out: "Mr. A, bro, we learn the same damn thing every year!" The American myth depended on the erasure of Native Americans, and no matter how hard I tried, as soon as I started to tell the story of our country, Native Americans kept slipping back into invisibility. I would start the lesson on Manifest Destiny and America's industrial growth gained quick momentum, burying the footprints of the vanquished. That was why it was such a blessing to have Johnny Smith tread new footprints across the floor of my classroom.

I would revisit the original sin of the Native American genocide each semester. Using examples of treachery and violence like smelling salts, I'd try to remind myself and students just how we got here. My Hmong and black students escaped direct culpability, even relating to the injustice with a sharper acuity. What I didn't have sensitivity for was the effect on my white students. And I still don't know to this day what it was. Like with the story of slavery, I could have instilled a sense of duty to help remedy things, or resentment. The future of the country might depend on which way it cut.

I remembered something else Johnny Smith said that his father had told him; "You can talk all day long and not say a thing in the English language." Doubtful that my lectures of Native American suffering and resilience would add up, I hoped our visits to sacred sites and with elders laid down a more subtle path forward. It taught the endurance of the earth, and wisdom. The humility to lower our heads and ask for guidance on the meaning of the "seventh direction." It was not the path of blame, but reconciliation.

We even took a bus later that spring to the far corner of Southwestern Minnesota. The kids piled out for an emergency bathroom break in a rural town. Farmland expertly squared off by the descendants of German settlers rippled out in all directions. We were headed to view ancient carvings on a small outcropping of reddish Sioux quartzite called the Jeffers Petroglyphs.

The collection of awkward black, Asian, Latino, and white students paraded back to the bus after laying siege to the solitary gas station bathroom for twenty minutes. On their way the kids passed the even-headed gazes of hard-working Lutheran farmers gassing up their pickups. Something to talk about over coffee at the town café. AM talk-radio might call it an invasion, but left to their own devices, the old-timers might say they saw some kids from the city passing through. (Who are the urban counterparts to these temperate old-timers? I imagined a group of elderly black Christians, standing outside a church in downtown Minneapolis, looking up to see a white, rural family heading from a parking lot to the stadium for a Minnesota Twins game.)

At Jeffers the kids took turns crossing the prairie, removing their shoes, and walking amongst carvings, some dating back 7,000 years. The sun shined down on them and one of the oldest continuously used sacred sites in the world. All around, horned turtles, bison, and thunder beings waited patiently for the voice of an elder to bring them to life. Even for us, the uninitiated, the atmosphere was packed with ancestral whispers, but their message was unintelligible, lost in the gentlest breeze.

There were masterful talkers in our group of students—Hmong kids who had heard the tales of Shamans, black kids weaned on the call and response of ecstatic preachers and family storytellers, Latino kids fed folklore from grandmothers in distant Mexican villages. They had their own pipeline to the ancestors.

I found myself worried about my quiet white students, and what heritage they were taking pride in. Swept along as the undisputed stars of American history, their story was at risk of becoming as dull as wallpaper, ignored like a textbook. They were the torchbearers of an increasingly unstylish status quo. While watching TV with my dad on visits, we started to notice a consistent pattern—the middle-aged white men in sitcoms and commercials always being cast as bumbling, out-of-step, and pitiful. Being white might have led to a safer, more cushy material life—a way of life affirmed by the color of the most politically and economically powerful people in the room. But the inspiring, hip, identity-affirming energy was assumed to be along the diverse fringes. Oddly, being white was not included in what was meant by 'diversity,' and frighteningly, neither were ideas.

White people weren't spawning the music, fashion, and dance trends. Yes, on the political and corporate level, they held most of the chips, but their white faces were being sidelined in the darker multi-cultural chic of pop culture. Being an 'other,' an 'outsider,' was at least something to hold on to. When your identity was taken for granted, as part of the white majority, you were never able to learn its contours. A white person was supposed to be who everyone else defined themselves by, but when you're everything, you're also nothing—you're basic. The category of white had no real shape—it was no wonder why many poor, young white men were feeling alienated. They were in a culture that told them they were kings, but when they looked around, they saw the trappings of pauperism and contempt for who they were.

It was not clear how a young white man like Landon could safely engage in identity politics, which made the whole project of identity politics precarious. I was nervous that the sense of belonging other kids were finding, would be elusive for him.

For a white kid—any kid really—to find pride in their past was not a simple task. Landon had to sidestep the wreckage of four hundred years plus of slavery and genocide to cultures in Europe. He could attempt to focus on the neutral traditions of his ancestor's home culture in Scandinavia—and divorce it from American history. He could embrace the inventive, hardworking roots his family had in the pioneer story, but would get with it the tainted advantages won through theft and treachery that had been backed by corrupt laws and the US Cavalry. Or…Landon could join the groups of anxious white people who have decided to double-down on the status quo, with no apologies. This sad alternative embraced the oldest stand-by identity in the country: superior race. White supremacy paraded itself around as forceful and confident—it had appeal. But in the end, it was another case of resentment, fear, and insecurity, where all problems were projected onto other groups. The same trap that black people fell into when they joined separatist groups, leaned into victimhood, or claimed the superiority of the black race.

It was not fair to tell a thirteen-year-old white kid that his great-grandfather had blood on his hands that he was responsible to wash off—that he was stained until society was cleared of inequity. It was a conundrum though. If African Americans and Native Americans still bore the damage of oppression, even in their genes, as some claimed, how could white people have escaped their own circuitry being warped by the past? Whether American's liked it or not they were all steeped in trauma. There was a frantic effort to confirm or deny its influence on the economic place in society many people of color found themselves, but just as deserving of attention was the moral toll it had taken on white people, the so-called victors.

I hoped that a white kid like Landon could bravely learn and decide *for himself* what debts were owed. I began to think it was a personal, psychological, quest that would lead us towards more racial harmony—not a systemic overthrow based on group generalizations. Because only on a personal level could debts be repaid without resentment, uncontaminated by coercion and the fear of being called a racist. But likewise, a black or Native kid should be able to decide whether they wanted collecting those debts to even be a part of their identity. It's a choice they should have as well. Because there are many people of color who appreciate the so-called "status-quo" of today, are grateful for how far we've come as a country, and mindful of the scale of struggles going on for people outside America's borders.

At Barn Bluff, the wind picked up and Landon's blonde hair flew in the same direction as the large American flag flapping on the forty-foot pole. I expected him to burst out singing a rock ballad from the 1980's. I loved his smile and gentle demeanor, and stood back watching him. I took out my new phone and a got a clip that would end up in the yearly eighth-grade graduation video in May.

It was a new flagpole that Landon was standing next to, just installed that year. The previous flagpole had succumbed to vandalism back in the sixties. A local veteran had recently taken on the restoration project. He was an old white man. He found out that the old cement foundation sat atop Native American burial mounds, so the new pole mount was moved sixty-three feet south. Measurable by inches, but progress.

THERE'S A TRUISM in social science circles; an era can't be named until it's over. When the thrust of law-making and action got diluted after Martin Luther King Jr.'s assassination, the Civil Rights Movement found its moniker but lost its momentum. A basketball or football dynasty seals off its legacy only after losing the championship the next year. Childhood "ends" and adulthood "begins" the first time you hear yourself saying, "When I was little…"

In the middle of May of my fourth year, Maloney, Ms. Tracy, Ms. Conley, Mr. Duvall, and I were asked to a meeting. Later, I would remember this meeting as the day we began to name an era. The meeting was in Maloney's science room, and when I entered, I saw two sharply dressed young professionals, and a white board polished to a shine. The man and woman were the assured, articulate types I saw in downtown Minneapolis in the summer—close to Target corporate headquarters, having beers at Brits Pub. I had a passing insecurity that Mr. Duvall would ditch us to join them—that he would leave our scrappy rebellion within public education, for the serious business of making money. And then, when he looked around his office and found no one like Ruby—he would realize his mistake. Mr. Duvall could try to fortify himself with the hologram of meaning that wealth affords—charity, volunteering, political contributions. But 'meaningful' work? That was the card we had as teachers. And, no matter what, we had that part of our lives covered.

There was an exciting, practical reason for the late spring meeting. Ms. D had the blueprints for a sprawling new school campus, and big grants were lined up to fund it. Corporate sponsors were drawn to our stories of success—i.e., the rising test scores. (We'd gladly be willing to *benefit* from companies trying to take part in meaningful work.) The philosophy of the school just needed to be refined. Our idiosyncratic formula needed easier handling qualities as it was promoted to donors that could help propel the move and make it sustainable.

Dreamy talk was made of $100,000 dollar salaries for teachers. I didn't flinch at the six-figure number when Ms. D first discussed it, and would have asked for a raise the next year. A hundred grand would be a reasonable start for a teacher in a country that valued education. If teachers were pegged as glorified babysitters, the low six-digit salary still left us underpaid. I thought for a moment

I would be able to have my cake and eat it, too—meaning *and* money.

When I took the most cursory glance at what other people did during a workday—besides nurses—I felt that we earned with our efforts salaries that could be thrice in size. Maloney however, considered himself a blue-collar worker, but he wouldn't have minded the boost, so he could at least have matched the hourly wage of a union plumber. With that kind of teacher salary, we maybe could have held onto talent like Mr. Duvall.

Sitting down next to my colleagues in Maloney's science room, I squirmed a little when I realized we were in a meeting with branding consultants hired by Ms. D. They earnestly needed our help in sketching out the qualities that made our school what it was. Ms. Tracy and Maloney kicked it off by trying to outline our collective passion. With carefully chosen words, they strained to describe a sort of fluid mission statement, consisting of tidbits of school folklore, and the permission granted by Ms. D to allow love and family values into the classroom.

I fumbled around myself trying to nail down a definition of our school culture. It was a network of free-flowing trust and freedom, born out of bold risks, forgiveness, and encouragement. All of it touched off by the tone set by Ms. D.

The consultants nodded their heads and made sounds of approval, filling the pristine whiteboard with words. Early on, I noticed that they were trimming down the sweep of our odyssey into catch phrases.

Before we knew it, we were brainstorming new names for the school.

Twenty-Six

LUCKILY OUR MOJO was such that the golden era of Ms. D's little school had not quite ended. After the meeting in May concluded, the search for a new name receded. We remained a vital, unwieldy entity, unable to be pinned down onto an appealing brochure.

Graduation night arrived, and we wished another set of irreplaceable eighth-graders goodbye. But why can't I remember all their names now? Why aren't I attending their college graduations and weddings? I had to admit I was not that kind of teacher. I viewed my students like people I met on my travels; people that I was lucky enough to have a chance encounter with on a train, or at a hostel. People I ate meals with, and shared great conversations, and even could have become dear friends with. But in the end, we honored each other with a hug and clean getaway. I don't remember making any promises or breaking them.

Maloney, on the other hand, was able to maintain nurturing relationships with many of the students—with the caveat that they didn't contact him until after they turned eighteen. I was able to put students out of my mind so quickly, I felt there might be something wrong with me, something cold. But as an introvert, I didn't have the emotional or social storage space for juggling a large network of former students. I leaned on my traveler's point of view. The kids and I were headed separate ways, and I satisfied myself that there was movement in their lives.

Despite my desire for clean breaks, we did give our eighth-graders long goodbyes. And after graduation that year, we had a special treat for them. Ms. Conley brought us all to her family cabin in Wisconsin for an overnight. Kids spent two sunny days at Ms. Conley's cabin clumsily paddling canoes in circles. When they floated too close to the dock, they were easy targets. I saw Adam and Javion line up together on the edge of the dock and leap off for a cannon ball attack. The canoes were swamped time and again. How often in life would these young people, having fun, splashing in the water, suddenly find themselves in a sinking boat?

I looked at Adam, cranking on the edge of the canoe so that it'd completely fill with water, while four girls screamed and swatted him with paddles. We'd helped him out a lot at Ms. D's school. He was happier, if not a better student. He was part of our community, but he was leaving now. How often would he be the cause of a boat flipping—and would there be kids, or a girlfriend, going down with him?

Another summer of bliss went by, with quick-fire road trips and breakfast burritos with Dan at The French Meadow. My son was in the glory days of childhood. He was old enough to run down the street *and* around the corner to press hard on the doorbell of his friend's house. I found myself feeling very free.

Pumped from my P90X workout challenge, I ran long stretches of the Winchell Trail—a dirt path established by the Dakota that traced the Mississippi gorge between the Minnehaha Waterfall by my house and St. Anthony Falls in what is now downtown Minneapolis. As a teacher, time was my luxury, and in July I felt I had all the time in the world.

Even though I knew it was coming, August managed to sneak up from behind me. It easily put me in a chokehold and dragged me to the ground. My face was pressed to the grass, grass that was still green. August forced me to turn my head towards September and the school year. I had no choice but to tap out and submit. I got up, brushed myself off, and put away the road atlas and camping gear. I dug in the closet for my school bag, where I had buried it deep at the end of May.

I had a consolation though. When I got in the car and drove to school on the last week of August for teacher preparation week, I knew I was going to a place that I loved, with people I trusted.

I walked in the doors of Ms. D's little school and picked up my free Horace Mann Teacher Planner that was sitting in my mailbox, and dropped my bag in my classroom. Then, as usual, I headed down to the dreary cafeteria for our beginning of the year meeting. The staff circled up and we began to share our tales of pilgrimage to the school. My fifth year as a teacher had officially begun.

Mr. Steven, an educational assistant who had taken over when Mr. Shane left, was a touch shaken when his turn came to share. The last school year, I had relied on Mr. Steven's confident and measured handling of student discipline. His favorite line after a rowdy kid continued to revolt was, "One and done." Pleading for a kid to comply was not Mr. Steven's bag. The kids therefore didn't wait for it, and usually started working instead. I had given so many worthless, meandering speeches trying to redirect students that I envied his brevity.

Like many of the teachers at Ms. D's little school, he was a devout Christian. At the circle he mentioned that he had spent time volunteering in East Africa that summer with his wife who was a doctor. During his trip to Africa, they had been at a refugee camp, and he had seen open suffering.

"There were kids with distended bellies and…" His eyes teared and he abruptly stopped.

A hush lingered. I waited for Mr. Steven to clap his hands, rub them together, and claim to be ready for a new school year. But he sat back quietly.

There was a distracted energy during the meeting, and I chalked it up to teachers still having half their heads in summer mode. Ms. D gave some updates about the state of school, and there was even mention of a waitlist to get into our school. A waitlist?

That was the ultimate sign that things were going in the right direction.

Seeing Ms. Conley, Mr. Duvall, and Maloney brought a smile to my face, but there was a shadow, a note of discord, in the larger group. But the meeting ended, and we went to our own rooms to get them ready for the year.

AT THE FIRST day of school assembly all the grades poured into the gym. Once they were seated Mr. Barnett hit play on the Black Eyed Peas hit, "I Gotta Feeling."

The teachers rose and did a dance routine to the song and the kids cheered. The doubts or weird vibes I'd felt at the meeting were gone and another year found its tune.

I had been less stressed during the run up to that school year. Not because I was more organized but because I knew I would be relying on hopscotching from one rich set piece of an outing or project to another. I could lay out the scope and sequence of the year's lessons only to see it turned to ruin the minute kids walked in the door with their own agendas. From where I stood, it was arbitrary what was included and excluded in the social studies standards and curriculum. Without a forceful agenda or compelling narrative, the bulleted topics on the standards never held together. And like I said, the day they lock down social studies standards will be a scary day in America, because that would mean an agenda *was* being enforced.

Instead, in my class we workshopped an open-ended screenplay. In it the students and I took turns writing about the sort of world we wanted and acted it out when we could. It was a world with a lot of art, meaningful questions, friendship, and time outside. Ms. D had moved me to a new room the year before and I had not rebuilt an altar. I'd learned that there was no need to spray paint anything in black because there was already a big altar that we could use. It was the shape of a planet. All I had to do was get my students outside where their footsteps would become prayers, the breaths of fresh air their offerings of gratitude, and what caught their eyes judged and forgiven for the beauty it did or didn't hold.

When we had to stay in the building, we asked other questions. Why were we in a room together? What made us Americans? Our purpose was contested every single day. We groped around in the darkness of the past, seeking out the handling qualities of history to try to make sense of our world. Some days we just gave up and hung out together. It wasn't a deft pedagogical scheme; I just didn't know, and so can you. The beauty of America was that we didn't need to know who we were; we could decide. The Constitution and Bill of Rights, in honest hands, left a space open for all of us to pick a story to believe in that let us sleep at night, and in the morning left us optimistic.

CAMP ST. CROIX was scheduled early that year. The weather was warm, and the kids were able to enjoy their sessions with the camp counselors. Kiara, a favorite of Ms. D, proved to be a master archer. As a teacher I didn't catalogue the gory details of her less-than-ideal home life. Eating ramen three meals a day was the tip of the iceberg, and I left it to others to overinvest in solving the monumental societal shortcomings that led to her mother's struggle, and then her own. But her mom kept trying and so did she, and I tried to do no harm for the hour or so that I was with her in class Monday through Friday.

"Yep," Ms. D told me one day, "Kiara will come into my office and walk around the table a few times between classes."

"Why?"

"She's just making sure I'm there. That's what she does."

At the archery range I saw Kiara standing with her back straight. The bow is pulled to her ear and her hand is brushing the combed-out poof of her black hair. It was the same hand with the thumb she always had in her mouth. The arrow flew into the target. It wasn't a bullseye, but it showed a hand that might become steady enough to get a job, pay the bills, maybe write a new chapter.

At another station Mr. K.O. threw on a hard hat and raced Curtis to the top of a climbing wall. K.O. won and started to roast Curtis. The two of them dangled with their crotches smashed into harnesses. They were slowly lowered to the ground like loud spiders.

"Man, you are really a sorry-ass! You let an old man beat you! Ha!"

"Be quiet bro, I want a rematch!"

On a ropes course Maloney tried an unorthodox technique, got flipped upside down and hung with his face two inches from the ground like Tom Cruise in *Mission Impossible*. Amelie's dimples flexed in a smile, and being half of Maloney's weight, she was able to climb and wobble on the ropes up past him for the win.

We ate mediocre lasagna in the cafeteria, sat through a reptile show given by a sleepy naturalist, and were soon sitting around the campfire. Student clusters of three sat wrapped in single blankets. Duane, a Hmong boy familiar with nights around a campfire stood close, nudging the logs with a stick. There were no talent-show antics this year. The beautiful night called for a different type of storytelling.

I'm not sure how someone can be a teacher and not know how to tell a story. I couldn't figure out what teachers were relying on in class. Repeated instructions? Step-by-step directions? Examples and modeling? Even a novice parent turns a spoonful of peas into an airplane.

The elementary teachers, who never came to Camp St. Croix, were better at holding on to the skill and made it work through tiny stories wrapped in fun and song. But as kids got older, especially in traditional public schools, it seemed that classrooms were packed with discrete facts and figures. The worst teachers lined them up and got students to choke the information down like dry chunks of meat and potatoes, solely through the threat of tests and grades.

My classes were filled with stories, not only because that's a big part of what social studies is, but because I didn't know how to hold the kids' attention otherwise. I sometimes exclusively counted on the 70,000-year-old human strategy for encoding information to do the work for me. I could have been deluding myself though. The reality was that students would often be confused after I finished a tale or analogy to illustrate some point. They were waiting for the *real* work to be assigned.

In my mind, the students were already done when I finished a story; listening, and the effort to understand *was* the work. But they had been trained to see work as not something the mind does, but a piece of paper that can be turned in to a teacher. They wanted to get the assignment done. The school day was long, and society had set the terms for success: fill in the blanks. I remember at the end of a triumphant storytelling performance in class a kid asked me, "So what am I supposed to *do*?"

Because of the success of Ms. D's school there were many adult visitors—the Education Commissioner of Minnesota even stopped in my room one day. Adult classroom visitors liked to ask my students the loaded question, "So what are you guys learning in social studies?" My students did not always know what to say. It was embarrassing for me in the moment, but also a badge of honor.

Storytelling, the educational cash-cow of pre-literate humanity, didn't lead to the quantifiable outcomes that the modern world craved. The result was that adults saw it as a fun but unproductive way of killing time with students, and the students relaxed a bit and listened because it was not really *work*. Storytelling, however, was shaped in the workshops of stone-age psychologists and perfected over millennia. A stubborn teenage mind was no match for its subtlety. As a story followed its only rule—the need for a beginning, middle and end—lessons slipped inside the mind.

Ms. Conley moved into the firelight, a sparkle in her eye. The flames were inviting, a natural setting for stories. Desks, books, computers, were nowhere in sight. There was no "Work Turn-in" basket. Kids rocked and hugged each other as the night cooled.

Above them the age-old audience of stars waited patiently for the storyteller to begin.

Other Loyalties

Ms. Conley unfolded her arms. The toe of her tall leather boot reached out to brush a pinecone across the dirt. She had played soccer in college, and it was an instinct.

"Once upon a time there was an old motel along the highway not far from here…"

The kids were experts at winding themselves up when it came to horror stories. As Ms. Conley dropped in the details—a woman alone, a dark hallway, a peephole, footsteps—students ratcheted up the tension with their own commentary.

"Her dumb self—she better not open the door."

"Hell no, I would not do that."

"Nah-uh, you better stop Ms. Conley."

"Shut up! I know that's you making that sound Jeremiah."

"I'm not walking back to the cabin when we done."

"Shh…Shut up! I want to hear what happens."

Ms. Conley left the kids with a sudden image of a bloody eye staring in at them from the peephole of the motel room door and sat back down. Her story, that perhaps matched her style as a teacher, was a crowd-pleaser, and accessible. Each kid understood what was going on in the story and in her classroom. That was her art. There was a sense of belonging each student had when she was in charge, and she looked them all in the eye, to make sure they were in the motel getting spooked with the rest of the class.

The shouts and disgusted turbulence that Ms. Conley's jump-scare ending produced subsided. There was an uncomfortable shifting among the adults, who dreaded being put on the spot. But by now the kids and everyone else knew who was going next: Maloney.

A master raconteur, he honed his craft before countless fires on trips with his family, Boy Scouts, and church youth groups. Each word was chosen with precision—like a carpenter fitting the jambs of a door. When the set-up was finished, Maloney led the kids over the threshold into a darker realm. As the tale unspooled, a lively haunting creeped over the camp—from the river, through the woods, and back from the past where some thieves and an old gypsy combined for a murderous night.

Maloney spoke dialogue with a 1950's wise-guy accent and painted a menacing picture of an ill-fated rowboat trip under the moonlight. I loved watching kids listening to a story—a form of benevolent hypnosis. A weird balance of paying attention and getting utterly lost in a new world played out across their faces.

Maloney's story left kids with an uneasy feeling. Instead of a jump scare they were tangled up in the moral ambiguity that the tale had ended with. Shadowy fingers reached out from the corrupted souls of the characters, leaving the kids quiet and sober, disturbed and fulfilled. They had something to chew on. They were left to wonder if they too had these shadows inside them.

How did Maloney's story reflect his style as a teacher? Packed with details, some crucial, some decorative, he required the kids to use their scientific minds to follow the mystery and find their footing. Could they separate causation from correlation, among the muffled cries, bloody, dripping blade, and single paddle left on a muddy riverbank?

Duane tossed a log on the fire, a brief veil of sparks separated me from the seated kids and when they burned out, I saw their eyes on me. I put on a coy act at first, and then heard them calling.

"Come on, Mr. A!"

I took a deep breath and placed myself in front of the fire—the holy lectern that would be ashes by morning, where nameless ancestors brought to life the untouchable forces that held the world together.

Following Maloney's cue, I moved them farther off the trail of terror. I'd fractured their peace of mind the year before with a "true" story about how Camp St. Croix had to close for a few years after an inmate escaped from the nearby jail and visited the camp with a hatchet.

I decided to make the full break from the Halloween colonization of campfire storytelling and told them the ancient Persian tale of "Mushkil Gusha—The Remover of Difficulties." It's a tale about a poor woodcutter, and his little daughter. He works all day

Other Loyalties

cutting wood which he brings down to the village to sell. With the money that he earns, he is able to buy a small amount of food for he and his daughter.

One day his daughter tells him that she wishes they could have some different, better food to eat. The old woodcutter goes out to cut twice as much wood and becomes exhausted and lost. When he had first set out, he had been full of hope, but that had not helped him. He starts to cry but finds that that is no use. Cold and hungry, he lays down and falls asleep.

Soon after, he wakes up and he is colder and hungrier than before. Since it's impossible to go back to sleep he starts telling himself the story of everything that had happened to him since his daughter asked him for a different kind of food. While he's telling himself the story of himself, he thinks he hears another voice, calling out from the dawn. The voice asks him what he is doing, and he replies that he is telling himself his own story.

The voice asks to hear the tale, and then instructs the old woodcutter to close his eyes and take a step. The woodcutter says that he does not see a step and the voice tells him to just do as he is told. He lifts his right foot, and when he sets it down, he finds that there is something solid under it. The woodcutter starts to go up what seems to be a staircase. The staircase starts moving up faster and faster, and when the woodcutter becomes frightened, the voice tells him to not open his eyes until he is told to do so.

When the woodcutter opens his eyes, he is in a desert surrounded by piles of pebbles that are red, blue, green, and white. The voice tells him to take as many pebbles as he can, close his eyes, and descend back down the staircase. When he opens his eyes he's back at the door of his cottage. He explains what happened to his daughter who is confused by the tale. But she is happy that he is safe, and they share their last bit of food together, a handful of dates.

When they finish, the old man hears the voice again, and it tells him that he has been saved by Mushkil Gusha—The Remover of Difficulties. It was now his duty to offer the needy some dates or give a gift to someone who can help the needy in the name of

Mushkil Gusha, and tell the tale each Thursday night. He must make sure that the tale is never, never forgotten. If this is done, and the people he tells the tale to do the same, then the truly needy will always find their way.

The next day he sells the extra bundles of wood he had collected for a good price and brings home some delicious new food. He and his daughter enjoy the food, and he tells her the tale of Mushkil Gusha. Life carries on like normal for the next week; he collects wood, and brings it to the market where he never has trouble finding a buyer. The next Thursday, as happens with humans, the old woodcutter forgets to tell the tale, and fails to help his neighbors when they come to the door and ask for help relighting their lamps. After shutting the door on his neighbors' faces, he discovers that the pebbles, which he had put in a corner of his cottage are starting to glow. He and his daughter cover them up with some rags, so no one else can see their treasure. In the morning the ordinary pebbles have turned to precious gems.

The woodcutter sells the gems and he and his daughter build a palace next to the king of their country. This king had a beautiful daughter who was a bit bothered by this palace that suddenly popped up seemingly out of nowhere. She sends her servants to investigate and when they return, they tell her, as best they can, how this came to be. The princess sends for the woodcutter's daughter, and though she is angry when they meet, they end up liking each other and become friends. They start meeting up by a stream to swim together and one day the princess takes off her valuable necklace and hangs it on a branch.

When the princess gets home, she can't find her necklace and accuses the woodcutter's daughter of stealing it. The woodcutter's little daughter is thrown in an orphanage, and the old woodcutter is arrested and put in a dungeon. After some time, he is brought to the town square where he is abused and yelled at by the townspeople. Over time they grow used to the presence of the old man and eventually ignore him—occasionally throwing him scraps of food.

One day he overhears that it is Thursday, and he realizes how much time had passed since he had told the story of Mushkil Gusha. Just as this thought entered his head, a nice man passed by and threw him a tiny coin. The old woodcutter thanks him but says that money is no use to him. What would be better is if the man could buy him a couple dates and sit beside him. The man goes and returns with some dates and the woodcutter tells him the tale of Mushkil Gusha. The man thinks that it is a strange tale and believes the old woodcutter must be crazy. But he is a kindly man, and when he returns home, he finds that all his problems are gone.

The next day, the princess finds her missing necklace by the stream and realizes her mistake. The daughter is brought out of the orphanage and the woodcutter is released and given a public apology. There are many more incidents in the tale of Mushkil Gusha, and it never really ends. Because of him, the tale is remembered, somewhere, by somebody, day and night, wherever there are people.

At Camp St. Croix, it was Thursday night.

The story had a strange effect. It did not entertain, rally together, and enliven the students, like Ms. Conley's story, nor did it fire up their minds like Maloney's. As a woman, did Ms. Conley's story and teaching style hinge on emotional risk-taking? She was more open and vulnerable with students than I was, and it seemed to lead to classes that were gelled and productive. Emotional risks were scary territory for me. As a man, did Maloney's style depend more on intellectual risk? A scientist must be okay with being constantly wrong, until a hypothesis pans out, and kids seemed much more open to trying and failing in his class than mine. These are run-of-the-mill gender stereotypes, the ones I'm supposed to guard against in service of the kids in my class. But where did that leave my story and teaching style?

The kids had been quiet and thoughtful while I told the story but not linked together or riveted. Was my style more touch-and-go, more subtle? The story had an ordinary message of kindness and generosity, woven into a tale of invisible staircases and piles of colorful pebbles. But the idea that an unseen force would come to their aid was not so far-fetched for students. They were on the edge of adulthood but still relied on adults to magically fill the refrigerator with "delicious" food, pay the heating bill, and arrive out of the sky to pick them up from the mall. They hoped that this same force would give them big hints about how to solve the problem of what to do with the rest of their lives. Had the story overlayed a transparent map onto their lives that somehow would help guide them, but they were hardly aware of? This all sounded like the claims of a charlatan. But the story of Mushkil Gusha was the sort of story kids heard from time to time in my classroom. At the very least they had learned to not wait for a punchline.

Maybe in their spare time, students wrestled with the meanings of the stories. There would inevitably come times in their lives when they'd be like the old woodcutter, completely alone, hungry, and lost. Would they know that these were the empty, anguished moments, when it was possible for them to finally be honest and tell themselves the story of how they got to where they were in their lives? Only then might great forces from the unseen world come to their aid. It wouldn't be their parents anymore. It wouldn't be the government. It might be themselves finally taking responsibility for their lives and becoming adults. It might be like Harry Potter, in *The Prisoner of Azkaban,* realizing that the figure across the lake that cast the spell that saved him from the life-sucking dementors, was, in fact, himself.

I had often told kids that the only thing I really cared about in class was that students were nice to each other. There were times that I thought that my expectations were too low, and this minimal requirement was evidence of it. Did it matter that I didn't have rigorous academic work centered in my room, or that I didn't force them to analyze the "deeper" meanings of stories, just let them sink in?

The fire crackled, and I heard Maloney sigh and say, "Ahh, Mooshkill-La-Goosha." I knew he'd appreciate that tale.

Other Loyalties

A few kids peeled off to go to the safety and familiarity of the cabins—exhausted from a day outside. Some others tiptoed away to plot and flirt. Low-key kids who preferred the company of adults lingered: Valentina, Amelie, Raya, Lucia, Brianna, Tabari, their names a form of storytelling themselves. We all stood around the red coals talking.

Finally, the wild screams from the field by the cabins lured us into the fray.

We all ran around for a couple hours. Maloney and I worked a rough perimeter, scaring kids and keeping them close to the cabins, like demented shepherds. Either side of the flimsy wooden doors of the cabins, groups of kids pushed to defend their territory, or to break in.

Around midnight I sat down on my bunk and counted the boys. Edgar's curly locks and round face appeared from under a sleeping bag.

"Is anyone still out there Mr. A?"

"I think that's about it."

Andy, a clean-cut Hmong kid, was digging out his toothbrush. He was following his mom's orders. I've been told by Hmong friends that boys can sometimes be spoiled in Hmong culture, but if Andy was being groomed for anything, it was a dapper hard-working entrepreneur or politician, with impeccable manners. Tou Mong, his buddy who always had a football in his hand and sports jersey on his back, agreed to walk to the bathroom with him.

When they returned, a couple kids asked if they saw anyone, worried that they might be missing something.

"No, there's nobody out," Andy said. "Just Jodie M. running around trying to scare the girls."

It had been a full day, a real day. Surely it was over. I started to untie my shoes. The visit from the branding specialists the year before had got me thinking. They were like the guy at the party who asks the seemingly harmless question, "Are you having a good time?" The question that kills the vibe. I felt dislocated by the lingering task of finding a new name for the school. It made me think that one day I'd be telling the story of Ms. D's little school to wide-eyed kids, in a traditional school, who would think that I was making it all up.

Just then there was a loud pounding on the door.

"Oh shit!"

"It's a raid!"

"Get the door! Block the door!"

Tou Mong hopped up and ran, followed by Tabari and Jeremiah.

Tou Mong lowered his shoulder to the door but suddenly stopped. Then he stood up, peeked through the window again, and opened the door. There, blazing in the porch light, was Ms. D. Like an ancient prophet, she had come to release us from the bondage of our assumptions about what nights were for, and what life was for.

"Ms. D!"

"Ms. D, what's going on?" Tabari asked.

"What are you guys doing in bed?" she asked. "Aren't you going to play midnight tag?"

Twenty-Seven

IN OCTOBER OF my fifth year teaching, my daughter was born. Ms. D's policy for time off for personal matters was "come back when you're ready." I had a student teacher who took over, one of three I had that year. Each one was better than I was at communicating with students. The kids' relief was apparent as soon as the student teacher got his lessons going. At last, class was held the way it was supposed to: a step-by-step march towards obvious goals.

Kendrick used to harass me about my, at times, inscrutable lessons, "Mr. A, why you making things difficult?"

"Man, if I make it easy, what do you think will happen?" I said.

"I'll get my work done and be able to chill."

"No."

"What chu' mean "no"?

"What would happen if I made it easy is that the question *and* answer would go from my mouth to your piece of paper."

"*Man*, that's what I'm talking about. Then I'd be done."

"But the lesson would have missed touching something."

"What?"

"Your own mind."

"Mr. A, you suspicious and you giving suspicious answers."

The student teacher gave Kendrick and other students a taste of measured, coherent lessons. (He also gave them the taste of Skittles and Starbursts when they followed directions—something I never did.) My own chaotic style, born out of my allergic reaction to doing unit by unit lesson planning, unsettled them. Comparing myself to the student teacher I started to feel like I had been selfish in my classroom. How many students had felt lost and "stupid" during my lessons? If they were hearty, like Kendrick, they could deal with my philosophical snobbery—but what about the rest?

Cynicism crept in, and for a dark moment, I considered taking the whole house down with me. Out of self-preservation, I never said it out loud, but I thought it might be a bad idea to have social studies taught in schools, period. At worst, it was fertile ground for propaganda and brainwashing—nationalism and conformity. With more force and top-down control students could easily be given marching orders to head towards a specific destiny for the country, which might be patriotic glory in a Darwinian global competition. The government could require the teaching of heroic anecdotes to supercharge the standard American narrative of progress. It would be a repetitive, jingoistic Top 40 playlist, that could drown out the folksy puzzle of our country's motto, *E pluribus Unum*. Did a country's unity depend on loyalty to a single identity imposed from above?

There were examples of what social studies education could look like at its worst. In the late 1950's, my father was in school during a burst of Arab nationalism in Egypt. He remembers getting pounded with slogans, and then, given a gun. A glance at the current aims of secondary social studies education in China reveals what can be called an educational security state. In this educational security state, strength and pride are emphasized. State-authorized memories make up the history curriculum and any examination of contemporary issues or criticism of the country is deflected onto adversaries like the US or Japan. In both the cases of Egypt and China, a social studies education serves the purpose of national unity. It makes clear just what an Egyptian or Chinese citizen looks like. But such an education neglects the skills needed in a democracy: independent thought, diversity of opinion, and a willingness to honestly examine society's problems in the open.

For years, social studies in America was viewed as a non-descript class on student schedules, that was irrelevant to their futures. There wasn't the urgency around the curriculum that has recently surfaced. Traditionally, it was a class period filled with fun facts and nerdy diversions for the rare kid who was a history buff. We were to touch on the milestones of US history in a bland way and prepare citizens to carry on passively, since the system seemed to be working—America was number one in the world after all. Why mess with the formula? Most students were bored, casually "hated" social studies (not like their visceral hatred of math), or felt they were in a class that meant nothing. But no real harm done.

Overseeing a potentially meaningless class could have been depressing, but I found it liberating. On the one hand, the branches of social studies—history, anthropology, geography, psychology—were dismissed as not being serious sciences, on the other they were a potential political flashpoint. I found that in the limbo that trapped social studies between being a "soft" science and culture-war hot spot, there was a hidden passageway. It led to a secret room, a third option, that no one knew about. I tried to hold my classes there.

It worked like this: it was natural for a kid to think it didn't make sense why they had to be in a classroom every day, and I would validate this feeling, agreeing that we might just be wasting our time. It was an uncomfortable feeling at first, acknowledging that we might be engaged in something pointless. But because the brain is a pattern-recognition machine it will engage with any sense-making challenge, whether it's a story, math equation, or block of time. In this secret room I tried to allow the brains of my students to work on this puzzle: Where are we sitting? How did we come to be sitting here? Do we have the power to not sit here? What are the costs of sitting here? How do we feel about sitting here? What would happen if we all stood up and left? Questions that, in the end, helped create the disciplines of social studies: geography, history, politics, economics, psychology, and sociology.

Like prisoners staring hard at the bricks in a wall day after day, our imaginations eventually turned the bricks into stepping-stones, and story panels.

When I presented students with weird questions, open-ended projects, and my own doubt and confusion about the nature of the world, they revolted at first because that's not how school is supposed to work. It's supposed to be a game where the all-knowing teacher doles out information and then the students repeat the information and reproduce it. That's why my more straightforward student teachers were embraced with such relief.

The student revolt to my approach was the first step in reconnecting them to a natural state of being, one in which the brain, evolved to handle problem-solving situations, seeks to arrange events and artifacts in a way that make sense—in order to survive. When students showed up each day there was no telling what we'd be doing—it produced anxiety and a type of mental exercise.

Knowing what I know now about traumatized kids, and their need for stability and predictability, I wonder how taxing and stressful my classes were for them. I refused to give straight answers, and the unresolved questions and choices I left floating around made some kids shut down for good, I'm sure. To make lessons easily accessible and orderly would have done these kids a lot of good—but it would have come at a price. To say the least, I relied heavily on Ms. Sasha, Ms. Tiffany, Mr. Steven, Mr. Hank, Ms. Danika, and everyone else who had to deal with my frustrated students.

Like Kendrick, some kids picked up on the fact that my room wasn't going to be a place where there was a right answer. Their status rank in my eyes did not depend on how well they lined up their ducks, or whether they were the first to raise their hands. They began to stop seeking me out as the source of knowledge in the room. Others concluded that I was unhelpful, and they were alone with their work. A few took their first baby steps into self-knowledge.

I tried to erase myself as the teacher. But in my quest to do no harm, to avoid indoctrinating students with the lies of the nation or my own lies, real harm was done to students who needed more concrete material. There was an array of students who struggled in my classes: very low readers, who didn't have the skills to do the independent work, kids dealing with trauma, but also straight-A students that thrived on the game of school, who could not figure out which boxes to check in my room.

I used to look at my confused students trying to engage in lessons in a way that was part of *their* plan, not mine. Like all of us, they searched for solutions that fit their worldview—but on occasion expanded it by taking on alternative perspectives. For example, one day I stood in front of a large world map and asked the students where power was in the world. I handed volunteers a sticky note that said 'power' and they placed it somewhere on the map and explained why. I was preoccupied with a critique of the effects of colonialism, lingering from my college days, and assumed my attitude had rubbed off on students by now. I fully expected a student to pin the tail on the power and wealth hording countries of Europe.

Thankfully, it wasn't long before students were sticking the notecard on sources of power that weren't on the map. Najah reached up, stuck the card above the map and shyly whispered, "The sun? Don't we need it for everything?" Amelie went up next, pulled the notecard off, but then stopped and left it, saying, "What about the moon too? Doesn't it make the tides go out in the oceans?" Mark, stepped up during third period, and found Jerusalem on the map. After pressing his thumb on the card to make sure it stayed, he said, "Probably what is behind a lot of stuff that goes on in the world is what people believe in, so maybe religion?" Finally, during the last class of the day, when we were all tired, Zion raised his hand. He took the card and stuck it onto Dante's forehead, and said, "This fool. He got the power to irritate me."

I tried to encourage some reluctant kids to participate but some just sat there with too much on their minds from stuff going on at home. I'd like to think it was a form of unconditional love between us, letting some students flounder so much, just go to sleep, or give up day after day with no consequences. But could it have been incompetence and laziness on my part? Why wasn't I demanding more or changing my style so I could reach them?

Thinking of my lax discipline and loose assignments, I didn't think I was capable of tough love—the kind I sometimes assumed these hold-out students needed. But tough love may have been at work in a way I didn't recognize as such. I'd only go so far to help a student—they had to stand up and meet me halfway.

I tried to provoke kids who never came to class prepared.

"Kevin, where's your pencil?"

"Man, I don't got one."

"You're like a samurai without a sword—you've showed up for battle empty-handed."

"This ain't no fight."

"What is it then?"

"It's second period."

"Kevin, *the pencil is mightier than the sword!*"

"Stop." He eyed the pencil I was waving around in his face. "Are you going to give me that so I can work?"

"Dante, where's *your* pencil?"

"I don't know."

"So, are you going to starve to death?"

"What?"

"The pencil is your tool to eat. It's your spoon—it's how you can feed yourself as a student!"

"Man, can I just get one?"

Later in the class period I'd circle back and see that the pencils were broken, thrown across the room, or sitting idly on the table.

"What happened?"

"This stuff is boring," Dante complained.

"But do you agree it still needs to get done?"

"Yeah."

"It's not that bad. Malcolm X changed his name a few times. Mother Theresa did too. That's all the essay is about. Why would someone change their name?" I took out another pencil. "Here's

Other Loyalties

another spoon. Do I need to spoon feed you or can you feed yourself?"

Kevin laughed.

"What you laughing at? You ain't done nothin' either. Look at your blank-ass page," Dante responded.

I took Kevin's paper and wrote a sentence starter: *I think people change their names because...* "There, I gave Kevin a spoonful of applesauce."

"You being disrespectful Mr. A," Kevin said, grabbing the pencil out of my hand. "Okay, go away. I'm working now."

"What about you Dante?"

"Don't touch *my* paper. I've got a mouth and hands—I ain't going hungry when they something good to eat." Dante pointed to the paper. "This here is dry as hell. I can't eat no dry food."

"Don't starve!" I called out, before running to another table before he could line up his comeback. Much of the work on paper was not very edible for Dante, skill-wise, nor culturally. Discussions, and interactive lessons were a better bet for him, they had sauce.

If I'm honest, there was a touch of disinterest too in my attitude as a teacher. I felt that if I was overly invested in the efforts of my students, I'd end up co-opting and influencing the direction of their work, creating a sort of intellectual brand empire that I wasn't interested in. If I stepped too far in between them and their thoughts and connected the dots it would be a form of theft. I didn't want to be in the way when something clicked. They should get that payoff, but it required a lot of groping around in the dark.

Ms. D told me a story about a teacher she couldn't stand back at a school in Wisconsin. The insights shared in this teacher's room always came with a price tag, and the students were made to feel indebted. The teacher, Ms. Anderson, would also take kids out on lots of exciting field trips. The problem was that, when they reached the top of an overlook or toured a cool factory, she'd announce, "Remember who took you here, *Ms. Anderson!*"

I think some of my attitude came from being a parent. By the time my daughter was born, my son was seven—at the tail end of childhood. When he was born, I had agonized that I wasn't ready to be his teacher. I wasn't the example I wanted be. I didn't have a parenting "brand."

The reality, I realized, was that it was too late—there'd be no time for polishing up—my life was incomplete and flawed. I would become a father as-is. Even a last-minute crusade before my son was born, gathering the holy tracts about parenting from the shelves of Barnes and Noble or blogs, would be useless. I knew that even if I said all the right things, kids don't listen, they watch.

The father my son would get was already baked into my being. The only thing to reconcile it was to underwrite the relationship with my son with unconditional love, and disinterest. By the time my daughter came around, I had a better idea of what my play would be as a father: just be myself. I remembered Ms. D's dictum, "You can only teach who you are…"

The conclusion was that if I could barely come to terms with how I would guide my own children, how nuts was it to think I could guide one hundred children that were not my own, in any way except unconsciously—from the depths.

As with my own children, I doubted students would come to know themselves on their own terms if I cared too much about where they were headed. Children needed things from adults, but where to draw the line? From the beginning children are trying to be free. Imagine a baby, born premature as all human babies are, and helpless for the first years of its life. Despite its weakness, its utter vulnerability, it kicks its legs when you grab its toes. Wiggling chaotically, the child already is trying to find its own way. The pain and confusion of birth sets it on a singular path— to move through this thing called life on its own terms. All the nursing, loving, holding, baby gates, texts to return home before dark, curfews, hiding of car keys, advice against motorcycling across South America instead of college, nomad resettlement, checkpoints, borders—cannot stop the eccentric, self-chosen desire to go where we want.

The instinct might be buried under a network of a thousand habits: a regiment of domesticity, government oppression and political apathy, and now a tar pit of digital comfort in the palm of our hands. But I believe to step the body in a direction of one's choosing is the crowning achievement of consciousness.

How does a teacher who believes this reconcile himself with a classroom and the obligation to enforce an agenda that requires a kid to stay put? How can this teacher tell a student to think this and not that?

Teachers take the meaningful nature of their jobs for granted. Working with kids is an important role in society, something that requires specialized training and licensure, like a lawyer or doctor. Teachers haven't gotten the same respect or salary because women have traditionally taken on the role. It follows that teaching and parenting are both underappreciated. Neither job is sufficiently supported by the government or culture.

Still, a conceit can take root when you're doing work that is *noble*.

The righteousness of teaching can be a trap. The sense of doing good work should allow teachers to sleep soundly at night. This would be true, if it weren't that they were burning the midnight oil to prepare for class. Triple-overtime, I'd found out from watching veteran teachers, was the norm.

But when teachers finally get to bed, they toss and turn all night worrying about the uncontrollable factors toying with a student's potential: neglect, homelessness, prenatal irresponsibility or ignorance, genetic predispositions. Instead of wising up and letting it go, teachers get up and mainline coffee all day, skip lunch, and search for the sparks of light clinging to the broken shards of creation—the hope children have—to make this world better.

That's how, as a teacher, I found myself at Kinko's laminating Civil War love letters at two-thirty in the morning, alongside college students printing out flyers for a punk concert. I was a member of the repair crew that had been working since time began, trying to persuade the young to become whole, so the world could too. In the middle of a savage war, the letters from soldiers told me that the heart was always crying out for something different.

That was the paradox of teaching: on the one hand I was trying to stay invisible so students could find their own way, on the other, I was responsible for the future of humanity.

What made the work possible at Ms. D's little school was that there was joy in it. But it wasn't until I took time off for the birth of my daughter that I realized both the toll it was taking and the arrogance it revealed.

A teacher must come to terms with something or be lost for good in the coffee-breath-swept wastelands, the purgatory of burnout. And it's this: it's not that you can't do it all—but is doing it all benefiting anyone?

Student teachers had taken the reigns of my class and it seemed that the kids were the better for it. All my attempts to insinuate meaningful questions into their world, may have had a distant cosmic payoff. But when I saw my student teachers at ease with the kids doing 'normal' lessons, I was reminded that disposition was more important than talent or intellect when it came to children.

Caring adults, who spoke in a straightforward way, kept kids sane. These types of people taught intuitively too, but their personalities harmonized more smoothly with the kids. It was like an ordinary, natural passing of the baton to the youth, one recognized by both parties.

They gave kids the information they needed to get by in the culture as it was; no grand strategies, just the basics—honesty, hard work, straight talk, and answers to questions. It was no surprise that two of my student teachers were rural folks, from small towns. They were not doing it all, they were not trying to change the world, they were doing just enough to make a small community tick—the classroom. For obvious reasons, my student teachers weren't conflicted about the nature of American identity. Could reflecting on this conservative point of view help

Other Loyalties

me as a teacher? Was the liberal pretense that I could transform the system, getting in the way of *teaching* kids?

IT WAS DECEMBER and I'd been back a couple weeks after paternity leave. Mr. Duvall pulled some strings and we got free tickets to see the play "A Christmas Carol."

We went on a crisp Tuesday morning for the matinee, but the kids were dressed in their Sunday best. They hopped off the bus in front of the famous Guthrie Theater in downtown Minneapolis. I got a clip of the suits and the heals striding up to the double doors on my camera phone. Like businesspeople, the attire provided a short-cut to respect. But for the brown and black students even choir robes wouldn't have prevented a few of the questioning eyes hitting them from the patrons in the lobby. The side-glance's passed and faded under the expectations that have slowly taken root in America since the Civil Rights Movement. A person might be grumbling or processing under their breath the presence of people of color, but they have few legal avenues left to act out on it—and that's worth noting. Were the legal battles against open discrimination the hard part—or did the hard part come now, with private decisions and struggles of the heart about who would be let in and left out?

Our arrival announced yet another mutually beneficial foray into a largely white place, like our trips to small towns. This time our diverse students and a white public grafted their existence onto each other in the high-ceilinged foyer of a premier theater company. What would it mean for the graft to 'take'? Later, I'd edit this arrival into a video called "Field-Trip-A-Thon." In it, Rashad's tie swings in slow motion with Jay-Z's "Empire State of Mind" playing in the background.

We took over a lounge before the show that had a bar and windows overlooking the Mississippi riverfront. Emilio sat on a stool at the counter. I hit record on my phone, and he gave me a nod. His pierced ears glinted under his newsboy cap. I don't know what life Emilio was fantasizing, but it probably involved Las Vegas, stilettos, stacks of cash, and a reflection of badass Tony

Montana, from *Scarface*, looking back at him from the mirror. I nodded back and moved on.

Mr. and Ms. D were decked out like the producers of a blockbuster movie, starring the beautiful children of their life's work. They strode across the red carpet, masters of shooting the breeze in both Wisconsin dive bars and cocktail lounges. Eventually we filed into the theater to watch a tale about injustice and redemption—a tale that fit America's story, but also humanity.

That was day one of the Field-Trip-A-Thon.

On Wednesday we went to the Science Museum to bask under the huge domed movie screen of the Omni-Theater. Lizzie's brother was the director of the museum and hooked us up with free tickets. Lizzie was the mother of Clayton, an angel-faced seventh grader, and was the one who would go caving under the streets of St. Paul with Maloney and Mr. Shane.

While at the museum I took a cheesy video of a group of kids sprawled out on the floor, putting together a giant puzzle of the earth from space, and another assembling the fossil bones of a long-gone species. In the video edit I inserted K'naan's song "Wavin' Flag," to play over those scenes of collective effort.

It was the theme song for the 2010 World Cup in South Africa. Reviewing the edit, I saw Keisha and Rashad, two eighth graders, fumbling with jumbo puzzle pieces that show a swirl of cloud over blue ocean. Keisha grabs another piece showing water and greenish land. It's a piece of East Asia —but the countries are unlabeled. I wondered if the joyful national flag waving of the soccer tournament would mutate into a death-match of geo-political rivalry that would send us into extinction with the dinosaurs.

That was day two of the Field-Trip-A-Thon.

On Thursday I had set up a trip to the Northwest Company Fur Post about an hour and half north of St. Paul. The temperature had dropped, and the yellow bus sped further up into the deep freeze. Filming the kids getting off the bus in untied Nikes, sweatpants, hoodies, and satin LA Laker's jackets, I braced myself to witness suffering.

Other Loyalties

There was a new group of students, half of whom were related to Kiara and Kendrick. They'd passed the word about Ms. D's little school to their cousins who'd signed up in the fall. There was Lamonte, Wyatt, Booker, and Nico. They had the same charm genes as their cousins but with rougher edges. They'd been in schools where the norm was dysfunction, and they assumed the relationships they would have with teachers would be adversarial.

I remember Lamonte and Nico's first days in my class. It was a jarring sneak peek at the showdown that black boys and teachers used to test each other's intentions at big public schools; you don't really want me here, and I don't belong here, so let's see how long we can shadowbox in the ring together.

One day in class, as Lamonte and Nico were busting up a lesson in the back by loudly talking over me, I stopped and said as frankly as I could, "You know guys, it's okay."

"What? What?" Nico said.

"You don't have to do this anymore."

"What chu mean though?" Lamonte said cocking his head.

"We don't have to play this game."

"What game you talkin' about bro?" Nico asked. It was a conversation. I could tell that I'd gotten a good recommendation from Kendrick—I'd cleared the first layer of security.

"Tug-of-war. Unless, of course, we start pulling on the same side."

Nico paused and for the first time looked up at the board, the rest of the students, and situation. For a second, I thought he'd invite me over to his side, his point of view, about why he was clowning in class.

But Lamonte, even more street-smart than Nico, slapped Nico's shoulder with the back of his hand. "Hold up Nico. This n---- talkin' bout' war? I better get my Glock then." They both laughed, and I lost them for the rest of the class.

It took a half a year to dismantle the game. We'd take turns letting go of control—letting one side win, by giving them the benefit of the doubt. I eased up on my stingy refusal to talk about my personal life and told them about my father's life in Africa one day. I knew Lamonte held onto this detail because a couple months later he brought it up in class. It was after I had students listen to the Bruce Springsteen song "American Skin," about the NYPD shooting death of Amadou Diallo, an unarmed immigrant from Guinea in West Africa.

When I stopped by Nico and Lamonte's table, a short debate unfolded between the two of them.

"Ain't yo' dad from Africa?" Lamonte said, before turning back to Nico.

"Yes, he's African," I replied, before quietly slipping in my usual line, "but we all are if we go back far enough."

"Yo' dad African?" Nico said, reminding himself of our earlier conversation.

"So is you *black*?" Lamonte asked me, before turning to Nico. "Is he black?"

"Wait, *is* you black?" Nico asked.

We all stopped, lost in a question, so easily answered by our eyes, yet such a dynamic factor in our lives. I glanced down at my olive skin. When I was growing up there wasn't a racial category on questionnaires that I could easily check off as a mixed person. North Africans were officially 'white' in census counts, but I didn't *feel* white.

"How would I know if I was black?" I asked, risking the certain type of brotherhood that Lamonte's question offered. I didn't know where my question was leading them—I didn't have some goal to get them to list off advantages or disadvantages of being black. The conversation was just an honest moment that I didn't want to end. It was what teacher's call a 'teachable moment,' an unplanned opportunity to offer insight. Except, I wasn't providing the insight—it was a collective effort.

Lamonte pushed his arms across the table and turned up his hands. "Like, have you been profiled? You know pulled over 'cause you was black?"

"Well, when I was twelve, I was in England with my soccer team. War had just broken out in Iraq. I was the only player to get pulled aside by airport security and questioned. Does that count?"

Nico and Lamont couldn't decide, but it was close. The blaring difference in our lives—the fact that I was on an international trip when I was their age—didn't occur to them. Being kids, they didn't pounce on a sweeping storyline of the privilege of my economic class and kept it local so to speak. They wanted a foothold—something to tell them if they could trust the person in front of them a little more.

I didn't ask if they had experienced profiling themselves. Was I selfish? There was a part of me that felt a little scuzzy afterwards. But guiding the conversation towards a sort of pandering performance of racial solidarity built on tales of victimhood, wasn't in the spirit of Lamonte's question. He was willing to connect—that was my takeaway.

Now at the trading post, Nico, Lamonte and I, were at the stage when we could talk and laugh together—mostly because of things like this *outside* of the classroom. The classroom was a poisoned chalice for Nico and Lamonte, and no matter how pure my intentions, poison leeched from the walls. Going outside was like living in a post-apocalyptic world without the death and destruction. The open air gave us room to imagine—a tantalizing blank slate—for society.

At the fur post I saw Nico through a row of pines. He was twice as tall as some of the sixth graders and was already on the radar of some college teams for both football and basketball. His group was playing the Ojibwe game called "snow snakes." Long wooden poles are slid along a track in the snow. The team who could slide theirs the farthest won.

His team was crushing the competition. Our group's guide, who was dressed in animal skins, smiled. She knew the story of George Bonga, born in 1805. He was one of the first black people to be born in the territory that would become Minnesota. The strange thing was that he was also said to have been one of the first "white" people to have been born in the territory. He even referred to himself as "white." The reason: the Ojibwe referred to anyone who was non-native as "white."

Bonga's father was African American, and his mother was Ojibwe, and he was a legend in the fur trading scene who spoke English, French and Ojibwe. Some said he could carry seven-hundred-pound parcels of fur on portages. He was a bridge between whites and tribes of the region before the tipping point when power fell permanently into the hands of the new white arrivals to the land.

I kept thinking of Bonga as Nico rotated through the activities: strapping on snowshoes for a walk among the birch, sizing up the kettles and cloth that native trappers could get for their beaver pelts at the storehouse, and sitting in a wigwam made of bark listening to old tales—something Bonga was said to love in his retirement at his lodge on Leech Lake, a lake in northern Minnesota.

Black people had been in Minnesota since the beginning, but somehow had still not arrived in the minds of the descendants of European immigrants. It's maybe why some of my black students said that they "stayed" somewhere not "lived" somewhere. No wonder Nico and Lamonte declined to sit down and play ball those first days in my classroom—they hadn't been getting signals much of their lives, that this place, Minnesota, could be their home.

Terrell had a runny nose, his shoes were encased in ice, and he was shivering uncontrollably. He'd started the year with us as a new seventh grader but had still not reconciled himself to these outings in the woods. Our guide was holding up the pelt of a skunk and repeating the word, "*Chicagoua, Chicagoua.* Does that sound familiar to anyone?"

Terrell, who had hidden half his face in his hoodie, perked up and said, "Chicago."

"Yes, that's it. It was the Illinois tribe's word for "skunk.""

Even the warm reference to the city where his relatives were couldn't ease Terrell's misery. I reluctantly let him step away from the group and go inside the interpretative center. I subscribed to

Maloney's take on natural consequences, but it was ten degrees, Terrell didn't have the gear for it, and he'd hung in there for most of the day. It was a show of effort that exceeded anything he'd done in class all year and I gave him his credit.

Soon, everyone was thawing out inside the building and having lunch. I turned my camera to a group cracking up as Wyatt somehow impersonated the sounds of a taxidermied beaver in a diorama. Maloney appreciated Wyatt's hectic energy and they had hit it off. With Maloney's help, Wyatt's probing mind had a place he could call home in the science room.

Ms. Conley hounded a few kids about picking up their lunch trash, hip-checking Maria who had left a bag of chips on a bench. Booker, a sixth grader who followed his cousin Kiara around, tried to get away with setting his milk carton on the ground. Ms. Conley deputized Kiara to tickle her cousin until he picked it up and put it in the bin. Then Ms. Conley put her arm around Ruby, who had pulled a Dum-Dum lollipop out of thin air and walked her to the idling bus—Ms. Conley in snazzy Mukluk snow boots, and Ruby in pink moonboots.

When the sky is clear and you look up, it's only a matter of time before you'll see a shooting star. That's what I did when we pulled into the school. I waited as students jumped off the bus. Terrell had survived, and I patted him on the shoulder as he limped onto the sidewalk.

Sure enough, a streak of light shot across the sky, as Tabari announced, "Mr. A, that was the best day of my life!"

Field-Trip-a-Thon had officially come to a close, and I rushed home to edit the new footage. The next week, after showing the kids the movie of themselves, I found out that Elisa was transferring schools. She was a strawberry-blonde girl with an overbite and ironic sense of humor that I loved.

"What happened?" I asked Mr. Duvall.

"Her mom thought we weren't doing enough academics. When we went out all last week that was it—she thought it was too much time away from class."

It was a warning perhaps, that not all parents were onboard with the middle school program. It was hard to believe that a parent wouldn't be worshipping our efforts with their children. But I had to check my arrogance again; it was possible there were other ways of doing things, that benefited kids. Or rather benefited the mindset of their parents.

Blood was thicker than the coffee running through the veins of teachers, who may have known, only in *some* cases, what was best for people's children. The only edge teachers had on parents when it came to education, was that teachers were paid, and in fact, had a professional responsibility to leave their stereotypes, personal biases, and beliefs out of the classroom as much as possible. When done right, this provided students a chance to find out what they thought about history, politics, and economics, in a space that was just a touch removed from the influence of their parents. One might even call that freedom.

Twenty-Eight

A FEW SUMMERS after Ms. D's little school was shut down, Maloney and I were driving up North to go camping. We'd both enjoyed the trips we'd gone on as colleagues and had taken up a tradition of a yearly adventure. We followed Interstate 35 into Duluth, and Lake Superior came into view. After a dull stretch of landlocked freeway miles, the huge outburst of blue water across the horizon never failed to surprise me.

My car tilted down through a series of hills to the harbor.

"So get this," Maloney suddenly said. "I was at Regions Hospital, checking on a friend."

"Downtown St. Paul?"

"Yeah. And all of sudden I see Nico. Remember Kendrick's cousin?"

"No way."

"So anyways, he runs up to me and says, 'Mr. Maloney, Mr. Maloney, you're not going to believe this.' And I'm like 'What? What?'"

I tapped the brakes.

"He says, 'Mr. Maloney, I got shot!'"

"Man, really?"

"He says, 'Look at this, look at this.' Then he lifts up his shirt to show me the bandage."

"Was it bad?"

"Well, he peels the bandage back and shows me where the bullet went in and exited, right on his side."

"What happened?'
"I don't know, he just told me, 'Mr. Maloney, they shot me.'"
I was troubled and grew quiet. Mr. Maloney grew up on the east side of St. Paul. He absorbed the facts of life that asserted themselves on the bruised and bloody bodies of young men who lived there a bit easier than me.

The car rolled parallel to the St. Louis River as its mouth opened into Lake Superior; *gitchi-gami* to the Ojibwe, meaning 'great sea.' Details of the harbor came into higher resolution. The rust-red tint of a one-thousand-foot cargo carrier pondered through the water towards its slip in the port.

I squeezed the wheel as the road curved through downtown. We passed over the 'Graffiti Graveyard,' a concrete gallery of spray-paintings and vagrant artifacts entombed under the interstate. Years before, Maloney had taken Ms. Tracy and I there when we were at a two-day conference on school forests at a state park nearby. After the presentations the other attendees headed to their lodgings to call their spouses and stare at the wood paneling on the walls until drifting off to sleep. Ms. Tracy and I piled into Maloney's car at midnight and held onto the madman's coattails.

At the Graffiti Graveyard we slipped through some rebar and hopscotched over the filth: single shoes, plastic bottles filled with strange liquids frozen solid, and other orphaned possessions of lost souls. The stench was held down by the subzero temperature. Maloney pointed to a sagging tent along a wall and offered twenty dollars to whoever would peek inside.

Colorful masterpieces were called forth from the darkness by our headlamps. On a support joist a tiny pictograph was caught in my beam. It was drawn with simple black strokes that sketched out train tracks. Their vanishing point was at the foot of a triangular mountain. The words above the drawing read, "Ride the ties." I swooned in the sub-zero air with the old-timey feeling of romantic adventure that I would get as a teenager.

George Bonga was born near Duluth, the place we were creeping around in the middle of the night. Bonga's father was a successful fur trader himself. Even then Duluth was a crossroads,

Other Loyalties

with the Ojibwe villagers that lived there drawn into a trade that reached to Europe.

There was a story told about Bonga—how he tracked down an Ojibwe man accused of murdering a mixed-blood, in what may have been a doomed love-triangle. For six days and five nights Bonga trailed him through the winter forest. Bonga finally caught up with him and brought the man back to Fort Snelling, where he was acquitted in the first trial to be held in the land that would become Minnesota. A black Indian, a white Indian, an Objiwe—all there at the birth of a new system of justice that would treat them as strangers for so long.

AFTER THE DECEMBER Field-Trip-A-Thon another personal matter kept me in Duluth off and on for a good part of January. In Arab culture an empty building can fill with mischievous spirits called *Jinn*. Looking back, I wonder if I was away too long from my classroom at Ms. D's little school.

Dennis, the Baptist preacher, my father-in-law, who helped me lay the cornerstone of my classroom—the bleachers—was spending his last days in hospice. The place was in a beautiful, wooded area on a hill above the city. He was able to meet his infant granddaughter and would host each visitor with warmth and energy even though he'd been surviving on ice chips for weeks.

Each morning our family would warily open the shades to his room to check the tree line. The staff at the hospice said that a buck would often appear on days when people passed. His pain was being well managed, and we felt blessed to spend a little more time with him, each morning when there was no sign of the buck.

I held his hand one afternoon, the long-haired, city guy with an Islamic upbringing. He, the devout Christian conservative, who had preached the gospel all his life, fighting the casual decay of the culture. We had always got along, and any sermons about unwed relationships and the fate of our unbaptized children were quietly delivered to my wife or not at all.

Love and faith were bigger than righteousness and dogma and the path for a friendship had been cleared. I didn't think much about my students. The daily worries of teaching felt a little insignificant, watching a good man pass before my eyes. Little did I know that similar feelings of sadness and gratefulness would enter my heart when Ms. D's school was driven into the ground.

AFTER MY FATHER-IN-LAW passed away, I returned to Ms. D's little school. It was late winter, and my third student teacher of the year was busy demonstrating how a class was smoothly run. Lucia was in the middle of presenting a project that she had understood and was clearly proud of when Mr. K.O. walked up to my desk.

He wasn't in showman mode, and I could tell something was weighing on him.

"Mr. A, nice to have you back."

"K.O. How have things been going?"

"You know, trouble with our sponsor, school board crap."

"The sponsor of the school?"

"Yeah, the three-year contract is up, and we were hoping to find a new sponsor, one that gets our philosophy a little better."

"Man, I should have checked with Project for Pride in Living. You know that place in Minneapolis that helps people train for jobs and build houses? I know the guy who started it. They might be up for it."

A flash of weary remorse crossed Mr. K.O.'s face.

"Should I check with them?" I asked.

"Yeah, it might be too late."

Now I remembered the vague rumblings over the years. The signposts of conflict that I always ignored. Because I didn't engage in gossip I missed out on some fundamental information: the news of who could be trusted, the clues about what's going wrong.

Mr. K.O. said that I could check with Project for Pride in Living, but I got the feeling that something sordid was already in motion that I have never fully understood to this day. With no natural impulse to go search for trouble, I lived with the fall-out of this unsettling meeting with Mr. K.O. for a couple months. I assumed that the problem-solvers of the school would iron it out: the women.

What I didn't bank on was a split that had taken place among the women that was impossible to repair. Power had been shared at our little charter school. Ms. D was generous: we all felt comfortable wielding power as long as it was good for kids. (I would schedule field trips without even asking anymore—sometimes forgetting to order buses. What did Ms. D do? Covered my butt by negotiating for some busses the day before trips, so that we could still go.)

But notes of resentment had somehow settled in among the staff, leaking into the mysterious superhighway of communication that bonds women. We know the worst violence happens in the family; if the love was real, so was the rift.

I PULLED IN the parking lot a bit late that fateful morning in Mid-March. It was filled with more cars than usual, but I didn't think anything of it.

The hallways were empty. I wasn't in the habit of doing morning rounds to chit-chat and funneled myself through the odd silence into my room. After a while kids started to amble in, slumped in chairs, or left again to search for friends.

It wasn't until midday, when I ran into Mr. Barnett in the stairwell, that I decided to ask about the subdued vibe I'd noticed. I hadn't seen Ms. D that day, but it was normal for her to be out crusading for charter schools or tracking down grants for us.

"Mr. A."

"Hey Mr. Barnett. So, what's this eerie feeling around here?"

"You weren't here for the meeting this morning."

"Meeting?"

"Yeah, so all these guys in suits show up and tell us there's an investigation."

"What?"

"And that we can't speak with Ms. D."

"..."

Mr. Barnett took in the confusion on my face. "Yep. Lawyers came and scared everyone."

"I don't get it."

"It's like a coup."

Mr. Barnett knew that I never delved into the nitty-gritty of drama, and I could see him gauging how much to say, or how far I wanted to be drawn in.

"So, Ms. D's not here?"

"Ms. D and Mr. D."

"I don't get it."

"I know."

In the power struggle between Ms. D versus our school sponsor and disgruntled staff, a decisive blow had been made. Ms. D was going to be removed as director of the school. An undisclosed accusation was used as a pretext for what some wanted to do all along—oust the heretic Queen.

Lawyers, archnemeses of kids who need danger and experience to grow, had finally been let in the gates of Ms. D's little school. They joined up with the protectors of the vulnerable—the responsible adults that sought to guard kids against the renegade Ms. D's unsafe plots and actions. But lawyers, and these "responsible" adults, are like the gargoyles atop a cathedral. Their power often turns inward, and they stifle kids from reaching the holy sanctuary that is the world outside of conventionality and the school walls. They keep kids safe from the dark, brilliant, explorations that build true values, character, and strength.

The evil that can grow inside a school does not come from misguided teachers, or even the asphyxiating fear of lawyers and accountants, or selfish parents conniving for their kid to outperform all their classmates without encouraging them to lend their classmates a hand. Evil is a room filling with the dusty build-up of shed skin, conversations that never happened because kids had to be quiet, emotions never felt because focus was solely on 'objective' facts, the molts of a hundred mean interactions between students because "values" were not supposed to be taught at

Other Loyalties

school. It is inertia, sedentary habits, the boredom of a million sitting kids on any given day. Energy that has turned to apathy, apathy that has turned to deviancy and rage. Rage that drives a kid to pick up a gun and take the world down with him. Life's vital force coming out sideways is what evil is.

As Mr. Barnett finished walking down the stairs and out of sight, that is what I feared was being extinguished at that very moment without Ms. D in charge; the raw, imperfect fire, of a leader who was honest to kids about what makes life worth living: striving for the good, with friends.

The mood at the school changed overnight as they say. Distrust, whispers, stony silences, contrived pleasantries, and anger filled the vacant space that Ms. D used to fill with a loud soul. I passed Ms. Soraira, the Venezuelan angel, later that week. Her face, losing color from her illness, was filled with pain and understanding. She rubbed my back, "Oh, Meester A."

I'm embarrassed that I didn't call the isolated Ms. D on my own right away. Maybe if I had been at the meeting and looked into the eyes of the lawyers, I could have sized up the situation better. But the secondhand reports of the specific threat from the lawyers to not talk to Ms. D filled me with a vague apprehension.

I walked around with a gnawing need to check in with Ms. D for a couple of weeks. It was like being turned back from the way home because of a snarling dog in your path. I was ashamed that courage fled so quickly.

Finally, one afternoon in the parking lot, Mr. Barnett handed me his cell phone.

"It's Ms. D," he told me.
"Really?"
"Yeah, it's okay, you can talk to her. I have."
I caught myself glance around and took the phone.
"Ms. D. I'm so sorry."
"I know Mr. A."
"What's going on?"
"I don't know. I really don't know what it is. I don't know anything."

"Well, we're thinking of you and will fight for you, Ms. D."
"Thank you, Mr. A."

EVEN THOUGH IT was not yet possible to spell out the conspiracy against Ms. D, it was its effects that preoccupied me. The accusation was sealed in a confidential legal report, but it was being wielded by Ms. D's adversaries like a secret weapon. The search for someone to blame for this situation was not as important to me as convincing people that our school without Ms. D would become something *unrecognizable*.

We had one last staff meeting before people stopped talking to each other. The two administrative staff who were leading the school in Ms. D's absence, gave a tight-lipped summary of the current investigation. Ms. Danika, Mr. Maloney, and a few other teachers described their willingness to support Ms. D.

There was a center of gravity in the room that I couldn't place. Most of the teachers, often full of helpful bursts of sensible advice, were very quiet—and I chalked it up to nerves.

Over the years I'd shared stories or analogies during meetings that had soothed or given perspective. Storytelling was the only tool for problem-solving that I had. It was my role and I stepped forward. After delivering a sermon on how the school without Ms. D was like a body without a heart, I stood for a moment longer before sitting down. A few faces turned up and I could see that they were touched. But it was a hollow reception—they had enjoyed the decorative wrapper of my words but hadn't eaten the message. I kept struggling to feel out the source of the gravity that was keeping people from coming to the obvious conclusion that the school was in mortal peril.

The next day, a few of us met at the food court of the Hmong Village Shopping Center after school to consider our options. Glowing signs for stuffed chicken wings, papaya salad, and pork belly with sticky rice, stretched along the wall above small, family-run food stalls. We crowded around a table.

Ms. Danika, who seemed to have a more realistic view of the type of fight we had on our hands, spoke first.

Other Loyalties

"The thing that could help is getting some type of lawyer to look into things from another side."

Maloney, finishing a bite of spicy Hmong sausage, said, "I'd throw in some money for that."

I glanced around at who had showed up for this clandestine meeting. Mr. Barnett, Ms. Conley and Mr. Duvall were there, Ms. Tracy and one of the kindergarten teachers, and a handful of others. Not as many people as I thought would come. Everyone wanted to help and nodded about the need for a lawyer—but how would teachers, even pooling their money, raise enough for a good lawyer? There was the fear of losing our jobs, and with it came the first note of resignation.

Then, before spring break, I naively wrote a letter saying that together we could make a last stand and sent it to the whole staff. At the time I thought the attack on Ms. D was coming from our sponsor, and some other outside forces. Long before this incident, I had overheard Ms. D grumbling about her incompatibility with the brittle sensibilities of our sponsor. I'd heard that Ms. D, not one to hold back, turned the screws a few times on our sponsor's representatives at board meetings. She had little time for the fussiness and moralizing that was the source of their complaints.

When the responses to my letter came in, many were missing. I realized that half the staff were ready to play along with the ouster of Ms. D by way of passivity, fear, or other factors that I have never understood: Ambition? Morality? Money? Jealousy? Grudges? Knowledge of the unknown transgression inside the confidential report?

As a social studies teacher I should have known that revolutions succeed when groups *inside* a country get outside help.

It was clear that there was a rough split between the elementary staff and their unruly partners in the middle school. But throughout that surreal spring, I'd be pulled into the rainbow-colored sanctuary of a first grade or kindergarten room. Unflappable teachers of six and seven-year-olds would express admiration for Ms. D and reveal that they'd had private talks with her.

Ms. Tiffany, a special education teacher, tiptoed into my own room after school one day, checked behind her, and thanked me for the letter I wrote. She had been talking to Ms. D all along and updated me. Ms. Tiffany was a small, cute, endlessly smiling blonde—it opened my eyes once again. My assumptions about the make-up of courageous people were all wrong. Her round, bespectacled face would go up alongside the bearded, grizzled lion-faces of the Afghan Mujahadeen, the fierce warriors who turned back the onslaught of the Soviet Army in the 1980's.

Some of my least favorite sentiments in the world now took up my time and mental space. Resentment and suspicion of my colleagues, and guilt that I hadn't been in tune with the school board turmoil. Meanwhile, school was in session. The staff, like feuding parents in the bitter death throes of a divorce, hid it all from the kids—who began to wonder where Ms. D was.

For the first time we had to lie to them.

I CAN ACCEPT that people have other loyalties. With the Baptist preacher, our other loyalties toward family, friendship, and the nameless beauty of a summer day fishing on the lake, allowed us to meet beyond the clamoring demands of religion, politics, and the culture war. To me that's the bread and butter of spiritual transcendence—and what good is spiritual transcendence unless it makes you more free and grateful for ordinary life?

The "other" loyalties expressed by people at Ms. D's school were overlapping in a tortured way. It was hard to tell which way these loyalties twisted. For parents at the school who were presented with rumors of an investigation, the loyalty was towards their kid's safety, but it collided with the happiness their kid had found at the school Ms. D built. The remaining administrators barricaded themselves behind the cold language of the law as they worried about legal problems for the school and themselves. Loyalty towards the institution braided together with self-preservation.

Teachers, committed to their students, livelihood, and career, had to weigh risking all that to honor their loyalty to Ms. D. She had given them a chance, helped them grow, and nurtured a couple of things that matter most in education: relationships, binding community rituals, and lesson ideas thought up in the middle of the night.

At a school, adult contradictions are harder to put up with—because the ones suffering are the kids. But I suppose these entanglements are true at most jobs. Suppose a hardworking businessman orchestrates an oil deal that will compound global warming. He drives home to tuck in his kids who have been enriched by an expensive, satisfying, and dynamic day at private school because he values education. They will inherit a future where climate change will upend organized human life and share it with kids who went to underfunded and overwhelmed public schools—those are loyalties at odds.

WORKPLACE CONFLICT WAS new to me, but I'd seen how a bad idea, backed by determined forces further up the hierarchy can carry the day. My college soccer coach was fired a year after winning the national championship and replaced by a man who was not up to the job. The reason: my old coach had personal friction with one of the athletic directors who wanted it to happen. Within months after the new coach stepped in, our talented team had disbanded—transferring to other colleges across the country and in my case overseas.

The climatic conflict at Ms. D's little school now had a date. The final school board meeting of the year was scheduled in May to decide the fate of Ms. D once and for all. Enough petty shenanigans, hurt, and tribalism had developed that the vibrant culture of the school lay in ruins. The details are a lousy archive not worth revisiting.

As the date of the school board meeting approached there was only one thing to do—take the kids outside.

Maloney, Ms. Tracy, Mr. J, Mr. Steven, and I loaded up the silver Caravans and pointed them towards the Franconia Sculpture Park, a farm plot turned into a bizzarro playground for artists handy with blow torches and hammers. For the past two years I had arranged for us to take the eighth graders there for a week-long workshop, where they designed and built a large sculpture to take back to the school. The money wasn't available this year, and we were set to cancel, but the Parent-Teacher-Organization covered the cost, believing it was an invaluable tradition for the eighth graders.

Franconia Sculpture Park was staffed by artists-in-residence who all lived in a big white farmhouse on the property. As we pulled in the gravel parking lot the eye-candy of offbeat, large-scale creations came into view: a tower of boomboxes, white pods suspended fifty feet in the air like an anime teeter-totter, a green lizard the size of an RV.

The sculptures each had a small placard with the artist's name and a paragraph declaring some conceptual pedigree. I preferred to enjoy the art the way the kids did. As they piled out of the vans, they gravitated to the pieces they could climb on and play with—the beauty of Franconia was that most of the art fit this category.

When my van pulled in the gravel parking lot I looked out to the middle of the field and I saw the pavilion where we would cut, solder, sand, and paint, far from our troubles. At the edge of the parking lot there was a small shed the size of a double-wide outhouse that served as the park's welcome center. A metal box labeled 'Donations' and a few flyers were visible inside it, and so was Carissa, our beautiful dreadlocked host. She stepped out of the shed and walked out with a smile to greet us.

Carissa had come out to Ms. D's little school earlier in the month to plan with the kids. The blueprint for their sculpture was ready, and we went straight to work. Miguel grabbed some goggles and began an apprenticeship at the bandsaw. Tina, Marina, Valentina, Lucia, and Cynthia began to break tile into the puzzle pieces of a mosaic. Mason, Hunter, and Marlowe helped move a pile of rebar under the kind guidance of a tattooed anarchist from the East Coast.

Kevin and Rashad had slipped on leather aprons and gloves that reached their elbows. Kendrick had on a welding helmet and was leaning close to the weld joint, in full concentration, as a radical feminist with a shaved head patiently demonstrated the craft.

I sat in the sun sanding wooden shapes with Maloney and Ms. Tracy. We cashed in on a situation where every single student was content and feeling useful, to have the sort of conversations people have in high school with their best friends.

"Do you ever just look at yourself in the mirror and think holy smokes, I exist?" Maloney said as he shaped the fin of a wooden fish with a square of sandpaper.

"Yes, totally." Ms. Tracy stopped and scratched the top of her hand. "You see yourself looking into your own eyes and wonder who is in there."

"You know, I look at myself, and see a sack of blood," Maloney marveled, "and think what am I *really?*"

The conversation was not seeded by a crises-of-meaning. It took on the light and curious air of a fledgling scientific inquiry. We took turns tossing deep thoughts back and forth like a beachball. When the thoughts got too heavy, filling with adult solemnity, we dropped them like medicine balls, and started a new topic. All the while the hum of kids at work was a song for us, that told us all was well—at least here, at Franconia Sculpture Park.

We made the hour drive back to the school in time to catch the buses. I ran into Mr. Duvall as I walked towards the room where the last board meeting was being held. The organizers of the meeting had refused to hold the meeting in a larger space knowing that a large contingent of Ms. D's supporters were planning on attending—parents, teachers, friends, and former students.

"Mr. Duvall."

"Hey Mr. A. How did it go today?"

"A nice refuge from this." I nodded ahead. "So, what do you think?"

"I just don't want it to get chippy."

We joined up with Mr. Barnett.

"Man, it's tense around here," I said.

"Yeah, I was over by the stairwell and saw some folks that gave me a funny look," Mr. Barnett grimly joked. "I said, 'Geez, are you guys going to push me down the stairs?'"

We pried our way into the overcrowded room, found a seam through, and posted up with the rest of the middle school staff. The board was sitting in a horseshoe formed out of student tables. There, pressed against a wall with her family, was Ms. D. It was the first time many of us had seen her in nearly two months.

I had a sort of generic, unkind view of lawyers even before this episode. Seeing them seated in Ms. Conley's classroom—the site of so much learning, irreverence, laughter, and hushed confessions of crushes—deflated me. Lawyers should rarely be let near kids or schools. (They're free to argue at the Supreme Court for desegregation, and student free speech, and the right of teacher unionization, but that's it!)

My deranged feelings toward lawyers come from my sense that the restrictions that stop the natural flow of learning in schools are a fossil record of lawsuits. Most red tape and pedagogical timidity found at schools reveals a history of butt-covering adults. Its reenforced by opportunistic parents trying to make a buck off the system.

Mistakes and learning, danger and heedfulness, cooperation and independence, were duets played with difficulty in our competitive and litigious society. A small charter school provided teachers a reprieve from the usual legal threats and a work environment that made bridging opposing forces a little easier. For one, it is free from both the cautious monitoring of unions, and the corporate conservatism and obliviousness of big district administrations. But also the oppressive expectations and specifications of private schools trying to please their paying parents.

At a small charter school there was a chance for innovation. Staring at the lawyers, sitting around the horseshoe at the board meeting I saw it slipping away. Did the group that invited them in really think a more conventional school would be better for kids?

Mr. K.O. was isolated at the meeting and every motion he made was smothered by the new board chair who, to his credit, kept the proceedings from unraveling into a verbal brawl. It was a hotbed of emotions, and the chairmen had no choice but to rely on the rhythm of procedure.

The time set aside for public comment opened and different figures stepped forward. A dad gave his reasons about why he wanted his name off an email thread that parents had started to inform them about what was happening at the school. That made it clear which side he supported.

An obese white mother took the floor. Her words poured out in the rushed way of those who aren't used to being listened to by a whole room.

"Ms. D phoned me up about something. She called me the wrong name." She let out a raspy smoker's laugh. A portion of the crowd who recognized that tendency in Ms. D chuckled. "But it don't matter. I don't know much but I know she loves my kids."

A wiry black grandmother, who had to take the bus and came in late, came to life by the door.

"I don't know what's goin' on, but I'm goin' to find out today. *Today!*"

People spoke from their hearts, at least the ones supporting Ms. D, but the gavel fell on the time for public comment. The flywheel of power went to work as Ms. D's detractors flexed their superior numbers on the board and voted to remove her as director.

My view is lopsided because I haven't spoken with any of my colleagues that had to make that vote. I don't know if it gutted them, or it was tinged with triumph. Maybe it was the icy mechanism of a duty fulfilled based on legal information I didn't have. I'm guessing it was a little of everything.

As we filed out to the hall, I saw Ms. Conley with tears in her eyes, and her arms folded tight across her chest. She had just given Ms. D a big hug.

Mr. Duvall was near and asked me, "Mr. A, I was waiting for you to speak. I was hoping you'd do one of your things—tell one of your stories."

"Yeah, Mr. A, how come you didn't speak?" Ms. Conley added.

"I had too much to say, that was the problem. I would've gotten myself in trouble."

"Yeah, that's understandable."

Threats to my job were never made and, until my last day a year later, I was never mistreated. Yet the harshness with which Ms. D was dispensed had left me feeling guarded. The capabilities of retribution were available to those who now had power, and my mortgage payment was real. I didn't want to admit fear influenced me and would bluster to friends about not being afraid of getting fired.

It was my first teaching job, and I had only gotten it because Ms. D was willing to gamble on a weird guy with a foreign name. Yet when I didn't speak, I felt like I had let the staff down. When the firepower of words was needed most, I had stayed quiet. There wouldn't be another chance before the school year ended when the staff was all together, friends and newly minted foes, where I could describe what we had created together before it disappeared for good.

After a couple minutes, Ms. Conley's room was empty again, the whole drama over in an hour. The mystery of the confidential indictment, which hung over the proceedings like a tropical storm named Kafka, would never be solved.

Outside the front doors of the school, Ayana was slipping fliers into the hands of parents passing by. She was the irrepressible mother of three girls at the school, two of which were in the middle school. She wasn't ready to give up on Ms. D.

"Hi Mr. A."

"Hey Ayana, thanks for doing that." I eyed the purple flier in her hand.

"Oh yes indeed."

Just then the chair of the school board walked through the doors, and a frisson of tension passed between everyone as Ayana backed away a little and smiled. A sense of civility wrestled itself into shape.

Maloney, clearheaded under duress did what was right and spoke to the new school board chair. "Well, that had to be hard."

"Yes, it was," the board chair said.

All four of us peered out from the top steps of the school at the dispersing crowd—four people who had to make their peace with decisions made.

The next morning, we sped off again to Franconia Sculpture Park in the silver Caravans, happy to leave the school behind. On Friday, Ms. Conley and Mr. Duvall brought the rest of the middle school up on a bus to see what the eighth graders had created. Three benches were inlaid with mosaics. One showed a set of waves—the nearest to the shore curled in a collection of blue tile pieces tipped with white shards. Seventh graders, Raya and Amelie ran their fingers over the rough finish and plotted what they would do for their eighth-grade sculpture next year. Would such an extravagance be supported next year by whatever administration replaced Ms. D?

Rising above the benches was a web of painted rebar. Attached to the web were individual wood and metal sculptures that each eighth grader had made.

"What is that?" Michael, a sixth grader, asked.

It's a question an artist should be happy to hear. The sound of someone trying to break into the meaning of a work of art with their eyes, struggling, and then trying with words.

"Bitch, what is *you*?" Rashad was proud of his welding and went on the defensive.

"I know what that is," Kendrick said, pointing to Michael's forehead.

"Hold up fam', I'm about to get some sandpaper and help this lil' G out. Polish his forehead down some." Rashad faked like he was about to leave to fetch some sandpaper.

Kendrick grabbed Michael, who tried to wiggle away. "No bro! No!"

Rashad acted like he had something in his hand and reached for Michael's head, before Michael broke free. Kendrick was cracking up, his dimples flashing.

Michael smiled, happy to get the attention of the older boys, and walked around the rest of the sculpture. Michael's sincere face filled with awe and confusion about the meaning of it all. Fulfilled, he spun away and ran to climb the giant lizard.

"Hey Mr. A, what'd you make?" Kendrick turned to me.

I pointed out my sculpture hanging on a strip of rebar that had been painted green. It was an owl that Miguel had cut on the bandsaw, with feathers made of door hinges that I'd drilled on in rows.

"That's tight. But you still suspicious."

It's not every day that someone takes an interest in you, and I'd miss Kendrick. We stood together a bit longer. Around us the entire middle school ran helter-skelter in the farm field, among the generous, touchable art—the opposite of the choked hauteur of an established museum.

The sculptures were like alien ships, each from a different galaxy, that had landed in a forgotten field. Ships built by aliens who knew what brought happiness to children. How like Ms. D's little school, settling into a humble neighborhood on the east side of St. Paul.

Mr. David, Mr. J, and Mr. Steven joined up with the hipster artists and some of the boys, to lift our massive sculpture onto a trailer to take to the school. Ratchets were laced through the rebar, and the three benches were slotted into the truck bed.

I hopped into the passenger seat and waved to Carissa. Mr. Steven picked his way over the gravel road and onto the highway. It was relaxing riding with Mr. Steven. I felt a strong bond with the few men who had ventured into education with me. A sensitive person myself, I felt like male educators were a brotherhood I wouldn't have to compete to the death with like men in a company or law firm. (Except for trying to bulk up a little, so I didn't look so wimpy next to Mr. Duvall.)

Other Loyalties

Mr. Steven was still smarting from getting the band-aid ripped off in the East African refugee camp, that exposed the worst of global poverty. He hadn't been the same, and I felt he'd be moving on soon to a new job. I started to sense that my time with many of my colleagues was coming to an end.

We passed the giant hat of a vintage Arby's sign and pulled in to check the straps.

"So what do you think is going to happen?" Mr. Steven asked.

"To the school?"

"Yeah."

"It's *already* happened."

Mr. Steven gave one more tug on the rope threading through the ratchet, and we climbed back in the truck.

At the school, we missed Mr. D, who had the Wisconsin farm boy know-how when it came to wrangling big hunks of metal. But we found a spot in front of the school and muscled the sculpture into place. The bell rang and the elementary kids poured out. The little kids understood the madness of the sculpture instinctually and swarmed around it. I caught a few glances from teachers that seemed skeptical about something so quirky being the public face of the school.

A second grader was testing the benches and tugging on the dangling mini sculptures made from wood. I knew him because my students had read Afghan folktales to him in kindergarten and first grade. He stood on the bench trying to see the back of a sculpture attached high up in the rebar web. His teacher shouted for him to go to his bus, and he jumped off the bench. I watched his little head with black hair, huge backpack and two tiny legs pumping away.

"Bye Mr. A!"

"Bye Luis!"

I got closer and saw that the piece he was studying was Maloney's. I went into the bushes to get behind the sculpture to see if there was anything written on the back. I recognized immediately that the precisely painted words were Maloney's subtle, private protest.

It read: "True art is what you have made of yourself. You are your own sculptor."

In a moment of low morale for me, the elegant middle finger hit the spot. It was not directed at any person, but at the spirit of parochialism that can creep into a school—cutting kids down to size to fit the narrow needs of the culture or the economy. And for Ms. D, Maloney's message was a salute for her efforts to not let it happen.

GRADUATION NIGHT ARRIVED. Families, some filled with members who hadn't finished high school, crowded into the gym. Many took the chance to play up this ceremony, with dinners and even an occasional splurge on a limo.

The eighth graders sat on stage in suits and new dresses, spotlight blaring down. Marina, with flowers in her hair, nudged Cynthia and whispered in her ear. They both looked out at the audience and pointed to a handsome former student who had come back to watch the ceremony.

Ms. D used to pull out all the stops for graduation night because she loved a good celebration, but the event would have to rely on our muscle memory this night. Ms. Danika and Mr. Barnett arranged a solo for Jamiyah and a rendition of the school song. Maloney, working all year after-hours, presented hand-drawn portraits of each kid.

With a single rose in each hand the night caught the thread of magic eighth graders had witnessed while watching their friend's graduate in years past.

I'd been asked to do the graduation speeches a few years back and would spend the month of May worrying scraps of paper to death trying to get the words right in time for the ceremony. When I had asked Ms. D why I was chosen she said, "The price was right!"

Parsing choice episodes from the year and pairing them with an analogy about mining for gems, I tried to illustrate the spirit of the departing class of eighth graders. I hoped my offbeat diversions weren't lost on the crowd of parents and relatives.

Other Loyalties

Afterwards, an auntie, lipstick on thick and neckline plunging, complimented my speech. I blushed and stared down at the gym floor where the black arc of the three-point line curved under my feet.

But one of the real highlights for the kids had been the video I put together of our trips outside that year.

Tired of getting roasted about my pink Nokia phone, I had exchanged it for an iPhone that could record video and would pull it out during our adventures. This year I had recorded Lucas and Landon rolling down a hill, crossing paths, crushing each other, and bursting into hysterics; Rashad's disgusted face looking into a box full of garter snakes; Cynthia staring up at the blue "room" behind a frozen waterfall; a snowshoe race between Kendrick and Maria. But mostly I'd caught the funny, candid moments when I shoved a camera in their faces—before they all began curating their lives for video a few years later.

For the montages in the video, they had to put up with songs from my musical tastes: MGMT's "Kids," Moby's "One of These Mornings," and The Verve's "Bittersweet Symphony."

That year I'd made a promise to Marlowe, Mason, and Hunter, who championed my *Beavis and Butthead* impersonations. They were the teenage characters of a mid-1990's animated show on MTV. Obsessed with boobs and heavy metal, Beavis and Butthead spent all day watching TV and committing petty vandalism.

Marlowe, Mason, and Hunter were sensitive and sophisticated young men. Their mild disaffection and bewilderment at life found a pressure valve in the dirtbag antics of Beevis and Butthead. The characters' approach to life was to simply determine if something "sucked" or not. Naysayers in their world were dismissed as "butt-munches" and "dill weeds."

I vowed to do the maniacal chortles of Beevis and Butthead at the end of my graduation speech. As I finished, with the mic still to my lips, I laughed deviously but no sound came out.

They accused me of breaking my promise. It "sucked."

Twenty-Nine

I KNOW NOW what a few of us remaining middle school staff were doing when we showed up in August, at the little school next to the old Catholic church, without Ms. D as our leader. It would be a sober year, where we'd ritually wash the middle school after its demise and prepare it for burial. And the distance between what the school used to be and what it now was would turn out to be very, very far. Like the distance between the living and the dead.

It was a bit dramatic to compare the change at Ms. D's little school to a death. But death was fresh on my mind, after watching my father-in-law slowly succumb to cancer. A recent experience with the death of one of my childhood friends reminded me how something alive could turn cold in the blink of an eye. The distance between life and death was not that great after all.

I learned about my childhood friend dying with a text message instead of a phone call. That's how it works these days. One morning while my phone was charging, the news that my first friend in life had died, waited indifferently for me to look. I brushed my teeth, fed the cat, and sat down for breakfast.

Only after taking a long drink of water, halfway through my bowl of oatmeal, did I glance down at the text from my father: "Last night Yousif passed away." I was asked by his family to help prepare Yousif's body for burial. In Islam, a person is to be washed in a specific way, anointed with camphor oil, and then wrapped in a clean white sheet within a day or two of leaving this world.

Other Loyalties

On my way to the funeral parlor, I reflected on the exuberant personality of my friend.

Yousif was an enthusiast, like Maloney and Mr. Shane. I could count on him to be excited about anything. Mostly it was about going fishing. We would get on our dirt bikes and speed down to Lake Calhoun in Minneapolis, now renamed Bde Mka Ska, after the original Dakota name for the lake. At our secret spot under the willow tree, Yousif and I began our quest to remove every sunfish from the lake.

After a couple of hours, we would speed home. Each of us would be holding onto a stringer full of tiny sunfish. In my garage we slid the fish off the stringers onto some newspaper. None of the fish were worth keeping. If we had filleted them, it would have been enough meat for a six pack of sushi rolls at the grocery store.

But there Yousif was, flipping a bluegill the size of a pet goldfish in his hands, celebrating the great catch. Crouched in the afternoon sun, in the dusty garage, he threw the tiny fish up in the air one more time and declared, "Oh yeah, my dad can put some salts and seasonings on these and it'll be a feast!"

At the end of May each year from when I was nine years old until twelve, we would go to a cabin for my birthday. It would be Yousif and I, and a couple unsuspecting white friends who were about to get a heavy dose of my uncle's brand of African village affection. In the van ride up, my uncle sat in back with the boys, telling us stories and playing games that were an excuse to slap somebody.

After twenty minutes my uncle removed his slipper and smacked Casey on the head, accusing him of farting. For the next three hours, each of us got repeated beatings. Eddie squeezed against the window but couldn't escape. Yousif screamed that he was innocent as the slipper cocked back and slapped down on his bare knee. Of course, it was my uncle who had been farting all along.

Once at the resort, the tradition was to walk into the woods behind the cabin until we got lost. This always disturbed the other kids a little, but Yousif and I competed to see who could get us deeper into the woods.

One year we hit the spring hatch for some type of caterpillar, and they rained onto our heads from the treetops as we walked. Yousif heroically volunteered to clean them off people's backs and necks, before bounding ahead. Soon we were confronted by a bog that smelled like a mixture of gasoline, poop, and mud. Yousif was the first to grab a big stick and wade into the mucky doom. At one point it reached our shoulders, but we made the crossing.

At the other end of the bog there was a creek. We found a giant snapping turtle in there and Yousif was seriously trying to figure out how to bring it back to the cabin, and then home as a pet. At the Watt Munisotaram Buddhist monastery, Billie made me think of Yousif, with his impulsive plan to take a cat home as a pet. In fact, many of our meandering hikes at Ms. D's little school reminded me of my childhood plunges into the woods with Yousif.

After setting the turtle down for a moment Yousif spotted a carp floating in a pool under a tuft of grass overhanging the creek. He asked me for my jackknife, picked up a stick, and immediately set about attaching it to the end. After five minutes he had a spear and was directing me to block off any escape routes the fish had.

After we admired and terrorized the turtle and carp for an hour or so more, we realized we didn't have any idea how to get back to the cabin. Yousif chose a direction and we followed him back into the woods until we bumped into a dirt road. It led to the lake, but we were nearly on the other side of it from our cabin. Yousif flagged down a man on a boat and we all hopped in. We smelled like gasoline, poop, and mud but with his back straight and all the confidence in the world, Yousif pointed way, way into the distance, and led us home.

The reason that I'm telling all this is simple. "My feet took me to my death," the Arab saying goes. When I saw my dear friend laid out in the basement of the funeral parlor, his bare feet were sticking out from the cloth. They reminded me of his energy. Seeing them motionless though, toes pointed to the ceiling, made the distance to travel between life and death feel very, very far, again. But all along, death stays close, just beneath the soles of our feet. If we're lucky, and can keep moving, each footstep leaves death behind.

I didn't know all the parts of the washing ritual and was glad when a black Muslim convert, with a stooped back, strode into the funeral home where I was waiting. He'd taken on the role of ferryman to the next world for many families in the Muslim community of Minnesota. I followed him down the stairs and was put at ease by the Malcolm X cadence of his speech and confidence of faith.

"Have you performed the *ghusl*, 'full ablution', before?" the man asked.

"No, I haven't had the experience."

"Okay, okay."

"I'll watch how you do it."

"Yes, yes, it's all a normal part of the journey."

"You're right."

Without hesitation he pushed open the door where Yousif's body was resting, waiting for its final washing. I took a deep breath and crossed the threshold.

Without turning he said, "You know, death is more real than life, so to speak."

It was true in a way; death helped us see things very clearly. And eventually I came around to accepting that the end of Ms. D's little school was the only way for us to see how glorious it was. But at the beginning of my sixth year at the school I was still in mourning, and denial and confusion were still in the air, clouding my vision.

I showed up early on Monday morning the last week of August, my face grim with the task of confronting a new reality. First off, the entire middle school had been moved from the second floor to the cafeteria, where a row of closet-sized rooms lined one wall. My old room had been spacious, with windows, and was right across the hall from Ms. D's office. When I arrived each morning,

I'd hear the tinkling drums and guitar chords of hits from the seventies and eighties coming from Ms. D's boombox.

Besides getting banished to the dreary basement, what else had changed? Ms. Conley wasn't there. When I asked her in the summer what she was going to do she laughed and announced, "Oh Mr. A, I don't know what I want to do with my life!" What would I do without her positivity around, during such a negative time?

Mr. K.O. and Mr. Barnett weren't there anymore. They had been the first to go. Sensing trouble early on, they'd laid the groundwork for a move to a charter school in Minneapolis. In their new school across the Mississippi, they closed the doors of their classrooms and did their thing. The kids loved them of course, and Mr. Barnett had helped a young music group hone their skills in his class. They ended up making the early YouTube hit, "Hot Cheetos and Takis."

Mr. Duvall's Teach for America assignment had ended. He had been gunning for a job at Google and I figured he'd soon be in the slipstream of certain success. But he had earned our respect. Like a preppy kid joining the Marines, us teachers had our doubts about the Teach for America recruit, but he'd shown guts on the battlefield. But he was gone, and Ruby had lost her guardian angel.

Early in the summer Maloney and I had been in contact, both trying to find lifeboats to other schools but couldn't nail anything down. I started desperately applying for jobs in Abu Dhabi and Costa Rica. Maloney had worked summer school and had moved the contents of my entire classroom downstairs to the cafeteria with the help of students. When I went incommunicado for a while, Maloney assumed I wouldn't be back, and I wasn't sure about him.

A pile of boxes, furniture, and bric-a-brac sat outside my tiny new classroom. My bleachers would have covered the entire floor space had I brought them in the room and were now stored at the back of the stage. The room was an airless, claustrophobic, monastic cell, where I'd live out my last days at the school.

I stood there in the dim light of the cafeteria wondering who else was still around.

"Hi Mr. A! We weren't sure if you were coming back."

It was the voice of Ms. Ashley, one of the Three Sisters, the dynamos that ran the elementary school. They were part of a common, but at times inexplicable phenomenon: suburban women who stick it out in city schools. I've seen it everywhere I've taught, and it isn't about job availability—because when some tire of the cultural friction and uphill struggle, they vanish to comfy gigs close to home. The Three Sisters cared, and had stayed, delivering a world-class education for class after class of kids.

Ms. Ashley had a clipboard in her hand, and I knew there was business to attend to. Looking at her blond hair, I thought of the 'Norns' again, the three goddess sisters of Norse mythology. Which one was Ms. Ashley? Was she Verdandi, the goddess whose name meant "what is coming into being"? What 'fate' was being weaved for me?

"Hey. Yep, I'm back," I replied, a bit coolly.

I was not sure how to behave towards someone who I perceived had hurt my friend Ms. D. That whole end of last year, I forced myself to be dry and curt with the people who had sided against Ms. D. My attitude was contrived and took a toll, as it didn't suit my nature. But anything else felt fake, especially acting like nothing happened.

After the falling out between the elementary and middle school staff in the spring, Maloney had said, "Well, I was friends with people before, and I will be friends with people after." I wish I could have taken his equanimous approach. But Maloney was more sociable, and he had laid groundwork that was stronger and more capable of withstanding the rift than me. He was the type to invest in morning rounds of chit-chat and jokes before the bell, sealing bonds with many more staff members than me over the years.

"How was your summer? Any more amazing adventures?" Ms. Ashley asked.

"Nothing too fancy…I did…'
"Mr. A!" She shouted cheerily.
"Yes?"
"How can I help you? What materials do you need for your class?"

I was too slow of a thinker for Ms. Ashley. She was a no-nonsense powerhouse. Intense and devoted to her students, I saw her as a kind of apprentice to Ms. D my first couple of years. She'd built a reading loft in her room and her kids were whipped into shape merely by her reputation. I even thought that if my son ever came to the school, I'd want him to be in her room, benefiting from order, calm, and the self-directed learning of a well-oiled classroom.

But if you want to understand something, look at the results. Ms. D was gone, and Ms. Ashley seemed to be one of the people in charge, or at least dictating spending of the school's budget. Ms. Ashley had watched Ms. D, who was in tears, pack up her office. I didn't know how much of a role she played but, painfully, I felt that I couldn't trust her anymore.

"I don't know. I've never spent money on books for my room."
"What?"
"Well, we got some copies of Joy Hakim's *A History of US* a few years back."
"Mr. A! Oh my god! You were never given textbooks to work with—something to go on? *What did you do all these years?* Let's get you some books. I can order whatever you need."

Ms. Ashley was a great teacher, but she had revealed that she didn't understand how we worked in the middle school—the sauce we had been cooking. Before stamping kids with society's agenda, we had opted to form a family and help them find themselves first. What was society's agenda? Some wanted kids to be taught a bland story of national glory that washed over them and left them scented with success and patriotism, and the mistaken view that all was well. Others wanted kids to be shown the worm-eaten underbelly of a rotting republic, that left them covered with a deep stench, and the mistaken view that all was broken.

Other Loyalties

In the middle were young people that had to live their lives and face the future. The middle school staff wanted to help students feel like they belonged no matter what, before making them start choosing sides. Political parties liked to promote the idea that one wouldn't belong anymore if they chose the wrong side—but we had other loyalties.

I eyed the crumpled packet of state social studies standards poking out of a light blue milk crate. I knew that somewhere buried in that crate was my *Age of Empires III* CD-ROM. The funny thing was that there were finally enough laptops in the school. I could have had Ms. Ashley order a few more copies of the game. At each screen, partners could have role-played the fates of different civilizations across the lands of North America. There had even been a new update of the game. In this version, kids could choose to be a Native American civilization. They were playable, like the British, French, and Spanish.

"Actually, Ms. Ashley, it'd be nice if…."

Just then a voice spoke over the intercom, "Ms. Ashley, please come to the main office."

Ms. Gina, whose voice we were hearing, had been nothing but encouraging to me from the day I set foot in the school. But in my mood of wariness and cynicism, I figured Ms. Ashley had made a plan with Ms. Gina to call down after five minutes. It was like the phone-calls young women give each other in the middle of dates to see if they need an excuse to bail. Ms. Gina was rescuing her sister from the new middle school dungeon, and the potentially hostile colleagues there, before it got too awkward.

I thought about Ms. D, and my feelings of protectiveness about her legacy, and understood where Ms. Ashley and Ms. Gina were coming from: friends looking out for each other.

Later that morning the circle of chairs was set up in the dim cafeteria as usual. There were a lot of new staff members and maybe they'd take part in the earnest tradition where we went around sharing our path to the school. I saw Mr. J and Ms. Soraira across the circle and my eyes softened a little. I took a sip of Minute Maid orange juice and waited.

Ms. Ashley began in a solemn tone, "We will now go around and share our deepest thoughts…"

Suddenly Ms. Rhodes and Ms. Gina popped up and headed for the stairs leading up to the gym.

"Or maybe not! Come on everybody!"

In the gym, rows of chairs faced the stage, and a goofy skit was set in motion.

"We need a volunteer!"

"Maloney!"

"Come on, one more!"

"Look there's Mr. A."

"Mr. A! Come on up!"

I hadn't raised my hand. My face was ashen, and I was still shaken from the jolt of being ripped out of the sacred circle in the dreary cafeteria. I cringed and jogged up on stage hoping no one noticed my unhappiness.

I sat on a chair, a contestant on a game show, and tried not to make eye contact with the staff below. Ms. Rhodes, dressed in a fairy costume, was twirling around me. She was the one who had baptized me by screaming "Diarrhea!" into my room during my first days as a teacher. We hadn't talked or met eye-to-eye since the previous spring. As she held out her wand to touch my forehead our faces met, her smile dropped, and a chord of sadness passed between us.

It was sensible to try to make a fresh start, even though I thought it'd be wise at some point for the staff to process what had happened the previous year. The firing of Ms. D was judged to be too radioactive to acknowledge and was left to fester in the background.

The new staff eventually picked up on the vibe, gathered bits of gossip, and were left to patch the story together on their own. In true Minnesotan fashion, conflict and emotions sank beneath the surface. The temperature dropped and the way people really felt was sealed under the ice that was like a giant mouth that had closed shut.

Other Loyalties

～

THERE'S ONE THING that can brighten a tomb, and this might sound macabre, but it's children. The first day of school of my sixth year teaching I waited for the sound of their footsteps coming downstairs to my new classroom—a shadowy rectangle beneath the stairs. A room that was the size of a burial chamber inside the Great Giza pyramid in Egypt I'd climbed into on a visit when I was seventeen.

It's said that in the early Pharaonic dynasties of ancient Egypt, members of noble families were selected to be buried with the King, along with servants, guards, and artisans. The whole thing about needing your entourage in the afterlife. The burial chamber of King Hor-Aha from five thousand years ago contained thirty-six graves. The bodies were determined to be of people all roughly the same age. It's as if an entire class were brought down into the limestone tunnels of the Valley of Kings and marched single file into the dusty chamber. There they were poisoned and laid down in rows, soon to arise in the underworld to carry on the mirror image of life on earth.

These thoughts of grandeur were the result of an ego problem, I decided. The middle school used to be royalty, commandeering resources and attention from Ms. D, and now we were put in our place. Instead of the age of adolescent self-discovery being celebrated, we were put back where society liked us best—out of sight. (Within a few years, social media and gaming would hide teenagers away for good. Adults wouldn't have to contend with the unpredictable joy of their bodies and voices stirring up the boredom of public life. They would be left to eat each other and themselves alive with the unchecked tendencies of their age group, amplified to the max, and pouring through their earbuds and screens.)

Tabari and Edgar showed up in the doorway.

"Hey Mr. A."

"Hey guys, good to see you."

"Dang, Mr. A."

Tabari took another scan of the new social studies room, saw me wedged in the corner, shook his head, and smiled.

"Dang dog, this is bogus."

"What happened?" Edgar asked. "Where are the bleachers?"

"Bro, does it look like the bleachers could fit in here?" Tabari said laughing.

Amelie and Dena squeezed past the boys. Both were beaming. They were the kind of girls who take school and run with it; maxing out projects; attending to the frilly, extra thoughts of teachers after basic instructions were done; and filling in the blanks of class time with personal reading books that were always in tow.

People talk about teachers needing to believe in their students, but it goes the other way too. It took the girls four seconds to tour the new room. But it didn't matter, they were happy *I* was there.

And just like that the room turned from a tomb into a mine. The strange mines that produce gems in proportion to one's effort. Me and the students would hammer away together in the mine that year. We did papier mâché, sewed, and crafted props for puppet shows about the lives of famous Americans. Amelie built a spaceship to take astronaut Mae Jemison into orbit, and it flew up against a starry backdrop drenched in tempura paint. Whenever possible we would ascend the steps of the cafeteria ourselves and climb out towards the sky.

The students even figured out a way to capitalize on the darkness of the new classroom. When December rolled around, it was time for the yearly Festival of Lights celebration. Each class would pick a country to represent and decorate their room accordingly.

I was happy that the festival, with its roots in Paganism and Eastern traditions, was still on the schedule. The fundamentalist inquisitors on the school board must have been appeased with Ms. D's vanquishment and overlooked this heathen celebration.

The festival was dear to the whole staff anyways and they would have insisted on keeping it. Teachers would have revolted like the peasants of the Middle Ages, who had refused to give up their solstice rituals even as they were converted en masse to Christianity. The all-night fire vigils, dancing, and offerings were part of the lifeblood of the peasant's culture. Instead of competing, the church co-opted these rituals, turned gods and goddesses into saints, and funneled the worship of the sun into the body of an exemplar of a man who was also divine.

The lineage of the traditions made no difference to me. The borrowing and merging of symbols was part of the human story. It can be read as a cynical political move by the early church, but the message was the same—darkness yields to light. The festival had a universality to it and was a welcome yearly ritual amongst the practical data points and subjects of public school. People have a need to slow down and gather; to acknowledge the dark, the suffering; and then beat it back with love and fire. We joined the ageless struggle between light and darkness under the guise of a yearly nighttime school event for parents.

Within the new reality of adult cliques at the school, and latent recriminations, fellowship resurfaced on the night of the festival. The celebration laid the groundwork to restart the new year with the basic process of becoming human again. And that relied on a touch of a force beyond us—or at least something larger than our troubles.

The elementary school went all out for the festival. Ms. Ashley even bought hats with thick black dreadlocks attached to them. The kids, many who were white, Latino, and Hmong, served jerk chicken to visitors, next to their black classmates, some with real dreadlocks. They all put on Jamaican accents and basked in the politically incorrect glory of imitating Bob Marley. (The other inquisitors, the politically correct, would come for the hats soon, I was sure.)

My eccentric homeroom had picked the moon as our "country," and the decrepit cell was transformed. We took out all the desks and I bought a couple packs of glow-in-the-dark stars, and some rolls of luminescent vinyl sheets. I even ran to the Science Museum to pick up packets of freeze-dried astronaut ice cream.

The kids cut out the adhesive paper and lined the perimeter of the room with a layer of neon green 'moondust.' They dotted the floor with craters and created boulders by bunching paper into circles and covering it with the glowing paper. The ceiling and walls filled up with stars.

When the night of the festival arrived, eighth grader Jeremiah revamped the hazmat suit I had used a few years back for an assembly and put on a white motorcycle helmet. Now an astronaut, he led small groups of elementary kids and parents through our classroom door and into a desolate and lonely valley of the moon.

In the darkened cafeteria, parents and students were milling around. Among them, the shadows of people I used to believe shared my purposes. A few former students had showed up to bask in attention, and make sure the school was now whack since they were gone. A.J. and Mason disappeared into Maloney's science room to share with him awesome high school adventures they'd had. Kendrick was holding court by a pillar.

There was some warmth powering the school again, but not quite enough to quell my uneasiness. I opened the door to go back inside to the lunar landscape. I'd put Dena in charge of turning on the lights for a few seconds between visitors to re-energize the phosphorescence of the glow-in-the-dark stars.

My timing was off, and as I stepped inside, Dena flicked on two strips of aging fluorescent bulbs, shedding plenty of light on each corner of the new tomb that was my classroom.

Thirty

AFTER THE FESTIVAL of Lights, it wasn't long until winter break. For a teacher, it's quite common to keep everything together until the last moment, and then on the first day of vacation, have a complete collapse of the immune system and get sick. Sometimes it's a mental collapse. A hardworking teacher, like a piece of meat, is beaten and tenderized by student needs, cooked slowly over the low heat of keeping up with weekly lessons, and singed by fingers of fire during 'full moon' spells of ridiculous behavior. When a chance to sit down arrives during break, the meat falls off in a pile and the teacher is left like a stripped bone.

I didn't succumb to the flu when break arrived. I was in good physical shape, having tried for two years to pass muster in the hall alongside Mr. Duvall. But the mental exhaustion of dealing with the unprocessed negative feelings at school had got to me. To soothe myself I went out one morning and bought a large mocha and sat down next to a fireplace at Caribou Coffee. Turning towards the gas-powered flame my knees started to heat up. I pushed aside the *New York Times* and spent some time with my own thoughts.

It seemed I'd reached a tipping point in my teaching career.

I had grasped how much needed to be done to make a class worth coming to. Once I realized that I wasn't doing enough for my students most of the time, I entered the crucible of this stage.

It felt like a face-off with time, sanity, and duty.

I had successful projects under my belt, but the students who had benefited from them had moved on—Kendrick, Javion, A.J., Cynthia, Jake, Mason, and the rest. Was it possible to lead another group down the same path all over again?

Our experiences had been eclectic, reliant on people and places, not precise lesson plans from a curriculum guide, computer files with saved unit plans, or banker boxes of supplies. Such experiences would be hard to recreate.

I considered the paths I could take as a teacher. I didn't have the entrepreneurial drive to hit the conference circuit or run teacher workshops. Cashing out and trying to get an administrative job would shield me from the let-down faces of kids bored by a crummy lesson, but I'd be left dealing with their rage against it as they acted out. Besides, as an administrator, the faces of those bored or angry kids would just be replaced with glum or disgruntled teachers in staff meetings. I'm sure administrators had wonderful reasons for taking their path, but I felt like I would be hawking the bits of knowledge I'd gleaned in a classroom to sound competent in front of adults—to little or no effect.

I could leave teaching altogether, but then some words of Professor Greenwalt came to mind, "Yes, the education system is troubled. But is it helpful to leave? Then you'll just be yelling from the sideline." The longer I was away from the class the more ill-informed I'd become, so that even the letters I might write to the editor regarding education policy, would be out of touch and useless. Even if the letters were persuasive—how could they compare to the influence one could have in front of actual students.

The whipped cream had melted into my mocha drink making it too sweet. I turned away from the fireplace and touched the heated denim of my pants. I was relaxed but knew five more months of the school year were ahead of me.

There was an option to forge ahead into the land of unsustainable expectations. It was the battle for perfection waged by many teachers, and always with a double-edged sword. The horizon looked burnt out, an apocalyptic wasteland, but I could link

Other Loyalties

arms with a small band of survivors in the school and keep giving kids the good stuff. We could double the coffee intake and die martyrs—together.

I noticed some teachers taking stock of the monumental tasks of public education. They took a step back, making a bid for survival within their careers until retirement. Society was not serious about the welfare of the young and had turned away from schools during a decades-long onslaught hitting both home and classroom—budget cuts, overcrowded classrooms, divorce, trauma, poverty, addiction, and finally capitulation to the complete tech hijacking of attention spans.

These pragmatic teachers seemed to make a pact with students to ride out the days. Their formula was mild competence, straightforward lessons that unfolded like a Lego instruction manual, lazy jokes, and choice time on Fridays. They subscribed to the teaching equivalent of easy jazz.

I wasn't worried that I was susceptible to this approach because an unexamined existence wasn't in the cards for me. I was just too awkward of a figure in a classroom to ever make the 'easy jazz' approach work. I knew this because during my first year at Ms. D's little school three eighth grade boys walked up to my tanker desk during my prep hour for some casual banter. I couldn't tell if they were asking me questions just to skip class or if Ms. D sent them to bug me.

It was hard to believe—but they had just wanted to talk. I felt like I had to do something, *teach* something to them.

"Mr. A, where are you from?" Xander, a skateboarder had asked.

"Well, give me some reasons why it matters, and I'll tell you," I answered.

"Like what do you do on a… Saturday?" Nick asked.

"I make sure I wake up—and then try to make something happen."

They exchanged sly glances and smiled.

"Mr. A, we like talking to you."

"Yeah, we just like talking to you man," added Rashad.

"Why don't we just do this more?" Nick asked.

They didn't know how nervous I was then. I didn't know what I was supposed to do. What did they need to hear at that moment? I was their teacher. But they didn't want a teacher; they wanted me. What *I knew* and who *I was*—it was enough for them. I was an example of a man at the dawn of the twenty-first century, and our culture had arranged for us to be in a room together to learn from each other. It was all enough.

At the time though, I gave the boys the impression that I wanted to get back to work. I still thought teaching meant filling up my Horace Mann Teacher Planner with lessons. Xander dropped his skateboard onto the hardwood floor, and they turned to leave—satisfied somehow. Or dissatisfied?

The enterprise of teaching was a little too complicated for me when I was conscious of being a teacher. I felt out of place standing in front of kids. It was the root of the panicked feeling that led me to buy a can of black spray paint all those years ago. I wanted them looking out at the world or inside themselves, not at me.

From the beginning the best I could do was throw open the doors as wide as they could go—to see if the world could help. At this inflection point of both my career and the school's history, the answer to getting by would have to be the same: go outside. I dumped my sugary drink into the trash, left the warmth of the Caribou Coffee shop, with its framed photos of the Alaskan wilderness, and took a walk.

ONE OF THE hurdles for us in getting kids outside at our school had always been cultural, these were city kids. Nature was a place with no familiar touchstones *until we made them*. Most didn't have a memory bank of campsites, family cabins, or favorite views from the shores of Lake Superior.

It was a place accessed by driving through suburbs that were wary of difference, and even more precarious rural landscapes. Once separated from the rec centers, malls, and churches—but more importantly the protective orb of extended family, cousins, and aunties—students were in what the Wilderness Act of 1964 itself defined as a place where "man himself was a visitor that does not remain." The apprehension our students had about visiting this wilderness was not made out of only historical or purely imagined slights. When we took a small group of kids up to go winter camping one weekend, we stopped at a well-known restaurant halfway between St. Paul and Duluth. Mr. Shane and Maloney, who were driving Kendrick, Jaden and Kevin, showed up first. I was in the second van. When my van arrived, we walked past display cases of donuts and pies and looked around for the other group. We strolled further amongst the tables and booths and couldn't find them.

Needing to use the bathroom, I walked to the back of the restaurant and found that they had been seated far away from all the other customers. Being isolated outside of the city for young black men was something haunted with the sounds of hound dogs. But crammed together in a booth in the far corner of this esteemed restaurant, the boys were laughing about it—what else could they do?

City life was grand: lots to do, Footlocker, sports teams, the Mall of America. I could understand why those boys would prefer it. But even so, when I pulled up a map of America, the vast majority of land was open. In between the small towns, suburbs and cities were blank spots on the map: national parks, state forests, regional parks, and reserves tucked into neighborhoods.

There was still space out there to walk in the footsteps of our ancestors—feeling a freedom of movement. Following quiet paths fit for people, not machines.

(A white country boy tearing up a trout stream on an ATV was taking it a little too far, but I felt his joy, abandoning the marked and paved roads dictating where he could go and what he could do. It was an attitude he probably caught from his father who might have played the rock n' roll song "Signs" that was covered by the band Tesla in 1990: "Signs, signs, everywhere there's signs/ blockin' out the scenery, breakin' my mind.")

For my students, if nature itself was seen as *not for them*, and the extent of their ventures outside stopped at the family barbecue in the city park, the conclusion wasn't good. These gatherings were life-saving citadels of security and peace, and good brisket. But it meant that the majority of America was not a place where they could feel at home.

Like Native Americans locked off their land, the city became a sort of reservation for people of color. A boundary set up by our continued belief about who owns the world.

AS A TEACHER, I kept a mantra in my head. Only once or twice did I mention it to other staff by saying it out loud: "If we go outside something bad might happen. If we stay in the classroom it's *guaranteed*."

The line reminded me of Abdi, who was one of the rare students at Ms. D's little school that had transferred out. His parents wanted to see more *visible* signs of academic rigor than we offered—stacks of homework and tests. One day, when he was still at our school, I complained to him that I couldn't do this or that over the weekend because I had to take care of my son. Abdi was confused.

In Somali culture, kids are normal. Families are part of the warp and weft of life. Sometimes in America I got the feeling that having a kid, or a family, was an alien prospect. People were oddly panicked about what to do with their new babies and raced to find experts, parenting videos, or saucy mothering blogs for advice. There was also the specter of abduction and danger that had been ratcheting up sense the 1980's. Parents behaved as if society viewed their kids as targets. I was one of them.

To Abdi's ears, the way I talked about my son sounded like I was discussing a UFO, not the circle of life first drawn and traversed near his ancestral homeland in East Africa. My insecurities about fatherhood and fears about the dangers the world posed to my son had made me think something "bad might happen" outside the house. It often led me to a self-imposed house arrest. Maybe it was the post-9/11 premium placed on the psyches of people with Muslim names like mine, but the attitude was suffocating me and my son.

Abdi's family had stared mayhem in the face in Mogadishu during the civil war there, and he'd seen his uncle shot in the back. He sized me up and said, "You got to go out man, just *bring your son*."

Since the early 2000's, as Somali families have moved out from Minneapolis to smaller communities in Minnesota, the usual array of reactions has followed them. Most white locals welcomed them, often drawing from a store of confidence and openness backed by faith. Others kept their skepticism to themselves. Soon the daily normality and banality of a family-centered people chipped away at their wariness of a new skin color and culture.

And, of course, there were those pulling on the alarms. America was under assault, and the sight of a purple hijab at a bus stop made them feel like their home was unrecognizable. Even the most ordinary acts were viewed as threatening when done by people who could *never* be real Americans.

In St. Cloud, a small city northwest of Minneapolis, a *New York Times* reporter spent some time talking to people about the new arrivals to the city. One lady, speaking about some people she saw at a park along the Mississippi, tried to give voice to the intangible fear she felt. "They were just"—she said, searching for the words to describe the offending behavior of the Somali-Americans. "They were just *walking around*."

AFTER RECOVERING FROM exhaustion over winter break, I decided to follow my old student Abdi's advice about just going out because it was the normal thing to do. I planned a foray for the middle school into the whitest of white worlds in Minnesota: ice skating. A warming house where the students could rent skates agreed to open early for us, and on a day when the temperature hovered near zero, we hopped on a bus and went.

The place was in Edina, a wealthy suburb of Minneapolis. The ice-skating course was the frozen man-made ponds and canals of a large residential and commercial development. Many South Asian tech workers lived in the apartments in the area, and the country's first ever indoor mall, Southdale, was across the street.

There was at least cosmetic diversity due to the economic activity of the area.

Still, it was a sight to watch the parade of colorful students enter a place with a single white worker. My intention was not a premeditated occupation of white space—a snotty collegiate take-over of a privileged activity, or middle-finger at the Man. The tables were not being turned on the white woman watching the warming house fill up with the diverse kids of our school.

There's a fear of being outnumbered that sours many good-intentioned white people on diversity. But this is not what I observed. What I saw was the initial surprise of a white woman in Edina. Her darting eyes and quick glance over property was a reflex ingrained in many middle-aged white Minnesotans who had grown up seeing mug shots of black people attached to a crime on the local news.

It was this white woman's return to composure and civility that I chose to focus on. She got past that initial, lower-level assessment of our students. The busyness of it all took over. She had a *job to do*; hand out skates. One by one, the kids poked holes in the racial wall between her and them with their excitement and innocence. Every smile from a black girl, happy with her skates, brought her closer to feeling that her own daughter could be standing there with her sassy friends.

If she had at first held her breath at the arrival of our city school, now the entire warming house was filled with our breath. She had only one choice in the new America: open her lungs and let the air in. And from the looks of it, she was breathing fine.

Out on the ice for the first time, friends clutched each other in suicide pacts, or pushed metal-frame skate trainers around with enormous grins, freezing their asses off. Kids even tried their hand at hockey, the ultimate white sport, before dipping back into the warming house.

Ryan, Lucas, and Jeremiah had some skating experience and disappeared down the winding canal that let out into larger ponds. I followed them through the landscaped stretch of ice and trees, bare now for over four months. When I found the boys, they were skating as fast as they could up to the snowbank lining a pond. Once they struck its edge they were launched into the snow. Jeremiah's Kermit the Frog hat went flying, hoodies became caked in snow. New office buildings towered above them, and a crowd laughing classmates soon gathered to admire the kamikaze show.

Skating back along the canal, I passed under a footbridge and glided past Edgar. In full concentration he took baby steps towards the action.

When we were done skating, we headed to a movie theater, all of us half-frozen. We were going to watch *The Life of Pi*, and it was Edgar that I pictured in the title role. In it, a young man from India, a romantic seeker, gets battered by the storms of life quite literally. As a teenager, he is caught in a shipwreck and forced to share a lifeboat with a full-grown Bengal tiger. Like the gentle Edgar, he would have to face up to the fact that life often traps us in a corner with things that snarl.

Maloney caught up with me before we entered the theater. "You know how much Lucas just spent at the concession stand?"

"No."

"Nineteen dollars!"

"Man."

"I could party for a week on that!"

Not all our students were poor, but none were rich. The sudden binges we'd see kids go on bewildered Maloney. His emphasis on the counterproductive side effects of the social safety net pointed to his tough love, realpolitik approach to uplifting his fellow man. The current configuration of welfare, unemployment benefits, and so on was disempowering for many, in his view. It was the first time I had encountered a humane type of conservative perspective. One that I grew fond of listening to.

On the bus ride home, I wondered which world was stranger to the students: the ice rink or the steamy zoo and botanical garden of Pondicherry, India where the film began. I pressed my back into the green vinyl seat and kept an ear open. The film didn't wrap up in a tidy way and I was curious whether this irritated or inspired the kids.

"Wait, was the tiger real?" I heard Amelie ask Haven.

"What do you mean—was it CGI?"

"No, was it really on the boat with the boy all that time in the ocean?"

"Yeah, I think."

"No, but you know when the boy was rescued in the end? He told his story to the Japanese guys—the ones investigating the shipwreck—and it sounded like the tiger wasn't there. It was really just another person the whole time."

"What?"

"Yeah."

"I did *not* get that."

"Mr. A?"

"Yeah." I turned around in my seat.

"Was the tiger real?" Haven asked.

Before I could answer Amelie shouted, "No! Ask Ms. Tracy—Mr. A is just going to confuse us even more!"

"Ms. Tracy?"

"Yes, Amelie?"

"Was the tiger real?"

"You mean, what did it represent?"

"NO! Was it *real*?"

Ms. Tracy, philosophical herself, was no help to them and they were left to decide on their own which parts of the fiction were true. Amelie and Haven huffed and puffed over it. Ms. Tracy took out her phone to make the usual call to the school: "Can you tell them to please hold the busses for a couple minutes? We're late, but we're almost back."

Since Ms. D had been ousted, the school that we were heading back to seemed, in some hard to measure way, more *real*. But it felt like it was the 'reality' that adults try to scare kids with. The view of reality that says, "You have to do this hard, boring, meaningless, work because that is how life is, and school is preparing you for it." When Ms. Ashley showed shock that I hadn't used a textbook with the kids for all my years at the school, she was maybe being more *realistic* than me, about what would prepare kids for high school, and the demands of a job. It was a practical viewpoint, that in the end may have better served many students.

When Ms. D was around, everything felt more like a dream. Imagination held center stage. The question was then, which was a more powerful tool to handle life: a cold, realistic, eye or imagination? I had made my choice at my homemade altar my first week of being a teacher. It was a promise to give back to students a part of themselves that adults seem so eager to sacrifice. The thing that allows children to be so happy and free thinking—their imaginations.

It wasn't just children that suffered when imagination was trampled on. I learned this on my trip to Egypt when I was seventeen. The trip also confirmed for me the importance of place in a lesson—and how that gave students experiences that were impossible to recreate. Time, place, and people mattered, and that was part of my trouble working with the state social studies standards and nailing down a curriculum that was supposed to last year after year.

On my trip I was in the Red Sea town of Hurghada, south of Cairo, Egypt. It was my junior year of high school and I had taken some time off to see what it was like in Africa, the birthplace of my father. I had climbed to the roof of my hotel at sunset and turned west. Three thousand miles of largely uninhabited space opened before me in an orange-red blast of rock and sand that reached to the Atlantic: the great Sahara Desert. The sky was marked with colors from a box of crayons not yet invented. One that held the color of my skin.

This may sound a little strange but the only way I can describe being in Africa was like being scalped, the top of my head sliced off by an ancient obsidian blade. Suddenly the moldy crust of all the "progress" we had made since our ancestors walked off the continent was gone. The sharp pain of the cut jerked me awake and what was left was the feeling of hot wind passing over hot blood, and then the cooling peace of a forgotten twilight. I could see why Victorian doctors sent sickly patients away from the sour damp of the British Isles for a "change of air" in the nineteenth century. I stood there breathing the dry air, and my insecurities and worries about high school were soothed.

I stayed on the roof while the stars slid into place and then walked to my room to pack. I'd be heading back to the city the next day, so I stepped out to see if I could find anything interesting in the small shops that lined the street.

As I walked along the street, I saw a man dozing on a chair. Beyond him were lit glass showcases. Delicate Pyrex glass vials filled with perfume lined the shelves. If I made any noise, I thought he'd wake up and seize me. Brushing the fragrance of Egyptian rose on my arm, he'd warn me that the girls would soon be chasing me down the street.

I noticed his dusty toes had slid halfway out of his flip-flops, a sign that he was taking his nap seriously. I passed safely—this far from the capital, the sales pitch was more laid back. In this guy's case the pitch was nearly horizontal.

I passed another shop and for the mere fact that the owner wasn't hovering by the door, I went in. The place was poorly lit, and I saw outlines of obelisks, pyramids, and papyrus scrolls. Even in the shadows I could tell they were of a cheap make. Behind the counter a middle-aged man was polishing a black stone bust of Queen Nefertiti. He greeted me and set down his rag. The sound of an old motorcycle passed the open door as another shopkeeper headed home.

I've never been a good shopper, so my air of disinterest wasn't a bargaining ruse. It had been my superpower in life really—the lack of a desire to buy things. My source of freedom. Strutting slowly through the store I appraised the multiplying number of objects I could live without.

In the tiny store in Hurghada, I lingered on some scarab beetle amulets. The scarab was a sacred symbol in ancient Egypt and its role in their world ran the gamut. The beetle stood in for the heart in mummies and was responsible for rolling the sun over the eastern horizon at dawn.

Other Loyalties

But the scarab is a dung beetle, a creature that lays its eggs in a ball of poop collected from herbivores. The idea of a sacred creature that made its name pushing poop around had poetry in it. It seemed like a tale of a humble creature uplifted by the grand imaginations of Pharaonic meaning-makers. But it was the beetle's own astonishing behavior that caught the attention of ancient Egyptians. They observed that the beetles use the sun and even the Milky Way to guide the transport of their dung balls.

The weathered shopkeeper turned towards me patiently, before picking his rag back up.

I lifted one of the turquoise beetles that sat on the glass counter. "How much for this one?"

He murmured a price.

For something that I didn't want to buy, it was too much. Feeling that I'd stayed too long, past the point of no return, I panicked about how to leave gracefully. I put the beetle back down on the counter, reached into my pocket and pulled out some pound notes. I set them on the counter, wished him good night and turned to go.

A flash of confusion passed over his stubbled face. Then in one motion he set down Queen Nefertiti, slid off his stool and straightened his back. Before I knew what was happening his hand was reaching back over the counter with my money in it. Then he said three words in muddled English.

"I am…businessman."

The jolt of dignity that radiated from him quickly coiled deep inside me. It still sits between my shoulder blades. It stirs sometimes when I start to trample the independence of others. It's what made me hesitate at the altar, at the cusp of becoming a teacher.

In the Egyptian's dusty shop there was no business going on. He may have not sold anything for days. Being a businessman was his own view of himself in the world. It was how he imagined himself. I had transgressed against his *imagination*.

March rolled around and there had been a string of heavy snowfalls, which meant the school boiler was still going strong.

Heat tended to pool in my tiny new classroom. For a string of days, it was in the mid-eighties when I checked the thermostat. It was like a villain had cut off the air supply and everyone was slowly wilting.

Students were working on another puppet show. As soon as I was done talking to them about next steps, they took their scripts and props they were painting out to the cafeteria tables, to escape the hot room and breathe.

The science room was empty, except for Ms. Tracy and a handful of kids retaking a test. Maloney had taken most kids out to help clear snow for elderly neighbors of the school. The doors of the English and math rooms were closed.

I didn't envy the new middle school staff. They were not able to tap into the creative momentum still flowing from when Ms. D was there. Plopped into the middle school where resentment was the strongest, they had to navigate the tension in the building without anyone spelling it out for them. Plus, they were hamstrung by the tentative demeanor that was usually affected by new hires.

I imagined the state of lethargy in the students roasting behind the closed doors of the English and math rooms. The good faith efforts of two new teachers battling against the fond memories kids had of Ms. Conley and Mr. Duvall. The only hope for the kids was to hold out for Maloney's class when they'd get to go out to shovel.

Later that week, the whole staff was down in the cafeteria for professional development. An earnest trio of teacher-presenters had been invited and were sharing their *secrets to success*. After a long day, the afterschool session was ill-advised, and the assembled teachers started to bleed out. Scanning my colleagues faces I saw the usual signs of decay that hit during hour two of any teacher training. Glazed eyes, compulsive coffee drinking and candy eating, and the fuzzy aura of a waking sleep. A sort of sleep that allowed the body to remain upright and passed as paying attention, that they learned from their students.

Other Loyalties

One person was sitting with their back straight and still commenting and asking questions: Maloney. They weren't the sort of questions and comments that are the performance of caring and concern that teachers feel compelled to do—the kind of *unnecessary* goodness, clarification, and engagement that makes a meeting drag on.

Maloney's engagement was the result of a philosophy towards life, one that doesn't get put aside casually. Bunkered down in my stuffy closet classroom, seeing out the days until summer vacation, it was an approach that I had to consider adopting, at my crossroads in teaching.

I became aware of Maloney's philosophy in the dying moments of a teacher meeting a year earlier. Sitting at a circular table, the middle school staff was at full strength with Ms. Conley and Mr. Duvall. We were pawing a problem around about a group of students. Half-hearted solutions trailed off mid-sentence, and somebody checked their watch. The situation was not critical, and we were at ease just sitting around together.

After a pause, Maloney pushed back from the table and before getting up said, "Well, like they say: Be all-in or leave." He rapped one fist gently on the table, rose, and called it a day.

Thirty-One

THE SIGNS WERE all there: it was time to go to Lilydale. The weather warmed a bit and Maloney and I had rallied to secure a bus for another visit. Everyone raced up from the basement classrooms and onto the bus. A few lucky wheelers-and-dealers got spots in a silver Caravan, and Mr. J peeled away. Mr. J was weathering the new reality at the school well but was heartsick like the rest of us and was happy to get out.

We had gone much of the year without a principal. The school was guided by an interim leader, and a committee that included the Three Sisters and the school accountant. But they were largely coasting on the hard work of Ms. D, like a new president bequeathed a humming economy.

Finally, just before spring officially arrived, the board had interviewed new directors for the school and took a vote. They elected a man who was legally blind. During his first few weeks at the school there were some heavy snowfalls, and one of the Three Sisters would pick him up when public transportation became unreliable.

He was a mild-mannered guy and we hit it off. His intentions were good, but he soon found out that his leadership was not really desired. The new forceful power center of the school was set and required him only as a figurehead.

In fact, Ms. Ashley told me bluntly, "The new director—he's useless."

There was something that the school board didn't seem to understand when they voted to hire the man: it's the eyes that make you blind, and the heart that lets you see.

It wasn't long before the blind man clearly saw a staff with broken morale. In a couple meetings with him I explained the need for healing that had never taken place since Ms. D was fired. He asked me in an email for more candid views. I described how working at the school that year had been like roaming the surface of a giant dead beast: a thicket of coarse hair, stink of rotting flesh, and the effort to make out the fading shape of magic. It was a desolate last walk over the carcass of a unicorn that I had been blessed to ride for five years.

It's tough to respond in a professional email to such words—but he did his best. He was clearly shocked by my description but did not indicate that I was out of line. He wrote, "I can tell that you are passionate about this school. That it means a lot to you, and that everyone is still suffering from what happened last year."

When Mr. J sped away towards Lilydale, I couldn't wait for the lumbering yellow bus we were on to catch up with him. Finally, we pulled in the dirt parking lot at the trail head.

Snowmelt from the top of the ravine had refrozen across our favorite path. A wide river of solid ice would have to be crossed. A slight slope meant that when kids lost their footing, they started to slide off the path into the young trees sticking through the ice. Rebecca, an eighth grader who read at a graduate level, was on her hands and knees, thinking her way across by finding divots in the ice. Halfway she turned to scoot on her backside.

Screams, laughter, and cursing echoed off the ice as it swept kids away back to the start or crashing into trees.

A sensible thing to do would be to turn around. But the challenge had been set, and a few kids were celebrating on the other side, and encouraging others. The spirit of Carter was still alive in the students. The winter fording continued and sure enough a handsome young seventh grader fell forward and bit clear through his lower lip.

Mr. J, part of the med team back-up always trailing behind the main group, had covered us so many times before. Maloney guided the stunned child back across the ice, into the care of Mr. J who took him to meet his dad at the hospital to get stitches.

I felt terrible when kids got hurt. It wasn't very often but I think I would have let it curb some of our adventures. It was Maloney who had the spirit to not hesitate and forge on. I knew he wasn't being callous with other people's children, because he took his own out on adventures with the same mantra: either live a life in fear or embrace the rare trip to the emergency room.

At the top of a steep ravine, scouts had found enough snow for us to butt-slide down the side of it. A line of kids hurtled down the ravine, while others were making their way back up. There was a small group huddled to the side, giggling, and peering down at their classmates taking a beating on the bumpy ride.

Maloney turned to one of them. "Just think Monique, one day you'll be an old woman sitting around looking back on your life and you'll go, 'Well, that was fun.'"

Monique took one more glance down the hill and said, "Alright y'all. If I die dress my body in Gucci."

"Girl! Your booty's about to get dirty as hell." Trina was a wiry firecracker, with glasses and a straight-shooting panache to her speech.

"Oh no, I ain't doing this!" Monique said as she sat down at the edge of the slide.

"You gonna die girl!" Trina warned one last time.

Monique screamed and sent herself bouncing down. At the bottom she brushed the snow and dirt off the lettering on her bottom that read, 'PINK,' and curled over in laughter. When she recovered, she yelled up, "Y'all better go down!"

"Hell no! You crazy!" Trina yelled back.

I imagined Monique and her friends as middle-aged professionals meeting up for a girl's weekend. It made me think of the group of black women from the same book club who were kicked off a Napa wine train in California for laughing too loud. One of the greatest perks of being outside was that the status quo sound barrier could be broken. The sky could absorb the joy of the girls as they let their happiness loose.

Jeremiah and Tabari led a repair crew that packed snow around a stump near the bottom of our homemade luge track. This mound turned into a jump that led to our second injury of the day—a bruised tailbone.

We had lucked out, getting by with cuts and bruises. A year after we took this last trip to Lilydale, two children died on a fossil-hunting field trip there. After heavy rains, a mix of sand and broken shale lost its hold, and a side of the bluff came tumbling down on top of them. What was incredible was that the father of one of the boys killed said that he didn't hold the school responsible. "Anything can happen," Lancine Fofana said.

After an investigation by two outside agencies, the city of St. Paul was cleared. They found no evidence that city officials knew the area held specific dangers that went beyond the general knowledge that erosion was occurring and landslides were a natural feature of riverside bluffs. Discussing the report, Mayor Chris Coleman said the undeveloped park was "an untamed, wild area," and that safety could not be guaranteed. "We can put up a sign. We can put up a fence. We can put up a gate. But we can't keep people from getting back into the 17 miles of wild area along the bluffs of the river in the city of St. Paul."

Lawyers offered their grim and necessary services to honor the dead through financial settlements—to paper over pits of grief with big checks. The money eventually received from the school district and city was used by the Fofana family to build a school back in Guinea, the country they had immigrated from.

Their son, Mohamed, had kept a journal during a two-month visit to the West African nation. He was troubled by the sight of kids begging on the streets. He wrote in a journal about what he would do in Africa when he grew up "I would build soccer fields for schools to play in."

In the immediate aftermath of the tragedy, it seemed to me that Mohamed's father had taken both a wise and instinctual view. *Anything can happen.*

THE GRACE OF Mohamed's father had the hallmarks of a religious view of life. A submission to higher forces that lit a path through the incomprehensible—or at least gave a person words to recite and hope to hold on to, while lost in the incomprehensible.

When I think about public education and what our aim truly was at Ms. D's little school, it was clear that we needed a better story, a myth to bolster our purposes. By sheer force of personality Ms. D was able to move us in a direction together without the details spelled out.

Mission statements in general varied slightly from school to school. But after all the wordsmithing, they ended up with smart but disembodied catchphrases about "critical thinking," "excellence and success," "lifelong learning," "21st century skills," "global citizens," and "change the world." The word "inspire" was in some statements, but the actual *stuff* of inspiration—the thing that would fuel the vision—was nowhere to be found.

The committees writing those statements couldn't be blamed. They had one hand tied behind their back—the hand that reaches into the unseen world. The hand that can yank us back to a perspective larger than us, that fills us with wonder, humility, and purpose. Ways of talking about life that were more compelling were problematic. They approached the realm of the spiritual tutti frutti, and were rightly regarded with suspicion by institutions that needed to keep church and state separate.

But in the early twenty-first century, the US was in a bind, its moral growth stunted, and civic life rotted by years of consumerism. Money was worshipped in the culture from top to bottom. A powerful story that served this god was that what America, and Americans, did was good, as long as some money was made. Martin Luther King Jr. warned about a culture that was too materialistic. He said that it is the "moral lag in our thing-oriented society that blinds us to the human reality around us and encourages us in the greed and exploitation which creates the sector of poverty in the midst of wealth."

Even within that very sector of poverty, the rural and urban poor, a fantasy swirled of decadent riches and easy living—just watch the music videos for country and hip-hop songs. The American god of money was prayed to in verses and hooks but had yet to answer in a meaningful way, except for the creators of the odd viral hit song.

But again, my arrogance had to be checked. As a teacher, to tell a young kid envisioning himself as a hip-hop star that he better think of a 'real' job, would be to transgress against his imagination. Telling a kid stuck in a trailer park, that he's wasting his time on his guitar, dreaming of being a rich country music star, would be the same crime.

Americans were slowly figuring out that the story of getting rich, the American Dream, was not only a bit hollow but near impossible for most of the country. As this dream faded, a gap in how Americans saw themselves appeared that was more dangerous than the organizing story of money—the green talisman the country had relied on to fill the void. A people without a convincing story will quickly seek out another, and in their haste latch onto the easiest one to understand—tribalism. Tribalism took different forms on different levels: race, creed, political party, nationality. It was the discordant story of more than one "chosen people," all jostling for attention and favor. Such a story has no broad audience appeal because people are only listening to the stories where *they* are the stars.

Private religious schools were on to something. They were providing a confident alternative story to the rank materialism of the culture. The brimming hodge-podge of good intentions, identities and narratives found in public schools were on the border of becoming incoherent. Private schools were able to guide their efforts by focusing on single tried-and-true religious stories. (Even if their path was narrowed by dogma, and entry required embracing certainties that could harden the heart towards others and close the mind for good.)

But religious schools were not an answer to a large, diverse nation. I imagined all public-school funds being released in vouchers to parents so that they could have the right to send their kid to any type of school. In my mind this would lead to a plague of dicey schools rising like pustules over the face of America. They would cater to the weirdest ideologies, agendas, and extremes. There would be no sieve, like the one that forces public school teachers to try and strip off their ideological and religious preconceptions before entering the classroom. An honest public school teacher can only make arguments with their conduct and character. After leaving out their biases and beliefs as best they can, teachers can safely offer students lessons that include the values that remain. Honor is one of them—and if a teacher can keep the sieve in place, they have demonstrated the value of honor well.

But with a voucher-based education free-for-all in the country, schools would become like the madrasahs of Afghanistan or Pakistan. American brand mullahs would compete for adherents, building their followers. Great storytellers, false prophets, run-of-the-mill hucksters, all weaving narratives but no collective tapestry, and no hope of keeping church and state separated. Yes, parents would have their say about what their kids learned by being able to select schools that catered to their most core beliefs (and assumptions). But with no common ground, or narrative shared with fellow citizens, schools would just be another thing to shop for—pick your color and name your price. And the result would be a citizenry incapable of holding a conversation.

I was not one of the imagined, 'socialist' public school teachers, creeping around infecting the youth, and agreed with many capitalist ideas, but capitalism was not very good at giving people meaning in their lives, (beyond the irreplaceable fulfillment of providing for oneself.) Yet I believed we still needed to keep religion out of public life, even if religions had a good track record of giving meaning to people's lives.

For now, the still strong public schools, filled with devoted teachers, would have to teach "critical thinking skills," "just the facts," and "social-emotional learning" and hope that the quest for purpose, enlightenment, and transcendence shined through between the lines. Perhaps, as only they can. And while they were at it, public school teachers were uniquely positioned to remind kids they were part of one country. For teachers, maintaining our neutrality was our patriotism.

THE GIRL WITH the bruised tailbone at Lilydale was ushered away and brought to a second waiting silver Caravan, driven by Mr. Kou. The rest of us walked toward a clearing near the old brickyard where clumps of cattails buffered a small lake. The kids had been quiet on the path down from the sliding area. Silence in a classroom could be easily misinterpreted. I wouldn't know if a student was bored, stumped, or thinking. At Lilydale, the silence could be trusted. Nature induced a different sort of silence in the kids—one that was reflective and observed, rather than imposed.

Monique and her friends had the freedom to be as loud as they wanted. But at one point I saw them with their arms linked walking along the dirt path. They were silent. The terrain around them was changing but staying the same—like a conversation—and it gave them permission to let their voices rest. Letting down their guard, footsteps and motion became the source of their confidence. I loved the loud expressions, attitude, and pinpoint verbal skill of big talkers like Monique and Trina. But I also valued a hike that was strenuous enough to make the girls realize that sometimes they needed to be able to hear their own breath.

Along the bluffs of the Mississippi River, we walked into the shared ignorance of our species, humbled together in awe and gratitude. Outside, it was easier to see creation, and how little we had to do with its internal engine, but how much we were a part of it.

It's not that people who live in the woods or the open spaces of rural America are closer to divinity—it's just a little easier to keep connected to our roots without all the noise and buildings in the way. By most accounts, those beginnings go back to the savannah 200,000 years ago. That is when we settled into the anatomical form we are in now. And it was brown feet that took the first tentative steps around humanity's cradle in East Africa.

In short, my city students had often felt out of place in our original home: nature.

I wonder when the moment was that humans became separate from the rest of creation. It would be nice to sum it up with the bite of an apple, but it was probably a gradual process—our alienation. A tool here, a shelter there. Drawings on cave walls of the animals surrounding us, and then paintings and carvings of supernatural creatures that don't exist at all: humans with beaks and tails, thunderbirds, and a lion-man. Storytellers pulled new worlds out of their imaginations, creating myths and totems that united larger and larger groups. A tribe here, a confederacy there. Pretty soon, we were inside farmhouses, fences, territory, kingdoms, cities, and nations, looking out at the wilderness.

Civilization, as impressive as it got, still fizzed along its borders with the wild. Coyotes slipped into the suburbs at night and ate cats, grizzlies sniffed around front porches, storm surges filled subway tunnels. We sprayed the swamps near towns with insecticide, built flood barriers, trapped or shot animals drifting onto our territory. Pushing back nature, and its untamed completeness, we threw the baby out with the bathwater.

The act of *creating* now appeared to come from the heads and hands of humans, but creation *itself* remained the domain of the spirit, mysterious and whole. Yet it was becoming harder to see creation amongst all our creating.

Maybe skyscrapers, grocery stores, cyberworlds, cars, are a temporary armor that has given us the safety to gather ourselves again, to *consciously* consider our next steps. Even the artificial environment of a twenty-first century classroom bursting with technology, could be seen as a weigh station where the young regrouped. From there we could discuss how they wanted to head into the future—with a bulldozer or footsteps, through a digital signal or in the flesh.

"This girl is on firrre!"

Behind me Trina belted the chorus of an RnB hit by Alicia Keyes. I snapped out of it.

"Look at Mr. A, he always be meditating on stuff," Monique said, her arms still linked with Trina's.

"He do, right?" Trina said, laughing.

"Why you so quiet all the time Mr. A!"

"What? I'm just walking."

"Ommm…" Trina mugged a Buddha pose with her fingers.

"Why are you harassing me? I'm just a guy on the path."

"*This girl is on firrre!*"

Monique and Trina skipped away to catch their friends.

When the silence got oppressive, when thinking hit a dead end, that other thing we didn't create but are a part of kicked in: soul. I was so grateful for how much my students taught me about that.

"*This girl is on firrre!*" I heard it one more time, through the trees, as the girls hopped out of sight.

For the time being I was happy that I was at a charter school—a small school in between the fissure of public and private. A threshold place. I felt that we'd found the spiritual drive behind community but didn't say it out loud. Left unnamed, the kids were not indoctrinated by an established spiritual approach to learning—but enjoyed its fruits.

Ms. D's little school, for a few improbable years, had threaded the needle.

Somebody tapped me on the shoulder.

I was awoken from my tree-hugging reverie and spun around. Just as I took a breath in, two handfuls of cattail fluff were thrown into my face. Cottony seeds filled my mouth and were sucked up my nose. A hundred seeds took root deep in my nasal passage. Unable to breathe, my life passed before my eyes, and a cattail sprouted from my grave.

Gagging and coughing, I heard hysterical laughter. I blew my nose hard. Squinting through watery eyes I saw the outlines of my assassins: Raya, Amelie, and Valentina. Beyond these three, cattails were being swung like swords, disintegrating over kid's heads. Bursts of fluff, tinged golden by sunlight, hung in the air above the battlefield.

Maloney stood on a mound of dirt, with a handful of cattail stems, like a weapons dealer delighting at the melee.

I spit out a gob of seeds and saw Maloney nod his head down a gravel road.

"I think there might be time for a splinter faction."

"A sortie?"

"Yep."

"Where?"

"The other side of the old railroad bridge."

Within minutes a group of fifteen kids were hustling down the road after us. Maloney did one of his sharp turns and we were off the road and climbing the side of the bluff. Halfway up we came to a hole in the ground. Maloney disappeared into it. I peered over the edge and saw a rope descending fifteen feet down a near vertical tunnel of limestone.

Kids will often ask about assignments in class, "Is this optional or required?" and "Will this be graded?"

It's hard to say which this was. That year I had neglected to teach many social studies concepts, as my packet of state standards languished in a drawer. But I knew the kids needed this lesson, and it was best taught by Maloney: the education of one's own judgement.

"Oh no, I am not going down that hole," Janelle said, even as her body leaned towards it.

"Girl, you know the Candyman's gonna be creepin' down there," Trina said.

"Mr. Maloney, why are you always trying to kill us?" Tabari yelled from the back of the group.

"Is Mr. Maloney gonna kill you or the Candyman?" Trina called back.

"How do you know? Maybe he is the Candyman?" Chloe said matter-of-factly. By eighth grade Chloe had found a style that she liked—a sort of sunny, gothic mix that suited her well. At a bigger city school, she may have been cast off, or ignored, as a

Other Loyalties

weird white girl, or in the suburbs, a 'freak.' But at our school she was right in the mix.

"Chloe, why you be saying that?" Janelle said shaking her head and peeking into the dark hole again. "It don't even matter now. We dying no matter what."

"Alright, who's next?" I disguised my anxiety in the fear and excitement of the kids and took on the role of ticket-taker at a fascinating but dodgy carnival ride.

One by one the kids dropped in. When their feet hit the sandy bottom and they glanced back up with wide eyes, it was a message for the next one to go. "Inspiration" was not a word on our school's mission statement; it was hard won each day—by Maloney's after-hours scouting of locales, and the kids own trust in themselves to stumble beyond their comfort zone. Even Janelle unhooked her arms from Jamiyah's, tested the rope, and vanished beneath the ground.

We followed Maloney's headlamp through a narrow tunnel into a church-sized cavern.

"Oh shit! What was that!"

A few kids ducked and groped for their friends in the dark.

"Bats!"

"Bats?"

"We woke them up."

"Ohmigod! Ohmigod!"

"Chill. They're gone."

"Crap, what else did we wake up?"

"Dude, don't say that."

The kids felt their way along the walls, their steps silent on the powdery ground. Damp, earthy air filled the cool blank space around them.

"Check this out." Maloney flashed his headlamp at a makeshift shrine: melted candles, rusted accessories, scraps of paper covered with gentle spells written in crayon, cans of Miller Lite, a plastic skull. It was a medley of Addams Family kitsch, Wiccan ritual, and would-be props from *The Goonies* film.

A water-stained Ouija board rested on an overturned milk crate. Amelie, Brianna, and Haven fiddled at its edge. As the kids acclimated, they ventured a bit further from the light of Maloney's headlamp, peering into the darkness of adjacent tunnels and caverns.

"What do you see in there?" I asked Tabari.

"I don't know, but I'm waiting for a zombie to jump out."

"Zombies are sitting at computers in the downtown offices above us."

"What?"

"All I see down here are signs of life."

Maloney was the last to pop back out of the hole onto the side of the bluff. As we walked down the dirt road to rejoin the rest of the group, Raya said quietly, "I don't think my aunt would have wanted me to do that."

I felt a little guilty, and half-wondered if the school would get a call from her aunt the next day. Would the new administration have our backs like Ms. D had?

It was the tricky thing about growing up—deciding when and where to take up sensibilities of your own. By middle school, most kids have learned to forge their parent's signature on permission slips. But Ms. D had done away with slips all together years ago, as we earned parents' trust. Raya's second thoughts about going in the caves was something to reflect on by herself. What risks would she or wouldn't she be willing to take in life?

I slept well that night—with the nostalgic feeling of exhaustion and satisfaction. It was a day that I would have loved to write about to Ms. D on a Weekly Reflection. I had no doubts that I'd done my job.

Thirty-Two

THE COPY MACHINE was halfway through the second ream I had fed into its tray. It was three hours after the bell on a Friday afternoon. My heart sank as I thought of my own children waiting for me at home. But my next week of lessons was now planned and there had been no paper jams in over an hour.

I pumped myself up and started singing Ice Cube's "It Was a Good Day."

I was teaching at a new public school on the east side of St. Paul. It had been two years since I left Ms. D's little charter school, and I was still adjusting to both the union pride and unavoidable administrative rigidity of Minnesota's second-biggest school district. The place of compromise, where labor and management met, was not thrilling, but did lead to institutional stability, and a measure of quality control when it came to teachers and schools.

The third-floor copy room at my new school doubled as a teacher's lounge. It was strange to have a space where kids weren't allowed. They were everywhere at Ms. D's. I figured the locked door to the room was on the advice of lawyers. Something about keeping kids away from access to test results and copies of confidential special education plans. I don't know a lot of students dying to transfer their classmates test scores or special education accommodations to Wikileaks, but I made sure I always locked the copy room door.

Not surprisingly, at this new school, I found myself among a group of teachers that immediately put me to shame with their talent, professionalism, and commitment. Granted, it was a new Montessori program they were trying to get off the ground, and many of them were stars at other schools that were recruited to take part in the daring goal of opening Minnesota's first public Montessori middle school in a lower-income part of the city.

The Montessori indulgence of viewing students as whole people, with their own needs, interests, and intrinsic motivation to learn, was snickered at by many teachers and administrators in the district. It was even thought to be a "crazy" idea by some. Certain kids in the city couldn't be trusted with self-directed learning—freedom within limits. And indeed, the new school was first conceived as a response to pressure from parents at a successful elementary Montessori school on a more well-off side of town.

When the district plopped the school in a neighborhood on the east side of St. Paul, most parents balked at sending their kids across the city. As the school experienced growing pains, the district, instead of supporting us, seemed to be hoping that the program would fade away. So instead of our school getting fed students from the Montessori elementary schools, half the families stepped through the doors with no idea what they were getting into.

As a parent it's probably a good idea to know if your child is signed up for the Peace Corps or military boot camp. Both are legitimate places to get new skills, learn discipline and service, and cooperation within a community. There's just a slight difference in style of going about it. At a Montessori school, kids are taught to listen to orders coming from inside themselves. Self-directed learning is an expectation that kids need to be prepped for from an early age, which means getting students from the Montessori elementary schools was vital for our new program to succeed.

In our society, low-income rural and urban kids are supposed to get boot camp, where the orders come from the outside. Many parents are even led to believe that's the only solution to the task of molding their child. When the Montessori school was 100 students over capacity and the wheels were coming off, even I started to wish for a drill sergeant to come to the rescue. We struggled to establish a climate of restorative justice, but a law-and-order mantra was whispered among teachers in private. One of the counselors confided to me that we needed someone to be "the hammer."

For the first time in my career, I wrote out some Office Referrals, reluctant to be starting a paper trail leading a kid deeper into the system. After breaking up a fight one day one of the angry students shoved a textbook in my face. I recorded my experience on paper and turned it in to the office—hoping some institutional lever would inflict the retribution that I could not. Two years later, this same student was in court for assaulting a teacher and the prosecution lawyer tried to contact me. The lawyer had picked up the paper trail. Was I going to testify against my former student? (Over time I learned to write out these referrals, cool down, and at the end of the day, recycle them. For better or worse. It was a lie to let the student think he could get away with hitting a teacher with a textbook, but after all, had writing the referral helped him in any way?)

The saga of the urban Montessori school that was left to die on the east side of St. Paul, is long and a bit sad, but the gist I'm sure, is clear here. The school was a dream *worth having* for the sake of the students, and hearing about the low morale at the other city schools, I was glad to be among the Montessori martyrs. We believed in what we were doing, even if it was failing.

I felt like I'd landed all right; the school pressed against the conventional, and the staff held fast to a humane vision of education. Yet my mind drifted back often to Ms. D's little school—to search for the lever within it that brought us clear of the nagging sense of failure in public education, right to the doorstep of the sublime. Waiting for my copies to finish I reached around in the past for the lever. Was it a confluence of a certain type of teacher? A philosophy? Ms. D's leadership? Sifting deep inside my memories of Ms. D's little school, a shape emerged bejeweled in unpredictable pulses of energy. My mind bucked as it touched something electric. I was scared. I felt heat and a creative force so full of potential to upend our society that I understood why it was hidden so well, and only shows itself to the pure of heart. When the uninitiated see it from the outside, they might call it madness.

A tiny red light appeared on the copy machine. I picked up a new ream of paper, checked over my shoulder, and broke open the packaging with a knee strike—a Muay-Thai kickboxing boost to get me through the final tasks of a long week. I loaded the tray, the room went quiet for a beat, and then the whir of the machine started up again.

The room filled with radiation, trace elements of ozone, nitrogen dioxide, and toner particles. The usual air supply of the teacher work room. This part of the building was nearly 100 years old. There were tall windows nearly reaching up to the ceiling and they were all closed. I was too obsessed with dicing up some card stock with the paper cutter to think of opening them.

I had been in the stuffy work room earlier that school day, sprinting up the stairs to make a copy in the dying moments of my dedicated prep hour. There was a new teaching assistant in the room on her lunch break.

She had eyed me for a second and then said, "Do you know that charter school over by…?"

"Yeah, I thought you were familiar for some reason," I said, jumping in.

"My kids still go there."

"How's it going for them?"

I lifted the cover, and a fluorescent beam shot out like the light from the Ark of the Covenant in *Indiana Jones*. I centered my original copy on the glass screen and closed it again before getting blinded or incinerated.

"Well, it's better," she answered. "You probably taught there when that *crazy* lady was principal."

I went silent, tucked my chin, and turned back to concentrate on pushing the right buttons on the machine. She couldn't have seen the smile on my face.

Other Loyalties

~

EACH FAST-FOOD RESTAURANT has an unmistakable smell, and I was engulfed in the oil and grease tincture that laced the air of a Culver's. We were about an hour out from the big rock where we would camp and cliff dive into Lake Superior.

A group of young men were waiting to dig into their Butterburgers—the bulk of whom were Latter Day Saints in their last years of high school. They were friends of Maloney's kids from the same temple, veterans of his high-adventure youth groups. The other young men who were there were all graduates of Ms. D's little school—Kevin, Jake, A.J., Mason, and Jaden—who were now in their early twenties. Maloney harangued them as trays of food started to arrive.

"So, we were winter camping last year…" Maloney began.

"Bro, was that the trip when I was sick as hell?" Kevin asked.

"Yep. Get this, Mason decides to sleep without a tent."

"I admit it was not a good decision," Mason conceded.

"But that's not the best part. He tried to do it in a deep-sea wetsuit I brought up!"

"I suffered immensely."

"Without a sleeping bag! Ha!"

They moved on to review the near misfortune of Kevin getting hit by a train near Palisades Park in South Dakota the summer before, trying to get a YOLO clip (You Only Live Once) for Instagram.

It had been nearly seven years since they had been our students at Ms. D's little school. During summer trips to the North Shore with Maloney, I'd seen them put on height and muscle, each making tentative inroads into lives of responsibility.

Before stopping at Culvers on the way up I caught up with Jake and Mason who were riding in my car. While driving, Jake's massive pale-skinned arms had caught in my periphery. Tattoos creeped over them—phrases, formulas for chemical compounds, symbols—different talismans inked on over the years. Added together, they had begun to map out a young man's quest to understand himself.

"Man, you've been working out."

"Yeah dude, I want to just get enormous. So fucking big that I can smash through the wall of a burning building to save someone."

Jake had been entrepreneurial since middle school. He had a streak of confidence and a sharp mind that had kept him advancing in life. As a seventh grader he bet me he could write a fifteen-page paper by the next day and did.

As I drove on, Jake described how he twisted his ankle during basic training for the army. He recited word for word the macho pep talk his sergeant gave him as he dragged his useless ankle behind him back to the barracks. As an eighth grader, he had done so much *parkour* with Maloney that his family doctor told him he already had the ankles of a thirty-five-year-old.

Jake fast-talked his way through the details of his work-out routine, to his pinned-together ankle, to the welding program he was in at a community college but also his thoughts of law school. Finally, he glanced down at his phone. He tapped commands into the Tinder app with lightning speed, read a message and said, "Dude, it's such a great time in history to be a horny guy in your twenties."

Jake bent over his phone to make arrangements, and I thought of my own hapless attempts to meet girls in my early twenties and wondered if I would have used such an app had it been around.

Mason had been in the back quietly adjusting the lens on his new camera and taking shots out the window. He was working at a pawn shop and had worked his way up to a managerial position.

The car passed a brown sign on the highway. It marked the trading post we had visited during the winter Field-Trip-A-Thon when they were in middle school. I glanced in the rearview mirror at Mason and asked what else he'd been up to over the past year.

Mason talked about keeping his beat-up car running and paying rent, and the ups and downs of having a girlfriend. As he spoke, with a deep voice, a man's voice, I pictured him sitting next to his father as a sixth grader, hood up, serious expression, but a twinkle in his eye. His father loved him so much. Mason's dad worked hard as the maintenance technician of an apartment complex, and the two would clash cinematically behind the scenes during his teenage years. But the bond was tight. They would go hunting together on some land they had up North.

"Yeah, last year we dug a trench, and put in a water trough. There's a place you can put firewood underneath."

"Nice."

"Yep. Hillbilly hot tub."

Mason went back to switching out the lenses on his camera, peering out at the passing trees, searching for overlooked beauty on the road north.

Our group was sitting in the middle of the Culver's in Two Harbors, a town on the shore of Lake Superior. Northern Minnesotans sat around the incongruent group of white, black, Asian, Arab and Latino's, like a frame. Booths along the windows were filled with grandparents and grandchildren, work crews in neon yellow vests on lunch break, and solemn couples rotating through the habits of their day.

Politeness and patience mixed with guarded judgements, as the different-colored Americans fed themselves with fast food. A woman with frizzy white hair glanced up at a loud laugh, a slang word caught in a man's ear and his head gave a tiny jerk, Kevin peeked at the large belt-buckle of a passing man, studies on the way fries were eaten by brown fingers secretly got underway from distant booths.

Each group pretended to ignore the other. The better natures of people were ready to be fair—but the lazy condemnation of differences was not far behind.

The city-country ballet had begun.

I don't know why this was the dynamic, but each group knew its role. It was a miniature painting of America. The churning, brimming diversity of the city producing loudly broadcast opinions, music, movies, fashion, entertainment, renewal—unaware of those in rural areas watching it all on satellite TV, and living lives that formed a culture of its own. When did their worlds cross except on Lil Nas X's, "Old Town Road"? A hit song that married hip-hop and country and gave the Billboard Charts trouble because executives didn't know what category to put it in. A grandfather stood by the soda fountain with a cup in his hand while a tiny blond girl pointed up at the Pepsi button. She reminded me of my daughter, and he had the look of Dennis, my father-in-law. While waiting my turn for a refill I looked back over at our group, and the people surrounding them. Country folk viewed themselves as *holding down the fort*, even as it aged around them, and desperately needed bursts of urban pizazz and immigrant optimism—the lynchpin of America's vibrancy from the start. City folks viewed themselves as *building a new fort*. They sped society towards sometimes-hasty change. Dismissing beliefs, values, and heroes tarnished by a modern view of the world, city folks sometimes trashed institutions worth keeping.

Tearing down statues turned up a lot of fresh dirt, but with no consensus on what to erect in their place, progress was thrilling but unstable. The most zealous mythmakers on both extremes of the political left and right were furiously trying to supply the lost citizens of America something to believe in—a clarified foundation for the country. Besides the golden arches of McDonald's that I saw across the parking lot, out of the Culver's window, what monument would we gather around?

The future would be contested until we could settle on a story about our past. But like I said, the day America locks down its story, and I as a social studies teacher must pass out a nationally mandated test, will be a scary day indeed.

America looks like both a failure and success to the world, an endless mess—but we're the ones figuring it out. We are the experiment that the rest of the world is counting on will succeed—because America, and its painful struggle to reconcile differences is the global future.

A sweet teenage worker, in a blue apron, wandered around with a tray of food. She squinted, trying to match the order with the numbers on the plastic A-frame tents that sat on tables next to people. She looked up again and set the tray in front of Maloney.

Maloney lowered his head, closed his eyes, and folded his hands—becoming a piece of holy origami formed by body and spirit.

For a moment, amid swashbuckling testosterone and racial tension, he paused and offered humble gratitude. Some of the young men stopped chewing for a second and some didn't, but they all took notice. Then, before anyone could get hung up about it, Maloney finished, lifted his head, and bit into his burger without hesitation.

Jake looked up at me and asked, "Mr. A, how come you don't pray before we eat?"

"To begin a prayer, you have to have ended one."

"Dude..." Jake shook his head.

It was the sort of answer expected of me. Or at least the lips of a character I had invented who was a slippery mystic. I had developed the persona way back before I even had to define myself as an adult working a job at Ms. D's little school.

Growing up I found out I had a knack for statements that ended dialogue, and it served me well as a shy person. I have a lot of respect for my friends who aren't silenced by my esoteric one-liners. We get on with the business of sharing the news, having some laughs, and brushing off the intractable, "deep," questions of life.

But there was the off chance that my statement to Jake had a basis in my true experience. Growing up as a practicing Muslim I prayed five times a day. It became easier to keep tabs on what I perceived as the presence of something larger than myself in the world. Prayers were scheduled pauses to remind oneself of it. There was a permeating quality to keeping up with so many formal daily prayers. Even in the hubbub of American junior high and high school I had to duck out to do my prayers. I had to find quiet spaces in basements, behind gas stations, in the stacks of libraries. And eventually, I had to repaint an altar in an old Catholic school classroom.

I trained myself to search for the unseen everywhere. I became wild-eyed, gullible, susceptible, primed, and ready to see the invisible. It was the feeling of climbing like an ant to the tip of a blade of grass. Once there, my antennas were swinging into the void, trying to latch on to a signal that would confirm what I knew was there, beyond the stars.

My search for the divine swallowed itself. It had become so broad it became that other word: life. In my twenties, when I stopped bowing my head to the ground five times a day, I wondered if that meant I had stopped *remembering*, or stopped *forgetting*. Maybe I just flickered between the two as my gratitude ebbed and flowed.

I decided that my answer to Jake *did* come from a made-up character—but it was a character I had come to admire. This mystic seeker was an aspirational part of me, a way of admitting that most of the time we don't worship as we should. A bit older now, I feel I'm back where I started—an ant crawling along a blade of grass. But I'm not heading to its tip. I've found enough right under my nose. A green path under my feet. My life as a small-scale adventurer, a part-time seeker, drummed up this pedestrian truth: Go to the place where *you are* first.

"This is a learning school, not a teaching school."

I don't know when I heard Ms. D say those words about her little school, but I often returned to them. When I stood in front of my classes at her school in a panic, thinking, *"I don't know, I don't know,"* it gave me permission to say out loud to my students, "I don't know." The teacher doesn't know.

Students hated not knowing. They squirmed and resisted. Ms. D's words gave me the confidence to say to my students, "I don't know, *and so can you.*" Teaching was not my job. It was learning. Learning that would be accomplished by them alone, us together, or not at all. And the first thing that should be learned was that life was bigger and better than us.

WE DUMPED OUR trash and filtered out to the parking lot of Culver's. The warm sun made movement easy, even after a greasy

Other Loyalties

feast. The boys piled in, and our caravan pulled back onto 35 Northbound.

Maloney had a trunk full of wetsuits culled from thrift-shops. Waning yuppie interest in trendy hobbies yielded a boon of high-end gear at the suburban outlets. Maloney seized on them and set up as a bootleg outfitter from his garage. Anyone up for a weekend adventure, he had covered.

The place we were going cliff jumping was on the backside of a rock formation near a place called Black Beach. It was another place from the Maloney Rolodex of Vanishing Secret Spots. Each year another one of these spots lost its status as the North Shore became more popular and developed. Within three years of this visit, Black Beach would be colonized by a campground with RV hook-ups. The beer coolers and Instagram day-trippers would overrun the place, as people recreated their sedate and tech-centric lifestyles in a pretty setting.

If there was one place where I suffered elitism it was the woods and wondered if I should blame Maloney. But I had grown to own it myself. I scoffed at state park campgrounds and trail signs and shook my head at the crowds at places like Old Faithful, when all of Yellowstone was available to hike. Yet when I went back to this specific spot near Black Beach after it had gotten popular, I saw that many of the people enjoying the "secret" beach, were Asian, black, and Latino—more diversity than I had ever seen on the North Shore. The scruffy kids piling out of a car from the city, trying to find the cliff jumping spot, could have been my own son and his friends. I had to eat my words.

It was progress. But change seemed to arrive all at once. The sensation of feeling suddenly outflanked was the thing that panicked some white people. It was the prospect of the city bursting its container and trickling out into the beautiful natural settings that were Minnesota's bounty. I felt the creeping judgement and fear when I scanned the packed beach. There was no hiding your skin on a beach. But I also sensed resignation and even acceptance. Times were changing fast, and I held out the hope that it was invigorating for some of the locals. After all, the new visitors were leading to an uptick in business opportunities in the towns along Lake Superior.

The black sand that the beach is known for is a result of sudden and drastic change itself—the iron mining that was brought to the region, which had so recently been the homeland of the Ojibwe people. The black color comes from taconite that was dumped into the water by the mining companies and rubbed itself off on the native sand. Yet now, the beach is touted as one of the most unique in Minnesota.

Again, the words of Johnny Smith's father came to mind, "You can talk all day long and not say a thing in the English language." *Misaabe-wajiw*, means "giant mountain" in Ojibwe, and became the name used for this area of Northern Minnesota, the Mesabi Iron Range. The "giant mountain" was transferred bit by bit to the shores of Lake Superior—first as chunks of high-grade ore from open pits and then as tiny pellets of taconite formed from the lower-grade ore underground. It was all dumped onto ships destined for the steel mills of Ohio, Indiana, and Pittsburg, where the raw ore took on new life as the bridges, skyscrapers, and tanks of American industrial and military might.

The feeling of a place changing—what are the right English words for that? The barbecue rib joint turning into a yoga studio. The worn-down front steps leading to a grandma's porch is pounded to chunks by a few swipes of a backhoe, trucked away, and sealed off by the metal and glass of a stylish condo. A secluded beach now bumping the latest hit from Post Malone. Engineers and computer programmers on high-end mountain bikes nosing around horse and ATV trails, forming an association with plans to chart out trail designations and restrictions.

We all missed the solitude of thinking we knew where we belonged.

When our caravan pulled up to Black Beach that day it was still mostly desolate. We squeezed into our wetsuits. Maloney set aside my favorite suit that had extra thick neoprene with an orange, yellow, and red patch on each shoulder. We called it the

Other Loyalties

"Disco Inferno." The suit was tight, and if the high jumps were going to take balls, I no longer had them.

At one end of the beach there was a narrow isthmus that led to a chunk of rock, the size of a small island, jutting into the water. One side was a sheer cliff reaching down to the water and the other was a tumble of boulders. We climbed the lichen-covered volcanic rock and pulled ourselves up using the handhold of a lone, stunted tree growing out of the side of the cliff. We shimmied through a narrow crack in the wall, climbed a little more, and then popped out on top where the shoreline of Lake Superior spread out below us.

We made our way over a patchwork of moss, weaving between Juneberry and hawthorn shrubs, to the other side of the island, where the waters of the Great Lake spread out before us farther than the eye could see. It was like we were on the orange, lichen-covered deck of a great ocean liner. The boys started scouting places to jump into the near-freezing waters of the lake. Maloney hopped down to a ledge and jammed a red rope into a crevasse so we could climb out of the water. He secured it by tying a knot called the 'monkey fist,' and turned to inspect the row of apprehensive young men.

The young Latter-Day Saints had been drilled by Maloney. They set their backpacks down, unscrewed the caps of Nalgene water bottles, and took a few sips before posting up near the highest cliffs.

Kevin had his Supreme brand snapback on and was smiling and shaking his head next to Jaden, whose face had gotten serious. Jake was silent for once, sitting off to the side on a slab of basalt zoning out on his phone. A.J. hadn't suited up yet, and Mason sat waiting stoically, his feet planted in neoprene booties.

Maloney attached his GoPro camera to a floatie and threw it as far as he could into the icy waters. "Who's going to be the first to go get that?"

That was the gist of it for the boys. Drive up, suit up, and choose a level of cliff to jump off, from five to fifty feet. They hemmed and hawed, searched for the split second when the mind became blank—pristine as the waters, as their lives when they were twelve— and broke free and leapt. They froze their asses off and laughed with friends. Posted YOLO clips on the quick and checked some comments on Instagram. Then, dared themselves to do something higher. They lived once, twice, three times, and more—all in one afternoon.

Incredibly the need to share on social media would wear off and phones were stored away in the folds of hoodies clumped on the rocks. The sun lowered in the sky, the wind calmed, and the young men noticed a different reflection besides themselves—the sky in the water.

LATER THAT NIGHT, around the campfire, I caught fragments of A.J., Jaden, and Kevin's lives. They spoke of classmates from Ms. D's little school who were in the early stages of being swallowed head-first by personal demons, pregnant, or just drifting. It was a stage of life where some found it hard to cope without wanting to steal away to light up a joint.

The boys were young men, and Maloney and I couldn't control their lives any more than we could when they were twelve. We could only walk with them a bit of the way and be there to check out the view when they were ready to look up from their troubles and move forward again.

A.J. was thoughtful, sensitive, and soft-spoken and I felt like I knew a little bit where he was coming from. There were times when he felt like buckling under the onslaught of a world that seemed to be in the midst of a lengthy mean streak. But the last update I got from him was a few pictures showing him flexing in the mirror, showing off his health and newfound discipline. A.J. was looking ahead again, and I was proud of him.

Jaden, anchored securely in his solid family life, was chipping away at a degree at community college and pursuing his love of basketball. On the way up we stopped to take a picture at the sign that read, "Black Beach." In the photo, Jaden has his arms stretched wide and his head held high. All he needed was a golden crown, and a caravan of a thousand camels, laden with gold, and he'd be Mansa Musa.

Kevin was making his way towards an environmental education degree and was doing side gigs as a guide for Outward Bound, a wilderness adventure company. He even found time to stand in line all night to buy limited edition Nikes that he turned around and sold for thousand-dollar profits.

Kevin told me once that he had some ancestors from the Blackfoot Nation. It may be a bit fanciful, but I imagined this gave him an edge to feeling at ease in the woods compared to some other students. If the past can cut one way into the future as trauma, it can cut the other into resiliency.

"How's Kendrick doing?" I asked.

"He's got an apartment." Kevin paused and looked up at me before adding, "He's living his life."

Kids peeled away one by one from the fire to their tents. Soon it was only Maloney and I. Set back in the woods we could see a glow coming from Kevin's tent. Through the thin polyester walls came the sound of helicopters. It was the opening scene from *Straight Outta Compton*.

Thirty-Three

IT WAS THE last day of my sixth year at the little school that used to be Ms. D's. I had arrived there early to drop off gear for the campout we were planning for after the eighth-grade graduation ceremony that was to take place that night.

As a charter school our day was longer, and we had more control over the calendar. Therefore, we accumulated 165 days of mandated "instruction" faster than the big districts. That was the number of days that state lawmakers believed amounted to a year of education. As far as I was concerned, 165 was a good number; the legislators had done well.

The sensible thing to do in Minnesota was close out the year before June, and Ms. D always had. That left three intact months of warm weather and summer. The heady spiral towards summer that year had an extra dimension, as the remaining old guard of the middle school hunted down jobs in other places.

I grabbed a tent and sleeping bag from my trunk and headed down the stairs to my room. For a moment I stood in the ambient light of the dreary cafeteria. The waxed floor beneath my beat-up Keen hiking shoes gave off a dull shine. A memory of one of our spring overnight lock-ins beat its way into my mind, as the sounds of Mr. Barnett's speakers echoed from the past. In fact, Mr. Barnett had brought in a whole DJ set-up with a multi-colored disco ball.

In the memory, it's after midnight, and I can see kids running up and down the stairs with bags of chips and pizza slices. They

Other Loyalties

dart into the gym to play "21" with Mr. J, Mr. Steven and Mr. David; watch *Madagascar* with Ms. Tiffany; deal out Pokemon cards in Mr. Duvall's; gossip and get their nails and hair done with Ms. Danika and Ms. Conley.

I'm down in the cafeteria as one of three chaperones for the dance party of the lock-in. Kids are in control of the playlist, but I boldly request a song from 1983 called *Send Me an Angel* by Real Life. The kids give me dirty looks but search it up. Ms. Tracy is dancing near a pillar. I know she'll appreciate hearing the new wave hit from Australia. Maloney is swinging his arms and painting the air with his fingertips on the other side of the floor, tripped out on the most kosher rave in history.

A billboard topper by Justin Bieber winds down as I follow globs of light wheeling across the floor: red and yellow, blue and green. The DJ finds my song and I close my eyes. It's a cliché—the junior high teacher dancing goofy. But in my mind, I'm melding to the chord strikes of a synthesizer, and feeling free. I can hear groups of kids laughing and calling out to me as they pass.

"Ahhh! Look at Mr. A!"

"Oh, hell no! I'm out."

"Mr. A! What dance is that?"

"That dude is on something."

"You go Mr. A! Do your thang!"

I keep my eyes closed, maybe because I don't want to lose the groove I'm in, but also because I trust my students enough to be vulnerable. They'd been asked to do the same when I had them close their eyes and stuff cotton balls up their noses in class. I was a chaperone with his eyes closed. If I peeked, I knew I would see them smiling because they understood deep down the need to dance.

I felt a soft hand on my shoulder. I shook loose the memory and was back standing with the tent and sleeping bag in my hands. Ms. Soraira had stepped away from a long line of preschool students picking up their breakfasts.

Along with Mr. Brandon, the giant, Ms. Soraira, the angel, was the first person besides Ms. D, that I had met that long ago

August when I was a brand-new teacher. She was buzzing around the empty school, cleaning, and organizing, with her three children helping, as I tried to size up the task of being a teacher. She would pop in my room throughout my years there and I would let down my guard, like I was in the presence of my favorite aunt. She was one of the quiet underground streams that kept the place alive and fed it the purest of waters.

"Meester. A, an' what about you? What are you doing next year?"

"I found something."

She gave me a long hug and smiled. The row of kids was snaking back upstairs, and she joined the tail end as it curved around the corner and out of sight.

When word got out that I was leaving the school I received an email from Ms. Ashley. She asked me what it would take to get me to stay. I was stunned. I felt that I had been unpleasant with people all year. At least to those who had been part of Ms. D's ouster. Ms. Ashley's message was reassuring; I hadn't let things get "chippy" as Mr. Duvall said. My dark thoughts about the mismanagement of the situation had not turned into perceivable acts of meanness—the alchemy for that required a taste for vengeance that I didn't have.

There was even a concession in Ms. Ashley's message, that I felt was sincere: "None of us will probably have a principal like Ms. D again in our careers. I get that."

THE LAST DAY went by in a blur of movie watching, snacking, and an extra-long recess. All the little kids went home on the busses, and then after a couple hours, the gym started to slowly fill for the graduation ceremony with aunties, uncles, cousins, siblings, grandmothers, moms and dads. The eighth graders were in bathrooms and classrooms putting on ties, doing makeup, and trying to mask their joy and nerves with jokes and flirting.

The day before, we had gone to our official 'School Forest', a stretch of trees at the edge of a city park about a half mile from the school. Maloney and the kids had formally adopted it a couple years before from the city of St. Paul with the help of the Department of Natural Resources.

The kids had played "Hunger Games," and during an escape an eighth grader named Melanie had gashed her leg on a stump. I saw her pass in an elegant silver and purple dress with a huge gauze bandage on her shin. The old adage about not wanting to die without a few scars came to mind.

That day at the park had ended early for Curtis and Emilio, who got into a scuffle while playing soccer. It had been so long since a fight had happened that I didn't really know what to do. Luckily, Mr. J ushered them both into the silver Caravan, shook his head at the justifications for violence they threw at him, and brought them back to school to cool off.

The logistics crew of the graduation ceremony was frenetically moving pieces into place: projector, sound system, extra chairs, cake. It was a night that usually carried its own happy rhythm, but this year it had an unwieldy, jangly feeling, like an old RV with fried brake pads. Orange extension cords vined across the floor and staff scurried over them—loose ends fraying both in their heads and hearts.

In a row below the stage was Maloney's hand-drawn portraits of the students. My contribution would come later with the yearly highlight film of outings. That's when I noticed that there was a lot of light coming through the scuzzy skylights of the gym. Nobody would be able to see the video on the small screen that had been set up near the stage. Gathering some large mats and long strips of black butcher paper, I pushed through the double doors of the gym onto the loading dock. Searching around, I found a tall ladder pressed against the building.

Before I could set down the mats and paper, I saw Maloney at my side reaching for the ladder. We hauled the stuff up to a ledge below the towering redbrick wall of the gym building. Pulling the ladder up we stretched it until it kissed the edge of the rooftop.

With the mats and paper rolled under our arms, we ascended step by step until we could throw a leg over the parapet. Standing up, a view of the church, rectory, parking lot, playground, and surrounding streets gave way to houses and the leafy neighborhood. Beyond them was the worn and fading pride of the working-class east side of St. Paul. The view dissolved into downtown in one direction and the suburbs in another.

We laid the mats and butcher paper over the frosted skylights, using fragments of bricks to hold them in place. Beneath our feet the gym was crowding with families, and I imagined staff scouring the building to make sure the eighth graders were prepared to march in. Then as the clock ticked, and the list of evening events was cued up, I imagine they began to wonder where on earth Maloney and Mr. A were.

I fussed around trying to pin down a corner of black paper when I noticed Maloney crouching in silence, his eyes scanning the gravel that topped the ballasted roof. He reached out a hand and plucked a pebble to examine and tossed it back down.

I'd seen the process before, but it was on backroads, or secluded beaches on the shores of Lake Superior. He waved a hand across the gravel, spreading it beneath his palm. Again, he picked up a stone he liked and brought it close to his face to inspect it. This one he dropped in the pocket of his dress shirt.

The sun was getting lower in the sky, but I decided to join him. Our footsteps crunched against the gravel as we shifted from place to place on our hunt. Two black crows in a tall oak squawked, unsettled to be eye-to-eye with humans this high up.

Time stopped. The analogies and metaphors always swirling through my head were brushed aside as I homed in on the rocks, searching for the ones that were translucent—the tell-tale sign of what we were looking for.

A lifetime can be spent searching for the shape of an honest moment to share with another person. This one took fifty million years to form but fit in a pocket. It could have been any old pebble and it wouldn't have changed a thing, but it was an agate.

AFTER THE CEREMONY the eighth graders hugged and kissed their families and snapped some photos. They changed into sweatpants and hoodies and crammed into the silver Caravans.

Early in the day Maloney and I had taken a few students and set up the tents at Willow River just across the border in Wisconsin. By the time we got there it was an hour to midnight. Kids chose their tents and Ms. Danika posted her chair by a large circular grate. Soon I saw the flash of large bags of Doritos and Twizzlers in the light of a raging fire. A few hours of stories, hide and seek, and ambushes, passed.

Some kids started to crash. Emotionally spent, and out of Monster energy drinks, they crawled into their tents. We had already taken one night-hike but now Maloney was offering another to the kids left standing. It included some of the usual steady hands: Amelie, Brianna, Haven, Raya, Edgar, Tabari, and Jeremiah.

We made it to the walkway on top of the Little Falls Dam. A reservoir spilled slowly through concrete before taking its natural form of a river again, winding through the darkened trees below. The kids were quiet. No one was complaining. They all wanted to be there, out searching in the middle of the night.

Near an open field by a beach there was a small building containing bathrooms. As we passed, Maloney nodded to a picnic table. At first, I didn't know what he was after, but then he nodded again towards the roof of the building.

AFTER THE ENTIRE middle school staff left the school, I'd get snippets of where people ended up and what they were up to. Over a few years Maloney taught at two other schools, before ending up at one closer to his house in the suburbs. He was durable and innovative and was able to put together great lessons and experiences for the kids, but he was hamstrung by nervous administrators, or just the ordinary parameters of a normal school.

They had a dragon but wanted him to operate as a microwave, gently warming leftovers—trapped inside a room.

As usual, Maloney took it in stride, and pressed his luck where he could. He kept his back lined straight against a touchstone of magic, fun, and productivity. Day after day, like a spring-loaded hammer striking quartz, kids were sparked to life inside his classroom.

Myself, I put up a good fight at my new school. The Montessori approach, although fussy and haughty at times, aligned pretty good with what we had tried to do at Ms. D's little school: work with the humans in front of us, using natural materials. Once the Montessori jargon was put aside, there was an accordance. Albeit without the touch of madness.

My "stuff" though—my lessons—began to feel watered down. My energy ebbed. I *love* kids, but I don't really like them if I'm acting like an adult. The reason it worked for me at Ms. D's little school is because we played so much—I had stayed a kid. It made being with my students so much easier.

I never figured out the small talk that puts kids at ease inside a room. Clear communication, the envious straightforward way my student teachers explained things, I hadn't mastered. Basic rituals and routines, after nearly two decades, I still didn't bother with properly.

Pacing the room at the Montessori school like a trapped lion, for the first time, I heard a kid ask, "Do you like being a teacher?"

It was unmistakable: the crossroads. *Be all in or leave.*

TWO IN THE morning at Willow River. Maloney and I rallied the kids around the heavy picnic table, lifting it together until it was under the roof line. We each climbed atop and pulled ourselves up and sat in a cluster near the ridge of the roof.

I saw Haven pushing her hands down to feel the soothing roughness of the shingles. Edgar and Tabari sat close, whispering. Amelie and Dena had their eyes opened wide. What were they dreaming of? I thought back to when I had the kids make Russian *matryoshka* nesting dolls of themselves out of different-sized plastic cups. I remembered Amelie, who was in sixth grade at the time, standing behind a row of all the "Amelies" she had inside herself: past, present, and future.

Above us was a better view of the starry sky. If there was a mission statement at Ms. D's little school, it was this.

Other Loyalties

In the morning we walked to Willow Falls. Kids spread out along the terraced rock shelfs, making their way behind the falling water and dipping their feet in small side rivulets. A shabby night's sleep was washed away by the cold water of the river, and the gorge came alive with shouts.

Some boys had wrestled a huge log into the river below the falls and were trying to ride it down the river like it was a knobby, old alligator. It kept rolling, toppling the boys into the weeds and muck.

A few other kids who had stripped to their boxers and swimsuits were splashing in a pool.

"Mr. A!" Emilio yelled. His pale belly hung over his shorts, and short black hair glistened on his head.

I nodded.

"Come on in!"

"Not today!"

He took a big swing at the water, like a disappointed uncle, and waved me over.

"Come *on!*"

I ducked behind a rock and found Maloney standing by a posted trail map.

"Want to take a short run?" he asked.

I checked the ratio of staff to students around the falls.

"Sure. Why not?"

Maloney pointed to a squiggly green oval on the map. I suggested a red one that didn't look like five miles. After one hour of sleep, it was like Navy Seal training. Maloney was the instructor and there was no way I was being left behind. The limits were out there, but there was no reason to turn back just because we knew that.

THE COUNTRY NEEDED a new story, a myth to hold it all together. In the news was a fresh tug-of-war over social studies standards. For better or worse I tried to steer clear of the certainties that it took to try to hammer down a curriculum for America that affirmed and pleased everybody. I wasn't sure giving every last self-described identity its own chapter or class was the way to correct the current imbalance. But the campaign to offer more of the truth about our history couldn't hurt. Well, it *would* hurt, but not as bad as staying the same.

Was America a novel or a collection of short stories?

It was clear one group had gotten more than their fair share of affirmation—but it didn't mean they still didn't need it. Everyone needed encouragement.

I didn't know the answers. It wasn't as simple as letting kids go outside. Nature wouldn't solve all our problems. But battered left and right by information, and sideswiped by the blind spots of technological progress, one refrain always sounded in my ears when I was planning at the start of each school year: What can humans do that computers can't?

Finding out what that was and making it the heart of the mission was something that Ms. D's little school seemed able to do. Our program didn't have the specific contours, direction, and force of storylines that tried to drag America back to a fabled past or rush it into a utopian future. It honored something I saw both city kids and rural people doing with lightheartedness: moving their warm bodies across the planet we share. Common ground was not something that needed to be found, it didn't require some bloody future struggle—it was waiting beneath our feet. Other loyalties, besides the political, were on my mind. And they did best in the open breeze, and Ms. D had left the windows *and* doors open.

When I first declared that I was going to try teaching, my sister told me about a dream she had one night. She described it to me over an Americano at a café in Minneapolis. She said that in the dream I had a golden classroom.

I couldn't figure out what the dream meant. After six years at the little public school on the east side of St. Paul, I understood. What makes a classroom glow, if it ever does, is not gold, not specific ideas or mystical radiance, but sunlight.

Other Loyalties

∼

AT WILLOW RIVER, the eighth graders climbed into the silver Caravans one last time and we headed back to the school. It was late afternoon. A few parents were waiting already, and kids had to say goodbye quickly. Most were so tired that it was a buffer to their emotions. They shoved their sleeping bags into backseats and collapsed into the front.

Another group lingered, some walkers and others yet to be picked up. Edgar had his moment of truth and saw the girl he had a crush on close a car door and disappear down the block. He hadn't told her how much he loved her. Now he was pacing and weeping.

I remembered the clock counting down in my head in middle school the last days of eighth grade—and my own desperation to show that I knew what love was to a girl I had a crush on.

I could only put a hand on Edgar's shoulder.

Soon Tabari and Jeremiah were carrying him away on a stretcher down the block. Arms around him, they headed to Tabari's house where he'd be rehabilitated with a binge of video games, Cheetos, and laughter. But the heartache was hard-won, and Edgar would keep it as a talisman to remember the fine feelings he was capable of, as life wore on and became coarser.

There was one student left, Emilio. I volunteered to stay until his ride came, and the rest of the staff took off to start their summers. The doors of the school were open, and Emilio and I stepped into the empty lobby. Lights were off and a musty smell was settling in. Lining the walls were the fading colors of dated student projects behind class display cases.

Emilio hadn't done much academic work in years. He was one of Mr. K.O.'s students. Mr. K.O. had roughed him up a bit and he'd made some inroads into reading, but in my class, nothing. Except for one day. It was when he was in seventh grade. Someone had cleared out a storeroom and there were boxes of books in the gym. He had skipped class and rummaged through them.

After dismissal he shuffled into my class and held out some beat-up paperbacks.

"Mr. A, I thought you might like these."

They were books by the Native American author Vine Deloria Jr.: *God is Red: A Native View of Religion*, and *Custer Died for Your Sins: An Indian Manifesto*. Emilio knew my preoccupations. It turned out he'd been paying some attention in class all along.

Emilio dropped his sleeping bag on the floor, picked up the phone at the front desk and tried to reach his brother. It'd be a while.

We both leaned against the front desk like old buddies at a bar. I remembered his dapper suit when we'd gone to see the show at the fancy theater downtown. Now he was in a rumpled white t-shirt, stained with dirt and cheese powder.

"So, what's the plan for next year?"

"I think my mom is calling that school next week. What's it called?"

I had a sinking feeling. All the behind-the-scenes work that used to be done by Ms. D to make sure our eighth graders found a high school that suited them hadn't been done.

"Man, you should get on that."

"Yeah. She's gonna call."

Emilio lowered his head and looked down at his hands. A long time passed. Then his face turned up and he glanced around at nothing in particular. "What do I do now?"

I wanted to say something to Emilio, give him an answer to his question. But that was not the type of teacher I was. The best thing I could do was *not* answer his question. The best thing to do was to let him keep it.

We heard a honk and went outside. Emilio ran around gathering his stuff and his brother was getting impatient. He barked at Emilio to get going. With an arm hanging out the window of an old Buick he reminded me of a Latino version of Ace, the tough older brother in the film *Stand By Me*.

Emilio piled his unrolled sleeping bag and pillow in his hands and headed down the front steps of Ms. D's little school. He turned back to say goodbye. But even after he got in and they started to drive away I kept waiting to hear the words that had powered the school for six precious years: "That was the best day of my life."

Author Photo by Wayne Moore

About the Author

KAREEM AAL is a writer and teacher. He lives in Minneapolis, Minnesota. His first book is titled *No True Love in Tehran: An American Trip to Iran*, which chronicles his adventures trying to get to Iran to visit a friend.

A REQUEST

If you enjoyed this book, please review it on
Amazon and Goodreads.
If you did not enjoy this book, please review it in
The New Yorker.

Reviews are very helpful to an independent author.

www.kareemaal.com

Made in the USA
Monee, IL
11 September 2022